3.8.50

THE IMAGE
AND
THE EYE

E. H. GOMBRICH

THE IMAGE
AND
THE EYE

*Further studies in the psychology of
pictorial representation*

PHAIDON
OXFORD

Phaidon Press Limited, Littlegate House, St Ebbe's Street, Oxford
First published in volume form 1982
This edition © 1982 by Phaidon Press Limited

British Library Cataloguing in Publication Data
Gombrich, E. H.
    The image and the eye: further studies in the
    psychology of pictorial representation.
    1. Art—Psychology   2. Visual perception
    I. Title
    701'.1'5   N71
    ISBN 0–7148–2245–0

Typeset in Monophoto Plantin by Keyspools Ltd, Golborne, Lancs.
Printed in Great Britain by Pitman Press Limited, Bath

Contents

Preface 7

Visual Discovery through Art 11

Moment and Movement in Art 40

Ritualized Gesture and Expression in Art 63

Action and Expression in Western Art 78

The Mask and the Face: The Perception of Physiognomic Likeness
in Life and in Art 105

The Visual Image: Its Place in Communication 137

'The Sky is the Limit': The Vault of Heaven and Pictorial Vision 162

Mirror and Map: Theories of Pictorial Representation 172

Experiment and Experience in the Arts 215

Standards of Truth: The Arrested Image and the Moving Eye 244

Image and Code: Scope and Limits of Conventionalism in
Pictorial Representation 278

Notes 299

Bibliographical Note 311

Sources of Photographs 313

Index 315

Preface

THIS VOLUME—the sixth of my collected essays published by the Phaidon Press—includes most of my papers dealing with the problems I first raised in *Art and Illusion: A Study in the Psychology of Pictorial Representation*. Since this book was based on my Mellon Lectures of 1956 and was published in 1960, I have had a good deal of time for second thoughts and revisions, some of which I mentioned in successive Prefaces to the English editions of 1967, 1971 and 1977. It turned out that not only students of arts and letters but also practising scientists asked me for clarifications and recapitulations and thus belied the pessimistic view that our intellectual world is split into two cultures which fail to communicate with each other. Accordingly, I was led to pay more attention to other visual tools, such as photography, diagrams and maps.

I thought it would be helpful to arrange these further studies roughly in the order in which they were written, without feeling too strictly bound by this decision. Thus the volume opens with a lecture on 'Visual Discovery through Art', given at the University of Texas (Austin), because I here look at the whole subject from a new vantage-point.

A lecture series on Time and Eternity arranged at the Warburg Institute, which also included talks on Relativity Theory, on Historiography and on Theology, prompted me to take up that topic—which was treated somewhat perfunctorily in *Art and Illusion*—in 'Moment and Movement in Art'. I also welcomed the occasion to elaborate the themes of Chapter 10 of that book in 'Ritualized Gesture and Expression in Art', read at a symposium organized by the late Sir Julian Huxley for the Royal Society. That meeting led in turn to the setting up of a study group of students of human and animal behaviour to which I contributed the paper on 'Action and Expression in Western Art'. I returned to this problem area in a discussion of physiognomic likeness entitled 'The Mask and the Face' in a lecture series held at Johns Hopkins

University in Baltimore in which I was joined by a psychologist and a philosopher.

An invitation to contribute to a special number of *Scientific American* on Communication resulted in an article on 'The Visual Image', which attempts to give a concise conspectus of this emergent discipline. I was faced with an even more intimidating task when I was asked by the Royal Society to give one of their Review Lectures on my field of research. I called this paper 'Mirror and Map'.

I was happy to continue a friendly debate with that great student of vision, the late J. J. Gibson, in a paper for his Festschrift entitled 'The Sky is the Limit', and to combine the discussion of perspective—which can never be far from any treatment of the visual image—with that of movement in another investigation, 'Standards of Truth: The Arrested Image and the Moving Eye', originally written in honour of the eminent psychologist Professor Hans Wallach.

'Experiment and Experience in Art' resulted from another 'ecumenical' initiative, a series endowed by the Richard Bradford Trust at the Royal Institution, to which again historians, critics, scientists and philosophers contributed. The last paper in this volume, 'Image and Code: Scope and Limits of Conventionalism in Pictorial Representation', was presented to a Congress on the Semiotics of Art at the University of Michigan, and accordingly addresses itself particularly to philosophers.

It was perhaps inevitable that in speaking to audiences which I could not expect to have read *Art and Illusion*, let alone my other essays, I had to summarize arguments and even mention examples I had used elsewhere. I can only hope that these will now function as *leitmotivs* demonstrating the unity of the subject. Even so, I decided to omit three further studies dealing with germane themes. The chapter I wrote for the volume on *Illusion in Nature and Art* (London, 1973), which I edited jointly with Richard Gregory, may well supplement some of the essays here, but since this publication is generally available I saw no need to reprint it. The essay, 'The "What" and the "How": Perspective Representation and the Phenomenal World', I wrote for *Logic and Art : Essays in Honor of Nelson Goodman* (New York, 1972) seemed to me somewhat too technical in its treatment of this rather arid problem to be included here. I also decided not to reprint the chapter 'The Variability of Vision', part of a contribution on The Evidence of Images in *Interpretation, Theory and Practice* (Baltimore, 1969), edited by Charles Singleton, largely because of the many illustrations it requires. I venture to hope, however, that those who may want to discuss and criticize my views in any detail will also take cognizance of these writings and, of course, of my book *The Sense of Order*, which concentrates on the perception of patterns rather than images.

In calling this collection *The Image and the Eye* I wished especially to draw attention to a shift in emphasis which has recently become noticeable in the study of perception. In the last few years the subject of the perception of images has attracted increasing interest. I was able in my later essays to profit from the book by John M. Kennedy, *A Psychology of Picture Perception* (San Francisco, 1974), but not from the most recent publication, still in course of progress, *The Perception of Pictures* (New York, 1980), edited by M. A. Hagen. I am happy that my volume will find more companions on library shelves, and I hope it will have furthered the debate about one of man's most basic and enjoyable gifts, the gift of image making.

Once more it is my pleasant duty in conclusion to thank kind helpers. Simon Haviland and Peg Katritzky of the Phaidon Press, Diana Davies, and the staff of the Photographic Collection of the Warburg Institute have been of invaluable assistance.

London, February 1982   E.H.G.

Visual Discovery through Art

I

NOT ALL art is concerned with visual discovery in the sense in which I propose to use this term here. Our museums show us a dazzling and bewildering variety of images which rival in range the creations of the living world of nature. There are whales among these images as well as humming-birds, gigantic monsters and delicate trinkets, the products of man's dreams and nightmares in different cultures and different climes. But only twice on this globe, in ancient Greece and in Renaissance Europe, have artists striven systematically, through a succession of generations, step by step to approximate their images to the visible world and achieve likenesses that might deceive the eye. I realize that most critics' admiration for this achievement has considerably cooled off in this century. Their taste has veered towards the primitive and the archaic. There are good and interesting reasons for this preference, to which I hope to return in a different investigation,[1] but taste is one thing, history another. The ancient world certainly saw the evolution of art mainly as a technical progress, the conquest of that skill in *mimesis*, in imitation, that was considered the basis of art. Nor did the masters of the Renaissance differ here. Leonardo da Vinci was as convinced of this value of illusion as was the most influential chronicler of Renaissance art, Giorgio Vasari,[2] who took it for granted that in tracing the evolution of a plausible rendering of nature he was describing the progress of painting towards perfection. It goes without saying that in Western art this evolution did not come to an end with the Renaissance. The process of the conquest of reality through art continued, at a varying pace, at least as far as the nineteenth century, and the battles fought by the Impressionists were fought over this issue—the issue of visual discoveries.

Lecture given at the University of Texas, Austin, in March 1965, in the series Program on Criticism.

One thing stands out from this story and demands a psychological explanation. It is that this imitation of visual reality must be a very complex and indeed a very elusive affair, for why should it otherwise have taken so many generations of gifted painters to learn its tricks? It was to explain this puzzle that I set out, in my book on *Art and Illusion*,[3] to explore the relation between visual perception and pictorial representation. It may be time to take stock once more and present some afterthoughts. Not that I see any reasons to repudiate the results of my investigations, such as they were. In fact, the reader who has worked through that rather groping presentation may have to put up with some recapitulations here. But I think that today I can render some of my explanations less elusive by anchoring them more firmly in an experience that is accessible to everyone. If I were to start the book today I would pivot the argument on the distinction between *recall* and *recognition*.

For the relevance of recognition to art, I can quote venerable authority, an authority, moreover, who wrote at a time when naturalistic paintings were still an object of wonder. Aristotle, writing in the fourth century B.C., discusses in his *Poetics* why 'imitation' should give man pleasure, why we enjoy looking at the perfect copies of things we find painful to behold in reality. He attributes this pleasure to man's inborn love of learning, which, as he politely concedes, is not confined to professional philosophers. 'The reason why we enjoy seeing likenesses is that, as we look we learn and infer what each is; for instance, that is a so-and-so.' The pleasure, in other words, is one of recognition. Naturalistic painting enables us to recognize the familiar world in the configurations of paint arranged on the canvas. Unlike Aristotle and his contemporaries, we may be so used to this experience that it no longer offers us a thrill. But most of us still feel the pleasure of recognition when the situation is reversed and we suddenly exclaim in front of a real scene, 'this is a so-and-so', a Whistler, perhaps, or a Pissarro.

Clearly, as historians we must approach this second experience through the first. For if Whistler or Pissarro had not been enabled to create on their canvases recognizable images of the visible world, we would not in our turn have been able to recognize their images in nature.

II

But though recognition is clearly an act of remembering, it must not be confused with that other aspect of memory: our power of recall. The difference is easily demonstrated with a little experiment which also introduces us to its bearing on art. Take paper and pencil and draw anything

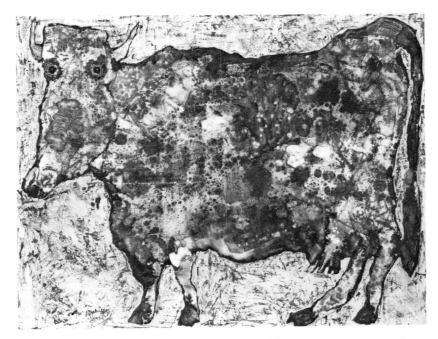

1. Jean Dubuffet: *The Cow with the Subtile Nose.* 1954. Oil and enamel on canvas, 89 × 116cm.
Collection, The Museum of Modern Art, New York,
Benjamin Scharps and David Scharps Fund

from memory with which you think you are utterly familiar; the design of the chairs in your study or the shape of an animal you know very well. Even without paper and pencil we can check our power of recall if we ask ourselves such simple but awkward questions as how exactly are the horns of a cow related to its ears.

Looking at the painting of a cow by the modern primitivist Jean Dubuffet (Fig. 1) you will discover that he has shirked this issue. His *Cow with the Subtile Nose* does not boast any ears I can discover. His *Cow with Fine Teats* (Fig. 2) certainly makes up for this deficiency, but is the relationship right? Surely not. And here is the important paradox to which I must draw immediate attention. Even where we find it hard to recall, we know when we *recognize*, and say, in Aristotle's words, 'this is a so-and-so'. And failing to recognize, we claim the right to criticize and to say, 'but cows don't look like this'.

It so happens that Dubuffet's curious creatures are not really primitive, but rather over-sophisticated pictures. He wants to 'show the appearance of objects as they have been impressed on a man's brain when his attention or consciousness did not intervene, or at least intervened only vaguely, or not more than in the daily life of any ordinary man who is normally preoccupied with all sorts of other things at the moment his eyes light upon any object.'[4]

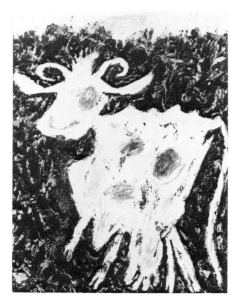

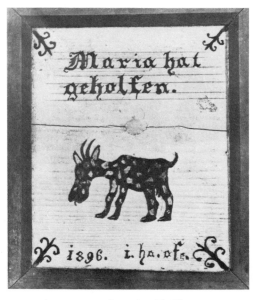

2. Jean Dubuffet: *The Cow with the Fine Teats*. 1954. Private Collection

3. Anonymous Austrian *Ex Voto*. 1896

We shall discover that there is a fallacy here. The man in the street may not be able exactly to recall a cow, but what he sees when he meets a cow is a very different matter. One thing is sure. Our difficulties of recall have nothing to do with the fact that we are men in the street, or streets, and not farmers in the fields. Take the *ex voto* of an Austrian peasant (Fig. 3). In this genuinely naïve picture, too, the animal is hard to recognize. Is it a cow or is it a goat? And yet, the peasant who painted this would know not only how to recognize cows and goats, he would even recognize every individual cow of his herd. He would also, of course, immediately recognize in a picture what he cannot recall, and so can we if we look at a painting by the most famous specialist in cattle painting, the Dutch seventeenth-century artist Paulus Potter (Fig. 4). It proves, if proof is needed, how immediate and effortless is recognition.

There is another paradox here connected with the first: the paradox that confused Dubuffet, and not only him. Recognition is easy, it is almost automatic, but, perhaps because of its automatic quality, largely unconscious. Not unconscious, to be sure, in the Freudian sense, but in the sense of those automatic processes to which we need not and often cannot attend. We do not know how and why we recognize a correctly drawn cow, but we soon notice if something is amiss in a real or a pictured cow. If the transition from cows to people is not too offensive, let me refer to the difficulties portrait painters so often experience. Troublesome relatives of their sitters will insist that there is still something around the mouth that is not right, that they still

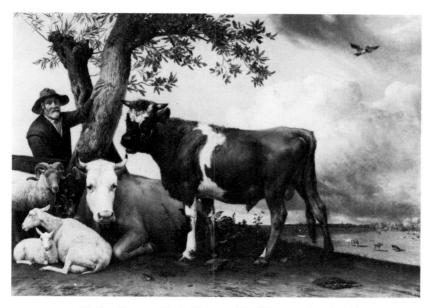

4. Paulus Potter: *The Bull*. 1647. The Hague, Mauritshuis

cannot quite recognize Uncle Jimmy. Yet they are rarely willing or able to say
why the mouth looks wrong to them. Maybe the painter will succeed in
satisfying them by working through a period of trial and error until, at last,
the mouth looks 'right'. Unlike the exasperated painter, I tend to believe that
the relatives probably knew what they were talking about. It is genuinely
disturbing to feel an element of strangeness unsettling a familiar sight. We
tend to notice at once if something in our room has been shifted, though few
of us could ever recall, let alone draw, the contents of our rooms.

This is the point at which art educators often start a little sermon. They
have become quite expert in creating in us a sense of guilt for failing to use our
eyes and never noticing the wonderful variety of the visible world which we
so lazily take for granted.[5] I am all for making people use their eyes, but
unless the sermon is carefully phrased it really makes little psychological
sense. The teacher whose pupil fails to attend to the lesson has a right to scold
him; but he would not get far if he asked him to attend to everything around
him: the flies on the ceiling, the hum of the traffic or the play of light on the
desk. It is of the essence of attention that it is selective. We can focus on
something in our field of vision, but never on *everything*. All attention must
take place against a background of inattention. A heightened awareness of
reality as such is something mystics may dream about, but cannot realize.
The number of stimuli that impinge on us at every moment—if they were
countable—would be astronomical. To see at all, we must isolate and select.

The true miracle, it seems to me, is that we still store so many impressions that recognition of the familiar is guaranteed.

It is clear that the distinction between the familiar and the unfamiliar must be of utmost biological importance, not only to man, but even to animals. Insects and birds must recognize their homeground and regard with suspicion any changes that may betoken danger. Whether they also have a power of recall is perhaps an idle question. Ours, as we have seen, is rather imperfect. But we have developed an instrument to overcome this disability, an instrument we retain largely in our grasp, namely, the symbol.

For though what we call reality is too rich and too varied to be reproducible at will, symbols can be learned and recalled to a surprising extent. The same person who could perhaps not recall the appearance of his own right hand may reproduce for you any number of Shakespeare's sonnets or cricket and basketball scores. The power of recall of symbols varies of course enormously, but thanks to their economy of elements, symbols are much more amenable to availability in storage. Think of music, perhaps the extreme example. Most people in our culture can recall a great variety of tunes at will; indeed, tunes will keep running through their heads and be whistled and hummed as a kind of mood music accompanying many of their waking hours.

Whatever can be coded in symbols can also be retrieved and recalled with relative ease. The tricks of how to draw this or that—a cat for instance—of which I speak in *Art and Illusion* at some length, can really be described as such simple methods of coding. The need for a schema is the need for a code.

There are many styles in the history of art that operate with ready-made memorizable codes alone, styles in which the artist learns from his masters how to represent a mountain or a tree, or the ox and ass at the manger according to a well-proven formula (Fig. 5). Indeed, the majority of artistic traditions operate in some such way. An older psychological art theory, including that of my teacher Emanuel Loewy, described these schematic images as 'memory images'. I now think that this description confuses cause and effect. It is not likely that anybody ever remembers reality in precisely that way, but images of this schematic kind admirably serve as codes that are aids in memorizing.

Of course, it is open to us, within limits, to codify and thus to memorize whatever we especially wish to recall. In inspecting a house we may think of buying, we will sketch a schematic diagram as an *aide-mémoire*, only to find to our annoyance that the diagram occasionally has superimposed itself on our memory of the place. We have to return to modify and enrich it.

Something of this kind can always be done in case of need. Once you have

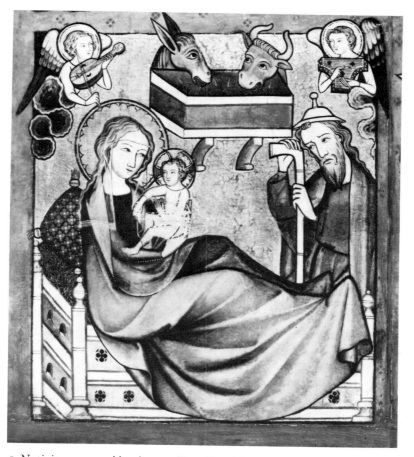

5. *Nativity. c.* 1340. Altenberger Altar. Frankfurt, Städelsches Kunstinstitut

noticed, for argument's sake, that you do not know enough about the relationship of those horns and ears of the cow, you can check and verbalize this information, or better still, enter it onto your schema and you are safe; safe, that is, until the next person asks you an awkward question about its nostrils—and the number of such potential questions is virtually unlimited.

Clearly, an expert cattle painter such as Potter would have been able to meet most of them head-on. He knew about cows, he could paint them by heart, and paint them so correctly that recognition accepted them as familiar and convincing.

In my book I chose for this process of approximation to nature the psychological formula of 'schema plus correction'. The evolution of naturalistic art can be seen in terms of this formula. I cannot expect this solution to be accepted by the reader before I have answered a question that may have irked him for some time: Is there not a fundamental difference between the so-called 'conceptual' styles that operate with a remembered code and those periods of naturalism to which Potter belonged? Is not the secret of Potter quite simply that he drew cattle from nature, even though he may later have used these sketches for his studio paintings? Is not all naturalism grounded on the discipline of drawing from the model or motif? And if these artists really trained themselves to observe and to draw what they saw in front of their eyes, what relevance has the distinction between recall and recognition to their type of art?

The answer must be one which every art teacher would give who has had to teach the traditional skills of representation—if such are still around. It is that, strangely enough, the difference between drawing from memory and drawing from life is only one of degree. Max Liebermann somewhere quotes his teacher as saying, 'What you cannot paint from memory you cannot paint at all.' It is true that in painting from the motif you have the inestimable advantage of easy comparison between your work and your model. You can always pause to see whether you recognize your motif in your picture or your picture in the motif. But though such comparisons will make it easier for you to spot mistakes, the example of the portrait painter I have mentioned shows that a feeling of discrepancy is one thing, the invention of a fitting code another.

There are many reasons for this difficulty, some of which I analysed at some length in my book. I also quoted Sir Winston Churchill, who rightly emphasized that even in painting from nature we must use our memory as we move our eye from motif to canvas. This would even be true of an artist copying a picture. But in painting from nature, more formidable psychological problems intervene. For psychologically it does not make much sense to say that we 'copy' what we see in the visible world. What we see extends in depth, while our painting surface is flat. The elements of what we see differ in colour. To invent a code of colour combinations distributed on a plane for the variety of experience in the real world is, of course, the achievement of naturalism. It is an achievement simply because, as I said several times in my book, the real world does not look like a flat picture, though a flat picture can be made to look like the real world. The reason for this paradox is discussed in psychology under the heading of the *constancies*. The name covers the totality of those stabilizing tendencies that prevent us from getting giddy in a world of fluctuating appearances. As a man comes to greet us in the street, his image will double in size if he approaches from twenty yards to ten. If he stretches out his hand to greet us, it becomes enormous. We do not register the degree of these changes; his image remains relatively constant and so does the colour of his hair, despite the changes of light and reflection.

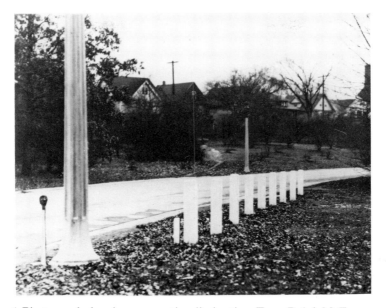

6. Photograph showing perspective diminution. From Ralph M. Evans,
An Introduction to Color (New York, John Wiley & Sons, 1948)

Even the amateur photographer knows something about this effect. He has learned how disappointingly small an object may look in his picture if he fails to move close enough for it to fill most of the field of vision. Painters, of course, have learned to break down the constancies by measuring the apparent size of an object against the brush held at arm's length (see Fig. 219). The novice who tries this simple technique for the first time is in for surprises if he knows how to watch his visual experience. And yet he would be mistaken if he inferred from this surprise effect that the methods he is taught only represent a 'convention', a fortuitous code that differs from the way we 'really' see the world. Arguments of this kind have frequently been used by critics of mathematical perspective. I believe them to be as misleading as is Dubuffet's claim that we never 'really' see a cow in the way Potter represents it. Both these criticisms fail to take into account that we know very well when a picture looks 'right'. A picture painted according to the laws of perspective will generally evoke instant and effortless recognition. It will do so to such an extent that it will in fact restore the feeling of reality, including—and this is most important—the constancies.

I am afraid I somewhat muffed this decisive point in my book by taking a poor example. I am all the more glad to be able to reproduce here the brilliant demonstration which originally convinced me of the crucial relevance of this transformation. It comes from the book *An Introduction to Color*, by Mr. Ralph Evans of the Kodak Laboratories in Rochester (Fig. 6).

All Evans has done is duplicate the image of the lamp-post in the background nearer the picture's lower edge and to do the same with the last of the row of posts. The effect is surprising indeed. Even with the illustration we must have recourse to measurement to convince ourselves that the lamp-post in the background is *really* so small and that the row of posts *really* diminishes to such an extent. The constancies operate even in a photograph. Yet nobody would deny for a moment that we have no difficulty in recognizing the familiar appearance of a suburban street when looking at the picture. Perspective diminution, however surprising, results in recognition. It is a valid instrument, and Vasari was right when he regarded perspective as a genuine discovery.

III

And yet there remains a question which Vasari failed to ask because he took the answer for granted. If only the tricks of naturalistic painting result in convincing images that make for effortless recognition, how can we explain the fact that most cultures are quite happy with schematic representations?

A humorous contemporary drawing, done in a medieval schematic style, which an unknown reader of my book kindly sent me from Australia, not only poses this question afresh, but may also contain the germ of an answer (Fig. 7). The caption tells us (as the king watches with exasperation while his meal slides from the table to the ground): 'It's the way they draw these wretched tables.'

To us, at least, the medieval convention suggests in fact that the table is tilted and that nothing could stand on it. If we could find out when this feeling first arose and when this kind of criticism would have been understood, we would be a long way nearer an explanation of why artists felt that the schema was in need of correction. Once this process was set in motion, the rest may have been a matter of trial and error, of taking thought, and trying again. *Il n'y a que le premier pas qui coûte.*

In my book I have tried to sketch an answer to this question as far as the beginnings of the Greek revolution are concerned. I shall try here to apply it briefly to the Renaissance, leaving it to another occasion to fill in the outlines.[6] My answer was that the purpose of art that led to the discovery of illusionistic devices was not so much a general desire to imitate nature as a specific demand for the plausible narration of sacred events.

Perhaps we should still distinguish here between various forms of pictorial

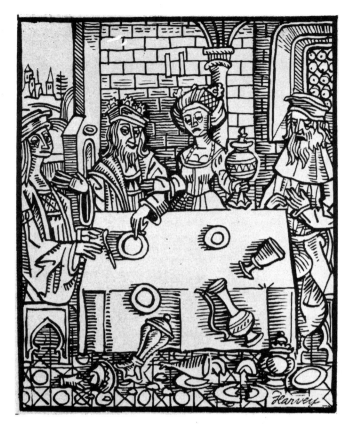

7. Harvey: 'It's the way they draw these wretched tables,'
The Bulletin, Sydney, Australia

narration. One may be called the pictographic method. Here the sacred event is told in clear and simple hieroglyphs which make us understand rather than visualize it. Within the context of such a style, it may be argued, the 'conceptual method' of drawing a table surface produces no discomfort. The hieratic figures of the Three Angels represented on the Romanesque tapestry as partaking of Abraham's meal (Fig. 8) may look pictographic to our eyes, but the scene as such is impressive in its solemn consistency. It is only where the artist aims more visibly at telling us not only *what* happened but *how* it happened that the conceptual method becomes vulnerable to criticism. The rise of naturalism, in other words, presupposes a shift in the beholder's expectations and demands. The public asks the artist to present the sacred event on an imaginary stage as it might have looked to an eye-witness. There is some evidence, I think, that this demand was in fact insistent around the time of Giotto's revolution. It is, of course, generally agreed that Giotto in his Biblical narratives aimed at such a dramatic evocation. We know that at first the effect of his art was stunned surprise at the degree of lifelikeness the

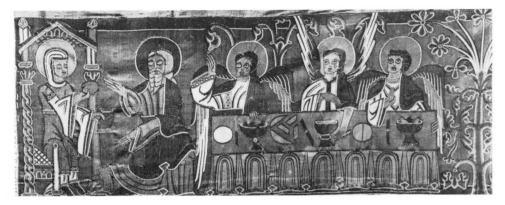

8. *Abraham's Hospitality.* 2nd scene of 12th century tapestry. Halberstadt Cathedral Museum

master's brush could achieve. But if I am right, it was this very success that made certain remaining inconsistencies in the spatial framework of his narratives more obtrusive. In front of his rendering of the Feast of Herod (Fig. 9), an irreverent wit might easily have asked whether the dishes were safe on that table. I do not know whether such a joke was cracked, nor even

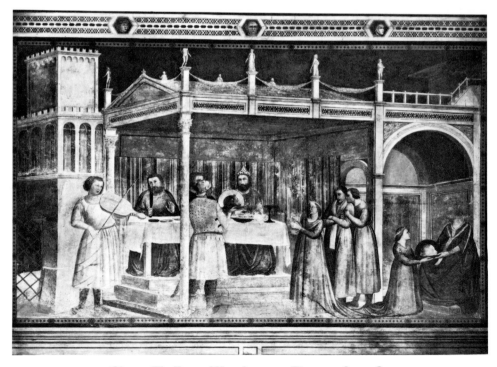

9. Giotto: *The Feast of Herod. c.* 1330. Florence, Santa Croce

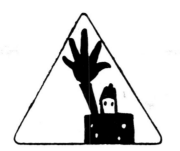

10. Pictographic road sign

whether such criticism of Giotto's method was in fact voiced.[7] But clearly, the invention of perspective three generations later eliminated this potential discomfort. Its rapid spread throughout Europe suggests at least that it met an existing demand. The closer the code came to the evocation of a familiar reality the more easily could the faithful contemplate the re-enactment of the story and identify the participants.

It is true that if this was the purpose it soon became overlaid by technical interest. The rendering of depth, of light, of texture and facial expression was singled out for praise by the connoisseur, and the problems of the craft became aims in themselves. But these aims, to repeat, were only achieved by a long process of trial and error that was guided by the critical scrutiny of paintings that failed to pass the 'recognition test'. The motive force we may imagine as underlying the growth of naturalism is not the wish to imitate natural appearances as such, but to avoid and counter the critic's impatient questions: 'What does this onlooker feel?'; 'What sort of fabric is his cloak?'; 'Why does he throw no shadow?'

Once we describe the rise of naturalism in terms of such scrutiny, it also becomes clear that there are rival functions of the image which do not elicit this kind of question at all. Even within the context of a sacred art, it may be didactic clarity that is demanded of artists designing images that should above all be as legible from afar as are Byzantine mosaics. Today there are such functions of the image as advertising (favouring some 'striking' effect) or diagrams and pictographic roadsigns (Fig. 10) which are better served by a reduction of naturalistic information. Accordingly, the poster and the pictographic illustration have gradually 'evolved' away from nineteenth-century illusionism.

IV

I think that in strictly definable contexts such as these, the term 'evolution' is more than a loose metaphor. Indeed, the schematic process I have sketched out here could be presented in almost Darwinian terms. The fitting of form to function follows a process of trial and error, of mutation and the survival of the fittest. Once the standard of either clear or convincing images has been set, those not conforming will be eliminated by social pressure.[8]

There is a real Darwinian parallel here which should not be overlooked. For the evolution of convincing images was indeed anticipated by nature long before human minds could conceive this trick. I am referring to the wonders of protective colouring and mimicry, of deterrent and camouflaging forms in plants and animals. As we have all learnt at school, and as we can see with amazement in zoological displays, there are insects that look exactly like the leaves of the tree which is their habitat (Fig. 11). There are caterpillars which, when they freeze into immobility, look deceptively like twigs; there are mammals which are so coloured that their dappled or striped skin merges surprisingly with the play of light in their native forest; there are harmless insects which deceptively imitate the shape and colour of dangerous species and thus manage to increase their chances of survival.

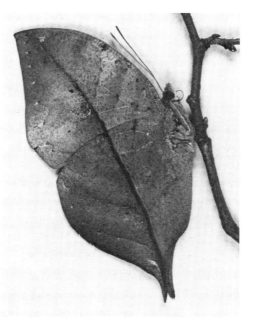

11. Indian leaf butterfly (*Kallima inachus*)

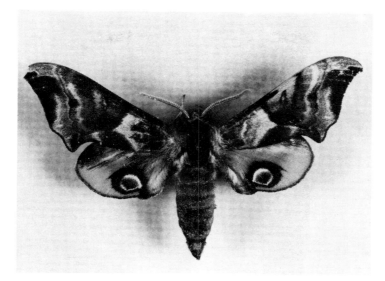

12. British eyed hawkmoth (*Smerinthus ocellata*)

The art historian and the critic could do worse than ponder these miracles. They will make him pause before he pronounces too glibly on the relativity of standards that make for likeness and recognition.[9] The eye and the brain of the bird from which protective colouring must hide the butterfly surely differ in a thousand ways from ours. And yet we can only assume that both for the bird and for us the butterfly and the leaf have become indistinguishable. The naturalistic style of these butterflies deceives a great range of predators including ourselves. Thus, in comparing earlier the bewildering variety of shapes in art with that of living creatures, I had a little more in mind than a mere illustration of multiplicity. For might it not be argued that the shapes of art are also arrived at through adaptation to various functions? I have spoken of the evolution of naturalistic styles in the animal world. Clearly nature is not always naturalistic in that sense. Some forms and colourings are explained by scientists as deterrents or attractants in a more general sense. Take the 'eyes' we frequently see on the wings of moths (Fig. 12). If we can believe the prevailing hypothesis, these have a deterrent effect on predators.[10] If you paint them out, the moths so treated are more likely to be eaten than those able suddenly to display these pairs of threatening eyes. It has been suggested that it is not accidental that the threatening shape takes this particular form.[11] Maybe predators are attuned from birth to the danger of this particular stimulus. A pair of large, watching eyes would signify a predator dangerous to them. But these, we might say, are not naturalistic in the same sense in which the imitated leaf is. They are rather in the nature of

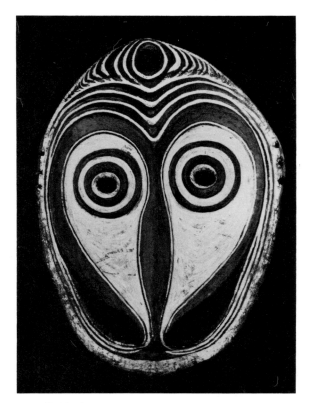

13. Gable decoration from a male tribal house in the
Sepik region of New Guinea. Stuttgart, Lindenmuseum

generalized, schematic—but expressive—images. They represent, if you
like, the Expressionist style of nature.

We may assume that evolution in art as well as in nature could also
approximate other specifications than that of effortless recognizability.
Maybe the immensely disquieting and expressive forms of those tribal styles
we call 'primitive' also evolved step by step towards awe-inspiring or
terrifying configurations (Fig. 13). Admittedly, there was nobody around to
express and formulate these standards. They may also have been less easy to
formulate. One might imagine that it was merely felt that certain masks,
images or ornaments were charged with more potency, more *mana*, than
others, and that those features that made for their magic power survived and
increased in the course of time.

And yet, I do not want to overstress the parallelism between human art and
the creativity of nature. The comparison seems to me as illuminating for what
the two processes may have in common as for their differences. In studying
the evolution of natural forms that extend over geological epochs, we have
learnt to beware of the teleological fallacy. Nature does not set itself aims.

Man does. Admittedly, he does so to varying degrees. It is fashionable to doubt this, too. We are constantly warned against indulging in parochial pride, and against seeing our culture as superior to other varieties. I confess that I am an unrepentant parochial. I believe that the birth of critical rationalism in Greek culture gave mankind a new tool towards the shaping of its own destiny, a tool that other cultures lack. We call it science. The evolutionary series of Greek and Renaissance painting differ from other evolutions precisely through the admixture of science. The science of anatomy, the sciences of projective geometry and of optics were called in to hasten the experimentation towards recognizable images. In the end, as we know, science overtook art in this respect through the evolution of photography, the colour film and the wide screen.

Maybe it is only in these periods of directed research that we can legitimately speak of 'visual discovery'. Indeed, what is usually described in these terms differs quite significantly from the unconscious process I have tried to characterize so far. It differs so much that it might appear at first sight to contradict and disprove my description of the processes of recognition and recall. For contrary to what this description would make us expect, there are visual discoveries which the public at first refused to accept as convincing.

The standard examples are the discoveries of the Impressionists, the methods of *plein air* painting which concentrated on coloured reflections and coloured shadows. These, we are told, did not at first look convincing. The public had to learn to see them by attempting their verification. Sympathetic observers noticed to their surprise that, having looked at Impressionist paintings, they, too, could recognize these coloured shadows in nature. The whole process seemed to be reversed. In fact, it was mainly this experience that led to the dismissal of Vasari's theories of learning as naïve, and to an increasing stress on visual relativism that I should like to criticize in my turn.

V

It is vital to my whole approach that I be allowed to specify a little more closely in psychological terms what is going on when, as the saying goes, the artist 'teaches us to see'. In the remaining sections, I should like to give at least a sketch of a tentative answer, knowing full well that it cannot be the whole story.

We must here return to the fact that recognition is largely unconscious and automatic. Even so, both logically and psychologically, this task of recognition is far from simple. For in fact, the stimuli can hardly ever be identical with those received before. A different angle of vision, a change in illumination, transforms the stimuli—and yet the impression of familiarity is not necessarily affected. Psychology discusses some of the stabilizing mechanisms involved here under the heading of the constancies with which we are already familiar. But the stability of recognition reaches beyond them. Take the most mysterious of all: our ability to recognize a familiar face in a crowd.[12] There is nothing more mobile to our senses than the human physiognomy, for every slight shift in its configuration has a strong expressive meaning. And yet, we also establish a framework of identity in change that is recognized through all the transformations of expression. It is the same face that now looks happy, now morose. It remains the same face even throughout the relentless transformations wrought on it by time and age. Familiarity is not to be confused with identity.

I have chosen the example of facial recognition because it may serve best to bring home even to the sceptic the plasticity of our visual experience. What we 'see' is not simply given, but is the product of past experience and future expectations. Thus, it may happen that we meet an old friend after many years and receive a shock—he has changed so much, we would hardly have recognized him. But after an hour, we do recognize the earlier face in the altered features, memory and impression merge again and we 'see' the old friend once more through, or across, the signs of age. Indeed, try as we may, we can hardly recover the first impression of strangeness, we no longer see him as unfamiliar.

And yet, the recognition of faces also teaches another lesson. The framework is more easily upset than we might expect. The unrecognizable disguise is not the mere fancy of old-fashioned dramatists. Change the hairstyle of a girl or add or subtract a beard, and recognition will be disproportionately difficult, as I have learned to my embarrassment when my students turned up thus transformed. Obviously, recognition demands some anchorage. Even in trying to remember the participants of a class, we look for some method of 'coding' these faces for recognition. Miss Smith is the girl with the ponytail; Mr. Jones, the boy with the moustache. Subsequent learning relies on this mark of identity that determines the *gestalt*.

We return here to the example of the portrait painter and his difficulty in achieving a likeness that is recognized as such by the sitter's relatives. Clearly, what is required is the choice of a code that coincides with the way these critics 'see' the sitter. I have suggested that their criticism may well be more valid than the painter is inclined to admit. But we may now add that the painter's own version may also win through. He may be able to persuade the

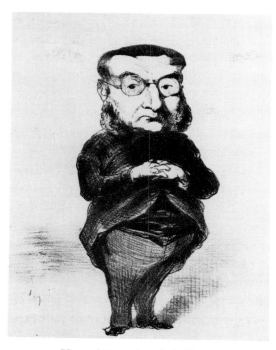

14. Honoré Daumier: *A. L. Coquerel.*
From *Charivari*, 3 October 1849

relatives of the validity of his own vision; looking at the sitter, they may suddenly recognize the portrait in him. Art has imposed a fresh vision on a face.

The most extreme case of this exploitation of the instability of vision is portrait caricature. It is also the most instructive, because the caricaturist need not be a great artist to seize upon those invariants which are all we generally remember of the appearance of politicians or actors. In distilling this framework into a simple code, he shows us the formula and helps the public figure to secure recognition. But the caricaturist can also transform his victim. He can single out characteristic invariants which we have yet never used for recognition, and in thus focusing our attention on these features, he teaches us a fresh code (Fig. 14). We then say that the caricaturist has made us see the victim differently—we cannot help thinking of the caricature whenever we meet the man.

It is in this direction that I propose to look for a solution to the problem of visual discovery in art. Its most striking effects presuppose a degree of plasticity in the way we 'see' the world which leaves recognition unaffected. This must be connected with the wealth of cues at our disposal for coding our visual experience. The painter, like the caricaturist, can teach us a new code of recognition, he cannot teach us to 'see'.

VI

Having stated the direction in which I think we have to go, I should like to proceed a little more slowly and to introduce a number of distinctions I failed to make in *Art and Illusion*.

I am afraid as a first step I must slightly reduce the importance generally attached to the artist and painter in this process of discovery. It is true, of course, that, being professionally concerned with visual experience, artists have played a conspicuous role in the discovery of unexpected features in the visible world. But there is no intrinsic reason why such discoveries need be coded in paint and not in words. Our coloured shadows are a case in point. As early as 1793, Goethe sent the German physicist and writer Lichtenberg a section of his colour theory dealing with the phenomenon of coloured shadows. Lichtenberg replied in a most interesting letter, in which he said that ever since receiving Goethe's paper he had been running after coloured shadows as he ran after butterflies as a boy. Lichtenberg discusses the general failure to notice these things 'because in our judgments which are based on visual impressions, sensation and judgment interpenetrate to such an extent that after a certain age it becomes hardly possible to separate them; every moment we believe that we perceive what we merely infer. It is for this reason that bad portrait painters lay in the entire face all over with pink flesh colour. They are unable to realize that there could be blue, green, yellow and brown shadows in a human face.'

I feel we would get further in our study of visual discoveries if we made some distinction between change of interest and change of perception. Lichtenberg's interest, once aroused, led him to notice things he had not noticed before. In itself, there is not much of a problem here. It can and does happen all the time. If you want to buy new curtains, you will probably notice curtains and their features that you would otherwise overlook. If you read about facial asymmetry, you will become aware of deviations from symmetry which you had never noticed. Some of these fluctuations are superficial and transitory, others more permanent. If fashion arouses interest in vintage cars, old cars will acquire a new look; if collectors should make news by paying high prices for a particular type of dustbin, we would begin to look at dustbins on our way to the office.

(Some five years after this lecture was given the London *Times* printed a report by Michael Leapman (24 August 1972) that about one third of New York's litter baskets had been stolen, since 'there seems to be something enormously camp and attractive about them'. I can only hope that my hypothetical prophecy did not contribute to this minor crime wave.)

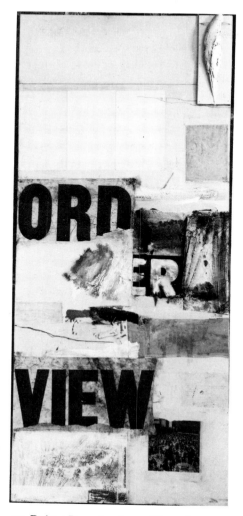

15. Robert Rauschenberg: *Hazard*. 1957.
Private Collection

Clearly, art is a frequent source of such novel interests. Contemporary artists such as Rauschenberg have become fascinated by the patterns and textures of decaying walls with their torn posters and patches of damp (Fig. 15). Though I happen to dislike Rauschenberg, I notice to my chagrin that I cannot help being aware of such sights in a different way since seeing his paintings. Perhaps if I had disliked his exhibition less, the memory would have faded more quickly. For emotional involvement, positive or even negative, certainly favours retention and recognition.

And yet, I would think, this experience of noticing things because artists have drawn attention to motifs still differs from visual discoveries at least in some degree.

I recently experienced the surprise of such a discovery. It may sound trivial enough as I describe it, but it will show that this function of art is not confined to representational painting. Our kitchen floor at home happens to have a simple black-and-white checkerboard pattern. As I was taking a glass of water from the tap to the table, I suddenly noticed the delightful and interesting distortions of this pattern visible through the bottom of the glass. I had never seen this transformation before, though I must have made this same movement hundreds of times. And suddenly I recognized the pattern and knew why I saw it now. I had visited an exhibition of the paintings of Lawrence Gowing, a painter who shares my interest in perception and was experimenting with abstracts. I had looked with interest at one of the paintings in which the illusion of space and light in a forest is created through the systematic distortion of a checker pattern (Fig. 16). It was a classic case of what might be called inverted recognition—the recognition not of reality in a painting but of a painting in reality. Clearly it was interest that had triggered

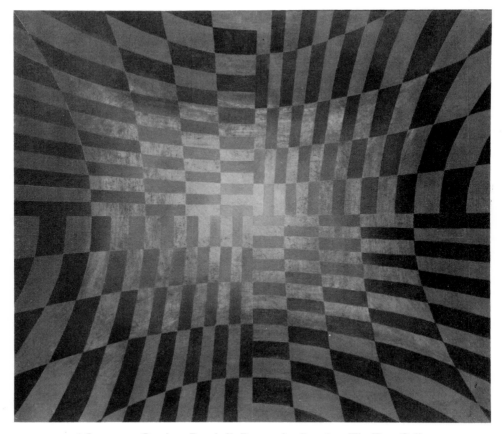

16. Lawrence Gowing: *Parabolic Perspective*. London, The Tate Gallery

it off. Without it, I might have taken a hundred or a thousand more glasses from the tap to the kitchen table without noticing the appearance of the floor through the bottom of the glass. Without noticing, not really without seeing. For of course I must have seen the pattern before, if we mean by 'seeing' that the stimuli must have reached my retina and my visual cortex. But I had attended to these as little as I attend to millions of other impressions that impinge as I move through the world.

I must draw attention to the difference between this and the former example, although it is only a difference of nuance. Rauschenberg may have created an interest in old billboards as possible motifs of artistic attention, but it would be stretching usage beyond common sense if I said in this instance that I had never seen billboards before. But this would be true of the pattern Gowing enabled me to arrest and to see. Moreover, he also enabled me to discuss and recall it. I suppose we might say his painting had unwittingly provided a symbol in which this fleeting impression could be coded and had thus isolated it from the stream of 'pre-conscious' or 'subliminal' perception. I thus experienced the thrill and shock of recognition when I encountered the configuration of the painting in this unexpected context, though I was not immediately aware of the cause of this isolation.

To probe a little deeper into this kind of visual discovery, we should, I think, investigate the effect of isolation from context, not only through art but also through other agencies. For isolation will easily break up familiarity and thus transform the experience. Take the example of our familiar room. Anybody who has ever moved house can tell how unfamiliar that old room can look when emptied of furniture. Not only unfamiliar, but strikingly different. Its very size seems to have changed. The once pleasant and cosy place seems to have shrunk into a small, stark cell. Admit the demolition firm, break down the walls and visit the foundations for a last time, and they will look tiny in relation to the total landscape. What was once a comfortable framework for your actions, as you moved from the easy-chair to your bookshelf, is now a speck on the terrain. The context completely transforms the experience. Yet it would be quite misleading to say you had never looked at your room before or never knew its real size. Your experience of familiarity was as real as is that of your unfamiliarity.

As far as images are concerned, the most convincing demonstration of this effect of context comes not, perhaps, from art but from photography. We all know that not all snapshots look convincing. Some isolate the phase of a movement from its context and look surprisingly unreal in consequence. Others give such a steep foreshortening that they look startling and almost unbelievable. Does it make sense then to say that this is what we really see in such situations? Yes and no. Interaction of cues can restore familiarity. We have the technical means now to put this surprising fact to the test. In Cinerama, the temporal and spatial context so closely simulates the experience of the real world that, far from finding steep foreshortening unrealistic, we tend to duck or blink as the object appears to approach us.

One answer to the question of how the same image can be both verifiably correct and yet unfamiliar surely lies in the effect of isolation. Here we can return to those famous coloured shadows of the Impressionists. In the sixth chapter of Zola's novel *L'Oeuvre*, the painter's rather simple-minded wife ventures to criticize him for painting a poplar quite blue. He makes her look at the motif and notice the delicate blue of the foliage. It was true, the tree was really blue, and yet she did not quite admit defeat; she blamed reality: there could not *be* blue trees in nature.

Was she so stupid? Her experience of familiarity, like that of everyone, was grounded on a knowledge of invariants, on what Hering called, a bit misleadingly, 'memory colour'. Psychologists—since the time of Goethe and of Lichtenberg at least—use artificial means for eliminating this mechanism, breaking down the interaction of cues and isolating the sensation as far as this can ever be done. They use what is called a reduction screen for defeating the constancies and demonstrating, for instance, the degree to which an illuminated surface changes its appearance as we tilt or move it in relation to the light source. Naturalistic painters have always used reduction in one way or another to break down the constancies. They tend to isolate and half close their eyes for this very purpose. But obviously, if they restore the context we do not experience surprise. The correct placing of the right values results in recognition. But there are both technical and artistic limits to this restoration, and hence the shock of incredulity.

If this shock results in interest, however, we can all be made to hunt for coloured shadows or other effects seen in paintings, as Lichtenberg did. We shall not need a reduction screen; interest and attention will do the isolating for us. And here the isolation really can lead to transformation—or, to use a more emotive word, to the transfiguring of reality.

VII

And yet, even this is not the whole story. For something more interesting might intervene to assist transformation through isolation. Briefly, isolation tends to increase ambiguity. In real life, it is the interaction of innumerable cues that generally allows us to find our way through the world with comparative ease. Yet it is a well-known fact that in certain situations we cannot tell whether an unfamiliar object seen in isolation is large and distant or small and close by, or whether an unevenly shaded area is hollow and lit from the left or protruding and lit from the right. Clearly, in reducing the richness of nature to suit his code, the painter will always increase the ambiguity of his individual stroke or mark. A line can stand for anything from a match to a distant horizon. In what are called 'conceptual' styles, every effort is made to reduce or eliminate these ambiguities and to secure the intended reading. Naturalistic styles mobilize all available means for the mutual clarification of cues and any obtrusive ambiguity counts as a fault to be eliminated. The master in the life class will draw attention to any passage that is not clear, any line that is not recognized for what it stands for. But once art has become emancipated from its purpose of illustration and evocation, this ambiguity acquires a new interest. From Impressionism to Cubism, the exploration of isolation and ambiguity has drawn increasing attention to the instability of the visible world. Once again these lessons can be recalled in real life situations—most easily in conditions of reduced visibility: in mist, in flickering light, or in unfamiliar situations. But increasing experience with the unexpected ambiguity of visual cues in paintings will alert us to the unsuspected ambiguity of visual cues in real life and thus lead to fresh discoveries. In recognizing such pictures in nature we learn about the complexity of vision as such.

Once again, painting has no monopoly here. I remember an unsettling experience of this kind that was elicited by a psychological experiment. I had just attended a demonstration of that intriguing visual teaser, Adelbert Ames's 'revolving trapezoid', in essence a flat foreshortened window frame that turns on its axis but looks stubbornly as if it swayed to and fro. As I walked cross-country, I happened to see a broken farm gate propped up in an inaccessible pond. It reminded me of the trapezoid and I suddenly realized that I could not tell its real shape, or position either. There was a moment of slight anxiety as I woke up to the fact that the same applied to distant trees or countless other configurations in my surroundings.[13] The passing shock has helped me to understand why we prefer to ignore this instability in our readings of the world.

Yet it is clear that if it were not for this instability it would make no sense to say that the painter can impose his vision on our world. He does it at those vulnerable points where coding is more or less optional. What is involved here is perhaps best illustrated with the help of a well-known textbook

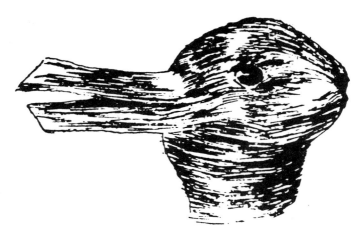

17. 'Rabbit or Duck?' From *Fliegende Blätter*

example of ambiguity, the notorious old 'rabbit or duck' figure I used in my book (Fig. 17). Clearly, in this most simple of cases we can elicit alternate readings depending on captions or a verbal description—but it might be even more effective to impose one of these readings through visual means.

I have not made any experiments, but I would predict that you could bring about a transformation merely by changing the visual context, either spatially, by drawing a duckpond or rabbit warren around the blot, or temporally, by showing a subject a series of pictures of rabbits, before projecting the ambiguous image; in which case, what we call mental set will surely do the trick and determine the reading.

It would be fascinating to go on from here and watch the final transition from interpretation to suggestion. In our figure, there is still an objective anchorage for the reading of either rabbit or duck. You might systematically reduce this anchorage and still make your subjects project an expected image, provided their initial conviction and desire is strong enough. For there is a natural transition here from interest to mental set, and thence to projection. The hungry rabbit catcher will scan the field for his quarry with such intensity that a clod of earth or a clump of leaves may tempt him, unless he has learned to hold his imagination in check. The degree to which a hunt or search can reorganize and transform cues was brought home to me—if I may continue my autobiography—when I was preparing this paper and looking in a library for a book with suitable illustrations of mimicry and protective colouring. Running my eyes along a line of miscellaneous books, I suddenly thought I had got it; I 'saw' a book with the odd but promising title 'Deceptive Beetles'—obviously some treatise on insect camouflage. Alas, as I looked more closely the title turned out to read *Decisive Battles*. I felt pretty silly, but I could not help wondering about the flexibility of the preconscious mind. Beetles to battles is not a surprising transformation; it involves the misreading of only two letters out of seven. But that, in this joy of false recognition, my preconscious had changed 'decisive' into 'deceptive' to keep the promise of a book on mimicry is almost disturbing.

Have I moved too far away from art? Not, I hope, if this extreme example of my folly illustrates the end of the spectrum, as it were, between perception and projection. I do not know if it is ever possible to separate the two completely. In scanning the world with interest roused by past experience, the previous impression and the incoming sensations tend to coalesce like two drops of water forming a larger drop. When paintings have aroused our interest in certain configurations, we may look for anchorage and confirmation and use every hint in a visual experience to find there what we sought. This may go for the 'conformist' as well as for the 'progressive'. The first will find his prejudices confirmed and recognize only the familiar code in the familiar world; this is what the innovators always complained of. But the other experience may be equally possible. The wish to find confirmation of some new experiment may make the progressive suggestible and may thus facilitate the artist's task of modifying his code. The premium in self-esteem that may be offered to those who can share a new way of seeing should not be overlooked as a determinant.

The experience of visual discovery I have tried to stalk is probably a compound of these elements. I especially mean the experience in which the normal relationship of recognition and recall is reversed, so that we genuinely recognize pictorial effects in the world around us, rather than the familiar sights of the world in pictures. The road to this experience led from interest to isolation and from isolation to increased ambiguity. In discovering an alternative reading of an isolated set of impressions, we receive a kind of minor revelation through recognition. Is this the thrill of learning of which Aristotle speaks?

I have so far steered clear of aesthetics, and it would be out of place to introduce it now. But we can be sure, I think, that this revelation is experienced as a new kind of beauty. It is well known that it was the admiration for the effects of Claude Lorrain, for his symbols of serenity and idyllic peace (Fig. 18), that first led the English connoisseurs of the eighteenth century to discover the beauties of what they called picturesque landscapes nearer home. Richard Wilson learned from Claude's code how to isolate and represent the beauties of his native Wales (Fig. 19).[14] In this momentous development that had its influence on the rise of Romantic nature worship in poetry no less than in art, prestige, new interests and new

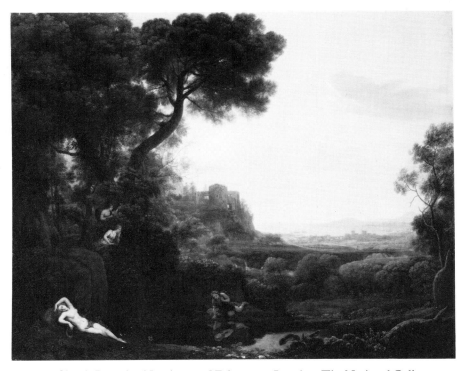

18. Claude Lorrain: *Narcissus and Echo*. 1644. London, The National Gallery

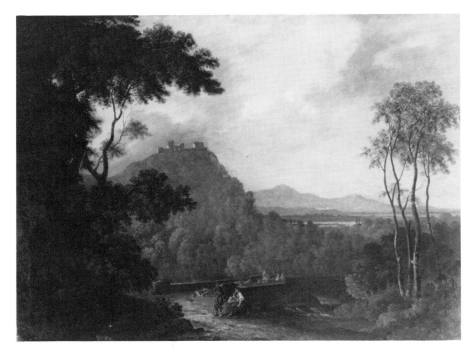

19. Richard Wilson: *Dinas Bran Castle*. *c*. 1770. Cardiff, The National Museum of Wales

visual experiences were no doubt intertwined in a way that is hard to disentangle. Wilson probably wished to see Wales in Claude's terms. But the very word 'picturesque' shows that one element involved was the thrilling and unexpected encounter with beloved pictures in what had previously looked like a familiar reality of the kind that is unconsciously recognized but not consciously recalled.

There is no reason to doubt that this process can and does go on. The world of visual experience is infinite in its variety and richness. Art can code reality correctly and yet paradoxically we have no cause to fear that artists need ever stop revealing to us new facets of this inexhaustible experience.

Moment and Movement in Art

WHILE THE problem of space and its representation in art has occupied the attention of art historians to an almost exaggerated degree, the corresponding problem of time and the representation of movement has been strangely neglected. There are of course some relevant observations scattered throughout the literature,[1] but no systematic treatment has ever been attempted. It is not the purpose of the present paper to supply this want, only to indicate how this neglect may have arisen and where we may have to revise our preconceptions if we are to approach the problem afresh. For it may be argued that it was the way in which the problem of the passage of time in painting was traditionally posed that doomed the answers to relative sterility. This tradition reaches back at least to the early eighteenth century, more precisely to Lord Shaftesbury's classic formulation in the *Characteristicks*.[2] Chapter I of *A notion of the Historical Draught, or Tablature of the Judgment of Hercules* (Fig. 20) opens with the statement that 'this Fable or History may be variously represented, according to the Order of Time':

> Either in the instant when the two Goddesses (VIRTUE and PLEASURE) accost HERCULES; Or when they are enter'd on their Dispute; Or when their Dispute is already far advanc'd, and VIRTUE seems to gain her Cause.

In the first instance Hercules would have to be shown surprised at the appearance of the two Goddesses; in the second he would have to be shown interested and in doubt, and in the third we would witness how he 'agonizes, and with all his Strength of Reason endeavours to overcome himself'. It is this Aristotelian turning-point that is recommended to the painter, though

Lecture given at the Warburg Institute in a series on Time and Eternity in June 1964.

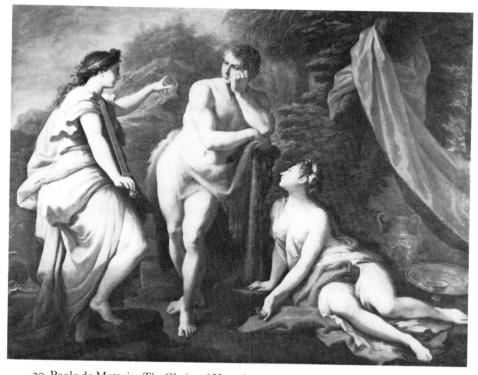

20. Paolo de Matteis: *The Choice of Hercules*. 1711. Oxford, Ashmolean Museum

Shaftesbury also discusses the fourth possibility of representing 'the Date or Period ... when Hercules is intirely won by Virtue'. He rejects it on the grounds of dramatic inefficacy and for the additional reason that in such a picture 'PLEASURE ... must necessarily appear displeas'd, or out of humour: a Circumstance which wou'd no way sute her Character.'

'Tis evident, that every Master in Painting, when he has made choice of the determinate Date or Point of Time, according to which he wou'd represent his History, is afterwards debar'd the taking advantage from any other Action than what is immediately present, and belonging to that single Instant he describes. For if he passes the present only for a moment, he may as well pass it for many years. And by this reckoning he may with as good right repeat the same Figure several times over ...
There remains no other way by which we can possibly give a hint of any thing future, or call to mind any thing past, than by setting in view such Passages or Events as have actually subsisted, or according to Nature might well subsist, or happen together in *one and the same* instant.

This absolute necessity, however, need not prevent the painter from representing movement or change such as the turning-point of the drama

Shaftesbury had recommended in his commission (Fig. 20). For 'the Artist has power to leave still in his Subject the Traces or Footsteps of its Predecessor . . . as for instance, when the plain Traces of Tears new fallen . . . remain still in a Person newly transported with Joy. . . . By the same means, which are employ'd to call to mind *the Past*, we may anticipate *the Future* . . .' In our case, for instance, the artist could show Hercules in doubt and yet indicate that his decision was to be in favour of Virtue:

> This Transition, which seems at first so mysterious a Performance, will be easily comprehended, if one considers, That the Body, which moves much slower than the Mind, is easily out-strip'd by this latter; and that the Mind on a sudden turning itself some new way, the nearer situated and more sprightly parts of the Body (such as the Eyes and Muscles about the Mouth and Forehead) taking the alarm, and moving in an instant, may leave the heavier and more distant parts to adjust themselves, and change their Attitude some moments after. This different Operation may be distinguish'd by the names of *Anticipation* and *Repeal*.

Shaftesbury admits that this rigorous standard of instantaneous action is often sinned against. He refers with amusement and contempt to the usual representations of Diana and Actaeon, in which the goddess is seen throwing water at Actaeon, whose horns are already growing although he is not yet wet.

It was Shaftesbury's formulation, no doubt, which influenced James Harris in his *Discourse on Music, Painting and Poetry*,[3] where the distinction is first made with all desirable clarity between the various media of art: music being concerned with motion and sound, painting with shapes and colours. Every picture is thus 'of necessity a *punctum temporis* or instant'. But though Harris calls a painting 'but a Point or Instant', he adds that 'in a Story well known the Spectator's Memory will supply the previous and the subsequent . . . [This] cannot be done where such Knowledge is wanting'. In fact he wonders whether any historical incident in a painting would be intelligible 'supposing history to have been silent and to have given no additional information'.

All these ideas were taken up by Lessing and woven into the fabric of his *Laocoon*, which systematically distinguishes between the arts of time and the arts of space. 'Painting can . . . only represent a single moment of an action and must therefore select the most pregnant moment which best allows us to infer what has gone before and what follows.'[4] Lessing, as I have tried to argue elsewhere,[5] did not write the *Laocoon* for the sake of this well-established distinction. What provoked him was the idea that poetry or drama should ever conform to the limitations of the visual arts. For these limitations, he thought, followed precisely from the restriction to one single moment. If there is to be one moment that will be transfixed and preserved for eternity it clearly must not be an ugly moment. The famous disquisition about the reasons why the marble Laocoon must not shout while Vergil can let his Laocoon groan and bellow is deduced from this *a priori* principle.

> The artist can never use more of ever-changing reality than one single moment of time and, if he is a painter, he can look at this moment only from one single aspect. But since their works exist not only to be seen but also to be contemplated, contemplated at length and repeatedly, it is clear that this single moment and single aspect must be the most fruitful of all that can be chosen. Only that one is fruitful however that gives free rein to the imagination. The more we see . . . the more we must believe ourselves to be seeing. There is no moment however in the whole sequence of an emotion which enjoys this advantage less than its climax. Beyond it there is nothing and thus to show the eye the extreme, means to clip the wings of the imagination. . . . Thus when Laocoon sighs the imagination can hear him shout, but when he shouts our mind can neither rise to greater intensity nor descend to a lower step without picturing him in a more tolerable and therefore less interesting state.[6]

Unconvincing as this casuistry may be, it was meant as a concession to Winckelmann, who had never failed to denounce the arch-corrupter Bernini, in whose works such as the *David* or the *Anima Dannata* the climax of movement and passion is indeed presented to the eye. As long as the arts of time remained free to depict these extremes, Lessing was quite ready to concede that the visual arts should concentrate on the moments of stillness instead.

These particular conclusions were implicitly challenged by the Romantics,[7] but as far as I know the underlying distinction between the arts of time and of space, of succession and simultaneity, remained unquestioned in aesthetics. Thus the artist was driven in the interest of truth to concentrate more and more on the task of giving, in Constable's words, 'One brief moment caught from fleeting time a lasting and sober existence'. These words were written in 1832.[8] A few years later photography was invented. But the early photograph with its long exposure time was not yet a threat to the artist who set himself the aim of catching time on the wing. When Ruskin wrote his chapter in *Modern Painters*, 'Of Truth of Water', to exalt the fidelity of Turner's renderings over the earlier conventions of Van der Velde or Canaletto, he regrets that he 'cannot catch a wave, nor Daguerreotype it, and so there is no coming to pure demonstration'.[9] However, he was clearly convinced that the Daguerreotype would prove Turner right if it ever could catch a wave.

And yet when the camera did finally catch up, it appeared to demonstrate the inferiority even of the most sensitive eye. The notorious issue over which the battle broke was the rendering of the galloping horse.[10] The photographer Muybridge, in 1877, went to great trouble to solve the problem of what really goes on in this rapid movement. He lined up twelve cameras along a racecourse in California in such a way that the passing horse would break a thread stretched across its path and thus release the shutter. The dazzling sun of California allowed a brief exposure, and in 1878 Muybridge could startle the worlds of art and of science with his demonstration that painters could not see. In particular the flying gallop, so frequent in the rendering of horse races, was claimed to be quite at variance with the facts. The reaction of painters and critics was ambivalent. Some said that it was the instantaneous photograph that looked unreal and that the experiment had proved the superiority of art. They pointed to the strangely frozen effect of instantaneous photographs. It is hard for us to recapture the puzzled curiosity which these once caused. We see so many pictures of football matches and athletic events in our papers that we have come to take these chaotic configurations for granted. Only once in a while does an action photograph really puzzle us with an impression of impossible movements. On the whole it is far from true that all snapshots look frozen to us. No wonder artists wanted to accept the challenge of the camera and tried to learn from it, thus endorsing the traditional view that the truthful image can or should render only what we actually manage to see in a moment.[11]

Now there certainly is a sense in which the instantaneous photograph represents the truth of that moment. Put a succession of snapshots taken at quick intervals into a revolving drum so that each is visible through a slot for about one-sixteenth of a second and we see the original event in motion. Thanks to this convenient illustration we can in fact pose Shaftesbury's problem in a very simple way. Suppose a news camera had filmed the Judgement of Hercules. Which of the frames would be suitable for publication as a still from the film? The answer is that none might do. The so-called 'stills' which we see displayed outside cinemas and in books on the art of the film are not, as a rule, simply isolated frames from the moving picture enlarged and mounted. They are specially made and very often specially posed on the set, after a scene is taken. That thrilling scene where the hero embraces his girl while he keeps the villain covered with a revolver may consist of many yards of film containing twenty-four frames per second of running time, but not one of them may be really suitable for enlargement and display. Legs fly up in the air, fingers are spread out in an ungainly way and an unintelligible leer comes over the hero's face. Far better to pose the scene carefully and photograph it as a readable entity which fulfils Shaftesbury's and Lessing's demands for anticipation and repeal, though the posed stills partly refute the theory that a real *punctum temporis* will easily combine all the necessary cues in one simultaneous assembly.

I do not want to overstate the force of this particular refutation. There are stills which are taken from the film frames and are perfectly legible, just as there are instantaneous photographs which do give us the perfect illusion of a coherent action. Conceivably the struggle of a man and his two sons with monstrous serpents might pass through the configuration of the Laocoon. But could anyone ever know this for certain? Do we not beg the most important question when we ask what 'really happens' at any point of time? We therewith assume that what Harris called a *punctum temporis* really exists, or, more radically, that what we really perceive is the infinite sequence of such static points in time. Once this is conceded the rest follows, at least with the demand for mimesis. Static signs, the argument runs, can only represent static moments, never movements which happen in time. Philosophers are familiar with this problem under the name of Zeno's paradox, the demonstration that Achilles could never catch up with a tortoise and no arrow could ever move.[12] As soon as we assume that there is a fraction of time in which there is no movement, movement as such becomes inexplicable.

Logically the idea that there is a 'moment' which has no movement and can be seized and fixed in this static form by the artist, or for that matter, by the camera, certainly leads to Zeno's paradox. Even an instantaneous photograph records the traces of movement, a sequence of events, however brief. But the idea of the *punctum temporis* is not only an absurdity logically, it is a worse absurdity psychologically. For we are not cameras but rather slow-registering instruments which cannot take in much at a time. Twenty-four successive stills in a second are sufficient to give us the illusion of movement in the cinema. We can see them only in motion, not as stills. Somewhere along this order of magnitude, a fifteenth or a tenth of a second, lies what we experience as a moment, something we can just seize in its flight. Compared with the speed of a computer we are indeed slow in the uptake.

The television screen is an even more impressive demonstration of this slowness of our perception and the duration of what we consider a 'moment'. When we watch the programme we are, in fact, watching a tiny spot of light traversing the screen from side to side 405 times in one-fifth of a second at a speed of about 7,000 miles an hour. This spot of light traces out the rectangular area on which the picture is seen. The camera scans the object with this beam which varies in intensity as it strikes brighter or darker objects, and these fluctuations are translated into electrical impulses and re-translated into a travelling scanning beam in the television set. At each moment of time, therefore, what we really see (if that expression had any meaning) would only be one luminous dot.[13] It could not even be called a brighter or less bright dot, since these notions introduce what has gone before and what comes after. It would be a meaningless dot. Actually if we want to pursue this thought to its logical conclusion the *punctum temporis* could not even show us a meaningless dot, for light has a frequency. It is an event in time, as is sound—not to speak of the events in the nervous system that transform its impact into a sensation.

These considerations may allow us to focus more sharply the philosophical problem that underlies the traditional distinction between the arts of time and the arts of space. As a process in time television certainly presents the travels of a meaningless flickering dot, and the extension in space of this dot turns out to be an illusion, founded on the sluggishness of our perception. Yet it is this sluggishness that overcomes the limitation of time, the *punctum temporis*, and creates a meaningful pattern through the miracle of persistence of memory.

It was no less a thinker than St. Augustine who pondered this miracle in one of the most famous meditations of his *Confessions*.[14] Famous, but still not sufficiently so. For if Shaftesbury and Lessing had profited from the lesson of St. Augustine's introspections they could not have created that fatal dichotomy between space and time in art which has tangled the discussion ever since.

What puzzled St. Augustine is precisely the elusiveness of the present moment flanked as it is by future time that is not yet, and past time that is no longer. How can we speak of the length of time, how can we even measure time since what we measure is either not yet or no longer in existence? It is Zeno's paradox from a new angle. For we do speak of long times, says St. Augustine, we also speak in poetics of long and short syllables, and everyone knows what we mean when we say that a long syllable in a poem is double the length of a short one. And yet I can only call the syllable long after it has ended, when it no longer *is*:

What is it therefore that I measure? Where is that short syllable by which I measure? Where is that long one which I measure? Both have sounded, have flown and gone, they are now no more: and yet I measure them . . . it is not these sounds, which are no longer, which I measure, but something that is in my memory that remains fastened there. It is in thee, my mind, that I measure the times. Please do not interrupt me now, that is do not interrupt thine own self with the tumults of thine own impressions. In thee, I say, it is, that I measure the times. The impression, which transient things cause in thee and which remains even when they have gone, that is it which being still present I measure.[15]

And as with the past, so with the future. 'Who can deny that things to come are not yet? Yet already there is in the mind an expectation of things to come.'[16] Then comes the famous introspective account of what happens in his mind when he recites a psalm.

Before I begin, my expectation alone extends itself over the whole, but so soon as I shall have once begun, how much so ever of it I shall take off into the past over so much my memory also reaches, thus the life of this action of mine is extended both ways: into my memory, so far as concerns the part I have repeated already, and into my expectation too, in respect of what I am about to repeat.[17]

When Professor Hearnshaw gave the presidential address at the British Psychological Society in 1956[18] he made this passage the starting-point for the discussion of what is technically known as 'temporal integration', the bundling together in one extended stretch of time of memories and expectations. Even in his own field he noticed a scarcity of literature on this all-pervasive problem, particularly in comparison with the 'extraordinary dominance of special concepts, notably in Gestalt psychology'. His explanation applies with equal force to our own field of study: 'Temporal integration cuts across faculty boundaries. It implies perception of the present, memory of the past, and expectation of the future—stimulus patterns, traces and symbolic processes—integrated into a common organization.' It is the kind of complex problem that research shies away from.

Not that the last hundred years have not yielded insights which allow us to pose St. Augustine's problem with more precision, though scarcely with the same beauty. We know for instance that where he speaks of memory that retains the present in the mind, we can and must distinguish between at least three types of such retention. The first is that persistence of a sense impression that is so relevant to television. This is, partly at least, a physiological process which makes the impression of light and sound persist for a moment when the actual stimulus is over. But apart from this, there is another kind of persistence or reverberation that is variously known as 'immediate memory', 'primary retention' or 'echo memory'.[19] It is an elusive concept, but one easily open to introspection. It happens that somebody says a few words which we fail to take in. But as we cast our mind back we find that the sound is still there, a few seconds later, and we can find out what the words were. This kind of immediate memory is a trace that disappears very quickly, but it is vital for our real understanding of St. Augustine's problem of what we measure when we measure the lengths of syllables in a poem or of tones in a melody just heard. These syllables or tones are still really there in a rather different sense from which things past are still stored somewhere in our mind. Indeed Hebb, in his book on the *Organization of Behavior*,[20] postulates two distinct kinds of memory. He would like to believe in some kind of reverberation of the stimulus preserving the memory until a more permanent trace is formed. Be that as it may, it really is evident that our impressions remain available for a brief span of time, the time that is known as the memory span or the specious present. Psychological experiments with the memorizing of nonsense syllables or digits show that subjects can hold a limited number over a few seconds, after which they vanish and are replaced by fresh incoming impressions. There is a fascinating paper by G. A. Miller called 'The Magical Number Seven plus and minus Two'[21] in which he puts forward the hypothesis that seven acquired its status precisely as the largest number of items we can generally hold at once. What matters to us in these experiments and speculations is that they corrode the sharp *a priori* distinction between the perceptions of time and of space. Successive impressions do in fact persist *together* and are not wholly experienced as successive. Without this holding operation we could not grasp a melody or understand the spoken word.

St. Augustine was right, moreover, when he found that the mind not only retains the past impression but also reaches out into the future. And again, more is involved here than a mere expectation extending over any length of time. Take St. Augustine's example of the recitation of a psalm. While we speak one line we are in a real sense making ready for the recital of future lines. Lashley has shown in a classic contribution to this subject[22] that the immediate future we are thus making ready for is as much really present in our mind as is the past. If it were not so spoonerisms would not occur. When Dr. Spooner said to a student 'You have hissed my mystery lesson' he proved that the letters to be spoken were already present together in his mind and got mixed up. One of Lashley's most interesting examples concerns typing mistakes. It happens for instance that we double the wrong letter in a word we perfectly know how to spell. The instruction to double, which is already waiting in the wings, as it were, misses its cue and is applied wrongly.

Here, where our own actions are concerned, we can speak of innervations stored in advance ready to go into action in some predetermined serial order or sequence—and surely it is much less surprising that this goes wrong occasionally than that it ever comes right. But even if we do not speak but listen to speech, if we do not play but listen to music, some representation of possibilities to come will be stored in readiness just waiting to be triggered off by the slightest confirmatory cue. There is the story of the unfortunate singer who discovered that he could not sing the highest note in an aria. So he stepped forward and opened his mouth wide and triumphantly while the orchestra made a loud noise. The public 'heard' the top note and applauded. The note was as much present in the public's mind at that moment as were the notes that led up to it. What would have happened if the singer had sung a false note instead? He would not only have hurt our ears in that moment, he would retroactively have spoilt the whole phrase even if the earlier notes had been provisionally classified and stored as acceptable.

Experiences of this kind illustrate why the old distinction between the arts of time such as music and poetry, and the arts of space such as painting and architecture, is so barren and misleading. In listening to music the moment is as it were spread out to a perceptual span in which immediate memory and anticipation are both phenomenally present. Some people feel this presence strongly as a spatial pattern, others less so. It hardly matters as long as we recognize that the understanding of music or the understanding of speech would not be possible if we lived in too narrow a present. For in music no less than in speech what comes after affects what has come before. There is a blasphemous musicians' joke attributed to Arthur Schnabel which demonstrates how the most heavenly theme, such as the opening of Mozart's G minor symphony, can be spoiled and destroyed by the simple doubling of the last note of the phrase. The same can be demonstrated in the hearing of speech where we really could not make sense of any sentence unless we scanned the recent sounds and revised our interpretation according to the way our expectations are confirmed or refuted by the next sound. Lashley gives two amusing examples for this influence of context on meaning: 'The mill-wright on my right thinks it right that some conventional rite should symbolize the right of every man to write as he pleases.' Here it is mainly the preceding words which influence our pigeonholing. But in his other instance the retroactive process comes into its own: 'Rapid righting with his uninjured hand saved from loss the contents of the capsized canoe.' The associations which give an unexpected meaning to the sound 'righting', as Lashley says, are not activated for at least three to five seconds after hearing the word. But as a rule the word is still present for this revision.

Psychological time is clearly something much more complicated and mysterious than the sheer succession of events. But if music and poetry are not so exclusively arts of succession as Shaftesbury, Harris and Lessing held, painting and sculpture are not as clearly arts of arrested movement. For, phenomenologically, that moment does not exist for the painter any more than it exists for the musician. If in hearing we assemble our impressions in some kind of short-term storage, before we confine them to memory proper, we do and have to do the same thing in seeing. Visual perception itself is a process in time, and not a very fast process at that. Measurements have been made of the amount of information the eye can take in at a glance and attempts have been made, especially by the late Professor Quastler, to give precision to these two concepts. His conclusion was that we generally vastly overrate the amount of information we process. 'What we actually see is a very rough picture with a few spots in clear detail. What we feel we see is a large picture which is everywhere as clear in detail as the one favourite spot on which we concentrate our attention. Roughly speaking the area of clear perception includes less than one per cent of the total visual field.'[23] We might add that the existence of the macula, the blind spot, was only discovered relatively late. Why? Because we can scan our surroundings for information and retain the result of previous scannings together with the anticipations of future impressions which can become critically important in confirming or revising a percept.

In that sense it is surely true to say that we never see what the instantaneous photograph reveals, for we gather up successions of movements, and never see static configurations as such. And as with reality, so with its representation. The reading of a picture again happens in time, in fact it needs a very long time. There are examples in psychological literature of the weird descriptions given by people of the same painting flashed on to a screen for as long as two seconds.[24] It takes more time to sort a painting out. We do it, it seems, more or less as we read a page, by scanning it with our eyes. Photographs of eye movements suggest that the way the eye probes and gropes for meaning differs vastly from the idea of the critics who write of the artist 'leading the eye' here or there.[25] Not that these aesthetic experiences need be entirely spurious or fictitious. They may be *post factum* reconstructions facilitated by retroactive revision. The most extreme and therefore the most instructive case of such retroaction on past sensations concerns the 'eidetic faculty'.[26] Eidetic children are able to inspect a picture for a few seconds and then to visualize it as on a screen even though it has been withdrawn. They can for instance subsequently read an inscription over a door or count the chickens in the yard even though they had not done

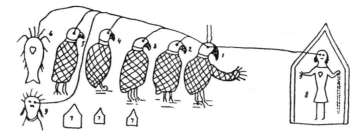

21. American Indian picture letter. From W. Wundt, *Völkerpsychologie* (I, 1, p. 247)

so during the exposure of the picture. But it has been shown that their memory is not simply a photographic reproduction. Many pictures portraying action result in an image where the action is carried to completion.

> In imaging a picture containing a donkey standing some distance from a manger, the donkey crossed over to the manger, moved its ears, bent its neck, and began to eat. Suggestions from the experimenter that the donkey was hungry sometimes served to set in motion a series of changes that surprised the imaging children themselves. It was as if they were not now looking at a static picture but at a living scene, for, as soon as the suggestion was given, the donkey would spontaneously race over to the manger. (After H. Kluver, 1926.)

We have here an almost pathological magnification of what goes on in all of us when we look at a picture. We build it up in time and hold the bits and pieces we scan in readiness till they fall into place as an imaginable object or event, and it is this totality we perceive and check against the picture in front of us. Both in hearing a melody and in seeing a representation, what Bartlett called the 'effort after meaning' leads to a scanning backward and forward in time and in space, the assignment of what might be called the appropriate serial orders which alone give coherence to the image.

In other words, the impression of movement, like the illusion of space, is the result of a complex process which is best described by the familiar term of reading an image. It cannot be the purpose of the present paper to explore this process afresh.[27] But one principle that applies to the reading of spatial relationships on a flat canvas can easily be shown to apply no less to the reconstruction of temporal relationships. It may be called the principle of the primacy of meaning. We cannot judge the distance of an object in space before we have identified it and estimated its size. We cannot estimate the passage of time in a picture without interpreting the event represented. It is for this reason perhaps that representational art always begins with the indication of meanings rather than with the rendering of nature and that it

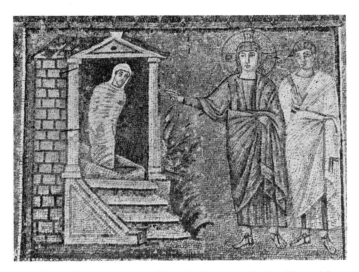

22. *Raising of Lazarus. c.* 520. Mosaic. Ravenna, S. Apollinare Nuovo

can never move far from that anchorage without abandoning both space and time. What else is the so-called 'conceptual image', the primitive pictograph of the child or the untutored, than the assertion of this primacy? A letter sent by the chieftain of an American Indian tribe to the President of the United States illustrates this principle (Fig. 21).[28] He is seen extending the hand of peace to the man in the White House. The indications of other creatures and huts signify that members of his totem and other tribes are now ready to live in houses and give up the life of nomads. Strictly speaking, then, there is no moment of time represented here—as little indeed as there is a real space in which the surrender takes place. And yet it is the gesture of the extended hand which ties the individual pictographs together into one coherent message and meaning. This meaning could be re-enacted in a real ceremony or represented in a realistic picture, but in every case it would have to centre on the chieftain's gesture or a symbolic equivalent which alone could convey to us that first there was war and now there is peace.

The narrative art of all periods has made use of such symbolic gestures to convey the meaning of an event.[29] Take the illustration in S. Apollinare Nuovo in Ravenna of the raising of Lazarus reduced to its essential elements—the figure of Christ, the mummy in the tomb, and the gesture of power that effects the change (Fig. 22). But is it different with a more ambitious rendering, such as Sebastiano's staging of the same event? (Fig. 23). Is it not all assembled round the gesture that makes the meaning cohere?

In a sense this appears to confirm Shaftesbury's and Lessing's idea that the successful illustration of a narrative will always suggest and facilitate repeal and anticipation, the scanning backward and forward in time that comes

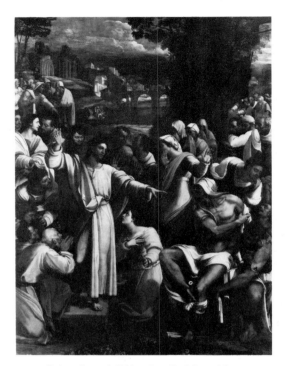

23. Sebastiano del Piombo: *Raising of Lazarus*.
1516–20. London, The National Gallery

from the understanding of an action. But we can also see more clearly why Shaftesbury was mistaken when he wrote that every painter 'when he has made choice of the determinate Date or Point of Time ... is afterwards debar'd the taking advantage from any other Action than what is immediately present, and belonging to that single Instant he describes. For if he passes the present only for a moment, he may as well pass it for many years.' There is a real difference between events assembled in one memory span and subordinate to one central perceptible meaning and events separated by years or even by hours. Just as music unfolds in phrases, so action unfolds in phases, and it is these units which are somehow the experienced moments in time, while the instant of which the theoreticians speak, the moment when time stands still, is an illicit extrapolation, despite the specious plausibility which the snapshot has given to this old idea.

If we ask ourselves what quality a snapshot must possess to convey the impression of life and movement we will find, not unexpectedly, that this will again depend on the ease with which we can take in the meaning that allows us to supplement the past and arrive at an anticipation of the future.[30] It must be the same with stills from films. A scene such as the extract from *Los Olvidados* (Fig. 24) is only too clear because we understand the logic of the

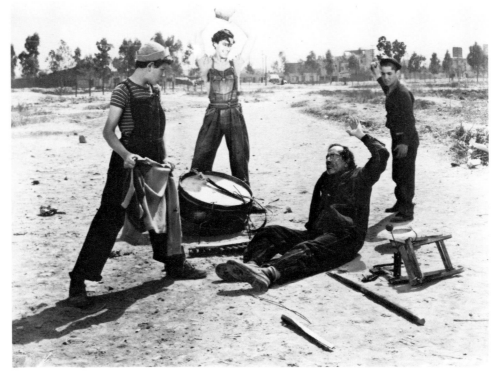

24. Scene from *Los Olvidados*. Collection, The Museum of Modern Art, New York, Film Stills Archive

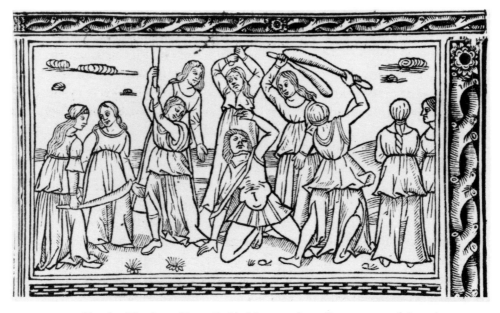

25. Death of Orpheus. From Ovid, *Metamorphoses* (Lyons, 1507, fol. 152)

situation, the threatening posture of the boys and the defensive gesture of the victim.[31] It is well known that this configuration has been often repeated in art in the context of battle-scenes and such subjects as the killing of Orpheus (Fig. 25). Did the producer of the film derive this formula from the classical *Pathosformel* which so interested Warburg?[32] Hardly. There are few other ways in which this meaning could be conveyed with such ease.

It would be interesting sometimes to ask oneself what objective time span is gathered together in this way by the meaning conveyed. Take the iconography of the Presentation of the Virgin: Giotto shows us St. Anne actually leading the Virgin up the step directly into the care of the High Priest (Fig. 26). The import of the action is emphasized by that dramatic device of bystanders not looking at the scene itself but at each other,[33] which extends the time span. They have seen what is happening and are now exchanging glances or remarks. In the Ghirlandaio (Fig. 27) the distance the Virgin has to traverse from her family to the waiting High Priest is larger, and so is the assistant crowd. The span increases in Titian's composition, but the gestures are the same (Fig. 28). Tintoretto (Fig. 29) changes the direction of the path and the intensity of the reaction among the beggars and cripples, but he too relies on the pointing action and the High Priest's gesture of welcome.

It is customary to describe this last type of composition as less static, more restless, *mouvementé* or *bewegt*, than the earlier examples, which strike us as comparatively calm, and possibly even posed as in a 'still'. The violent movement of some of the figures and particularly their instability clearly contributes to this impression that a moment has here been caught that could not have lasted more than a split second. But we also feel that the composition itself, the comparative complexity of the arrangement and the steep curve of the steps, enhances this reaction. After all we might easily describe the architecture itself in terms like 'dynamic', as if we experienced the forms to be in motion.[34] Though these belong to the commonplaces of criticism, it is not quite easy to account fully for this terminology. Why is symmetry experienced as static, asymmetry as unstable; why is any lucid order felt to express repose, any confusion movement?

It is unlikely that there is one cause underlying these reactions or, indeed, that they are not at least partially conditioned by cultural conventions. But one would guess that here, as so often, the metaphors we use can guide us at least some way. Balanced objects can remain static where lopsided ones will fall any moment, and so the tendency is to seek for the reassuring balance and to expect a rapid change where it is absent. It is curious how easily this experience is transferred, as if by analogy, to other configurations. A leaflet for amateur photographers[35] rightly points out that a sailing-boat

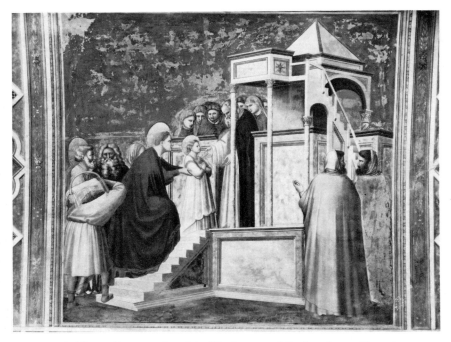

26. Giotto: *Presentation of the Virgin. c.* 1306. Padua, Arena Chapel

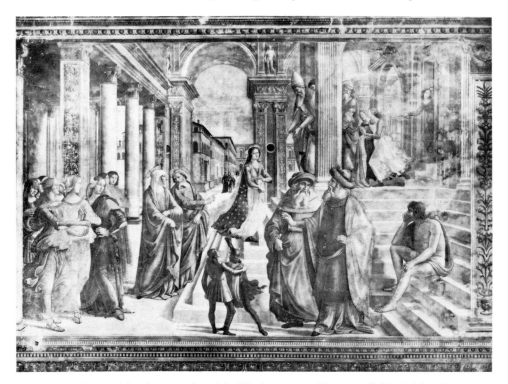

27. Ghirlandaio: *Presentation of the Virgin. c.* 1490. Florence, S. Maria Novella

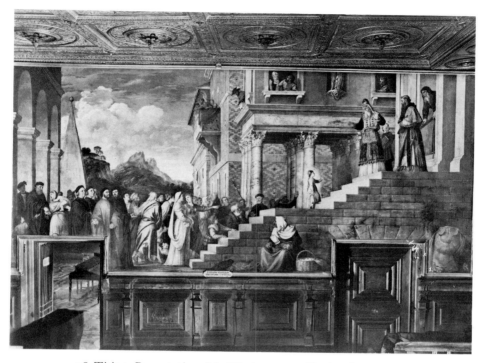

28. Titian: *Presentation of the Virgin. c.* 1535. Venice, Accademia

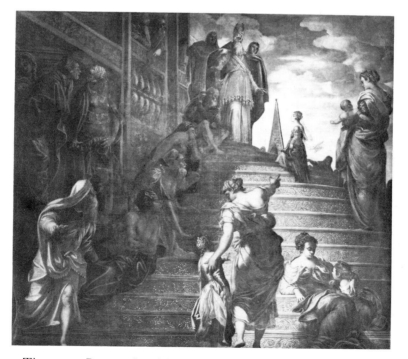

29. Tintoretto: *Presentation of the Virgin. c.* 1552. Venice, Madonna dell'Orto

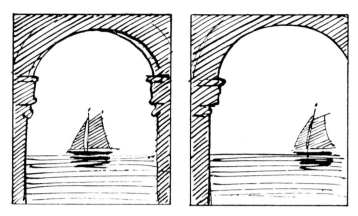

30. Setting and movement

photographed in the centre of a picture will look becalmed, one shown off-centre will appear to move (Fig. 30). Of course this applies with much greater force to sailing-boats than, for instance, to trees, which suggests that even here meaning has a large share in the resultant impression.

Even so we seem to be presented with a strange paradox—the understanding of movement depends on the clarity of meaning but the impression of movement can be enhanced by lack of geometrical clarity. The most interesting test case here is an experiment made by Donatello. The dancing *putti* of his Prato pulpit (Fig. 31) are gay and sprightly enough, but when the master came to develop the idea in the *Cantoria* (Fig. 32) he deliberately used the daring device of placing the dance behind a row of columns. For most observers the effect of turbulent movement is enhanced by this partial masking. It is an effect cleverly exploited in the signs of the Winter Olympic Games at Grenoble in 1968 (Fig. 33). Could it be that another analogy contributes to this effect? That the difficulty we experience

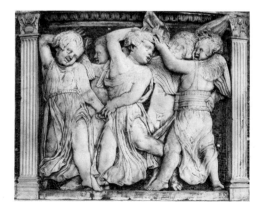

31. Donatello: Pulpit. Detail. 1434–8. Prato, Cathedral

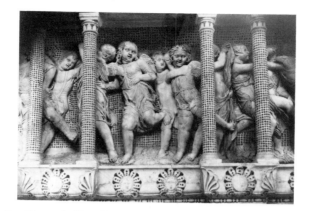

32. Donatello: *Cantoria*. Detail. 1433–40. Florence, Museo dell'Opera del Duomo

in following and integrating the scene fuses with memories of the difficulty we might experience in reality in sorting out the bodies and limbs of a whirling dance? In both cases, after all, the eye would send back to the brain the message 'hard to catch' and so the two might be interchangeable. Maybe Donatello consciously or unconsciously exploited an additional effect that arises out of such masking—the effect known to psychologists as the Poggendorf illusion (Fig. 34). A line that appears obliquely to pass behind a band or rectangle frequently looks as if its continuation were displaced. And so the possibility exists that the leg of the child really seems to have moved while we scan the composition. There must be yet other reasons why incompleteness can contribute to the impression of rapid movement. The 'snapshot effects' of Degas sometimes give the impression that the artist was so intent on fixing a motif on the canvas that he had neither time nor opportunity to seek an advantageous viewpoint. The incompleteness becomes an indication of the painter's hurry, of his own preoccupation with

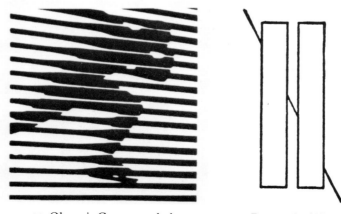

33. Olympic Games symbol   34. Poggendorf illusion

time, which is contagious. We, too, speed up our scanning, and it can happen in the process that the incompleteness of familiar forms actually arouses our anticipations in almost hallucinatory manner precisely as the experiments with eidetic children describe it. It is again the effort after meaning which leaps ahead of the actually given and completes the shape as we tend to complete a sentence or a musical phrase. Hence, perhaps, the increase in the impression of speed and movement which is felt by many observers when they look at the less complete and less legible side view of the Discobolos (Fig. 36) and compare it with a frontal photograph (Fig. 35).

If these devices hint at the possibilities of narrowing the temporal span of the moment represented while enhancing the effect of movement, the victory of the camera in all these methods was bound to make the artist seek for further fields of experiments. The Futurists, of course, with all their glorification of speed and movement, followed the camera rather tamely in their imitations of double exposures. Even Duchamp's famous *Nude descending a Staircase* remains a rather cerebral affair. It needs a great artist to articulate this elusive impression of movement in images of a fresh significance, and here as elsewhere it was Picasso who came up with the most

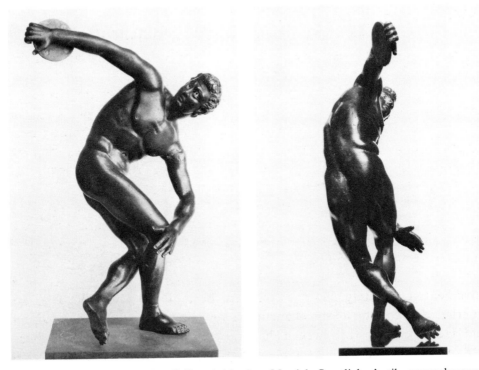

35, 36. *Discobolos*. Front view (*left*) and side view. Munich, Staatliche Antikensammlungen

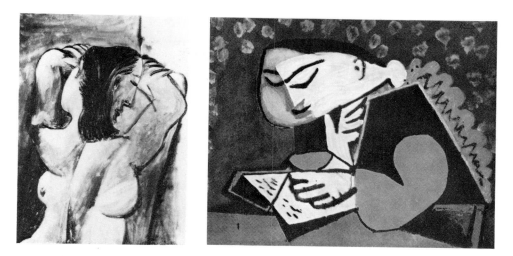

37. Pablo Picasso: *Sleeper turning*. From Zervos, *Picasso* (11, 1960, Fig. 198, p. 85).
38. Pablo Picasso: *Girl reading*. Private Collection

interesting and most varied solutions. In Cubism he played with the idea of various aspects of an identical object, but this programme—so far as it ever was a programme—is little more than a pretext to lead the effort after meaning a hectic chase through a labyrinth of ambiguous facets which both obscure and reveal the still life on the table, recalling the process of vision itself rather than the thing seen.

But it is in some of his later paintings that Picasso seems to have been most successful in giving us a feeling of successive images without sacrificing the meaning of their common core.[36] The *Sleeper turning* (Fig. 37) is such an example, but his greatest triumph here is, perhaps, the *Girl reading* from the early 1950s (Fig. 38). The strange ambiguity of beauty and plainness, of serenity and clumsiness in these conflicting aspects does not immediately suggest a succession of viewpoints in time, but precisely because they are here held in provisional simultaneity they present a novel and convincing victory over that man-made spectre, the *punctum temporis*.

For whatever the validity of these individual devices and however subjective the effect of movement one or the other may produce in some observers, one thing is certain: if perception both of the visible world and of images were not a process in time, and a rather slow and complex process at that, static images could not arouse in us the memories and anticipations of movement. Ultimately this reaction must be rooted in the difficulties we experience in holding all the elements in our mind while we scan the visual field. Hence even abstract art can elude the static impression at least in those extreme cases which exploit fatigue and after-images to produce a sensation of flicker and make the striations and patterns dance before our helpless eyes.

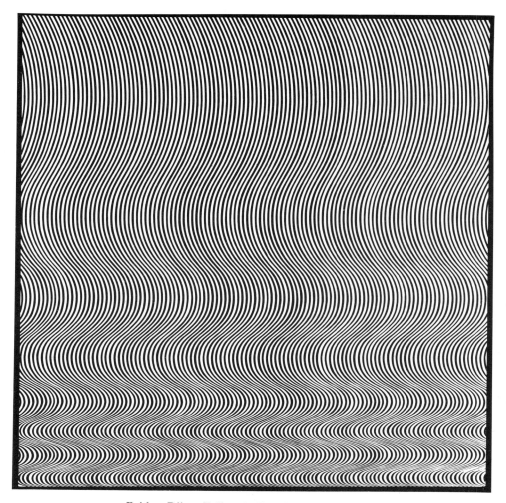

39. Bridget Riley: *Fall*. 1963. London, The Tate Gallery

An explanation of these phenomena experienced before the black and white paintings by Bridget Riley[37] (Fig. 39) is still being sought,[38] but even the first attempts throw a fascinating light on the complexity of visual processes. Experiments such as these are wholesome reminders of the inadequacy of those *a priori* distinctions in aesthetics which were the subject of this paper.

Ritualized Gesture and Expression in Art

I HOPE I may dispense with the ritual of an introduction and plunge *in medias res* with the aid of my first illustration, an anti-war poster of 1924 by the German expressionist artist Käthe Kollwitz (Fig. 40). It shows the various aspects of gesture and expression I should like to single out for discussion. The young man on the poster surely exhibits those symptoms of mass emotion that Konrad Lorenz has recently analysed so convincingly in the penultimate chapter of his book on aggression:[1] the heightened *tonus*, the

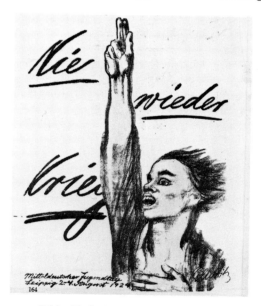

40. Käthe Kollwitz: *Nie wieder Krieg.* 1924

A contribution to a Discussion on Ritualization of Behaviour in Animals and Man organized for the Royal Society by Sir Julian Huxley in June 1966.

rigid posture, the raised head with the forward thrust of the chin, even the bristling hair, all the physical reactions that accompany the emotion of mass enthusiasm or *Begeisterung*. If we retain the term *symptom* for these visible signs, we may use the term *symbol* for the other kind of visible sign, the gesture of the hand with two outstretched fingers which conventionally accompanies the swearing of an oath in central Europe, a ritual in the narrow cultural sense of the term. If natural symptom and conventional symbol can be seen as the two extremes of a spectrum[2] we would, I believe, have to place the gesture the young man performs with his left hand somewhere in between these extremes. The hand on the heart is a widespread gesture of sincerity and protestation that has even become a formula in German speech, *Hand aufs Herz*. English is more specifically ritualistic here, with 'cross my heart', a formula that neglects the symptomatic element of the hand gripping the heart in one of those autistic gestures[3] indicative of stress, reinforced, perhaps, by the feeling of the heartbeat that accompanies a 'heavy heart'. But as so often with physical symptoms of emotions, these are still subject to conscious control, they are sufficiently plastic to be moulded by cultural traditions.[4] Few of us, for instance, would seriously make this gesture, for in our anti-

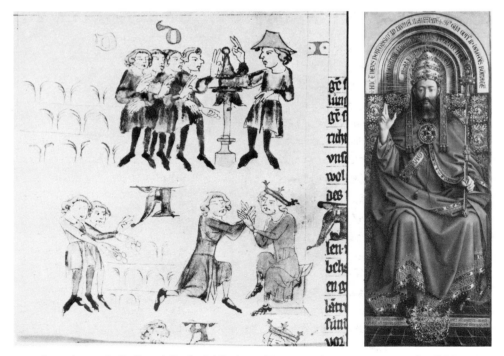

41. *Swearing on the Relic* and *Oath of Allegiance*. From a 14th century manuscript (MS. 32). Dresden. After Amira, *Der Dresdener Sachsenspiegel* (1902, pl. 15).
42. Van Eyck brothers: *God the Father*. From the Ghent Altarpiece. 1432. Ghent, Cathedral of St. Bavo

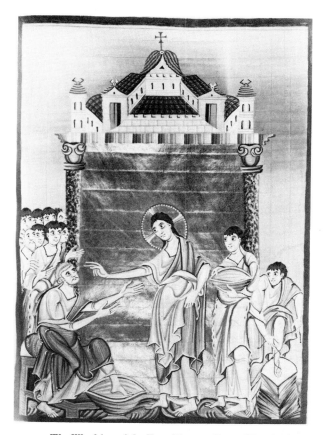

43. *The Washing of the Feet.* From a Gospel Book of
Otto III. *c.* 1000, German. Munich, Bayerische Staatsbibliothek

rhetorical culture it would suggest hamming. Within the context of a political
poster, of course, understatement would be out of place and the hand on the
heart is effective enough. And so, to turn to the other elements of gesture that
concern the student of art, are the traces of the artist's own emotional state,
what might be called the graphological aspect.[5] This element can be seen to
modify and transform the conventional symbols of lettering: '*Nie wieder
Krieg*' (No More War) is obviously written in the same state of tension that
we see in the face of the young man. The underlining mounts to a crescendo,
as would the voice of the man pronouncing his oath, and the writing contrasts
altogether with the script imparting factual information below. Needless to
say, this distinction between emotive symptom and conventional symbol as
ends of a spectrum is an abstraction, the symbolic ritual of oath-taking is
charged with all the symptoms of the emotion both in the way the upraised
arm is tautened and the way it is drawn with emphatic strokes.

But if we can agree on some such distinction we may find it easier to discuss

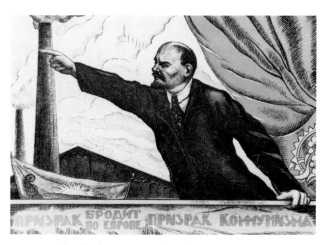

44. *Lenin*. Anonymous Russian poster. *c.* 1920.
After Polanski, *The Russian Revolutionary Poster* (Moscow, 1924)

their interaction in art and in life. For the representational element of art, of course, mirrors life at least up to a point. It makes use of gestures that have their meaning in human intercourse. The gesture of the oath is quite an interesting case.[6] It is represented in the Bayeux Tapestry and frequently shown among the formalities of a German legal manuscript of the fourteenth century, the *Sachsenspiegel*,[7] where the swearing fingers touch the holy relic upon which the oath is taken (Fig. 41). But the position of the fingers is not specific to the oath. We all know it as the Christian gesture of blessing[8] exemplified by the majestic painting of God the Father from the Ghent Altarpiece (Fig. 42). The gesture here is more relaxed, of course, than that of the oath on the expressionist poster, but its very calm adds to the impression of a gesture of power.

Originally this position of the fingers signified neither blessing nor the oath. It accompanied any solemn spoken pronouncement and belongs to the repertory of movements recommended by ancient teachers of rhetoric.[9] In medieval narrative art it comes therefore to function simply as a 'speaking gesture'. An Ottonian miniature (Fig. 43) shows Christ thus explaining to St. Peter the new ritual of washing the feet, illustrating the account in the Gospel of St. John (13: 8, 9), 'Peter saith unto him, Thou shalt never wash my feet. Jesus answered him, if I wash thee not, thou hast no part with me. Simon Peter saith unto him, Lord, not my feet only, but also my hands and my head.' His eloquent gesture recalls once more the range between the symbolic and the more spontaneously expressive, the 'initiated action' of the apostle, grasping eagerly what he is offered. Perhaps it is in considering the difference between these gestures that we can also come nearer to explaining the peculiar speaking gesture—it may be described as a gesture of unambiguous non-action, the hand is immobilized and can neither grip nor push. We still used this conventional speaking gesture of '*aufzeigen*' at school in Vienna, to signify that we wished to speak.

Its most important distinctive feature is the raising of two fingers, which renders it more artificial but also more humble and innocuous than the pointing hand, which indicates a degree of emphasis that can be unbecoming.[10] The Baptist thus reinforces his words written on the Isenheim Altar (Fig. 45), and the Revolutionary in his shrill didacticism (Fig. 44), but children are still taught, I believe, that pointing is rude, because in some form it implies a command, a sign of dominance universally understood.

The speaking gesture, by contrast, which accompanied solemn pronouncements and thus survived at least up to this century in the specialized rituals of the oath and the blessing, is certainly part of a particular tradition, a symbol of a gesture language. The literature about these languages, alas, is

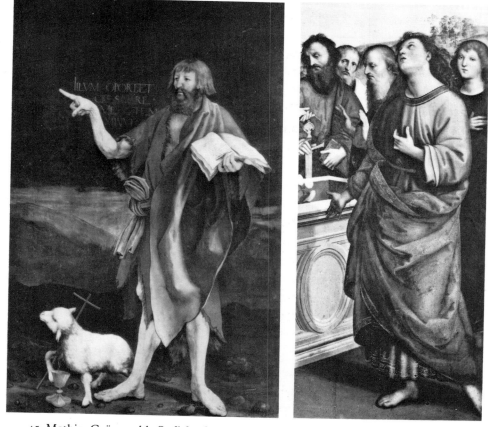

45. Mathias Grünewald: *St. John the Baptist.*
From the Isenheim Altar. *c.* 1515. Colmar,
Musée d'Unterlinden. Photo O. Zimmermann

46. Raphael: Figure from *The
Coronation of the Virgin. c.* 1503.
Rome, Pinacoteca Vaticana

patchy and undeveloped.[11] I would not know, for instance, where to look for information about the frequency in real life of that other gesture of the hand on the heart. As an historian of art I know it as a formula in a particular tradition, that of Western religious art (Figs. 46 and 53).[12] I doubt if it occurs with quite the same meaning in either ancient or Eastern art.

This raises the whole vexed question of the relation between the gestures we see represented in art and those performed in real life.[13] It is a vexed question for two reasons, one because in many cases art is our principal source of information about gestures, and secondly because art arrests movement and is therefore restricted in the gestures it can show unambiguously.[14] You cannot paint even the shaking of the head we use in the West for 'no'.

One thing is certain, there were great periods in art when artists considered it their task to make the figures in their painting speak through gestures. Dante describes the rendering of certain scenes he sees in Purgatory as *visibile parlare* (*Purgatorio*, x, 95), 'visible speech', because the attitude of the figures so clearly expressed their mind, and Leonardo da Vinci never ceased urging that, as he put it in the *Trattato della pittura*,[15] 'the most important in painting are the movements originating from the mental state of living creatures, the movements, that is, appropriate to the state of . . . desire, contempt, anger or pity . . .' (fol. 48). He advises artists to 'take pleasure in carefully watching those who talk together with gesticulating hands, and get near to listen what makes them make that particular gesture . . .' (fol. 125). He

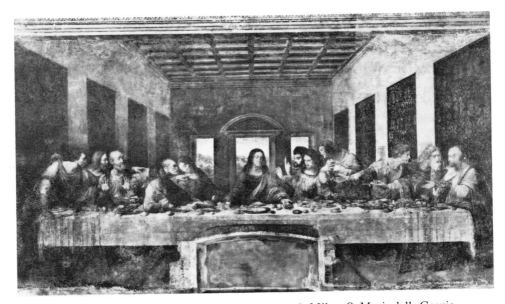

47. Leonardo da Vinci: *The Last Supper*. 1495–8. Milan, S. Maria delle Grazie

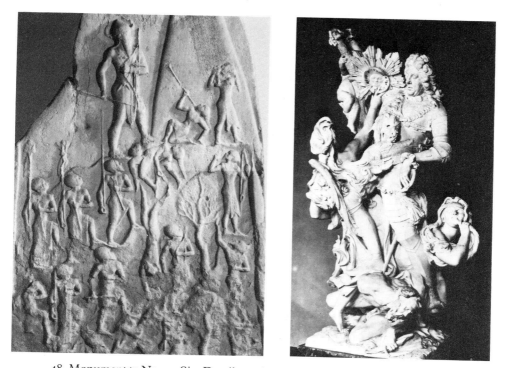

48. Monument to Naram Sin. Detail. 23rd century B.C. Paris, Musée du Louvre.
49. Balthasar Permoser: *Apotheosis of Prince Eugene of Savoy*. 1718–21.
Vienna, Österreichische Galerie im Belvedere

even goes so far as to advise studying deaf-mutes, who have no other means of communication (fol. 46).

He applied his own precept in his *Last Supper* (Fig. 47), which shows the reaction of the Twelve Apostles to Christ's announcement of the impending betrayal, a painting which none other than Geothe retranslated into a masterly dramatic dialogue.[16] I do not want to dwell too long on his famous example, beyond saying that clearly Leonardo made use of that intermediate range of gestures that lie between the spontaneous symptom of emotions and the conventionalized. It has always been felt that these are typically Mediterranean gestures, the protestation with hands towards the breast, the shrinking back in horror, the warding off with upraised hands, but clearly even these could not convey their meaning in the context if we did not know the Gospel story. The likelihood, moreover, that even in the Mediterranean such as announcement would result in such configuration is small, despite the attempt in the film *La Viridiana* to bring it to life in a group of beggars.

Yet, with great respect to Leonardo and the academic teachers who have followed him in his incessant advice to the artist to study life in the raw, it seems to me that observation alone would never have resulted in such works.

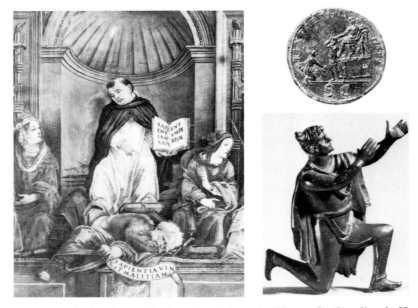

50. Filippino Lippi: *St. Thomas Aquinas*. Detail from *St. Thomas Confounding the Heretics*. 1489–93. Rome, S. Maria sopra Minerva.   51. Surrendering barbarian. Coin of Trajan. Early 2nd century A.D. London, The British Museum.   52. Kneeling captive. Roman, early Imperial. Paris, Bibliothèque Nationale

Life in movement is just too rich and too manifold to allow of imitation without some selective principle. Random snapshots of people in random situations could never have given us that narrative art that was considered the artist's highest task. I admit that I am biased here. For I have also argued in another context, in my book on *Art and Illusion*,[17] that the painter's starting-point can never be the observation and imitation of nature, that all art remains what is called conceptual, a manipulation of a vocabulary, and that even the most naturalistic art generally starts from what I call a schema that is modified and adjusted till it appears to match the visible world.

I should like to propose as my principal hypothesis that as far as gesture is concerned the schema used by artists is generally pre-formed in ritual and that here as elsewhere art and ritual, using the word in its narrow cultural sense, cannot easily be separated.

Within the context of this symposium, the transition from action to ritual and hence into art can perhaps be followed in an age-old formula, that for triumph, which shows the victorious ruler trampling on his defeated foe, as on this Mesopotamian Stele of Naram Sin (Fig. 48). I am afraid this is not artistic licence. I remember reading that even in Byzantium the ritual of triumph sometimes included the barbarous ceremony of the Emperor publicly setting his foot on the neck of the vanquished ruler. Art, I am sorry to say, preserved this gesture of ritual domination even beyond its natural life. Many monuments to victorious heroes like Balthasar Permoser's statue of Prince Eugene of Savoy (Fig. 49) show the victor setting his foot or his knee on the writhing body of the defeated, no doubt with the lingering feeling that the perpetuation of the humiliation will also perpetuate the victory. Even within the realm of spiritual conflict this ritualistic image is preserved, as in a fresco by Filippino Lippi in Rome, where it is St. Thomas Aquinas (Fig. 50) who is shown trampling victoriously on that arch-heretic Averroes, with whose interpretation of Aristotle he disagreed.

Such extremes, admittedly, leave not much room for gesture in the stricter sense of the word, but the preceding stage of a ritualized gesture of submission is even more frequent in art, contrasting the victorious hero with the defeated foe who sues for mercy or displays otherwise in his attitude all the signs of self-humiliation. In Roman art this contrast between authority and submission is such a leading theme that a long book has recently been published with the significant title *Gesture and Rank in Roman Art*.[18] The place in the pecking order of a military society is clearly visible in the relationship of postures and gestures that befit the leader and the led. Needless to say, this ritualized relationship of command and submission is also capable of spiritualization. The stereotyped gesture of surrender which displays the helplessness of the vanquished who 'throws up his hands' in an appealing movement showing him unarmed and incapable of further aggression (Fig. 51) is also the most important source of gestures of worship and prayer before the Godhead. Indeed the representation of a barbarian with upraised hands in the Bibliothèque Nationale (Fig. 52) has been described as surrendering by Brilliant and as praying by Ohm.[19]

No doubt the gesture of praying with folded hands also belongs in this category. Its evolution and transformation really parallel the process of ritualization that is the subject of this symposium, because few who use it today will think of the original purpose of this sign of surrender, delivering oneself more or less 'bound hand and foot', or at least ready to be bound without offering resistance. In India the origins of this gesture are lost in the distant past, but it appears to have been unknown to classical antiquity and even to the early Christians, who still prayed with upraised hands. It has been suggested that its gradual ascendancy in the Middle Ages was due to the influence of the feudal ritual of the oath of allegiance in which the liegeman placed his hands between those of his Lord (Fig. 41), an act of submission that is illustrated in legal manuscripts and is still performed at graduation in Cambridge. Isolated representations of figures praying with folded hands can be found in Western art since about A.D. 1000,[20] but at least one authority

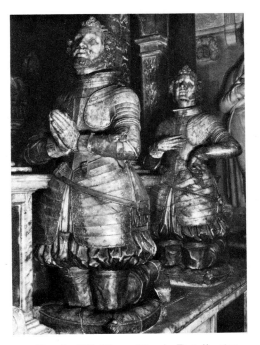

53. Tomb of Sir Henry Norris. Detail. 1603.
London, Westminster Abbey

traces its more general adoption to St. Francis of Assisi, who may have inspired its incorporation in the ritual of the Mass.[21] Be that as it may, from the thirteenth century on innumerable images of saints, donors and worthies perpetuate the act of submission in ecclesiastical art on tombs (Fig. 53), altars and illustrations. To us, its original meaning has merged with the general expression of a mood. The folded hands evoke the atmosphere of piety and contemplation that transcends a narrow ritualistic interpretation.[22] Owing, however, to the association of prayer with a request to the deity, the gesture has also become one of begging in central Europe.[23] Small children are taught in Austria to accompany their '*bitte*' ('please') with a movement of the hands that can easily develop into impatient and insistent clapping—the final change from submission to the signalling of a demand. As far as art is concerned, the very frequency of the gesture allows us to illustrate the difference between the cheapened formula that can embarrass us in devotional art (Fig. 54) and the way a great artist such as Rembrandt can mysteriously restore its original validity in his wonderful etching of David in prayer (Fig. 55).

I here come to the second point I wanted to make in this brief survey. Important as are the areas of contact between ritualized behaviour in animal and man, and far-reaching as is their bearing on a study of art, I could not agree to an equation of that discharge of emotion that occurs in ritual with the motivations of human art. Whatever may be true of so-called primitive societies where art may mainly serve the canalizing of collective emotions, for the individual in our kind of society the ritual is not only a help but also a hindrance in that discharge. We may be happy in the ritual of applause at the end of a lecture or concert, but when we stand face to face with the performer we are embarrassed to hear everyone say, 'thank you for a most interesting lecture'. We are embarrassed precisely because it is a ritual and we know that it is used after good and bad lectures alike. We try as we approach the lecturer to make our voice more charged with symptoms of sincere emotions, we press his hand in raptures, but even these tricks are quickly ritualized and most of us give up and lapse into inarticulacy. It takes a Rembrandt, or, on a lower level, a Käthe Kollwitz, to repeat a ritualized gesture in a way that is felt to be charged with genuine expression, not *only* a ritual, but a symptom as well.

I suspect that animals are rarely plagued by this feeling of inadequacy when they perform a ritualized act of submission or ingratiation. For animals probably lack that distinctly human achievement, the lie. The Judas kiss, the use of a ritual of love as a signal of aggression is not within their range. What we mean by expression in human behaviour and particularly in human art

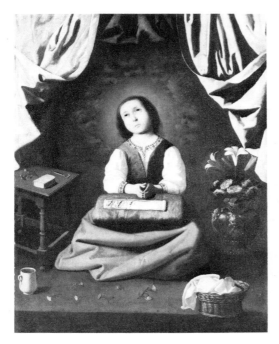

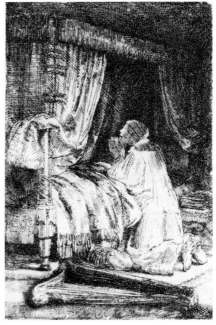

54. Zurbaran: *The Virgin as a Child. c.* 1630. New York, The Metropolitan Museum of Art, Fletcher Fund, 1927

55. Rembrandt: *David in Prayer.* 1652. Etching. London, The British Museum

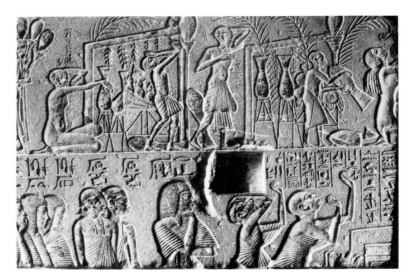

56. Relief from the tomb of a priest. Detail. Egyptian, nineteenth dynasty.
Berlin, Staatliche Museen

implies some kind of correspondence between inwardness and outward sign.
How often have not religious leaders and reformers decried ritual when they
found this correspondence wanting, how often have not critics done the
same. In the study of animals I am sure this very distinction would be invalid.
Professor Lorenz rightly insists that for the goose the friendship ritual *is* the
friendship. We cannot separate the behaviour and its inwardness, as it were.
Even in man, I believe, that duality has its limits. There is surely much truth
in the James-Lange theory which stresses the extent to which behaviour
reacts back on the emotions. It may really be difficult to 'smile, and smile, and
be a villain', or to feel sad while doing a gay dance; difficult, but it can be done.

And yet no student of art, I think, should neglect this more complex
relationship that exists in human society between emotion and its expression.
I may here take for an illustration the most typical ritualized behaviour that
certainly influenced the language and conventions of art, I mean the ritual of
mourning the dead. It both sums up my hypothesis about the roots of
expressive gesture in ritual, and illuminates the complexities of the situation.

It comes perhaps as a surprise to encounter so vivid an expression of
emotions within the rigid conventions of Egyptian art (Fig. 56), even though
the relief dates after that period in the eighteenth dynasty in which these
restraints were much relaxed in the El Amarna revolution. Even so it is
relevant to both my themes that what we have in front of us is not so much a
symptom of personal grief as its enactment in the ritual of wailing that plays
such a part almost everywhere in primitive societies in the discharge of
emotions.[24] Wailing-women are still hired for the purpose of such rituals in

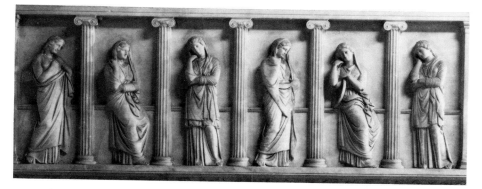

57. Sidonian sarcophagus. Mid 4th century B.C. Istanbul, Archaeological Museums

the Middle East to increase the lament. The tearing of hair, the scattering of ashes, the mutilations of garments and even of the body, all these are the appropriate ritual that not only expresses but produces the emotion. I suppose a good wailing-woman learns to experience the grief she is paid to express and so does the artist who perpetuates the wailing in stone. But what matters is not his feeling but his awareness of the ritual. Now one gesture of mourning we see on the Egyptian relief, the heavy head supported by the hand, carried over into Greek art,[25] as in the famous Sidonian sarcophagus (Fig. 57), where the wailing-women are perpetuated in stone in a timeless

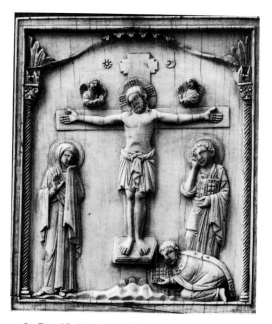

58. *Crucifixion*. Byzantine ivory. 10th century.
Berlin, Staatliche Museen

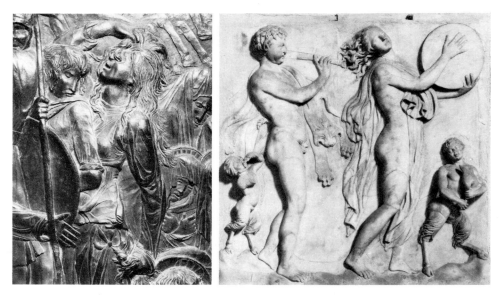

59. Donatello: *A Mourning Woman under the Cross*. Detail from the pulpit relief. *c.* 1460–70. Florence, S. Lorenzo.   60. Dionysiac revels. Roman Imperial relief. Rome, Musei Vaticani

lament. The figure on the right with her head on her hand prefigures the ritualized gesture of mourning that entered the vocabulary of medieval art,[26] belonging to the Virgin and St. John under the Cross, as on Byzantine medieval ivories (Fig. 58).

Clearly it needs a real artist to recharge such a formula with emotion, to attune the whole body and *tonus*, the colour and composition, to the expression of grief that is part of the ritual. Donatello's reliefs on the San Lorenzo pulpits are a sublime example of that intensity of emotion that expresses itself in these gestures of abandon (Fig. 59).

It was the conviction of Aby Warburg,[27] the founder of the Warburg Institute, that this new feeling for the language of the body, its expressiveness in extremes, was in itself engendered through fresh contact with the monuments of ancient ritual, the representations of the Dionysiac thiasos with its maenads dancing in ecstatic frenzy (Fig. 60). Warburg was certainly right that these renderings of a ritual were much admired and studied by Renaissance artists trying to penetrate the language of emotive symptoms.[28] He was also right in stressing the dangers that arose in art through an inflation of these gestures, that crescendo of frenzied gesticulation that characterizes some of the Baroque. It was an inflation that inevitably produced the reaction of a return to the gold standard of classical restraint, the taste of our generation for Piero della Francesca's calm.

Aesthetic problems of this kind are usually treated by critics under the categories of 'sincere' versus 'theatrical' expression. I am not sure that this is right. Both the rhetorical and the anti-rhetorical, the ritualistic and the anti-ritualistic, are in a sense conventions. Indeed what else could they be, if they are to serve communication between human beings?

I have left myself very little time to apply these findings, such as they are, to the situation in contemporary art and criticism which shuns any ritual except, perhaps, the ritual of father-killing, and which still is left with the dilemma of expression and ritual unsolved. It matters little that it is no longer the gesture in narrative contexts that is the problem but that graphological gesture to which I drew attention at the outset, that alleged symptom of the artist's emotion that is discharged in the brush-stroke of an artist such as Van Gogh with his magnificent flaming lines.

Today it is this gesture-trace that is to carry expression, according to a theory of painting that is itself not uninfluenced by the more ritualistic philosophy of Chinese calligraphy. Tachism and Action Painting, if I understand these movements, have made a ritual of Dionysiac frenzy in the throwing and pouring of paint as a sign of ecstasis. But like all purely expressionist theories the theories of abstract expressionists were caught in the dilemma to which I referred before, the dilemma of being human and being aware of what others do. It may have been liberating for Jackson Pollock to break all bonds and pour his paint on the canvas, but once everybody does it, it becomes a ritual in the modern sense of the term, a mere trick that can be learned and gone through without emotion. In trying to avoid this dilemma we get anti-art and anti-anti-art, till we are all in a spin of ritualistic innovation for its own sake. The dilemmas that underlie this crisis are real enough, I believe. We cannot return to the anonymous ritual of mass emotion as we are enjoined to do on the other side of the Iron Curtain. But we can, I hope, face these issues and learn from the study of behaviour that neither the total sacrifice of conventions nor the revival of collective ritual can answer the needs of what we have come to mean by art.[29]

Action and Expression in Western Art

1. THE PROBLEM

'It only lacks the voice.' This traditional formula in praise of works of art would suggest that painting and sculpture might present ready-made material for the student of 'non-verbal communication'. But, alas, painting not only lacks speech, it also lacks most of the resources on which human beings and animals rely in their contacts and interactions. The most essential of these, of course, is movement. Art can represent neither the nod nor the headshake. The sudden blush or the frequency of eye contact are equally outside its range. Indeed one may well wonder how art could ever have acquired the reputation of rendering human emotions.

The answer I shall propose in this paper will inevitably correspond to the one I have suggested elsewhere.[1] I have argued that the creation of images which satisfy certain specific demands of verisimilitude is achieved in a secular process of trial and error. 'Making'—I suggested—'comes before matching.' Art does not start out by observing reality and trying to match it, it starts out by constructing 'minimum models' which are gradually modified in the light of the beholder's reaction till they 'match' the impression that is desired. In this process the resources which art lacks have to be compensated for by other means till the image satisfies the requirements made on it. Seen in this light we need not doubt that works of art have in fact satisfied succeeding generations who approached them with different demands, but with a desire for the convincing rendering of human expression. Indeed the literature on art testifies to the triumph of painting and sculpture over the limitations of their media. Works of art have traditionally been praised precisely for 'only lacking the voice', in other words, for embodying everything of real life except speech.

A paper presented to a study group on non-verbal communication set up by the Royal Society under the chairmanship of W.H. Thorpe in 1970.

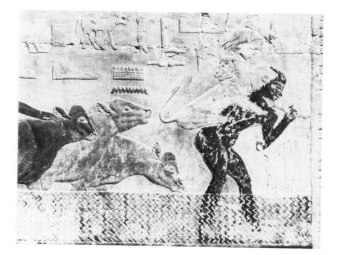

61. *Return of the herds*. Detail of relief from the
Tomb of Ti. Egyptian, fourth dynasty

To dismiss this reaction simply as a conventional exaggeration would exclude the student of non-verbal communication from the realm of art. It seems more fruitful and also more cautious to accept this reaction as a testimony to the combined power of convention and conditioning in creating a semblance of reality, a model to which men have responded as if it were identical with a life situation.

If art is thus seen as an experiment in 'doing without', an exercise in reduction (conventionally referred to as 'abstraction'), it is clear that the history of styles cannot be seen simply as a slow approximation to one particular solution. Different styles concentrate on different compensatory moves, largely determined by the function the image is expected to perform in a given civilization.

The most obvious way of compensating for the absence of speech is of course by the addition of writing, and this method was used with varying intensity in ancient Egypt, in archaic Greece, in medieval art where scrolls come out of the mouth of figures to show what they are saying, and once more in the modern comic with its 'balloons'. We may leave these on one side as evading the problem of 'non-verbal' communication.

2. LEGIBLE INTERACTION

There are at least two requirements for a 'still' to be legible in terms of expressive movements. The movements must result in configurations that can be easily understood and must stand in contexts which are sufficiently unambiguous to be interpreted.[2]

An example (Fig. 61) which dates from the third millennium B.C. may illustrate these postulates all the better because the interaction depicted is not cultural but 'natural' and concerns 'non-verbal communication' among animals. The Egyptian relief from the fourth dynasty shows a man carrying a calf on his shoulders which turns its head at a group of cows, one of which lifts her head towards it and appears to low. The movements represented are not only easily legible as significant deviations from the normal or expected postures of the animals, they also leave us in no doubt as to their expressive significance. We know that the man is taking the calf from the cow and thus we almost hear it low. If we asked somewhat pedantically how we can be sure, we would have to say that the man could not very well walk backwards in order to take the calf to the cow – quite apart from the fact that we would not know why he should do so, while we know very well why he takes the calf away.

Many of the resources of art for the depiction of expressive interaction are shown in this little group. It reminds us from the start that the transition from physical interaction to anticipatory movements is a gradual one, there is no intention on the part of the cow and the calf to express their reaction to the separation, only movements attempting to overcome it. It is up to us whether we interpret these movements as purposive or expressive.

3. ACTION AND EXPRESSION ON THE STAGE AND IN ART

This insight is an old one. It was developed with much subtlety by the eighteenth-century actor J. J. Engel, to whose *Ideen zu einer Mimik* (1785–6) Karl Bühler[3] has paid a justified tribute. Speaking of positive or negative reactions to an 'external object', Engel observes that they are both marked by an 'oblique position of the body'.[4]

> When desire approaches the object either to possess it or to attack it, the head and the chest, that is the upper part of the body, is shifted forward, not only because this will enable the legs to catch up more quickly, but also because these parts are most easily set in motion and man thus strives first to satisfy his urge through them. Where disgust or fear makes him shrink back from the object the upper part of the body bends backwards before the legs have started moving . . . A second observation which will always be confirmed where a vivid desire is at work is the following : it always tends towards the object or away from the object in a straight line . . .

Engel describes the human parallel to our animal example—the interaction between the child standing on tiptoes stretching its arms towards the mother and the mother bending down and extending her hands encouragingly towards her darling. He then proceeds to analyse reactions to more distant objects, the posture of the listener who tries to overhear a conversation, the gaping onlooker. In all these movements of orientation the most active part of the body is turned towards the object of attention.

Engel's analysis of the conflicting pulls of contrary drives strikingly foreshadows the descriptions of modern ethologists.[5]

When Hamlet follows the ghost of his father his longing for the desired discovery of a dreadful family secret has the overwhelming preponderance; but this longing is weakened by his fear of the unknown being from a strange world, and increasingly weakened the nearer the prince comes to the ghost and the further he moves away from his companions. Hence his movement should only be lively when he breaks away from his companions with a threat. When he begins to walk, it should be without hurry or heat though still with firmness and determination, gradually his step should become more cautious, more soft and should bestride less space, the whole movement should be more inhibited and the body increasingly pulled back into a vertical position.

Nor is Engel unaware of the problem of the role of convention in expressive movements which must indeed obtrude itself on his kind of analysis. Having asserted that a lowering of posture is used by all nations as an expression of reverence, he discusses with honesty and circumspection anthropological evidence from Tahiti which appears to contradict this claim.[6]

As an actor, Engel also has many things to say about human reactions to internal states, to imagined situations and objects, the clenched fist of the revengeful rival who anticipates his coming fight, the movement of horror or of love in the actor's monologue. But he is also very much aware of the role which speech plays in explaining and communicating these reactions and sceptical even about the chances of pure mime. About painting, he explicitly forbears to speak.[7]

It was shown earlier in this volume[8] that Engel had an important predecessor in Lord Shaftesbury, who had attempted to bridge the gap between the movements of life and the 'stills' of painting by suggesting how the past and the future could somehow be made visible in the rendering of a transitory moment. In his *Characteristicks* (1714) he discussed the ways a painter could represent the story of the choice of Hercules (see Fig. 20), in which the hero is confronted by Pleasure and Virtue and decides for the latter.

Whatever we may think of his *a priori* analysis, it reminds us of the relevance of our two initial postulates, the need for legibility and for clear contextual clues. In art the two are obviously interdependent. The clearer the situational clues (as in our animal example), the less may there be need for perfect legibility, and vice versa.

4. SYMBOLIC AND EXPRESSIVE GESTURES

It is well known that 'primitive' or 'conceptual' styles of representation show much concern for clarity and legibility. But it will be found that some of the devices adopted towards this very end may interfere with the lucid rendering of expressive movement. The conventions of ancient Egyptian art strenuously excluded the rendering of foreshortening.[9] Every human figure had to be shown in a clear silhouette which looks somewhat distorted to us, precisely because every part of the body is so turned as to present its most lucid, 'conceptual' shape. It is partly for anatomical reasons that these needs interfered less with the rendering of animals and their movements and thus allowed the artist of our example to depict his little tragedy so movingly. Where human figures are shown interacting in violent motion, as in representations of teamwork, or of fighting, the needs of legibility sometimes lead to a wrenching and twisting of the body which somewhat hampers the convincing rendering of expressive gestures.

In the representation of social interaction recourse had therefore to be taken to social symbolism. Notoriously the important personage in Eygptian art is represented larger than are those on the lower rungs of the hierarchy. He is frequently marked with a sceptre or other insignia while those he commands or supervises are represented in submissive postures. Moreover it is well known that all civilizations have developed standardized symbolic gestures which approximate the vocabulary of a gesture language.[10] I have suggested above[11] that these ritualized gestures of prayer, of greeting, of mourning at funeral rites, of teaching or triumph are among the first to be represented in art. They are much more easily fitted into the conventions of a conceptual style, such as the Egyptian, than are the spontaneous movements of human interaction. These 'performative' gestures are self-explanatory actions which set up a clear context and are not concerned with the passage of time.[12] The King stands before his God, the Noble receives tributes, the dead are bewailed: all these are types of juxtaposition which lend themselves to unambiguous representation even within a style which excludes the realistic approach to the human body in action.

It is well known that it is to Greek art that we must look for the conquest of appearances. I have suggested in *Art and Illusion* that the striving for this mastery was determined by the function of art within Greek civilization, where it required the illustration or even the dramatic evocation of

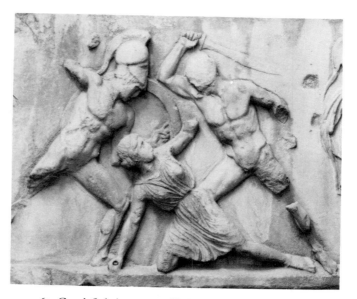

62. Greek fighting group. Halicarnassus Mausoleum.
c. 350 B.C. London, The British Museum

mythological stories as told by the epic poets.[13] Be that as it may, Greek art certainly developed devices which compensate for the absence of movement not by symbolic expression but by the creation of images of maximal instability. Bodies are made to take up positions which we know from experience to be incapable of being maintained, muscles are tautened like a drawn bow, garments begin to flutter in the wind to indicate speed and transitoriness. By itself such a style need not be relevant to our topic, for theoretically the interaction of figures could remain on a purely physical level, fighting groups grappling and parrying blows, or athletes wrestling. But even in such situations it is no more possible than it was in our initial animal example to separate action from communication. We see the victim of aggression trying to ward off the coming thrust with a gesture of self-protection that also suggests pleading, we see the victor in an attitude of domination that suggests triumph or pride (Fig. 62). A study of these and similar motifs in ancient art reveals the need for a compromise between the conflicting demands of maximal legibility and maximal movement.[14] The attitude of both aggressor and victim must be transitory, but lucid, and those solutions which best do justice to these demands will tend to be adopted as a formula on which only slight variations need be played. Thus the moment in which 'non-verbal communication' between human beings was first specifically observed and rendered in art can never be determined with any degree of precision.[15] What matters is the degree of empathy expected and aroused.

If it really became the task of Greek art to turn the beholder into an eye-witness of events he knew from Homer and other poets, it is clearly not fruitful to look beyond this demand for a hard and fast distinction between physical and psychological interaction.

5. NARRATIVE AND INTERPRETATION

We do not know how the Egyptians viewed the separation of the calf from its mother, but it is obvious that I have sentimentalized the scene in calling it a little tragedy. No empathy is likely to have been expected on the part of the beholder; even in human scenes there is little evidence of such a demand. It is this appeal to our responses which distinguishes Greek narrative art of the sixth and fifth centuries B.C. from most earlier styles. The fright of Eurystheus who (on a hydria in Paris) has crept into a vat and lifts his hands in horror as Hercules brings Cerberus (Fig. 63); the joy of Theseus' sailors (on the François Vase in Florence) gesticulating and throwing up their arms in pleasure as they land in Delos (Fig. 64); the sorrow of Ajax (on a cup in Vienna) who hides his head in grief when he loses his case for the arms of

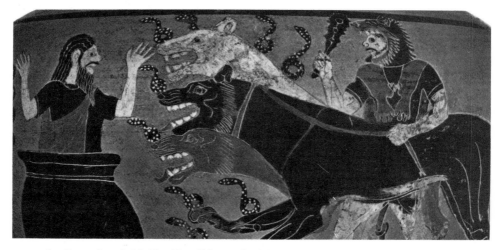

63. *Eurystheus in his Vat*. Detail from a hydria. *c.* 530 B.C. Paris, Musée du Louvre

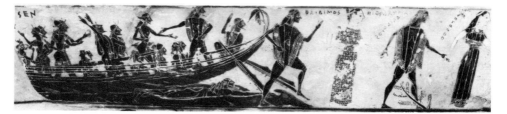

64. *Theseus' sailors landing on Delos*. Detail from the François Vase. *c.* 570 B.C.
Florence, Museo Archeologico

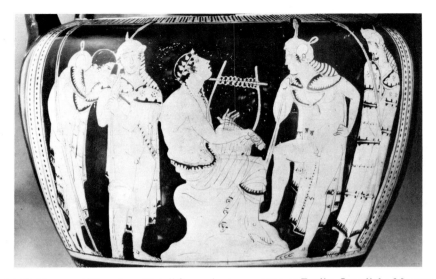

65. *Orpheus and Thracians*. Detail from a krater. *c.* 450 B.C. Berlin, Staatliche Museen

Achilles; the rapt attention of the Thracians (on a wine bowl in Berlin) who hear Orpheus sing (Fig. 65); the Satyr (on a jug in Oxford) who dances with joy as he finds a nymph asleep—all these are examples taken from Greek vases[16] leading up to the period in the early fourth century when Xenophon in the *Memorabilia* represented Socrates discussing the subject of expression with the painter Parrhasios and the sculptor Cleiton. In both these little dialogues the artists must have their attention drawn to the possibility of representing not only the actions of the body but through the body the 'workings of the soul'.

'How could one imitate that which has neither shape nor colour . . . and is not even visible?' asks the puzzled Parrhasios, and is told of the effect of emotions on people's looks: 'Nobility and dignity, self-abasement and servility, prudence and understanding, insolence and vulgarity, are reflected in the face and in the attitudes of the body whether still or in motion.'[17]

The injunction has been repeated in countless variations throughout the literature of art which is based on the classical tradition. Not only are particular works of painting or sculpture praised for their mastery in conveying the character and emotions of the figures portrayed, many treatises on art since the Renaissance (e.g. by Alberti, Leonardo, Lomazzo, Le Brun) contain sections in which the outward symptoms of the emotions or 'passions' are described and analysed. Interesting as these discussions are for the history of our studies,[18] it must be admitted that most of them bypass the crucial difference between art and life which was our starting-point. Expressive movements are movements and once we lack the explanatory sequence to tell us how this configuration started and where it leads to, ambiguity will increase to an unexpected extent, unless, of course, the absence of movement is compensated for by situational cues. Eurystheus in his vat may be extending his hands because he cannot wait to stroke Cerberus, the sailor who throws up his arms for joy on landing in Delos may have been hit by an arrow, Ajax may be hiding his head to conceal not his sorrow but his laughter in having brought off a splendid trick, the Thracians may be bored by Orpheus' songs and even the Satyr may jump and clap his hands in order to wake the sleeping nymph. There is a humorous book called *Captions Outrageous* (by Bob Reisner and Hal Kapplow) attempting such re-interpretations of famous masterpieces with more or less wit. Psychologists, moreover, know from the varying readings of the *Thematic Apperception Test*[19] how great is the spread of possible interpretations of any picture unless a firm lead is given by the context or caption. Experiments have shown that if we isolate an individual figure from the snapshot of an emotional scene it will only exceptionally allow us to guess the elements of the situation.[20] Even facial expression when isolated from casual snapshots turns out to be highly ambiguous. The contorted face of a wrestler may look in isolation as if he were laughing, while a man opening his mouth to eat may appear to be yawning.[21]

Thus art stands in need of very clear and unambiguous cues to the situation in which the movement occurs. In particular we have to know whether a movement portrayed should be interpreted as predominantly utilitarian or expressive. Fig. 67 is easily misinterpreted as a gesture of submission, that is an expressive movement of extreme obeisance. We have to know the context, the story of the Gathering of Manna, to understand why the man is cowering on the ground and stretching out his hands – he is trying to grab as much as possible of the miraculous food that has fallen from heaven. A representation of interacting people is not necessarily self-explanatory. It must be interpreted and this interpretation implies setting the movements into an imaginary context.

In most periods of art such a context is given by situational cues which are familiar to members of the culture. The painter and the sculptor make use of a good deal of symbolic lore to mark a personage as king or beggar, angel or demon, they introduce further emblems or 'attributes' to label individuals so that no difficulty arises in recognizing Christ or the Buddha, the Nativity or the Rape of Proserpina.

Take the relief of Orpheus and Eurydice (Fig. 66) after a Greek composition of the fifth century B.C. First we must recognize the protagonists by what are called their 'attributes', the singer's lyre, or the traveller's hat of

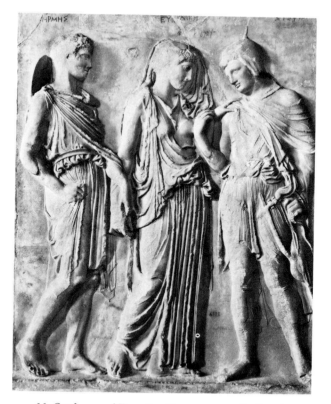

66. *Orpheus and Eurydice*. Roman copy of a Greek
5th century relief. Naples, Museo Nazionale

Hermes, the guide of the dead. Only then can we identify the episode here represented, the fatal moment when Orpheus has disobeyed the condition imposed on him and has looked back at Eurydice, who is therefore taken back to Hades by the god. Thus we may 'compare and contrast' it without irreverence with our Egyptian example (Fig. 61). The Greek work does not deviate much from that 'conceptual' clarity that presents the posture of every figure at its most legible, it is in fact in subtle departure from this normal position that the relationship of the three actors is most delicately conveyed. These small deviations are in the direction postulated by Engel's analysis. Hermes is seen to bend back slightly as he gently takes Eurydice by the wrist to return her to the realm of Hades. The two lovers face each other, her hand rests on the shoulders of the guide who had failed her, her head is slightly lowered as they gaze at each other in a mute farewell. There is no overt expression in their blank features, but nothing contradicts the mood we readily project into this composition, once we have grasped its import.

Such a subtle evocation must rely on the kind of beholder who would also know how to appreciate the reworking of a familiar myth at the hands of a

Sophocles or Euripides. The relief, in other words, is not really created to tell the story of Orpheus and Eurydice but to enable those who know the story from childhood to re-live it in human terms. This reliance on suggestion is characteristic of the great period of Greek art in which every resource of expressive movement was used to convey the interaction of individuals. These resources were lost or discarded as soon as art was predominantly used to drive home a message and proclaim a sacred truth.

6. THE PICTOGRAPHIC STYLE

During declining antiquity, with the rise of Imperial cults and, above all, with the development of Christian art, we can observe the re-emergence of frankly conceptual methods and a new standardization of symbolic or conceptual gestures.[22] These gestures of prayer, instruction, teaching or mourning, help rapidly to set up the context and to make the scene legible. The Emperor sacrificing, the general addressing the army, the teacher instructing his pupils, the defeated submitting to the victor, all these are types of juxtaposition which lend themselves to as unambiguous a representation for those who know the conventions of gesture language, as do scenes of combat for those who do not. Such impressive legibility is demanded where the rendering of a holy writ almost forbids that free dramatic evocation that Greek art had evolved. Moreover it needs much mastery on the part of the artist and the beholder to isolate and interpret expressive movements in the context of vivid interaction. Thus late antique and early Christian art generally played safe in the illustration of narrative texts. An almost pictographic idiom was distilled from the freer tradition of classical art. The need for unambiguous messages stilled the vivid and subtle interplay of action and reaction that marked the masterpieces of the earlier style.[23] Instead we are frequently shown the protagonist, Christ, a saint, or a prophet or even a pagan hero, standing erect, with a gesture of 'speaking' or command, the centre of the scene to which all other figures must be related.

To the student of non-verbal communication this extreme 'pictographic' convention is of interest precisely because the need to turn art into a 'script for the illiterate'[24] brings out both the potentialities and the limitations of the medium and can serve as a point of reference in the consideration of other styles.

The pictographic style takes no chance with naturalism. There is no pretence, implied or overt, of presenting a snapshot of a given scene such as might have been seen and photographed by an imaginary witness. In fact the style makes it easy to show up the fallacies in this conception of art discussed in the previous essay which have haunted criticism since Lessing's *Laocoon*.

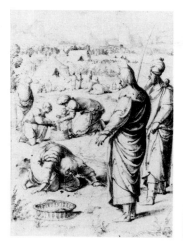

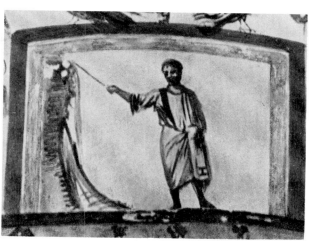

67. Aertgen van Leyden:
The Israelites in the Desert.
c. 1550. Berlin, Staatliche Museen

68. *Moses Striking the Rock.* From the Catacombs.
4th century. Rome, Via Nomentana,
Coemeterium Maius

Neither the prayer nor the speech, the wailing or the submission is imagined to be recorded at a particular moment of time. The assembled pictographs relate to a story in the past which is now accomplished and complete. Christ stands with extended hand in front of an edifice that contains a mummy, to symbolize the Raising of Lazarus (see Fig. 22). Moses is seen with outstretched hand holding a rod, while water gushes from the rock as in many catacomb paintings (Fig. 68). It would be foolish to ask whether the act of striking is over or whether the artist has anticipated the effect by showing the jet of water. The juxtaposition simply conveys the story of the water miracle much as a brief narrative would. One might in fact translate the pictograph into a sentence in which the protagonist is the subject, the action the verb and the tomb or rock the object. The pictograph – to use a distinction I have found useful – represents the 'what' but not the 'how', the verb but not the adverb or any adjectival clause.

7. THE CHORUS EFFECT

There are several ways in which art can introduce these enrichments to convey not only the fact of the event but also some of its significance, and these invariably draw on the resources of 'non-verbal communication', that is on expressive as distinct from symbolic movement. Perhaps the most general method in art has been to clarify the meaning of the action by showing the reaction of onlookers. When Christ brings Lazarus to life, his two sisters prostrate themselves before Him in awe and gratitude while the crowd shows by their gestures and movements that they are witnessing a

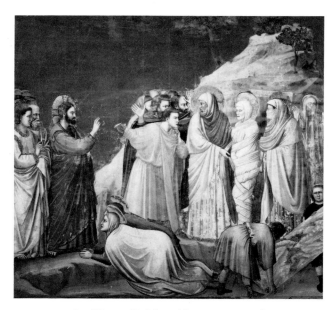

69. Giotto: *Raising of Lazarus. c.* 1306.
Padua, Arena Chapel

miracle. (Not to mention the bystanders holding their noses to remind us that the corpse was already far gone! Fig. 69.) When Moses strikes water from the rock, the Elders who had come to witness the scene throw up their arms in wonder and the thirsting Israelites extend their eager hands to drink (Fig. 70). There are many themes of Western art which can best be described in terms of this formula of action and reaction, the reacting crowds providing the 'chorus' explaining the meaning of the action, and, in doing so, setting the key for the beholder's response. The student of expression can here verify some of the analysis by Shaftesbury and Engel mentioned above. The orientation of the figures towards or away from the central event can express admiration, aggression, flight or awe. But art, like the stage, has also explored less obvious reactions in the depiction of great events – the 'autistic' gestures of the contemplative, the fearful movement of the hand to the head, the abstracted look of those immobilized by surprise and, to mention a frequent but very subtle formula, the way a bystander may turn away from the main event to look into his neighbour's eye as if to make sure that others, too, have seen the same and are equally moved (see Fig. 26).[25]

8. EXPRESSION AND EMPHASIS

Needless to say, it is somewhat too schematic to call purposeful movements 'action', and movements which are an expression of an inner state 'reaction'. Both action and reaction can be more or less communicative of psychological

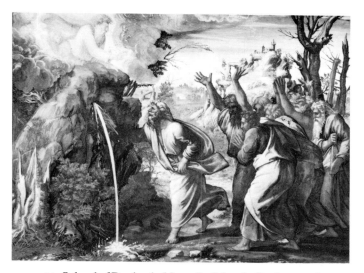

70. School of Raphael: *Moses Striking the Rock. c.* 1518.
Vatican, Musei e Gallerie Pontificie

states, provided we have sufficient context to interpret them. This is a point
where the 'language' of gestures can be compared with the language of words
– every symbolic movement also has a 'tone' which conveys character and
emotion; it can be tense or relaxed, urgent or calm. There are countless
traditional subjects in Western art which allow us to study these possibilities
of what Dante calls 'visible speech'. Describing a relief representing the
Annunciation he says: 'The angel that came to earth with a decree of peace . . .
appeared before us so truthfully carved in a gentle gesture that it did not
appear to be a silent image. One would have sworn that he said "Ave" . . . and
onto her attitude there was impressed that speech "Ecce ancilla Dei" exactly
as a figure is sealed onto wax . . .' (*Purgatorio*, x, 34–45).

In what I have called the 'pictographic' mode this exchange would be
expressed simply by the Angel extending his hand in a speaking gesture while
the Virgin's reaction and response were confined to a lifting of her palms in a
movement of surprise (Fig. 71). But on reading the gospels the artist would
find more about the supreme moment of the Incarnation, he would read that
on seeing the angel 'she was troubled at his saying and cast in her mind what
manner of salutation this should be' before the final submission, 'Behold the
handmaid of the Lord; be it unto me according to thy word'.[26]

Any artist who wanted to depart from the pictographic method of narrative
to emulate the representation Dante had seen in his vision had therefore to
feel his way like an actor trying to express a complex emotion – the way fear
and wonder turn into unquestioning acceptance.

We happen to know through the writings of Leonardo da Vinci that the right extent of departing from pictographic clarity towards the Greek style of dramatic evocation was a subject of debate among artists of the Renaissance. Chiding those of his fellow artists whom he regarded as mere 'face painters' – specialists in portraiture – Leonardo comes to speak of his favourite topic, the need for universality in an artist and especially the importance of observing the expression of mental states. Those Florentine artists of the *quattrocento* who had gone furthest in exploring the representation of movement encountered a certain amount of opposition in the name of 'decorum'. Alberti in the 1430s speaks in general terms of the need for restraint, since figures throwing their limbs about look like 'duellers'.[27] Filarete,[28] paraphrasing this remark some twenty years later, identifies the target of these strictures – he says that Donatello's disputing Apostles are gesticulating like jugglers. Now Leonardo, who must have heard similar remarks passed about his own paintings, goes over to the counter-attack. Specialists in portraiture, he remarks, lack judgement in these matters because their own works are without movement and they themselves are lazy and sluggish. Thus when they see works showing more movement and greater alertness than their own, they attack them for looking as if 'possessed' or like morris dancers.[29] Admittedly, Leonardo concedes, there can also be excesses in the other direction.[30]

> One must observe decorum, that is the movements must be in accord with the movements of the mind . . . thus if one has to represent a figure which should display a timid reverence it should not be represented with such audacity and presumption that the effect looks like despair . . . I have seen these days an angel who looked as if in the annunciation he wanted to chase Our Lady out of her chamber with gestures which looked as offensive as one would make towards the vilest enemy, and Our Lady looked as if she wanted to throw herself out of the window in despair.

A painting in Glasgow (Fig. 72) from the workshop of Botticelli almost answers to Leonardo's satirical description.

But Leonardo, being Leonardo, did not remain content with these polemical remarks. He went on reflecting on the problem posed by such disparate judgements about works of art and came to the conclusion that the reactions of his fellow artists were invariably connected with their own style and temperament. 'He who moves his own figures too much will think that he who moves them as they should, makes them look sleepy, and he who moves them but little will call the correct and proper movement "possessed".'[31]

It is interesting to watch Leonardo himself groping for the 'correct and

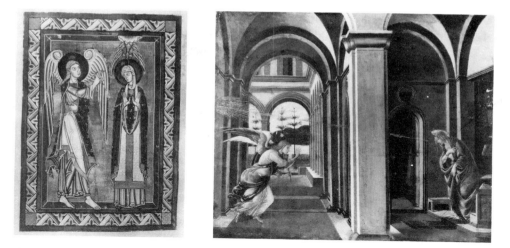

71. *The Annunciation*. From a Swabian Gospel MS. *c.* 1150. Stuttgart Landesbibliothek.
72. School of Botticelli: *The Annunciation. c.* 1490. Glasgow, Art Gallery and Museum.

proper' rendering of 'timid reverence' in an early study for an *Adoration of the Magi* (Fig. 74). Once more it may be instructive to recall the 'pictographic' mode of illustrating the Biblical episode on early Christian sarcophagi, where the Virgin and Child are approached by three identical figures in the recognizable garb of the Magi in the symbolic act of paying homage (Fig. 73), their hands carrying the presents often covered by a cloth. For Leonardo, of course, the symbolic act must also be expressive of what goes on in the minds of the Kings who have come from afar to greet the newborn Saviour. He varies the gesture of presentation and submission from the upright and rather unmoved youngster in the left-hand corner who does not even look at the child, to the old King who humbles himself as he moves

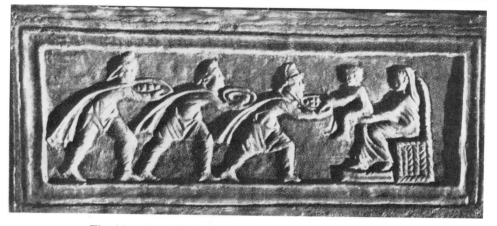

73. *The Adoration of the Magi*. Detail from a sarcophagus. 4th century.
Ravenna, S. Giovanni Battista

forward on his knees to extend his gift. But the right degree of emphasis is obviously only one of the needs the artist seeks to satisfy. He also takes great care that the posture and movement remain completely legible, turning the actors in such a way as to present the clearest silhouette. None of these attitudes is really a movement caught on the wing; each could be taken up and held in a *tableau vivant* and it is this among other things which Leonardo clearly wanted if the figures were not to incur the justified strictures of excessive movement.

Comparing his solution with that of his contemporaries one might imagine that the criticism that Leonardo's figures looked too lethargic might have come from Botticelli, whose later style is indeed almost 'possessed' (Fig. 76). The opposite objection, that Leonardo's own figures are 'gesticulating like mad', might have come from his other Florentine rival Ghirlandaio, whose *Adoration* provides a foil of stolid immobility to Leonardo's dramatic gestures (Fig. 75).

Leonardo's interesting observations can be generalized to apply not only to the varying standards of artists, but also to those of other critics. We all know that the Northerner will tend to find the expressive movements of the Latin nations over-emphatic and theatrical. In writing about Leonardo's *Last Supper*, Goethe[32] had to remind his German readers of this characteristic of Italian culture, and I have found that contemporary English students can be

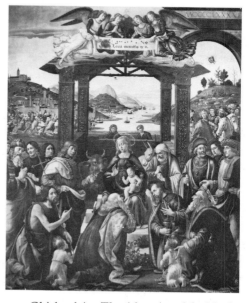

74. Leonardo da Vinci: Study for
The Adoration of the Magi. c. 1481.
Drawing. Paris, Musée du Louvre

75. Ghirlandaio: *The Adoration of the Magi.*
1488. Florence, Ospedale degli Innocenti

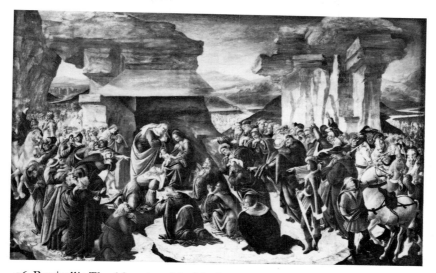

76. Botticelli: *The Adoration of the Magi. c.* 1500. Florence, Galleria degli Uffizi

incredulous if they are told that Leonardo may really have intended the intensity of gesticulation he used in the *Last Supper* (see Fig. 47) to convey the disciples' reaction to Christ's words that one of them would betray Him.[33] We certainly judge the emotional import of an expressive movement by comparing it with some mean, just as we do the loudness of speech or other dimensions of emphasis.

Thus the style of movement represented in art will depend on a great many variables including the current level of emphasis, or the demand for restraint, which varies in its turn not only from period to period and nation to nation but also from class to class. Few aspects of 'manners' and behaviour were more eagerly discussed in treatises on acting and on art than this question of 'decorum'.

Nobility, on the whole, implied restraint or at least a stylized type of emphasis, while the vulgar could disport themselves more freely and more spontaneously, as in pictures of carnivals, of taverns, of the barber pulling a tooth. Naturally the resources of expressiveness continued to be adapted to different ends in conformity with these different ideals. It has been claimed[34] that the Church of the Counter Reformation favoured the representation of martyrdoms to rouse the beholder. It is certain that the seventeenth century in Italy developed new formulae for extreme and ecstatic states.

By that time, of course, art may be said to have largely returned to a function akin to its role in classical Greece. It was not mainly there to tell the sacred story to the illiterate but rather to evoke it in a convincing and imaginative way to those who knew it. It is characteristic of art that ultimately the display of resources may become part of a novel purpose. This

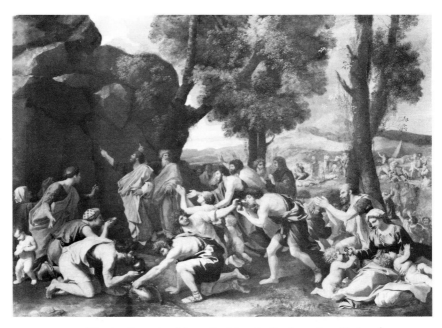

77. Nicolas Poussin: *Moses Striking the Rock. c.* 1637. Duke of
Sutherland Collection (on loan to the National Gallery of Scotland)

is certainly true of the rendering of expressive movement. The artist's
mastery in conveying human emotions was so much admired that the
illustration of a sacred or secular story becomes rather the occasion for the
exercise of such mastery. Just as the libretto of the average opera was chosen
to allow the composer to express or depict the widest range of human
passions in his music, so the subjects selected by post-Renaissance artists
were frequently intended to permit a maximum of dramatic effects.

Naturally in art no less than in drama these effects in their turn were
subject to the rules of 'decorum', particularly in seventeenth-century France.
When Poussin illustrated the story of Moses striking the rock (Fig. 77)—as
he did three times in his life—he took great care that the thirsting Israelites in
the desert were made to express their response to the miracle with nobility
and restraint. His rendering of the Gathering of Manna was the subject of a
famous academy discourse by the painter Le Brun, who stressed the
conformity of the various types to classical precedents.[35] The very
approximation of pictorial representations to the stage, however, also
produced a reaction. Epithets such as 'stagey' or 'theatrical' are not
necessarily words of praise when applied to works of art, and the gradual
eclipse suffered by academic art with its 'grand manner' is closely linked with
the reaction against classical rhetoric in favour of a less formal and less public
display of emphatic emotion.

9. INWARDNESS AND AMBIGUITY

The tradition of Northern art, less immediately affected by classical influences, had earlier on developed pictorial devices which appealed to this taste for a more inward, more lyrical and less dramatic expression in art. Instead of concentrating on expansive movement, the artist relied on the characterization of physiognomies and facial expression. A type of composition appeared towards the end of the fifteenth century in which the *dramatis personae* are shown in close-ups and all the psychological interaction must be read in the features.[36] Thus the artist may concentrate on representing the expression of devotion in the heads of the three Magi who offer their gifts to the Christ child (Fig. 78) or on contrasting the fierce aggression of Christ's tormentors with the Saviour's patience.

Northern art, like the drama of Shakespeare, was altogether less hemmed in by classical rhetoric and decorum and this may explain the fact that in painting too the greatest portrayer of human reactions is to be found in the

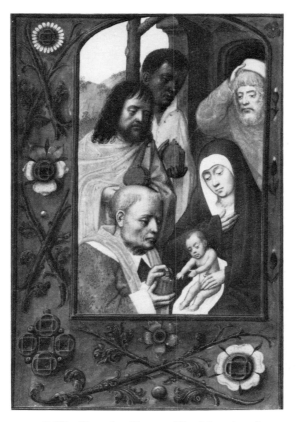

78. The Hortulus Master: *The Adoration of
the Magi. c.* 1490. Munich, Bayerische Staatsbibliothek

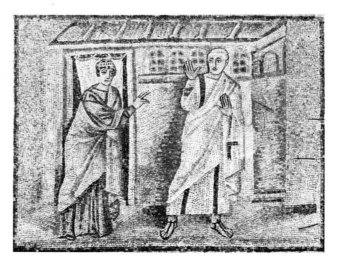

79. *St. Peter's Denial. c.* 520. Mosaic. Ravenna, S. Apollinare Nuovo

Protestant North, in Rembrandt, who had studied and absorbed both traditions. Once more it is instructive to compare his way of narration with the 'pictographic' method of early Christian art. One of the mosaics of S. Apollinare Nuovo (Fig. 79) illustrates the Denial of Peter (Luke 22: 54–62).

> Then took they him, and led him and brought him into the high priest's house. And Peter followed afar off. And when they had kindled a fire, in the midst of the hall, and were set down together, Peter sat down among them. But a certain maid beheld him as he sat by the fire and earnestly looked upon him, and said, This man was also with him. And he denied him, saying, Woman, I know him not. And after a little while another saw him, and said, Thou art also of them. And Peter said, Man, I am not. And about the space of one hour after another confidently affirmed, saying, Of a truth this fellow also was with him: for he is a Galilaean. And Peter said, Man, I know not what thou sayest. And immediately, while he yet spake, the cock crew. And the Lord turned, and looked upon Peter. And Peter remembered the word of the Lord, how he had said unto him, Before the cock crow, thou shalt deny me thrice. And Peter went out, and wept bitterly.

The Ravenna mosaic represents the essential elements in the story. The maid raises her hand in a speaking gesture towards St. Peter, who shrinks back and vividly signals his denial. Rembrandt (Fig. 80) evokes the entire scene by the camp fire, but at first glance it would seem that he is less intent on translating speech into movement. The maid holds a candle close to Peter's face to scrutinize his features but he merely lifts one hand in a movement which is much less unambiguous than that of the early Christian mosaicists. Indeed,

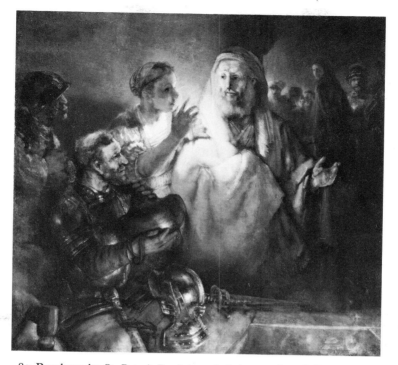

80. Rembrandt: *St. Peter's Denial. c.* 1656. Amsterdam, Rijksmuseum

taken in isolation the figure may simply be shown to speak or even to make an inviting gesture asking one of the other figures to come forward. But the figure is not in isolation and thus Rembrandt compels us to picture the whole tragic scene in our mind, the anxious old man sadly facing the inquisitive woman and the two tough soldiers whose presence amply accounts for his denial. But what makes the picture particularly unforgettable is the barely visible figure of Christ in the dark background, who has been facing His accusers and is turning round, as the Bible says, to look at His erring disciple. It is the absence of any 'theatrical', that is of any unambiguous, gesture which prevents us from reading off the story as if it were written on scrolls and involves us all the more deeply in the event. The very element of ambiguity and of mystery makes us read the drama in terms of inner emotions and once we are attuned to this reading we increasingly project more intensity into these calm gestures and expressions than we are likely to read into the extrovert gesticulations of the Latin style. The painting by Rembrandt demands quiet scrutiny and prolonged meditation. Moreover, it demands much more active participation on the part of the beholder, who must know the Biblical story and have pondered its universal significance if he is to understand the poignancy of Peter's expression and of Christ's unseen gaze.

Speaking somewhat schematically, it may be argued that from the

Renaissance to the eighteenth century the function of art was conceived in the same way as it had been in ancient Greece—the artist should show his mettle by interpreting known texts. It was the 'how' and not the 'what' that the connoisseur admired and pondered. He appreciated the way the painter rendered a particular episode from the Bible or from the Classics and desired to share and understand the reaction of participants through an act of imaginative empathy. It is here, of course, that Rembrandt is supreme precisely because he has discovered and developed the perfect mean between the unrealistic pictographic gesture and the indeterminate representation of an enigmatic movement.

The importance for art of mobilizing the beholder's projective activities in order to compensate for the limitations of the medium can be demonstrated in a variety of fields. The indeterminate outlines of Impressionist pictures which suggest light and movement are a case in point. Such experiments should be of interest to the psychologist of perception for what they tell us about our reactions to real-life situations. This may also apply to the study of non-verbal communication. There is no reason to think that in such real situations the most unambiguous gesture or expression is also the most telling or moving. We learn to appreciate ambiguity, ambivalence and conflict in the reactions of our fellow human beings. It is this richness and depth of our response that a great artist such as Rembrandt knows how to evoke. Provided therefore we do not make the mistake of looking in the greatest works of dramatic narration for a realistic record of movements such as actually occur in non-verbal communication we can study these illustrations with much more profit than the limitations of the medium would allow one to expect.

This is true despite the fact that an inventory of expressive movements used in old master paintings would be likely to reveal a surprisingly limited range. The reasons for this restriction should have become clear from the preceding examples. Perhaps the most decisive of them is the need for conceptual clarity in the posture presented to the beholder, which rules out a large range of movements in which limbs would be too much foreshortened or hidden for the movement to explain itself. Needless to say, neither this nor any other rule is absolute, and subsidiary figures can often be shown in postures of greater complexity or obscurity. However, the astonishment with which the first snapshots were greeted shows that the average observer rarely notices, let alone remembers, the more transient movements, which were therefore excluded from the traditional vocabulary of art. We must stress once more that in this as in other respects the realistic rendering of life situations did not arise from simple imitation but from the adjustment of a conceptual or pictographic tradition.

10. ALTERNATIVE FUNCTIONS

I have emphasized the interdependence of art and function because its recognition helps us to escape from a dilemma which still haunts the history and criticism of art. Originally this history was told in terms of progress, interrupted by periods of decline. It is this conception of history that we find in the authors of classical antiquity and in those from the Renaissance to the nineteenth century, who describe the gradual acquisition of mastery in the rendering of the human anatomy, of space, of light, texture and expression. To the twentieth century, which has witnessed the deliberate abandonment of these skills on the part of its artists, this interpretation of history has come to look naïve. No style of art is said to be better or worse than any other. We may accept this verdict within limits provided it does not tempt us into an untenable relativism concerning the achievement of certain aims – and the rendering of non-verbal communication is a case in point.

We have a right to speak of evolution and of progress in the mastery of certain problems and in the discovery of perfect solutions. Kenneth Clark, in a perceptive essay,[37] has singled out such a problem, the meeting and embrace as it occurs in the story of the Visitation, and has shown its progressive perfection towards what may be called a 'classic' form. We can acknowledge such perfection without forgetting the possibility of alternative solutions once a shift in the problem occurs.

Unfortunately the history of art has tended for too long to fight shy of this type of investigation. We have no systematic study of eye contacts in art[38] and even the exact development of facial expression is all but unknown. Clearly it would not be possible for this essay to reduce these large blank patches on the map of our knowledge. All that can still be done, in conclusion, is to point to their existence and to the location of some of them.

I have mentioned one at least by implication: there must be a great difference between a painting that illustrates a known story and another that wishes to *tell* a story. No history exists of this second category, the so-called anecdotal painting which flourished most in the nineteenth-century salon pictures. Indeed twentieth-century critics have covered the whole genre with such a blanket of disapproval that we are only now beginning to notice this phase in the history of art.[39]

It is likely, however, that the student of non-verbal communication would find a good deal of interest in these systematic attempts to condense a typical dramatic scene into a picture without any more contextual aids than, at the most, a caption. Clearly many of these painters must have profited from a study of the realistic stage rather than from an observation of life, but the fact remains that they made use of a very much enriched vocabulary. The painting by Haynes King, *Jealousy and Flirtation* (1874, Fig. 81), hardly stands in need of a caption. The flirting girl with her inviting look, her hands resting on her head, is immediately intelligible as is the awkward but pleased reaction of the young man. The expression of jealousy may be a little too obvious and genteel, though the 'autistic' gesture of the girl's left hand is expressive enough.

Or take *The First Cloud* (1887) by Orchardson (Fig. 82). It would be interesting to test the interpretations of this scene by subjects who do not know the caption. One could certainly think of alternative interpretations, for after all we only see the woman from the back and have to project into her movements whatever we read in the man's expression. According to Raymond Lister 'she is walking off in a huff . . . the man's eyes following her with a somewhat puzzled though obstinate expression . . .'[40] At any rate his expressive posture is a novelty to art.

It would be interesting to trace the development of these novel means and in particular to examine the role which book illustration on the one hand and

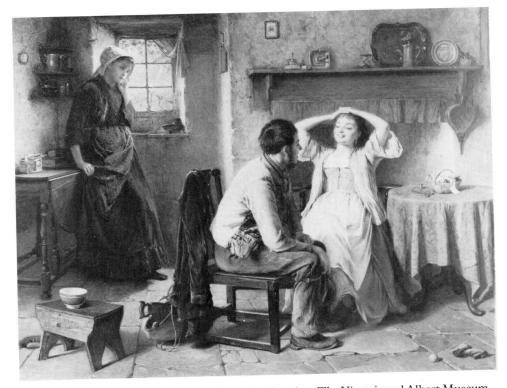

81. Haynes King: *Jealousy and Flirtation*. 1874. London, The Victoria and Albert Museum

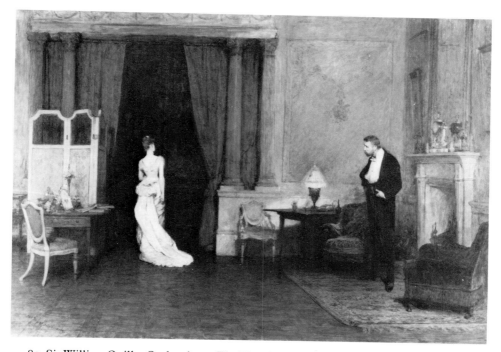

82. Sir William Quiller Orchardson: *The First Cloud.* 1887. London, The Tate Gallery

photography on the other played in this development. One thing seems to me sure. Given the story-telling function of anecdotal art we should be enabled also to trace another series of progressive skills in this as in any other type of representation. In fact, if we go back to the roots of this art in the genre paintings of the Netherlands and if we stop to examine the methods used by the first deliberate story-teller, William Hogarth, we will in all likelihood find that there is a gradual process of enrichment and refinement regardless of whether we like or dislike the ultimate result.

One could think of other topics and social functions which have driven the artist towards the exploration of non-verbal communication. Advertising, for instance, frequently demands the signalling of rapturous satisfaction on the part of the child who eats his breakfast cereals, the housewife who uses a washing powder or the young man smoking a cigarette. It has equally specialized in the exploration of erotic enticement, the 'come hither look' of the pretty girl or the inviting smile of the secretary who ostensibly recommends a typewriter. Clearly the commercial artist and the commercial photographer are likely to know a great deal about the degree of realism and stylization that produces the optimum results for this purpose and also about the changing reactions of the public to certain means and methods. Finally we may point once more to the unexplored realm of the 'comics' with their own conventions of facial expressions and gestures which have penetrated into 'pop' art. Art is long and life is short.

POSTSCRIPT

In conclusion a further elucidation of the use of the term 'expression' in relation to art may be useful. The traditional usage here adopted, which applies this term to the expression of the emotions of the figures in a dramatic illustration (*Laocoon*, the *Pietà*), has indeed been partly superseded by the approach of twentieth-century aesthetics, which so frequently regards the work of art as an expression of the artist's inner states.[41] To these may be added the most ancient usage which relates art predominantly to the emotions it is capable of arousing.[42] The interplay of these usages can best be exemplified in the history of musical theory. The Greeks (including Plato) concentrated on the *effects* of music on the emotions, which ranged from magic efficacy to the creation of moods. The dramatic theory of music favoured by the revivers of opera in the Renaissance and the Baroque stressed the power of music to *depict* or paint the emotions of the noble hero or the desolate lover. It was only in the Romantic period that music was interpreted as an expression of the composer's moods and sentiments. It will be observed that this change of attitude may leave the correlation between certain types of music and certain types of emotion unaffected: the proverbial trumpet call may be seen as arousing, depicting or manifesting war-like feelings. Interest in these aspects changes with the changing social functions of music. It is the same with the visual arts. The magic function of arousal may reach far back to apotropaic images and survives in religious, erotic and commercial art. Interest in art as an expression of the artist's personality and emotion presupposes an autonomy of art only found in certain societies such as Renaissance Italy. Indeed Leonardo's observations on the link between an artist's character and his dramatic powers quoted above (page 92) point the way to this evaluation.

The Mask and the Face:
The Perception of Physiognomic Likeness in Life and in Art

THIS ESSAY takes its starting-point from a chapter in my book on *Art and Illusion*, the chapter entitled 'The Experiment of Caricature'.[1] Caricature had been defined in the seventeenth century as a method of making portraits which aims at the greatest likeness of the whole of a physiognomy while all the component parts are changed. It could thus serve me for a demonstration of equivalence, the proof that the images of art can be convincing without being objectively realistic. I made no attempt, however, to investigate more precisely what was involved in the creation of a striking likeness. It does not look as if anyone has explored the whole vast area of portrait likeness in terms of perceptual psychology. There must be reasons for this omission even beyond the appalling complexity of the problem. Somehow concern with likeness in portraiture bears the stamp of philistinism. As I mentioned before it evokes the memory of quarrels between great artists and pompous sitters whose stupid wives insist that there is still something wrong around the mouth. These dreaded discussions, which may be much less trivial than they sound, have made the whole question of likeness a rather touchy one. Traditional aesthetics has provided the artist with two lines of defence, which have both remained in vogue since the Renaissance. One is summed up in the answer which Michelangelo is reported to have given when someone remarked that the Medici portraits in the *Sagrestia Nuova* were not good likenesses—what will it matter in a thousand years' time what these men looked like? He had created a work of art and that was what counted.[2] The other line goes back to Raphael[3] and beyond to a panegyric on Filippino Lippi, who is there said to have painted a portrait that is more like the sitter than he is himself.[4] The background of this praise is the Neo-Platonic idea of

One of three lectures on Art, Perception and Reality given at Johns Hopkins University in October 1970.

the genius whose eyes can penetrate through the veil of mere appearances and reveal the truth.[5] It is an ideology which gives the artist the right to despise the sitter's philistine relatives who cling to the outward husk and miss the essence.

Whatever the use or abuse to which this line of defence has been put in the past and in the present, it must be granted that here, as elsewhere, Platonic metaphysics can be translated into a psychological hypothesis. Perception always stands in need of universals. We could not perceive and recognize our fellow creatures if we could not pick out the essential and separate it from the accidental—in whatever language we may want to formulate this distinction. Today people prefer computer language, they speak of pattern recognition, picking up the invariants which are distinctive of an individual.[6] It is the kind of skill for which even the most hardened computer designers envy the human mind, and not the human mind only, for the capacity of recognizing identity in change which it presupposes must be built into the central nervous system even of animals. Consider what is involved in this perceptual feat of visually recognizing an individual member of a species out of the herd, the flock, or the crowd. Not only will the light and the angle of vision change as it does with all objects, the whole configuration of the face is in perpetual movement, a movement which somehow does not affect the experience of physiognomic identity nor, as I propose to call it, physiognomic constancy.

Not everybody's face may be as mobile as that of Mr. Emanuel Shinwell, whose characteristic changes of expression during a speech were caught by the candid camera of the London *Times* (Fig. 83), but the example would seem to justify the reaction that we have not one face but a thousand different

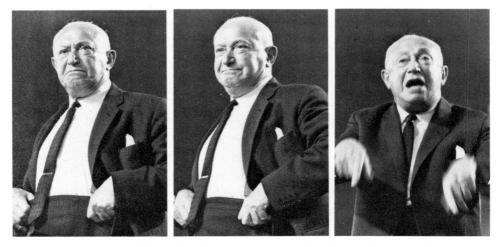

83. *Emanuel Shinwell making a speech.* From *The Times*, 7 October 1966

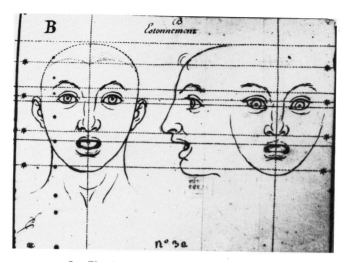

84. Charles Le Brun: *Astonishment.* 1698

faces.[7] It might be objected that the unity in diversity here presents no logical or psychological problem, the face just shows different expressions as its mobile parts respond to the impulse of changing emotions. If the comparison were not so chilling, we might compare it to an instrument board with the mouth or the eyebrows serving as indicators. This was indeed the theory of the first systematic student of human expression, Charles Le Brun, who based himself on Cartesian mechanics and saw in the eyebrows real pointers registering the character of the emotion or passion (Fig. 84).[8] On this reading of the situation, there is no greater problem in our recognizing Emanuel Shinwell in different moods than there is in recognizing our watch at different hours. The framework remains and we quickly learn to separate the rigid bone structure of the head from the ripples of changes which play on its surface.

But clearly this explanation operates at best with a gross over-simplification. The framework does not remain static; we all change throughout our lives from day to day, from year to year. The famous series of Rembrandt's self-portraits from youth to old age shows the artist studying this relentless process, but it is only with the coming of photography that we have all become fully aware of this effect of time. We look at the snapshots of ourselves and of our friends taken a few years ago and we recognize with a shock that we all have changed much more than we tended to notice in the day-to-day business of living. The better we know a person, and the more often we see the face, the less do we notice this transformation except, perhaps, after an illness or another crisis. The feeling of constancy completely predominates over the changing appearance. And yet, if the time-span is long enough this change also affects the frame of reference, the face itself, which a vulgarism actually calls the 'dial'. It does so most thoroughly throughout childhood when proportions change and we first acquire a proper nose, but it also does so once more in old age when we lose our teeth and our hair. Yet all growth and decay cannot destroy the essence of the individual's looks—witness two photographs of Bertrand Russell, as a child of four (Fig. 85) and at the age of ninety (Fig. 86). It certainly would not be easy to programme a computer to pick out the invariant, and yet it is the same face.

If we watch ourselves testing this assertion and comparing the two pictures, we may find that we are probing the face of the child trying to project into it, or onto it, the more familiar face of the aged philosopher. We want to know if we can see the likeness or, if our attitude is one of scepticism, we want to prove to ourselves that we cannot see it. In any case those who are familiar with Bertrand Russell's striking features will inevitably read the comparison from right to left, and try to find the old man in the young child; his mother, if she were alive, would look in the features of the old man for the traces of the child, and having lived through this slow transformation, would be more likely to succeed. The experience of likeness is a kind of perceptual fusion based on recognition, and here as always past experience will colour the way we see a face.

It is on this fusion of unlike configurations that the experience of physiognomic recognition rests. Logically, of course, anything can be said to be like any other thing in some respect, and any child can be argued to be more like any other child than like an old man, indeed any photograph can be argued to be more like any other photograph than any living person. But such quibbles are only helpful if they make us aware of the distance that separates logical discourse from perceptual experience. Rationally we are free to categorize things in any number of ways and order them according to any quality they may have in common, be it weight, colour, size, function, or shape. Moreover, in this ordering activity we can always specify in which respect one thing is like another.

That physiognomic likeness which results in fusion and recognition is notoriously less easy to specify and analyse. It is based on what is called a global impression, the resultant of many factors which yet in their interaction make for a very particular physiognomic quality. Many of us would be unable to describe the individual features of our closest friends, the colour of their eyes, the exact shape of their noses, but this uncertainty does not impair our feeling of familiarity with their features, which we would pick out among a thousand because we respond to their characteristic expression. Clearly we must not confuse this experience with the perception of contrasting

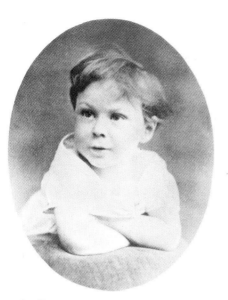

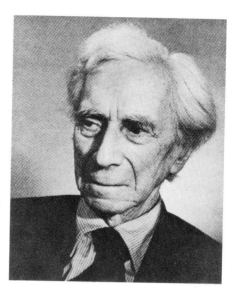

85. *Bertrand Russell at the age of four*   86. *Bertrand Russell at the age of ninety*

expressions on a person's face. Just as we can generalize on a person's voice or on the duct of his handwriting through all the varieties of tone or line, so we feel that there is some general dominant expression of which the individual expressions are merely modifications. In Aristotelian terms it is his substance, of which all modifications are mere accidents, but it can transcend the individual in the experience of family likeness so marvellously described in a letter by Petrarch. Petrarch discusses the problem of imitating the style of an admired author and says that the similarity should be like that between a son and his father, where there is often a great difference between their individual features 'and yet a certain shadow, or what our painters call the *aria*, reminds us of the father as soon as we see the son, even though, if the matter were put to measurement, all parts would be found to be different.'[9]

We all know such examples of family likeness, but all of us have also been irritated by the talk of visiting aunts about baby looking 'exactly like' uncle Tom or aunt Joan, assertions which are sometimes countered with the remark 'I cannot see this.' For the student of perception such discussions can never be boring, the very disagreement about what they see is grist for the mill of those of us who look at perception as a nearly automatic act of categorizing in universals. What people experience as likeness throws light on their perceptual categories. Clearly we do not all have the same impression of a person's *aria* or characteristic face. We do see them differently according to the categories with which we scan our fellow creatures. This fact, perhaps, accounts for the central paradox in the field of physiognomic perception, the one which is implied in the distinction between the mask and the face: the experience of the underlying constancies in a person's face, which is so strong as to survive all the transformations of mood and age and even to leap across generations, conflicts with the strange fact that such recognition can be inhibited with comparative ease by what may be called the mask. This is the alternative category of recognition, the cruder type of likeness which can throw the whole mechanism of physiognomic recognition into confusion. The art which experiments with the mask is of course the art of disguise, of acting. The whole point of the actor's skill is precisely this: to compel us to see him or her as different people according to the different roles. The great actor does not even need the mask of make-up to enforce this transformation. A great impersonator such as Ruth Draper was able to transform herself from scene to scene with the simplest of means. The illustrations show her as two women in the life of one businessman, the haughty wife (Fig. 87) and the devoted secretary (Fig. 88). The scarf, the costume, and the wig may help, but what really effects the transformation is the difference in posture, in the whole *tonus* of the persons represented.

Sociologists have increasingly reminded us of the truth that we are all actors, we all obediently play one of the roles which our society offers to us— even the 'hippies' do. In the society with which we are familiar we are extremely sensitive to the outward signs of these roles and much of our

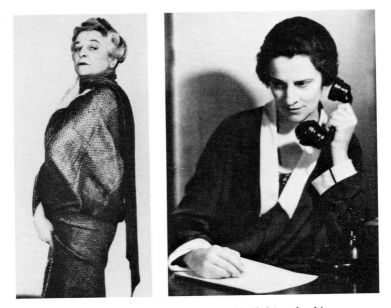

87, 88. *Ruth Draper as the businessman's wife (left) and as his secretary.*
Photographs by Dorothy Wilding and Nicholas Murray

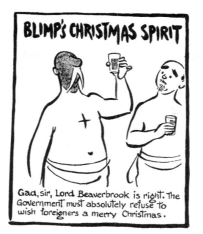

89. David Low: *Colonel Blimp*. 1936

categorization proceeds along these lines. We have learned to distinguish the types with which our writers and satirists keep us in touch: there is the military type, David Low's Colonel Blimp of blessed memory (Fig. 89), the sporty type, the arty type, the executive, the academic type, and so all through the repertory of the comedy of life. Clearly this knowledge of the cast permits a great economy of effort in dealing with our fellow creatures. We see the type and adjust our expectations: the military red-faced man will have a booming voice, like strong drink, and dislike modern art. True, life has also taught us that we must be prepared for such syndromes to be incomplete. In fact, whenever we meet the exception to this rule and find the perfect embodiment of a type we are apt to say, 'this man is so much the typical Central European intellectual it just is not true.' But it often is true. We model ourselves so much on the expectation of others that we assume the mask or, as the Jungians say, the *persona* which life assigns to us, and we grow into our type till it moulds all our behaviour, down to our gait and our facial expression. It seems there is nothing to exceed the plasticity of man except, of course, the plasticity of woman. Women work more consciously on their type and image than most men used to do, and often they try by means of make-up and hair style to shape themselves in the image of some fashionable idol of the screen or of the stage.[10]

But how do these idols shape their image? The language of fashion gives at least a partial answer. They look for a distinctive note, for a striking characteristic that will mark them out and attract attention through a new kind of piquancy. One of the most intelligent of stage personalities, the late Yvette Guilbert, described in her memoirs how she deliberately set about in her youth to create her type by deciding that, since she was not beautiful in the conventional sense, she would be different. 'My mouth,' she writes, 'was thin and wide and I refused to reduce it through make-up, because at that time all the women of the stage had tiny heart-shaped mouths.'[11] Instead, she emphasized her lips to contrast with her pale face and to bring out her smile. Her dress was to be simple as a shift, she wore no ornament, but she completed her striking silhouette by adopting the long black gloves which became famous (Fig. 90). Thus her image, which was a deliberate creation, met the artist half way, because it could be summed up in those few telling strokes we remember from the lithographs of Toulouse-Lautrec (Fig. 91).

We are approaching the area of caricature, or rather that borderland between caricature and portraiture which is occupied by images of stylized personalities, all the actors on the public stage who wear their masks for a purpose. Think of Napoleon's forelock and of that gesture of standing with the hand tucked into his waistcoat which the actor Talma is said to have suggested to him. It has remained a godsend to impersonators and cartoonists seeking a formula for a Napoleonic aspiration—and so have the tricks adopted by the lesser Napoleons we have had to endure.

It hardly matters how trivial the distinctive trait may be which is taken up,

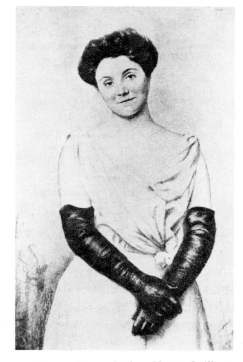

90. Bennewitz von Löfen: *Yvette Guilbert.*
1896. Pastel

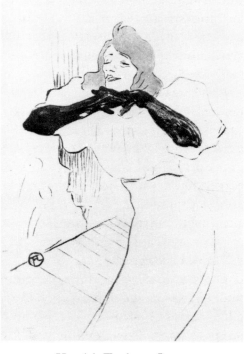

91. Henri de Toulouse-Lautrec:
Yvette Guilbert. 1894. Lithograph

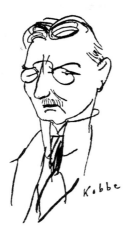

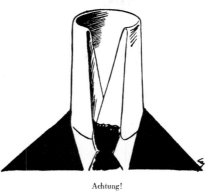

Achtung!

Ein Stehkragen taucht wieder auf!

92a. 'Kobbe': *Hjalmar Schacht*.
From *Der Montag Morgen*,
10 March, 1924

92b. Caricature of Schacht. From
8 Uhr Abendblatt, Berlin,
13 June 1932. Caption reads:
'Look out! A high collar has
turned up again!'

provided it remains consistently identifiable. Hitler's financial wizard, Hjalmar Schacht, was apparently in the habit of wearing a high starched collar (Fig. 92a). The collar itself somehow evokes the social type of the rigid Prussian moving in the company of upright executives (Fig. 92b). It would be interesting to find out by how much the height of Schacht's collar exceeded the average of his class; at any rate, the deviation stuck and gradually the collar came to replace the likeness of the man. The mask swallowed up the face.

If these examples suggest anything, it is that we generally take in the mask before we notice the face. The mask here stands for the crude distinctions, the deviations from the norm which mark a person off from others. Any such deviation which attracts our attention may serve us as a tab of recognition and promises to save us the effort of further scrutiny. For it is not really the perception of likeness for which we are originally programmed, but the noticing of unlikeness, of that departure from the norm which stands out and sticks in the mind. This mechanism serves us in good stead as long as we move in familiar surroundings and have to mark the slight but all-important differences which distinguish one individual from another. But once an unexpected distinctive feature obtrudes itself the mechanism can jam. It is said that all Chinese look alike to Westerners and all Westerners to Chinese. This may not be strictly true, but the belief reveals an important feature of our perception. One might indeed compare the effect with what is known as the masking effect in the psychology of perception where a strong impression impedes the perception of lower thresholds. A bright light masks the

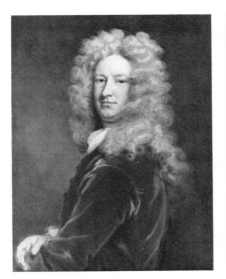

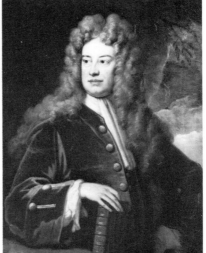

93. Sir Godfrey Kneller:
Sir Samuel Garth. c. 1710. London,
National Portrait Gallery

94. Sir Godfrey Kneller:
John Somer. c. 1702–10. London,
National Portrait Gallery

modulations of the dim nuances in the vicinity just as a loud tone masks subsequent soft modulations of sound. Such unaccustomed features as slanting eyes will at first rivet our attention and make it hard for us to attend to the subtle variations. Hence the effectiveness also of any striking and unusual mark as a disguise. It is not only all Chinese who tend to look alike to us but also all men in identical wigs such as the members of the eighteenth-century Kit-Cat Club displayed in the National Portrait Gallery in London (Figs. 93 and 94).

How far do such portraits represent types or masks, and how far are they individual likenesses? Clearly there are two difficulties in answering this important question, one obvious, the other perhaps less so. The obvious difficulty is the same with all portraits of people before the invention of photography—we have very few objective controls about the sitter's appearance except occasionally a life—or a death—mask or a tracing of the shadow as a silhouette. We shall never know whether we would recognize Mona Lisa or the Laughing Cavalier if we met them in the flesh. The second difficulty springs from the fact that we ourselves are trapped by the mask and therefore find it hard to perceive the face. We have to make an effort to abstract from the wig to see how far these faces differ, and even then changing ideas of decorum and deportment, the social mask of expression, make it hard for us to see the person as an individual. Art historians often write of certain periods and styles that portraits at that time were confined to types rather than to individual likeness, but much depends on how one decides to use

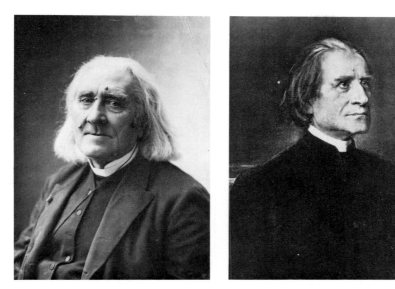

95. *Franz Liszt*. Photographed by Nadar   96. Franz Lenbach: *Franz Liszt*

these terms. Even the stereotypical images of tribal art have been known to embody an individual distinctive feature which would escape us since we neither know the person represented nor the stylistic conventions of the tribe. One thing is sure, moreover: it is almost impossible for us to see an old portrait as it was meant to be seen before the snapshot and the screen spread and trivialized the likeness. We can hardly recapture the full significance of an image commissioned and made to sum up the sitter's social status and career, and to preserve his features as a memorial to his descendants and as a monument to later ages. Obviously in such a situation the portrait had quite a different weight. The artist's reading of the sitter's features would impose itself during his life-time and would totally take over after his death in a manner we can neither hope for, nor need fear, since the multiplicity of records we have will always counter such a psychological take-over bid.

No wonder the coming of the camera found the artists and their friends in a bewildered and aggressive mood. Some of the arguments used against the possibility of a photographic likeness produced in the nineteenth century look surprising to us, for many now will prefer Nadar's splendid portrait of Franz Liszt (Fig. 95) which shows the great virtuoso, warts and all, to the rather theatrical painting by Franz Lenbach (Fig. 96), but, again, we must admit that we have never known Liszt. Here the question is really whether we can even see photographs in the same way in which they were first seen. The candid camera and the television screen have completely changed our mental set towards the image of our contemporaries. Such intimate snapshots as those showing our modern Franz Liszt, Sviatoslav Richter, at rehearsals in shirt-sleeves (Fig. 97) would not only have been technically impossible in the nineteenth century, they would also have been psychologically unacceptable, they would have struck our grandfathers as both indecorous and totally unrecognizable.

But though the snapshot has transformed the portrait it has also made us see that problem of likeness more clearly than past centuries were able to formulate it. It has drawn attention to the paradox of capturing life in a still, of freezing the play of features in an arrested moment of which we may never be aware in the flux of events. Thanks to the work of J. J. Gibson in the psychology of perception we have become increasingly aware of the decisive role which the continuous flow of information plays in all our commerce with the visible world.[12] Hence we also understand a little more wherein rests what might be called the artificiality of art, the confinement of the information to simultaneous cues. To put the matter crudely—if the film camera rather than the chisel, the brush, or even the photographic plate had been the first recorder of human physiognomies, the problem which language in its wisdom calls 'catching a likeness' would never have obtruded itself to the same extent on our awareness. The film shot can never fail as signally as the snapshot can, for even if it catches a person blinking or sneezing the sequence explains the resulting grimace which the corresponding snapshot may leave uninterpretable. Looked at in this way, the miracle is not that some snapshots catch an uncharacteristic aspect, but that both the camera and the brush can abstract from movement and still produce a convincing likeness not only of the mask but also of the face, the living expression.

Clearly the artist or even the photographer could never overcome the torpor of the arrested effigy if it were not for that characteristic of perception which I described as 'the beholder's share' in *Art and Illusion* and to which I have also referred in this volume. We tend to project life and expression onto

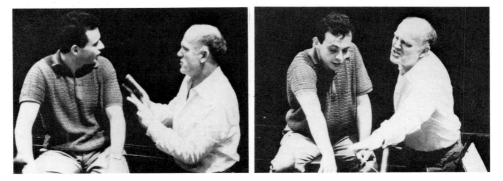

97. *Sviatoslav Richter*. Photographed during rehearsal

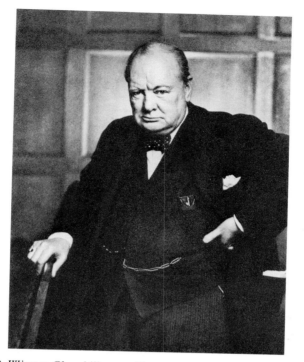

98. *Winston Churchill*. 1941. Photographed by Karsh, Ottawa

the arrested image and supplement from our own experience what is not actually present. Thus the portraitist who wants to compensate for the absence of movement must first of all mobilize our projection. He must so exploit the ambiguities of the arrested face that the multiplicities of possible readings result in the semblance of life. The immobile face must appear as a nodal point of several possible expressive movements.[13] As a professional photographer once told me with a pardonable overstatement, she searches for the expression which implies all others. A scrutiny of successful portrait photographs confirms indeed this importance of ambiguity. We do not want to see the sitter in the situation in which he actually was—having his portrait taken. We want to be able to abstract from this memory and to see him reacting to more typical real-life contexts.

The story of one of the most successful and most popular photographs of Winston Churchill as a war leader (Fig. 98) may illustrate this point. We are told by Yousuf Karsh how unwilling he found the busy Prime Minister to pose for this photograph during a visit to Ottawa in December 1941. All he would allow was two minutes as he passed from the chamber of the House to the anteroom. As he approached with a scowl, Karsh snatched the cigar from his mouth and made him really angry. But that expression, which was in reality no more than a passing reaction to a trivial incident, was perfectly suited to symbolize the leader's defiance of the enemy. It could be generalized into a monument of Churchill's historic role.[14]

Admittedly it is not very usual for photographers to exploit the ambiguity or interpretability of an angry frown. More often they ask us to smile, though folklore has it that if we say 'cheese' this produces the same effect around the mouth. The arrested smile is certainly an ambiguous and multi-valent sign of animation and has been used by artists to increase the semblance of life ever since archaic Greece. The most famous example of its use is of course Leonardo's *Mona Lisa*, whose smile has been the subject of so many and so fanciful interpretations. Maybe we can still learn more about this effect by comparing common-sense theory with unexpected but successful practice.

Roger de Piles (1635–1709), to whom we owe the first detailed discussion of the theory of portrait painting, advises the painter to attend to expression:

> It is not exactness of design in portraits that gives spirit and true air, so much as the agreement of the parts at the very moment when the disposition and temperament of the sitter are to be hit off. . . .
>
> Few painters have been careful enough to put the parts well together: Sometimes the mouth is smiling, and the eyes are sad; at other times, the eyes are chearful, and the cheeks lank; by which means their work has a false air, and looks unnatural. We ought therefore to mind, that, when the sitter puts on a smiling air, the eyes close, the corners of the mouth draw up towards the nostrils, the cheeks swell, and the eyebrows widen.[15]

Now if we compare this sound advice with a typical eighteenth-century portrait such as Quentin de la Tour's charming pastel of his mistress Mlle Fel (Fig. 99), we see that her eyes are by no means closed as in a smile. And yet the very combination of slightly contradictory features, of a serious gaze with a shadow of a smile results in a subtle instability, an expression hovering between the pensive and the mocking that both intrigues and fascinates. True, the game is not without risk, and this perhaps explains the degree to which the effect froze into a formula in the eighteenth-century portraits of polite society.

The best safeguard against the 'unnatural look' or the frozen mask has always been found in the suppression rather than the employment of any contradictions which might impede our projection. This is the trick to which Reynolds referred in his famous analysis of Gainsborough's deliberately sketchy portrait style, which I quoted and discussed in *Art and Illusion*. Photographers such as Steichen have aimed at a similar advantage by a combination of lighting and printing tricks, to blur the outline of a face and

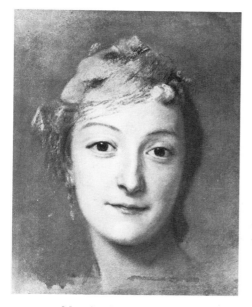

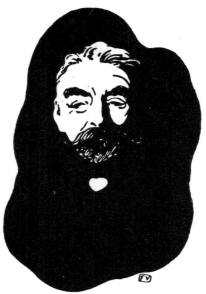

99. Maurice Quentin de la Tour:
Mademoiselle Fel. c. 1757. Pastel.
St. Quentin, Musée Antoine Lécuyer

100. Félix Vallotton: *Mallarmé.*
1895. Woodcut

thus to mobilize our projection, and graphic artists, such as Félix Vallotton in his portrait of *Mallarmé* (Fig. 100), have also aimed at similar effects of simplification, much discussed at the turn of the century.[16]

We enjoy this game and we rightly admire the painter or the caricaturist who can, as the saying goes, conjure up a likeness with a few bold strokes, by reducing it to essentials. But the portrait painter also knows that the real trouble starts when you have to proceed in the opposite direction. However skilful he may have been with the first rough outline, he must not spoil the sketch on the way to the finished portrait, because the more elements he has to handle, the harder it is to preserve the likeness. From this point of view the experience of the academic portrait painter is almost more interesting than that of the caricaturist. A remarkably circumspect and revealing report on the problem of catching a likeness can be found in a book by Janet Robertson, whose paintings belong to the tradition of formal portraiture:

> . . . there are certain errors one learns to look for as the possible cause of untrue expression. Does there seem too 'sharp' a quality? Check carefully that the eyes are not too close together; is the look, on the other hand, too 'vague'? Make sure they are not too far apart—often, of course, the drawing can be correct, but overemphasis or underemphasis of shadows may seem to draw the eyes together or widen the distance between them. If, in spite of a conviction that you have drawn the

mouth correctly, it still somehow looks wrong, check the surrounding
tones, especially that on the upper lip (i.e., the whole region between
nose and mouth); an error in the tone of this passage can make all the
difference in bringing the mouth forward or sending it back, a matter
that affects expression at once. If you feel there is something wrong and
you cannot locate it, check the position of the ear . . . Now, if the ear is
placed wrongly it alters the whole impression of the facial angle and you
may remedy a jowly look or a weak look by correcting that error without
touching those features with the expression of which you have been
struggling in vain.[17]

This description by a painter who had the humility to listen to lay criticism
is so instructive because it spells out certain relationships between the shape
of the face and what the author calls its expression. What she means has less
to do with the play of expressions than with what Petrarch called the *aria* of
the face. We remember that this 'expression' is not the same as its
expressions. The distance of the eyes or the angle of the face are, after all, a
matter of bone structure, which is unalterable, and yet, as the painter found,
they radically influence that overall quality one might perhaps call the
dominant expression. The facts are not in doubt. Long before psychological
laboratories were even thought of, artists made systematic experiments
which established this dependence. I have paid tribute in *Art and Illusion* to
the most thorough and sophisticated of these experimenters, Rodolphe
Töpffer, who established what I have proposed to call Töpffer's law, the
proposition that any configuration which we can interpret as a face, however
badly drawn, will *ipso facto* have such an expression and individuality.[18]
Almost a hundred years after Töpffer, the psychologist Egon Brunswik in
Vienna launched a famous series of experiments to probe this kind of
dependence (Fig. 102). His studies confirm the extreme sensitivity of our
physiognomic perception to small changes; a shift in the distance of the eyes
which would perhaps be unnoticeable in a neutral configuration may
radically affect the expression of the mannikin, though how it will affect it is
not always easy to predict.

Brunswik, moreover, in a subsequent discussion of his own and other
people's findings was careful to warn against generalizing his results:

Human appearance, and especially the face, constitutes as tight a
package of innumerable contributing variables as might be found
anywhere in cognitive research.

He goes on to remind us that any new variable introduced may nullify the
effect observed in the interaction of others. But—and this was the burden of

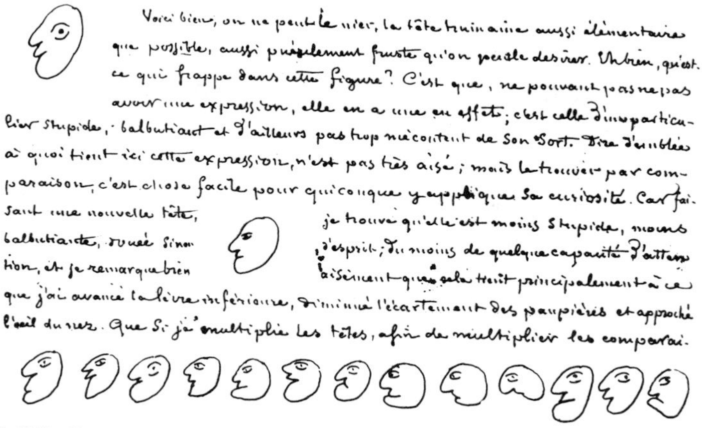

101. R. Töpffer: *The Permanent Traits.* From his *Essay de physiognomie*, 1845

his difficult methodological book—'the situation is the same for all high-complexity problems of life and behaviour.'[19]

In a sense, one might say, Brunswik encourages the innocent humanist to rush in where angels armed with the tools of factor analysis fear to tread. The mutual interaction of variables in the face has been handled, as we have seen, by portrait and mask makers alike. Brunswik refers his scientific readers to a book by a make-up expert. Indeed I would not be surprised if experience in these fields could throw light on unexpected places.[19a] Take the problem of headgear and the way it affects the apparent shape of the face. In widening the area around the face two conflicting psychological mechanisms might come into play. The effect of contrast exemplified in a well-known illusion (Fig. 103) might make the face look narrower. Alternatively we remember the Müller-Lyer illusion (Fig. 104) which suggests that an addition on either side must rather appear to broaden the face. Now if it is true that the slightest shift

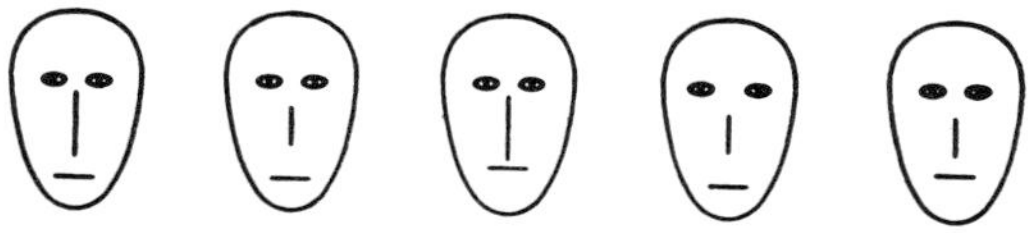

	T7	W7	D7	W4	G7
Sad	1st				
Old	1st				
Bad	6th	5th			
Unlikeable	3rd	1st	7th		
Ugly	6th	2nd	1st		
Unintelligent		3rd	7th	1st	
Unenergetic					1st

102. *Schematic heads.* After Brunswik and Reiter

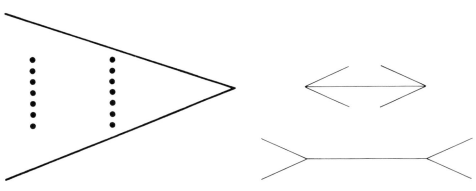

103. *Contrast illusion*. After M. D. Vernon   104. *Müller-Lyer illusion*. After M. D. Vernon

in the distance of the eyes results in a noticeable difference of expression and if Janet Robertson is right that eyes further apart give the face a vague expression, this observation might enable us to decide between these mutually exclusive alternatives. Let us try and screen off the monstrous coiffure of one of Velázquez's portraits of a Spanish princess, whose appearance usually strikes one as sadly pudding-faced (Fig. 105). Does not her gaze acquire more life, intensity and even intelligence when we remove the sideway extensions (Fig. 106)? The eyes, apparently, move together, which suggests that the effect conforms to the Müller-Lyer illusion.

It is in this area of the interaction between the apparent shape and the apparent expression that we must look for the solution of our problem, the

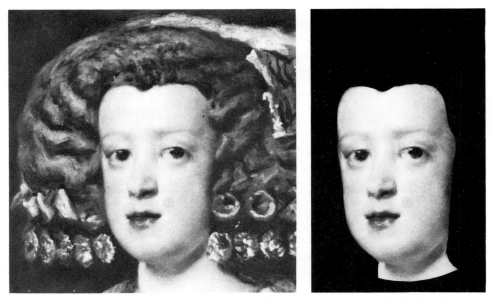

105. Diego Velázquez: *Portrait of the Infanta Maria Theresa. c.* 1651. Paris, Musée du Louvre.   106. Diego Velázquez: *The Infanta Maria Theresa*, without coiffure

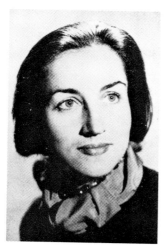

107. *Françoise Gilot.*
1951. Photograph

108. Pablo Picasso:
Françoise Gilot,
'*Femme Fleur*'. 1946.
Private Collection

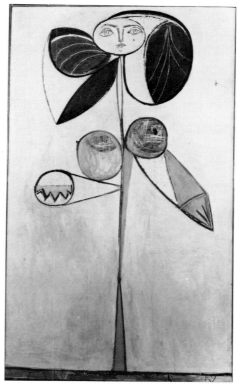

problem of the artist's compensation for the absence of movement, his creation of an image which may be objectively unlike in shape and colour and is yet felt to be like in expression.

There is a telling account given by Mme Gilot of Picasso painting her portrait (Figs. 107 and 108) which supports this assertion to a striking degree. The artist, we hear, originally wanted to do a fairly realistic portrait, but after working a while he said: 'No, it is just not your style, a realistic portrait would not represent you at all.' She had been sitting down but now he said: 'I do not see you seated, you are not at all the passive type, I only see you standing.'

Suddenly he remembered that Matisse had spoken of doing my portrait with green hair and he fell in with the suggestion. 'Matisse isn't the only one who can paint you with green hair,' he said. From that point the hair developed into a leaf form, and once he had done that, the portrait resolved itself in a symbolic floral pattern. He worked in the breasts with the same curving rhythm. The face had remained quite realistic all during these phases. It seemed out of character with the rest. He studied it for a moment. 'I have to bring in that face on the basis of another idea,' he said. 'Even though you have a fairly long oval face, what I need in order to show its light and its expression is to make it a wide oval. I'll compensate for the length by making it a cold colour—blue. It will be like a little blue moon.'

He painted a sheet of paper sky-blue and began to cut out oval shapes corresponding in varying degrees to this concept of my head: first, two that were perfectly round; then, three or four more based on his idea of doing it in width. When he had finished cutting them out, he drew in on each of them little signs for the eyes, nose, and mouth. Then he pinned them onto the canvas, one after another, moving each one a little to the left or right, up or down, as it suited him. None seemed really appropriate until he reached the last one. Having tried all the others in various spots, he knew where he wanted it, and when he applied it to the canvas, the form seemed exactly right in just the spot he put it on. It was completely convincing. He stuck it to the damp canvas, stood aside, and said, 'Now, it's your portrait.'[20]

This record gives us some hints about the lines along which the transposition from life into image may occur. It is a balancing of compensatory moves. To compensate for her face not being really round but oblong, Picasso paints it blue—maybe the pallor is here felt to be an equivalent to the impression of slimness. Not that even Picasso felt able to find the exact balance of compensations without trying them out: he tested a number of cardboard shapes. What he was searching for is precisely the equivalent, equivalent at least for him. This, as the saying goes, is how he saw her, or as we should rather say, how he felt her. He groped for the solution of an equation between life and image, and like the conventional portrait artist he tried to catch it by playing with the interaction between shape and expression.

The complexity of this interaction explains not only why women try on new hats in front of a mirror but also why likeness has to be caught rather than constructed; why it needs the method of trial and error, of match-mismatch to trap this elusive prey. Here as in other realms of art equivalence must be tested and criticized, it cannot be easily analysed step by step and therefore predicted.

We are far removed from what might be called a transformational grammar of forms, a set of rules which allows us to refer the different equivalent structures back to one common deep structure as has been proposed in the analysis of language.[21]

But though such a transformational grammar will always prove a will-of-the-wisp, maybe the problem of portrait equivalence allows us still to go one or two small steps forward. If the problem of likeness is that of the equivalence of the dominant expression, this expression or air must remain the pivot around which all the transformations turn. The different sets of variables must combine to the same result, it is an equation in which we are confronted with the product of y and x. Increase y and you must decrease x, or vice versa, if you want the same result.

There are many areas in perception where this situation obtains. Take size and distance which together produce the retinal size of the image; if other cues are eliminated we cannot tell whether an object seen through a peephole is large and far or near and small, we have no values for x and y, only for the product. Similarly with colour perception, where the sensation is determined by both the so-called local colour and the illumination. It is impossible to tell whether the patch of colour seen through a reduction screen is a dark red seen in bright light or a bright red in dim light. Moreover, if we call y the colour and x the light we never have any of these variables neat as it were. We cannot see colour except in light, and therefore that 'local colour' which figures in books on painting as 'variously modified by light', is a construction of the mind. Yet, though it is logically a construction, we feel quite confident in our experience that we do and can separate the two factors and assign their relative shares to colour and illumination. It is on this separation that the so-called colour constancy is pivoted, just as size constancy is pivoted on our interpretation of the object's real size.

I think that a somewhat analogous situation exists in the perception of physiognomic constancies, even though, as Brunswik has told us, the number of variables there is infinitely larger. Granted that this is so, I propose as a first approximation to isolate the two sets which I have mentioned before, the mobile and the static ones. Remember the crude analysis of the face as a dial or instrument board in which the mobile features serve as pointers to changing emotions. Töpffer called these features the impermanent traits which he contrasted with the permanent traits, the form or structure of the board itself. In one sense, of course, this analysis is quite unreal. What we experience is the global impression of a face, but in responding to this resultant I would suggest we separate in our mind the permanent (p) from the mobile (m). In real life we are aided in this, as we are aided in the perception of space and of colour, by the effect of movement in time. We see the relatively permanent forms of the face standing out against the relatively mobile ones and thus form a provisional estimate of their interaction (pm). It is this dimension of time, above all, that we lack in the interpretation of a still. Like many pictorial problems, the problem of portrait likeness and expression is compounded here, as we have seen, by the

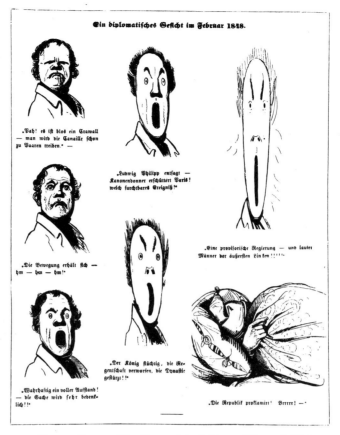

109. Kaspar Braun: *The News of 1848*. From *Fliegende Blätter*

artificial situation of arrested movement. Movement always assists in confirming or refuting our provisional interpretations or anticipations, and hence our reading of the static images of art is particularly prone to large variations and contradictory interpretations.

When somebody is disappointed we say 'he pulls a long face', an expression vividly illustrated in a German caricature of 1848 (Fig. 109). Naturally there are people who have a long face, and if they are comedians, they can even exploit this disappointed look to good effect. But if we really want to interpret their expression we must assign any feature to one of the two sets of unknown variables p or m, the permanent (p) or the mobile (m), and this separation may sometimes go wrong.

The difficulty in solving this equation may in fact account for the astonishing diversity of interpretations we sometimes encounter in relation to works of art. A whole book was written in the nineteenth century collecting the varying readings of the facial expression of the Roman portraits of Antinous.[22] One of the reasons for this diversity may be the difficulty in assigning a place to my two variables. Is Hadrian's favourite slightly pouting his lips (Fig. 110), or has he simply got such lips? Given our sensitivity to nuance in such matters, the interpretation here will in fact alter the expression.

A glance at the history of physiognomics may help to clarify this discussion a little further. Originally physiognomics was conceived as the art of reading character from the face, but the features to which it paid attention were exclusively the permanent traits. Ever since classical antiquity it had mainly relied on the comparison between a human type and an animal species, the aquiline nose showing its bearer to be noble like the eagle, the bovine face betraying his placid disposition. These comparisons, which were first illustrated in the sixteenth century in a book by della Porta,[23] certainly influenced the rising art of portrait caricature because they demonstrated the imperviousness of physiognomic character to a variation of elements. A recognizable human face can look strikingly 'like' a recognizable cow (Fig. 111).

There is no doubt that this pseudo-scientific tradition relies on a reaction which most of us have experienced. In one of Igor Stravinsky's less charitable conversations he talks of 'a worthy woman who naturally and unfortunately looked irate, like a hen, even when in good humour.'[24] One may question whether hens look irate, maybe peevish would be a better word here, but no one would easily deny that they have an 'expression' which an unfortunate woman may share. In terms of our first approximation we may say that the permanent shape of the head (p) is interpreted in terms of a mobile expression and that this is the psychological root of the physiognomic superstition.

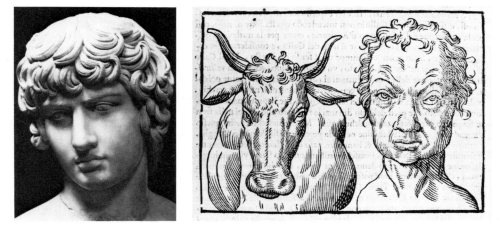

110. *Antinous*. Roman sculpture. Early 2nd century A.D. Naples, Museo Nazionale.
111. *Physiognomic comparison*. After G. B. della Porta, 1586

Humourists will always exploit this tendency of ours to project a human expression onto an animal's head. The camel is seen as supercilious, a bloodhound with its wrinkled forehead looks worried, because if we were supercilious or worried our features would arrange themselves in this way. But here as always it is dangerous to equate inference or interpretation with a deliberate intellectual analysis of clues.[25] It is precisely the point that we respond to such configurations more or less automatically and involuntarily though we know perfectly well that the poor camel cannot help its supercilious looks. So deep-seated and instinctual is this response that it pervades one's bodily reactions. Unless introspection deceives me, I believe that when I visit a zoo my muscular response changes as I move from the hippopotamus house to the cage of the weasels. Be that as it may, the human reaction to the permanent features of non-human physiognomies, which is so well documented in fables and children's books, in folklore and in art, suggests very strongly that our reaction to our fellow creatures is closely linked with our own body image. I am here led back to the old theory of empathy, which played such a part at the turn of the century not only in the aesthetics of Lipps and of Vernon Lee but also in the writings of Berenson, Wölfflin, and Worringer. This doctrine relies on the traces of muscular response in our reaction to forms; it is not only the perception of music which makes us dance inwardly, but also the perception of shapes.

Maybe the idea dropped out of fashion partly because people got tired of it, and partly because it was too vaguely and too widely applied. But as far as the perception of expression is concerned I personally have no doubt that our understanding of other people's facial movement comes to us partly from the experience of our own. Not that this formulation solves the mystery which lies in the fact that we can imitate an expression. How does the baby which responds to its mother's smile with a smile translate or transpose the visual impression sent to its brain through the eyes into the appropriate impulses from the brain to move its own facial muscles in a corresponding way? I suppose the hypothesis would hardly be gainsaid that the disposition to perform this translation from sight to movement is inborn. We do not have to learn smiling in front of a mirror, indeed I would not be surprised if the varying styles of facial expression we all can observe in different nations and traditions were transmitted from generation to generation or from leader to follower by unconscious imitation, by empathy. All this tends to corroborate the hypothesis that we interpret and code the perception of our fellow creatures not so much in visual as in muscular terms.

It may seem somewhat perverse to approach this far-reaching hypothesis by way of our freakish response to the imagined expression of animals, but this would not be the only case where a malfunction has helped to reveal a psychological mechanism. We obviously were not endowed with our capacity for empathy in order to read the souls of the beasts, but to understand our fellow humans. The more they resemble us the more likely will we be able to use our own muscular response as a clue to understanding their moods and emotions. Such a standard is necessary precisely because we will go wrong if we cannot separate our two variables. We must know from experience and perhaps from inborn knowledge what is a permanent trait and what an expressive alteration.

But would this hypothesis help us also to solve the main problem we are after, the detection of that physiognomic constancy which we called the characteristic expression of a person and which Petrarch described as the *aria*? I think it may, if we are ready to amend our first approximation which only recognized the two variables of the permanent and the mobile traits. Once more we may here hark back to the history of physiognomics to gain a leverage. When the crude superstition of animal physiognomics first came under fire in the eighteenth century, its critics, notably Hogarth and his commentator Lichtenberg, rightly stressed the second of my variables.[26] It is not the permanent traits which allow us to read a character but the expression of emotions. But these mobile expressions, so they argued, gradually mould a face. A person who is frequently worried will acquire a furrowed brow, whereas a cheerful person will acquire a smiling face, because the transient will pass into permanence. There is something, perhaps, in this common-sense view but it savours too much of eighteenth-century rationalism to be fully acceptable. Hogarth, in other words, regards the face in the same light as Locke regards the mind. Each is a *tabula rasa* before individual experiences write their story onto its surface. It would certainly never be possible to arrive from such a view at an explanation of physiognomic constancy. For what this account omits is precisely the object of our quest, whether we call it character, personality, or disposition. It is this all-pervasive disposition which makes one person more prone to worry and another more likely to smile—in other words, every one of these 'expressions' is embedded in an over-all mood or feeling tone. There is a difference between the smile of an optimist and that of a pessimist. Needless to say, these moods in their turn are subject to fluctuations, some are reactions to external events, some reflect inner pressures. But we now begin to see in what respect the two unknown variables of our first approximation were too crude. They failed to take account of the hierarchy that extends from the permanent frame of the body to the fleeting ripple of a mobile expression. Somewhere within this hierarchic sequence we must locate what we experience as the more permanent expression or disposition that constitutes for us such an important element in the 'essence' of a personality. It is this, I believe, to which our muscular detector is so suited to respond, for in a sense these more permanent dispositions are probably muscular in their turn.

Once more we may remember that the link between 'character' and body build belongs to an age-old belief in human types and human 'complexions' or 'temperaments'. If these beliefs do so little justice to the variety and subtlety of human types, this is at least partly due to the poverty of linguistic categories and concepts for the description of the inner as opposed to the external world. We just have no vocabulary to describe the characteristics of a person's attitudinal framework, but that does not mean that we cannot code these experiences in any other way. What is so characteristic and distinctive of a personality is this general *tonus*, the melody of transition from given ranges of relaxation to forms of tenseness, and this in its turn will colour a person's speed of reaction, gait, rhythm of speech, and account for instance for that link between personality and handwriting we all feel to exist, whether or not we believe that it can be specified in words. If our own internal computer can somehow integrate these factors in a corresponding state we would know where to look for that invariant that normally survives the changes in a person's appearance. Here, in other words, we may have to look for that unwritten and unwritable formula which links for us Bertrand Russell at four and at ninety, for behind all these variations we sense a common signature tune. It is the same alertness, the same degree of tension and resilience we sense in both positions, and it is this which evokes in us the unique memory of that particular person. In a way, perhaps, the inability of many people to describe the colour of a person's eyes or the shape of a nose, however well they may know him, constitutes a negative confirmation of this role of empathy.

If this hypothesis could be established, the same unity of response might also account for the experience of likeness in portrait and caricature across the variations and distortions we have observed. Indeed we may now be in a position to return to that paradigm of the caricaturist's trick which I discussed but did not explain in *Art and Illusion*.[27] It is the famous pictorial defence by the caricaturist Philipon, who had been fined 6,000 francs for having lampooned Louis Philippe as a *poire* (Fig. 112), a fathead, and pretended to ask for which step in this inevitable transformation he was to be punished? Though reactions of this kind are not easily verbalized it may still be possible to describe the likeness that is felt to exist between these stages in muscular rather than in purely visual terms.

Take the eyes which radically change their size, position, and even slant,

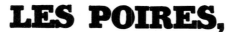

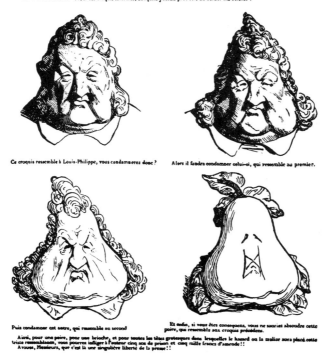

112. Charles Philipon: *Les Poires*. From *Charivari*, 1834

from the first picture to the last. Clearly by moving them together and increasing their steepness they are made to take over also the indication of the frowning forehead which increases in the third picture, only to be omitted as redundant in the last where we are made to feel the frown in the evil eyes of the *poire*. Regarding them as pointers for muscular movements, we can imagine ourselves achieving this expression of the last phase only by knitting our brows and dropping our cheeks which corresponds to the feel of sluggish malice that belongs to the face from the first. The same is true of the corners of the mouth. In the first picture the mouth still smiles, but the heavy flesh pulls the sides down and creates a response in us—or at least in me—which is perfectly evoked by the scrawled features of the last picture, from which all traces of a false bonhomie have disappeared.

This role of our own bodily reaction in the experience of equivalence may also help to account for the outstanding feature of caricature, its tendency to

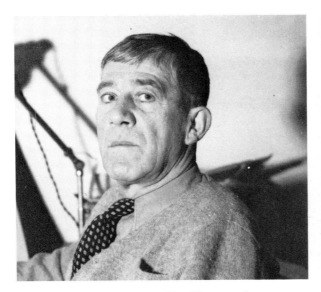

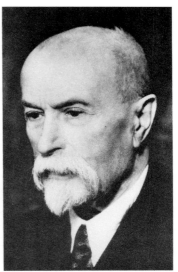

113. *Oskar Kokoschka*. Photograph

114. *Thomas G. Masaryk.*
1935. Photograph

distortion and exaggeration: for our inner sense of dimensions differs radically from our visual perception of proportion. The inner sense always exaggerates. Try to move the tip of your nose downward and you will feel you have acquired a very different nose while the actual movement you achieved was probably no more than a fraction of an inch. How much the scale of our internal map differs from that of the eye is best (and most painfully) experienced at the dentist's when the tooth he belabours assumes well-nigh gigantic proportions. No wonder the caricaturist or expressionist who relies on his inner sense will tend to alter the scales; he can do so without impairing the sense of identity if we can share his reactions in front of the same image.

Such a theory of empathy or sympathetic response does not preclude the misunderstanding of expressions. On the contrary, it helps to explain it. If Louis Philippe had been a Chinese, the slant of his eyes would have meant something different, but empathy might also have let us down in interpreting its exact nuance.

No doubt empathy does not offer a total explanation of our physiognomic reactions. It may not account for the impression of a narrow forehead as a sign of stupidity, nor is it clear whether it is acquired or is inborn, as Konrad Lorenz has postulated other physiognomic reactions to be (see Fig. 119). [28]

But whatever the limitations of the hypothesis here put forward, the student of art can at least contribute one observation from the history of portrait painting which strongly suggests that empathy does play a considerable part in the artist's response—it is the puzzling obtrusion of the

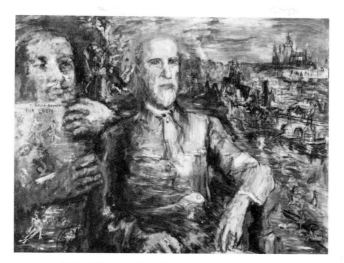

115. Oskar Kokoschka: *Thomas G. Masaryk.* 1934–6.
Pittsburgh, Museum of Art, Carnegie Institute

artist's own likeness into the portrait. When the Prussian ambassador to England, Wilhelm von Humboldt, was painted by Sir Thomas Lawrence in 1828, his daughter reported after a visit to the master's studio that the upper half of the face, forehead, eyes and nose were much better than the lower half which was much too rosy and which, by the way, resembled Lawrence, as (she found) did all his portraits.[29] It may not be easy at this distance of time to test this interesting observation, but the situation is different with a great contemporary master of portraiture, Oskar Kokoschka (Fig. 113). Kokoschka's self-portraits testify to his grasp of his essential features, the face with its long distance between nose and chin. Many of Kokoschka's heads have these proportions, including his impressive portrait of Thomas Masaryk (Fig. 115), whose photographs show a different relation between the upper and the lower half of the face (Fig. 114). Objectively, therefore, the likeness may be faulted, but it may still be true that the same power of empathy and projection which is here at work also gives the artist special insights which are denied to artists who are less involved.

It is not frequent for an art historian to be in the position of offering supporting evidence for such a general hypothesis, but it so happens that I had the privilege of listening to Kokoschka when he spoke of a particularly difficult portrait commission he had received some time past. As he spoke of the sitter whose face he found so hard to unriddle he automatically pulled a corresponding grimace of impenetrable rigidity. Clearly for him the understanding of another person's physiognomy took the way over his own muscular experience.

Paradoxically this involvement and identification here exert the opposite

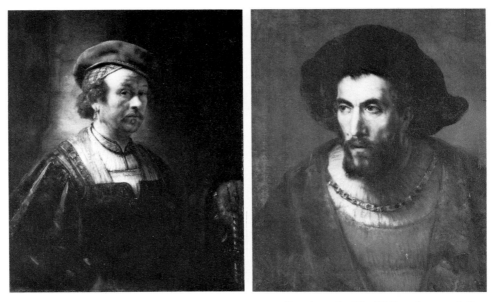

116. Rembrandt: *Self-Portrait. c.* 1650.
Washington, The National Gallery of Art,
Widener Collection

117. Rembrandt: *The Philosopher. c.* 1656.
Washington, The National Gallery of Art,
Widener Collection

pull from that we observed in the recognition and creation of types. Here it was the deviation from the norm, the degree of distance from the self that was found decisive. The extreme, the abnormal, sticks in the mind and marks the type for us. Maybe the same mechanism operates in those portrait painters who are quick in seizing a characteristic trait without seeking much empathy. These would not be self-projectors like Kokoschka, but rather self-detachers or distancers (if there is such a word), but both could pivot their art on their self.

The very greatest of portrait painters probably must have access to the mechanisms of both projection and differentiation and have learnt to master them equally. It surely is no accident that a Rembrandt never ceased throughout his life to study his own face in all its changes and all its moods (Fig. 116). But this intense involvement with his own features clarified rather than clouded his visual awareness of his sitters' appearance. There is an outstanding variety of physiognomies in Rembrandt's portrait œuvre, each of his portraits capturing a different character (Fig. 117).

Should we here speak of character? One of the leading portrait painters of our own day once remarked to me that he never knew what people meant when they talked about the painter revealing the character of the sitter. He could not paint a character, he could only paint a face. I have more respect for this astringent opinion of a real master than I have for the sentimental talk

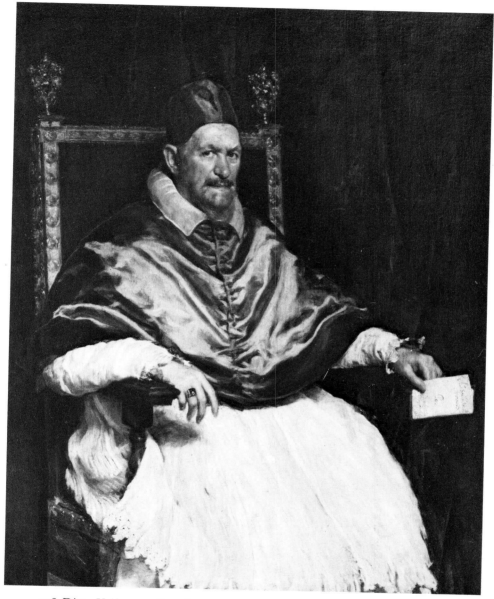

118. Diego Velázquez: *Pope Innocent X. c.* 1650. Rome, Galleria Doria Pamphili

about artists painting souls, but when all is said and done a great portrait—including some by that painter—does give us the illusion of seeing the face behind the mask.

It is quite true that we know next to nothing of the character of most of Rembrandt's sitters. But what has captivated art lovers who have stood in front of the greatest portraits of our artistic heritage is the impression of life that emanates from them. A surpassing masterpiece, such as Velázquez's great portrait of Pope Innocent X (Fig. 118), never looks arrested in one pose, it seems to change in front of our eyes as if it offered a variety of readings, each of them coherent and convincing. And yet this refusal to freeze into a mask and settle into one rigid reading is not purchased at the expense of definition. We are not aware of ambiguities, of undefined elements leading to incompatible interpretations, we have the illusion of a face assuming different expressions all consistent with what might be called the dominant expression, the air of the face. Our projection, if one may use this chilling term, is guided by the artist's understanding of the deep structure of the face, which allows us to generate and test the various oscillations of the living physiognomy. At the same time we have the feeling that we really perceive what is constant behind the changing appearance, the unseen solution of the equation, the true colour of the man.[30] All these are inadequate metaphors, but they suggest that there may be something, after all, in the old Platonic claim, so succinctly expressed in Max Liebermann's retort to a dissatisfied sitter—'this painting, my dear Sir, resembles you more than you do yourself.'

The Visual Image : Its Place in Communication

OURS IS a visual age. We are bombarded with pictures from morning till night. Opening our newspaper at breakfast, we see photographs of men and women in the news, and raising our eyes from the paper, we encounter the picture on the cereal package. The mail arrives and one envelope after the other discloses glossy folders with pictures of alluring landscapes and sunbathing girls to entice us to take a holiday cruise, or of elegant menswear to tempt us to have a suit made to measure. Leaving our house, we pass billboards along the road that try to catch our eye and play on our desire to smoke, drink or eat. At work it is more than likely that we have to deal with some kind of pictorial information: photographs, sketches, catalogues, blueprints, maps or at least graphs. Relaxing in the evening, we sit in front of the television set, the new window on the world, and watch moving images of pleasures and horrors flit by. Even the images created in times gone by or in distant lands are more easily accessible to us than they ever were to the public for which they were created. Picture books, picture postcards and colour slides accumulate in our homes as souvenirs of travel, as do the private mementos of our family snapshots.

No wonder it has been asserted that we are entering a historical epoch in which the image will take over from the written word. In view of this claim it is all the more important to clarify the potentialities of the image in communication, to ask what it can and what it cannot do better than spoken or written language. In comparison with the importance of the question the amount of attention devoted to it is disappointingly small.

Students of language have been at work for a long time analysing the various functions of the prime instrument of human communication.

This study appeared in a special issue of Scientific American *on Communication, 1972.*

Without going into details we can accept for our purpose the divisions of language proposed by Karl Bühler, who distinguished between the functions of expression, arousal and description. (We may also call them symptom, signal and symbol.) We describe a speech act as expressive if it informs us of the speaker's state of mind. Its very tone may be symptomatic of anger or amusement; alternatively it may be designed to arouse a state of mind in the person addressed, as a signal triggering anger or amusement. It is important to distinguish the expression of an emotion from its arousal, the symptom from the signal, particularly since common parlance fails to do this when speaking of the 'communication' of feeling. It is true that the two functions can be in unison and that the audible symptoms of a speaker's anger may arouse anger in me, but they may also cause me to be amused. On the other hand, someone may contrive in cold blood to move me to anger. These two functions of communication are shared by human beings with their fellow creatures lower down on the evolutionary scale. Animal communications may be symptomatic of emotive states or they may function as signals to release certain reactions. Human language can do more: it has developed the descriptive function (which is only rudimentary in animal signals). A speaker can inform his partner of a state of affairs past, present or future, observable or distant, actual or conditional. He can say it rains, it rained, it will rain, it may rain, or 'If it rains, I shall stay here'. Language performs this miraculous function largely through such little particles as 'if', 'when', 'not', 'therefore', 'all' and 'some', which have been called logical words because they account for the ability of language to formulate logical inferences (also known as syllogisms).

Looking at communication from the vantage point of language, we must ask first which of these functions the visual image can perform. We shall see that the visual image is supreme in its capacity for arousal, that its use for expressive purposes is problematic, and that unaided it altogether lacks the possibility of matching the statement function of language.

The assertion that statements cannot be translated into images often meets with incredulity, but the simplest demonstration of its truth is to challenge the doubters to illustrate the proposition they doubt. You cannot make a picture of the concept of statement any more than you can illustrate the impossibility of translation. It is not only the degree of abstraction of language that eludes the visual medium; the sentence from the primer 'The cat sits on the mat' is certainly not abstract, but although the primer may show a picture of a cat sitting on a mat, a moment's reflection will show that the picture is not the equivalent of the statement. We cannot express

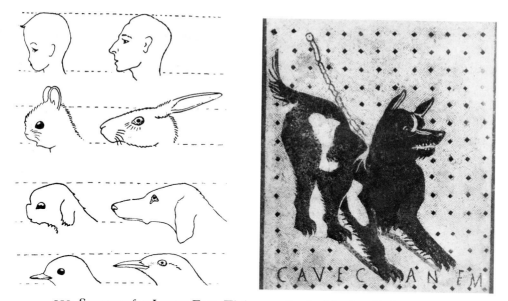

119. *Sequence after Lorenz*. From Tinbergen, *Study of Instinct* (Oxford, 1943).
120. *Cave Canem*. Mosaic of a dog. From Pompeii. Naples, Museo Nazionale

pictorially whether we mean 'the' cat (an individual) or 'a cat' (a member of a class); moreover, although the sentence may be one possible description of the picture, there are an infinite number of other true descriptive statements you could make such as 'There is a cat seen from behind', or for that matter 'There is no elephant on the mat'. When the primer continues with 'The cat sat on the mat', 'The cat will sit on the mat', 'The cat sits rarely on the mat', 'If the cat sits on the mat . . .' and so on ad infinitum, we see the word soaring away and leaving the picture behind.

Try to say the sentence to a child and then show him the picture and your respect for the image will soon be restored. The sentence will leave the child unmoved; the image may delight him almost as much as the real cat. Exchange the picture for a toy cat and the child may be ready to hug the toy and take it to bed. The toy cat arouses the same reactions as a real cat— possibly even stronger ones, since it is more docile and easier to cuddle.

This power of dummies or substitutes to trigger behaviour has been much explored by students of animal behaviour, and there is no doubt that organisms are 'programmed' to respond to certain visual signals in a way that facilitates survival. The crudest models of a predator or a mate need only exhibit certain distinctive features to elicit the appropriate pattern of action, and if these features are intensified, the dummy (like the toy) may be more effective than the natural stimulus. Caution is needed in comparing these automatisms to human reactions, but Konrad Z. Lorenz, the pioneer of ethology, has surmised that certain preferred forms of nursery art that are described as 'cute' or 'sweet' (including many of Walt Disney's creations) generate parental feelings by their structural similarity to babies (Fig. 119).

Be that as it may, the power of visual impressions to arouse our emotions has been observed since ancient times. 'The mind is more slowly stirred by the ear than by the eye,' said Horace in his *Art of Poetry* when he compared the impact of the stage with that of the verbal narrative. Preachers and teachers preceded modern advertisers in the knowledge of the ways in which the visual image can affect us, whether we want it to or not. The succulent fruit, the seductive nude, the repellent caricature, the hair-raising horror can all play on our emotions and engage our attention. Nor is this arousal function of sights confined to definite images. Configurations of lines and colours have the potential to influence our emotions. We need only keep our eyes open to see how these potentialities of the visual media are used all around us, from the red danger signal to the way the décor of a restaurant may be calculated to create a certain 'atmosphere'.[1] These very examples show that the power of arousal of visual impressions extends far beyond the scope of this article. What is usually described as communication is concerned with matter rather than with mood.

A mosaic found at the entrance of a house in Pompeii shows a dog on a chain with the inscription *Cave Canem* (Beware of the Dog) (Fig. 120). It is not hard to see the link between such a picture and its arousal function. We are to react to the picture as we might to a real dog that barks at us. Thus the picture effectively reinforces the caption that warns the potential intruder of the risk he is running. Would the image alone perform this function of communication? It would, if we came to it with a knowledge of social customs and conventions. Why, if not as a communication to those who may be unable to read, should there be this picture at the entrance hall? But if we could forget what we know and imagine a member of an alien culture coming on such an image, we could think of many other possible interpretations of the mosaic. Could not the man have wanted to advertise a dog he wished to sell? Was he perhaps a veterinarian? Or could the mosaic have functioned as a sign for a public house called 'The Black Dog'? The purpose of this exercise is to remind ourselves how much we take for granted when we look at a picture for its message. It always depends on our prior knowledge of possibilities. After all, when we see the Pompeiian mosaic in the museum in Naples we do not conclude that there is a dog chained somewhere. It is different with the arousal function of the image. Even in the museum the image might give us a shadow of a fright, and I recently heard a child of five say when turning the pages of a book on natural history that she did not want to touch the pictures of nasty creatures.

Naturally we cannot adequately respond to the message of the mosaic unless we have read the image correctly. The medium of the mosaic is well suited to formulate the problem in terms of the theory of information. Its modern equivalent would be an advertising display composed of an array of light bulbs in which each bulb can be turned either on or off to form an image. A mosaic might consist of standardized cubes (*tesserae*) that are either dark or light. The amount of visual information such a medium can transmit will depend on the size of the cubes in relation to the scale of the image. In our case the cubes are small enough for the artist to indicate the tufts of hair on the dog's legs and tail, and the individual links of the chain. The artist might confine himself to a code in which black signifies a solid form seen against a light ground. Such a silhouette could easily be endowed with sufficiently distinctive features to be recognized as a dog. But the Pompeiian master was trained in a tradition that had gone beyond the conceptual method of representation and he included in the image information about the effects of light on form. He conveys the white and the glint of the eye and the muzzle, shows us the teeth and outlines the ears; he also indicates the shadows of the forelegs on the patterned background.[2] The meaning so far is easy to decode, but the white patches on the body and, most of all, the outline of the hind leg set us a puzzle. It was the convention in his time to model the shape of an animal's body by indicating the sheen of the fur, and this must be the origin of these features. Whether their actual shape is due to clumsy execution or to inept restoration could only be decided by viewing the original.

The difficulty of interpreting the meaning of the dog mosaic is instructive because it too can be expressed in terms of communication theory. Like verbal messages, images are vulnerable to the random interference engineers call 'noise'. They need the device of redundancy to overcome this hazard. It is this built-in safeguard of the verbal code that enables us to read the inscription *Cave Canem* without hesitation even though the first *e* is incomplete. As far as image recognition is concerned it is the enclosing contour that carries most of the information. We could not guess the length of the tail if the black cubes were missing. The individual cubes of the patterned ground and inside the outline are relatively more redundant, but those indicating the sheen occupy a middle position; they stand for a feature that is elusive even in reality, although the configuration we now see could never occur.

However automatic our first response to an image may be, therefore, its actual reading can never be a passive affair. Without a prior knowledge of possibilities we could not even guess at the relative position of the dog's two hind legs. Although we have this knowledge, other possibilities are likely

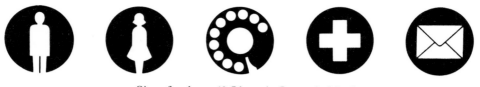

121. Signs for the 1968 Olympic Games in Mexico

to escape us. Perhaps the picture was intended to represent a particular breed that Romans would recognize as being vicious. We cannot tell by the picture.

The chance of a correct reading of the image is governed by three variables: the code, the caption and the context. It might be thought that the caption alone would make the other two redundant, but our cultural conventions are too flexible for that. In an art book the picture of a dog with the caption E. Landseer is understood to refer to the maker of the image, not to the species represented. In the context of a primer, on the other hand, the caption and the picture would be expected to support each other. Even if the pages were torn so that we could only read 'og', the fragment of the drawing above would suffice to indicate whether the missing letter was a *d* or an *h*. Jointly the media of word and image increase the probability of a correct reconstruction.

We shall see that this mutual support of language and image facilitates memorizing. The use of two independent channels, as it were, guarantees the ease of reconstruction. This is the basis of the ancient 'art of memory' (brilliantly explored in a book by Frances Yates[3]) that advises the practitioner to translate any verbal message into visual form, the more bizarre and unlikely the better. If you want to remember the name of the painter Hogarth, picture to yourself a *hog* practising his *art* by painting an *h*. You may dislike the association, but you may find it hard to get rid of.

There are cases where the context alone can make the visual message unambiguous even without the use of words. It is a possibility that has much attracted organizers of international events where the Babylonian confusion of tongues rules out the use of language. The set of images designed for the Olympic Games in Mexico in 1968 appears to be self-explanatory,[4] indeed it is, given the limited number of expected messages and the restriction of the choice that is exemplified best by the first two signs of the array (Fig. 121). We can observe how the purpose and context dictate a simplification of the code by concentrating on a few distinctive features. The principle is brilliantly exemplified by the pictorial signs for the various sports and games designed for the same event (see Fig. 33).

We should never be tempted to forget, however, that even in such usages context must be supported by prior expectations based on tradition. Where these links break, communication also breaks down. Some years ago there was a story in the papers to the effect that riots had broken out in an underdeveloped country because of rumours that human flesh was being sold in a store. The rumour was traced to food cans with a grinning boy on the label. Here it was the switch of context that caused the confusion. As a rule the picture of fruit, vegetable or meat on a food container does indicate its contents; if we do not draw the conclusion that the same applies to a picture of a human being on the container, it is because we rule out the possibility from the start.

In the above examples the image was expected to work in conjunction with other factors to convey a clear-cut message that could be translated into words. The real value of the image, however, is its capacity to convey information that cannot be coded in any other way. In his important book *Prints and Visual Communication*[5] William M. Ivins, Jr., argued that the Greeks and the Romans failed to make progress in science because they lacked the idea of multiplying images by some form of printing. Some of his philosophical points can hardly be sustained (the ancient world knew of the

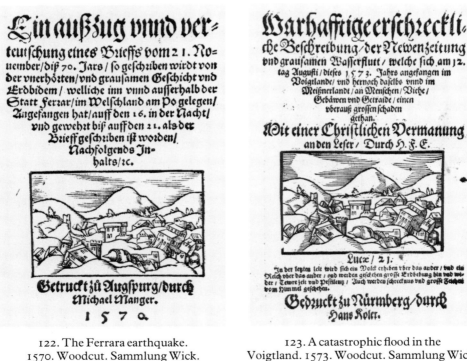

122. The Ferrara earthquake.
1570. Woodcut. Sammlung Wick.
Zurich, Staatsbibliothek

123. A catastrophic flood in the
Voigtland. 1573. Woodcut. Sammlung Wick.
Zurich, Staatsbibliothek

multiplication of images through the seal, the coinage, and the cast), but it is certainly true that printed herbals, costume books, news-sheets and topographical views were a vital source of visual information about plants, fashions, topical events and foreign lands. But study of this material also brings home to us that printed information depends in part on words. The most lifelike portrait of a king will mislead us if it is incorrectly labelled as being somebody else, and publishers of early broadsheets sometimes re-used woodcuts showing a city devastated by a flood to illustrate an earthquake or another disaster (Figs. 122 and 123) on the principle that if you have seen one catastrophe, you have seen them all.[6] Even today it is only our confidence in certain informants or institutions that allays our doubts that a picture in a book, a newspaper or on the screen really shows what it purports to show. There was the notorious case of the German scientist Ernst Haeckel, who was accused of having tried to prove the parallelism of human and animal development by labelling a photograph of a pig's foetus as that of a human embryo. It is in fact fatally easy to mix up pictures and captions, as almost any publisher knows to his cost.

The information extracted from an image can be quite independent of the intention of its maker. A holiday snapshot of a group on a beach may be scrutinized by an intelligence officer preparing a landing, and the Pompeiian mosaic might provide new information to a historian of dog breeding.

It may be convenient here to range the information value of such images according to the amount of information about the prototype that they can encode. Where the information is virtually complete we speak of a facsimile or replica. These may be produced for deception rather than information, fraudulently in the case of a forged banknote, benevolently in the case of a glass eye or an artificial tooth. But the facsimile of a banknote in a history book is intended for instruction, and so is the cast or copy of an organ in medical teaching.

A facsimile duplication would not be classed as an image if it shared with its prototype all characteristics including the material of which it is made. A flower sample used in a botany class is not an image, but an artificial flower used for demonstration purposes must be described as an image. Even here the borderline is somewhat fluid. A stuffed animal in a showcase is not an image, but the taxidermist is likely to have made his personal contribution through selecting and modifying the carcass. However faithful an image that serves to convey visual information may be, the process of selection will always reveal the maker's interpretation of what he considers relevant. Even the wax effigy of a celebrity must show the sitter in one particular attitude and

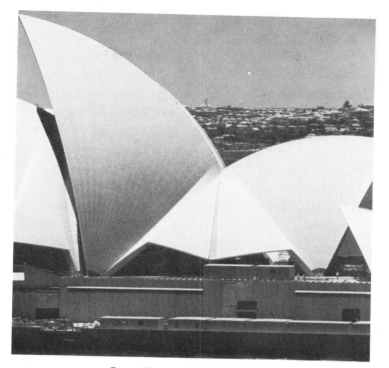

124. Opera House. Sydney, Australia

role; the photographer of people or events will carefully sift his material to find the 'tell-tale' picture.

Interpretation on the part of the image maker must always be matched by the interpretation of the viewer. No image tells its own story. I remember an exhibit in a museum in Lincoln, Neb., showing skeletons and reconstructions of the ancestor of the horse. By present equine standards these creatures were diminutive, but they resembled our horse in everything but the scale. It was this encounter that brought home to me how inevitably we interpret even a didactic model and how hard it is to discard certain assumptions. Being used to looking at works of sculpture, including small bronze statuettes of horses, I had slipped into the mental habit of discounting scale when interpreting the code. In other words, I 'saw' the scale model of a normal horse. It was the verbal description and information that corrected my reading of the code.

Here as always we need a jolt to remind us of what I have called the 'beholder's share', the contribution we make to any representation from the stock of images stored in our mind. Once more it is only when this process cannot take place because we lack memories that we become aware of their role. Looking at a picture of a house, we do not normally fret about the many things the picture does not show us unless we are looking for a particular aspect that was hidden from the camera. We have seen many similar houses and can supplement the information from our memory, or we think we can. It is only when we are confronted with a totally unfamiliar kind of structure that we are aware of the puzzle element in any representation. The new opera house in Sydney, Australia, is a structure of a novel kind, and a person who sees only a photograph of it will feel compelled to ask a number of questions the photograph cannot answer (Fig. 124). What is the inclination of the roof? Which parts go inward, which outward? What, indeed, is the scale of the entire structure?

The hidden assumptions with which we generally approach a photograph are most easily demonstrated by the limited information value of shadows on flat images. They only yield the correct impression if we assume that the light is falling from above and generally from the left; reverse the picture and what was concave looks convex and vice versa (Fig. 125). That we read the code of the black-and-white photograph without assuming that it is a rendering of a colourless world may be a triviality, but behind this triviality lurk other problems. What colours or tones could be represented by certain greys in the photograph? What difference will it make to, say, the American flag whether it is photographed with an orthochromatic or a panchromatic film?

Interpreting photographs is an important skill that must be learned by all who have to deal with this medium of communication: the intelligence officer, the surveyor or archaeologist who studies aerial photographs, the sports photographer who wishes to record and to judge athletic events and the physician who reads X-ray films. Each of these must know the capacities and the limitations of his instruments. Thus the rapid movement of a slit

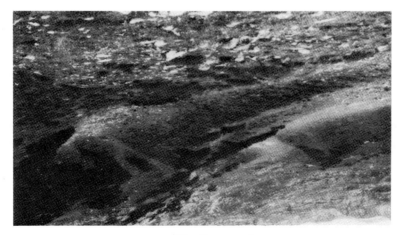

125. Depth reversal

shutter down the photographic plate may be too slow to show the correct sequence of events it is meant to capture, or the grain of a film may be too coarse to register the desired detail in a photograph. It was shown by the late Gottfried Spiegler that the demand for an easily legible X-ray image may conflict with its informative function.[7] Strong contrast and definite outlines may obscure valuable clues (see Figs. 203 and 204). Needless to say, there is the further possibility of retouching a photographic record in the interest of either truth or falsehood. All these intervening variables make their appearance again on the way from the negative to the print, from the print to the photo-engraving and then to the printed illustration. The most familiar of these is the density of the halftone screen. As in the case of the mosaic, the information transmitted by the normal illustration process is granular, smooth transitions are transformed into discrete steps and these steps can either be so few that they are obtrusively visible or so small that they can hardly be detected by the unaided eye.

Paradoxically it is the limited power of vision that has made television possible: the changing intensities of one luminous dot sweeping across the screen build up the image in our eye. Long before this technique was conceived the French artist Claude Mellan displayed his virtuosity by engraving the face of Christ with one spiralling line swelling and contracting to indicate shape and shading (Fig. 126).

The very eccentricity of this caprice shows how readily we learn to fall in with the code and to accept its conventions. We do not think for a moment that the artist imagined Christ's face to have been lined with a spiral. Contrary to the famous slogan, we easily distinguish the medium from the message.

From the point of view of information this ease of distinction can be more vital than fidelity of reproduction. Many students of art regret the increased use of colour reproductions for that reason. A black-and-white photograph is seen to be an incomplete coding. A colour photograph always leaves us with some uncertainty about its information value. We cannot separate the code from the content.

The easier it is to separate the code from the content, the more we can rely on the image to communicate a particular kind of information. A selective code that is understood to be a code enables the maker of the image to filter out certain kinds of information and to encode only those features that are of interest to the recipient. Hence a selective representation that indicates its own principles of selection will be more informative than the replica. Anatomical drawings are a case in point. A realistic picture of a dissection not

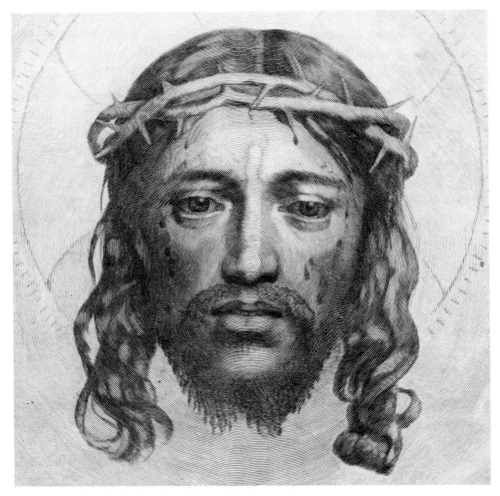

126. Claude Mellan: Detail from *The Napkin of St. Veronica*. 1735. Engraving.
London, The British Museum

only would arouse aversion but also might easily fail to show the aspects that
are to be demonstrated. Even today surgeons sometimes employ 'medical
artists' to record selective information that colour photographs might fail to
communicate. Leonardo da Vinci's anatomical studies are early examples of
deliberate suppression of certain features for the sake of conceptual clarity.
Many of them are not so much portrayals as functional models, illustrations
of the artist's views about the structure of the body. Leonardo's drawings of
water and whirlpools are likewise intended as visualizations of the forces at
work.[8]

   Such a rendering may be described as a transition from a representation to
diagrammatic mapping, and the value of the latter process for the
communication of information needs no emphasis. What is characteristic of

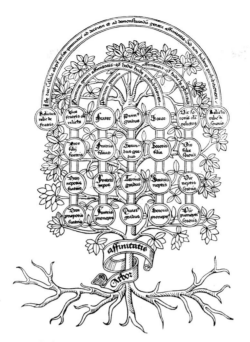

127. Johannes Andrei: *Tree of Affinities*. 1473.
Woodcut. New York, The Pierpont Morgan Library

the map is the addition of a key to the standardized code. We are told which particular heights are represented by the contour lines and what particular shade of green stands for fields or forests. Whereas these are examples of visible features, standardized for the sake of clarity, there is no difficulty in entering on the map other kinds of feature, such as political frontiers, population density or any other desired information. The only element of genuine representation (also called iconicity) in such a case is the actual shape of the geographical features, although even these are normalized according to given rules of transformation to allow a part of the globe to be shown on a flat map.

It is only a small step from the abstraction of the map to a chart or diagram showing relations that are originally not visual but temporal or logical. One of the oldest of these relational maps is the family tree. The kinship table was often shown in medieval treatises of canon law because the legitimacy of marriages and the laws of inheritance were in part based on the degree of kinship (Fig. 127). Genealogists also seized on this convenient means of visual demonstration. Indeed, the family tree demonstrates the advantages of the visual diagram to perfection. A relationship that would take so long to

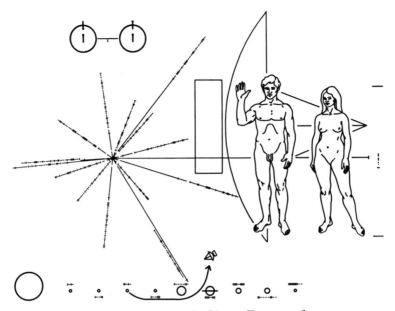

128. Pictorial plaque on the *Pioneer* F spacecraft. 1972

explain in words we might lose the thread ('She is the wife of a second cousin of my stepmother') could be seen on a family tree at a glance. Whatever the type of connection, whether it is a chain of command, the organization of a corporation, a classification system for a library or a network of logical dependencies, the diagram will always spread out before our eyes what a verbal description could only present in a string of statements.

Moreover, diagrams can easily be combined with other pictorial devices in charts to show pictures of things in logical rather than spatial relationships. Attempts have also been made to standardize the codes of such charts for the purpose of visual education (particularly by Otto and Marie Neurath of Vienna, who sought to vivify statistics by such a visual code).[9]

Whether the developed practice of such visual aids is as yet matched by an adequate theory is another matter. According to press releases, the National Aeronautics and Space Administration has equipped a deep-space probe with a pictorial message 'on the off chance that somewhere on the way it is intercepted by intelligent scientifically educated beings' (Fig. 128). It is unlikely that their effort was meant to be taken quite seriously, but what if we try? These beings would first of all have to be equipped with 'receivers' among their sense organs that respond to the same band of electromagnetic waves as our eyes do. Even in that unlikely case they could not possibly get the message. We have seen that reading an image, like the reception of any other message, is dependent on prior knowledge of possibilities; we can only recognize what we know. Even the sight of the awkward naked figures in the illustration cannot be separated in our mind from our knowledge. We know that feet are for standing and eyes are for looking and we project this knowledge onto these configurations, which would look 'like nothing on earth' without this prior information. It is this information alone that enables us to separate the code from the message; we see which of the lines are intended as contours and which are intended as conventional modelling. Our 'scientifically educated' fellow creatures in space might be forgiven if they saw the figures as wire constructs with loose bits and pieces hovering weightlessly in between. Even if they deciphered this aspect of the code, what would they make of the woman's right arm that tapers off like a flamingo's neck and beak? The creatures are 'drawn to scale against the outline of the spacecraft', but if the recipients are supposed to understand foreshortening, they might also expect to see perspective and conceive the craft as being farther back, which would make the scale of the manikins minute. As for the fact that 'the man has his right hand raised in greeting' (the female of the species presumably being less outgoing), not even an earthly Chinese or Indian would be able to interpret correctly this gesture from his own repertory.

The representation of humans is accompanied by a chart: a pattern of lines beside the figures standing for the 14 pulsars of the Milky Way, the whole being designed to locate the sun of our universe. A second drawing (how are they to know it is not part of the same chart?) 'shows the earth and the other planets in relation to the sun and the path of Pioneer from earth and swinging past Jupiter'. The trajectory, it will be noticed, is endowed with a directional arrowhead; it seems to have escaped the designers that this is a conventional symbol unknown to a race that never had the equivalent of bows and arrows.

The arrow is one of a large group of graphic symbols that occupy the zone between the visual image and the written sign. Any comic strip offers examples of these conventions, the history of which is still largely unexplored. They range from the pseudo-naturalistic streaking lines indicating speed to the conventional dotted track indicating the direction of the gaze, and from the hallucinatory medley of stars before the eyes after a blow to the head to the 'balloon' that contains a picture of what the person has in mind, or perhaps just a question mark to suggest puzzlement. This transition from image to symbol reminds us of the fact that writing itself evolved from the pictograph, although it became writing only when it was used to transform the fleeting spoken word into a permanent record.

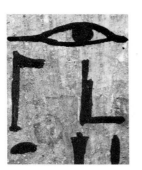 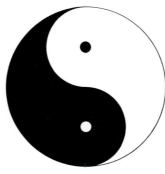

129. Osiris in Egypt-   130. Yin and Yang symbol   131. Great Seal of the
ian hieroglyphics   United States of America

It is well known that a number of ancient scripts drew for this purpose on both the resources of illustration and the principle of the rebus: the use of homophones for the rendering of abstract words. Both in ancient Egypt and in China these methods were ingeniously combined to signify sounds and facilitate reading by classifying them according to conceptual categories. Thus the name of the god Osiris was written in hieroglyphics as a rebus with a picture of a throne (*'usr*) and a picture of an eye (*'iri*) to which was adjoined a picture of the divine sceptre to indicate the name of a god (Fig. 129). But in all ancient civilizations writing represents only one of several forms of conventional symbolism, the meaning of which has to be learned if the sign is to be understood.

Not that this learning need be an intellectual exercise. We can easily be conditioned to respond to signs as we respond to sights. The symbols of religion such as the cross or the lotus, the signs of good luck or danger such as the horseshoe or the skull and crossbones, the national flags or heraldic signs such as the stars and stripes and the eagle, the party badges such as the red flag or the swastika for arousing loyalty or hostility—all these and many more show that the conventional sign can absorb the arousal potential of the visual image.

It may be an open question how far the arousal potential of symbols taps the unconscious significance of certain configurations that Freud explored and Jung was to link with the esoteric traditions of symbolism in mysticism and alchemy. What is open to the observation of the historian is the way the visual symbol has so often appealed to seekers after revelation. To such seekers the symbol is felt both to convey and conceal more than the medium of rational discourse. One of the reasons for this persistent feeling was no doubt the diagrammatic aspect of the symbol, its ability to convey relations more quickly and more effectively than a string of words. The ancient symbol of yin and yang illustrates this potential and also suggests how such a symbol can become the focus of meditation (Fig. 130). Moreover, if familiarity breeds contempt, unfamiliarity breeds awe. A strange symbol suggests a hidden mystery, and if it is known to be ancient, it is felt to embody some esoteric lore too sacred to be revealed to the multitudes. The awe surrounding the ancient Egyptian hieroglyphs in later centuries exemplifies this reaction.[10] Most of the meanings of the hieroglyphs had been forgotten, but the method of writing the name of the god Osiris was now believed to have symbolic rather than phonetic significance and the eye and sceptre were interpreted to mean that the god was a manifestation of the sun.

The reader need not look further than a U.S. dollar bill to see how this association was tapped by the founding fathers in the design of the Great Seal (Fig. 131). Following the advice of the English antiquarian Sir John Prestwich, the design expresses in words and image the hopes and aspirations of the New World for the dawn of a new era. *Novus ordo seclorum* alludes to Virgil's prophecy of a return of the Golden Age, and so does the other Latin tag, *Annuit coeptis*, 'He [God] favoured the beginning.' But it is the image of the unfinished pyramid rising toward heaven and the ancient symbol of the eye suggesting the eye of Providence that gives the entire design the character of an ancient oracle close to fulfilment.

Interesting as the historian must find the continuity of a symbol, such as the eye on the Great Seal, reaching back over more than 4,000 years, the case is somewhat exceptional. More frequently the past influences symbolism through the stories and lore in the language. Cupid's darts, Herculean labours, the sword of Damocles and Achilles' heel come to us from classical antiquity, the olive branch and the widow's mite from the Bible, sour grapes and the lion's share from Aesop's fables, a paper tiger and losing face from the Far East. Such allusions or clichés enable us to 'cut a long story short' because we do not have to spell out the meaning. Almost any story or event that becomes the common property of a community enriches language with new possibilities of condensing a situation into a word, whether it is the political term 'Quisling' or the scientific term 'fallout'. Moreover, language carries old and new figures of speech that are rightly described as images: 'The sands are running out', 'The pump must be primed', 'Wages should be pegged', 'The dollar should be allowed to float'. The literal illustration of these metaphors offers untold possibilities for that special branch of symbolic imagery, the art of the cartoonist.[11] He too can condense a comment into a few pregnant images by the use of the language's stock figures and symbols. Vicky's cartoon showing Italy as Hitler's 'Achilles' heel' is a case in point (Fig. 132).

Like the successful pun that finds an unexpected but compelling meaning

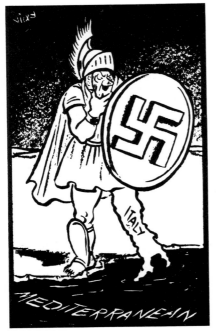

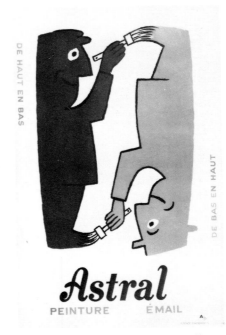

132. 'Vicky': *Achilles' Heel*. 1942.   133. Raymond Savignac: *Astral Peinture Email*.
140 × 100cm. Offset poster. Collection, The Museum of Modern Art, New York,
Gift of the designer

in the sound of a word, Vicky's cartoon reminds us that Italy has a 'heel', and what else could it be but an Achilles' heel? But even if we can count on some familiarity with the shape of Italy and the story of Achilles, the aptness of the cartoon might need a good deal of spelling out forty years after its initial appearance. If there is one type of image that remains mute without the aid of context, caption and code, it is the political cartoon. Its point must inevitably be lost on those who do not know the situation on which it comments.

A glance at the imagery that surrounds us does not bear out the claim that our civilization lacks inventiveness in this field. Whether we approve or disapprove of the role advertising has come to play in our society, we can enjoy the ingenuity and wit used by commercial artists in the use of old symbols and the invention of fresh ones. The trademark adopted for North Sea gas in Britain cleverly combines the trident, that old symbol of Neptune, with the picture of a gas burner (Fig. 134). It is interesting to watch how this idea was first coded as a realistic representation and then reduced to essentials, the increase in distinctiveness making it both more memorable and easier to reproduce (Fig. 135).

Freud's analysis of the kinship between verbal wit and dreamworld could easily be applied, as Ernst Kris has shown, to the condensation of visual symbols in advertising and cartoons.[12] Where the aim is first and foremost to

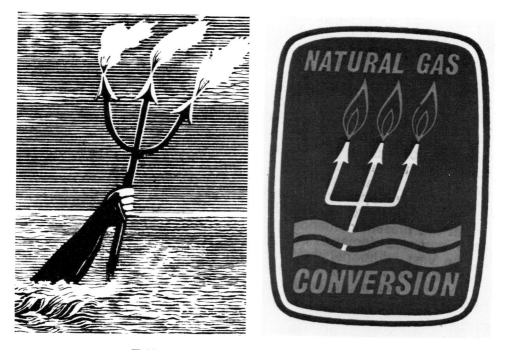

134, 135. Trident trademark, adopted in Britain for North Sea Gas.
Realistic version (*left*) and abstract version

arrest the attention, condensation and selective emphasis are used both for their power of arousal and for their surprise effects. The incomplete image and the unexpected one (Fig. 133) set the mind a puzzle that makes us linger, and enjoy and remember the solution, where the prose of purely informational images would remain unnoticed or unremembered.

It might be tempting to equate the poetry of images with the artistic use of visual media, but it is well to remember that what we call art was not invariably produced for purely aesthetic effects. Even in the sphere of art the dimensions of communication are observable, although in more complex interaction. Here too it is the arousal function of the image that determines the use of the medium. The cult image in its shrine mobilizes the emotions that belong to the prototype, the divine being. In vain did the Hebrew prophets remind the faithful that the heathen idols were only sticks and stones. The power of such images is stronger than any rational consideration. There are few who can escape the spell of a great cult image in its setting.

The strength of the visual image posed a dilemma for the Christian church. The church feared idolatry but hesitated to renounce the image as a means of communication. The decisive papal pronouncement on this vital issue was that of Pope Gregory the Great, who wrote that 'pictures are for the illiterate what letters are for those who can read.' Not that religious images could function without the aid of context, caption and code, but given such aid the value of the medium was easily apparent. Take the main porch of the cathedral of Genoa (Fig. 136), with its traditional rendering of Christ enthroned between the four symbols of the Evangelists (derived from the prophet Ezekiel's vision of the throne of the Lord as it is described in the Bible). The relief underneath will tell the faithful from afar to which saint the church is dedicated. It represents the martyrdom of St. Lawrence. For all its impressive lucidity the image could not be read by anyone unfamiliar with the code, that is, with the style of medieval sculpture. That style disregards the relative size of figures for the sake of emphasizing importance through scale, and it represents every object from the most telling angle. Hence the naked man is not a giant hovering sideways in front of a grid. We must understand that he is stretched out on an instrument of torture while the ruler commands an executioner to fan the flames with bellows. Without the aid of the spoken word the illiterate, of course, could not know that the sufferer is not a malefactor but a saint who is marked by the symbol of the halo, or that the gestures made by the onlookers indicate compassion.

But if the image alone could not tell the worshipper a story he had never heard of, it was admirably suited to remind him of the stories he had been told

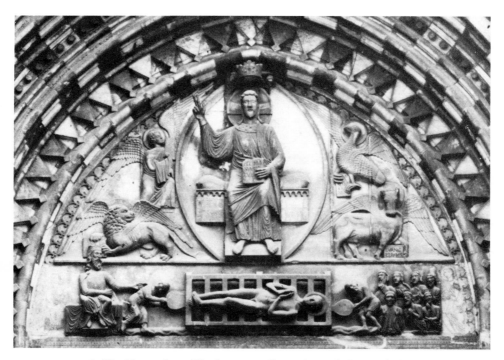

136. *The Martyrdom of St. Lawrence.* Central portal, Genoa Cathedral

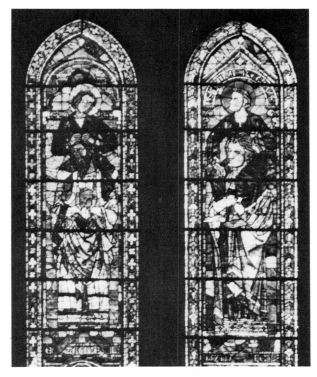

137. Stained-glass lancet windows.
Early 13th century. Chartres Cathedral

in sermons or lessons. Once he had become familiar with the legend of St. Lawrence even the picture of a man with a gridiron would remind him of the saint. It only needed a change in the means and aims of art to enable a great master to make us feel the heroism and the suffering of the martyr in images of great emotional appeal. In this way pictures could indeed keep the memory of sacred and legendary stories alive among the laity, whether or not they were able to read. Pictures still serve the purpose. There must be many whose acquaintance with these legends started from images.

We have touched briefly on the mnemonic power of the image, which is certainly relevant to many forms of religious and secular art. The windows of Chartres show the power of symbolism to transform a metaphor into a memorable image with their vivid portrayal of the doctrine that the apostles stand on the shoulders of the Old Testament prophets (Fig. 137). The whole vast genre of allegorical images testifies to this possibility of turning an abstract thought into a picture.[13] Michelangelo's famous statue of Night (Fig. 138), with her symbolic attributes of the star, the owl and the sleep-inducing poppies, is not only a pictograph of a concept but also a poetic evocation of nocturnal feelings.

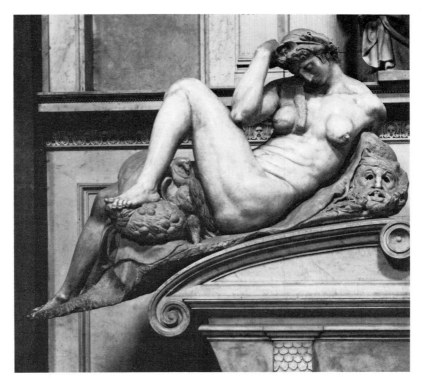

138. Michelangelo: *Night*. Detail from the Tomb of
Giuliano de' Medici. 1524–31. Florence, San Lorenzo, Medici Chapel

The capacity of the image to purvey a maximum of visual information could be exploited only in periods where the styles of art were sufficiently flexible and rich for such a task. Some great artists met the demands of naturalistic portraiture and faithful views with consummate mastery, but the aesthetic needs for selective emphasis could also clash with these more prosaic tasks. The idealized portrait or the revealing caricature was felt to be closer to art than the wax facsimile could ever be, and the romantic landscape that evoked a mood was similarly exalted over the topographic painting.

The contrast between the prose and the poetry of image making often led to conflicts between artists and patrons. The conflict increased in acerbity when the autonomy of art became an issue. It was the Romantic conception of genius in particular that stressed the function of art as self-expression (even though the catchword is of later date). It is precisely this issue that remains to be discussed here, since it will be remembered that the expressive symptom of emotions was distinguished in the theory of communication from the dimension of arousal or description. Popular critics who speak of art as communication often imply that the same emotions that give rise to the work of art are transmitted to the beholder, who feels them in his turn.[14] This naïve idea has been criticized by several philosophers and artists, but to my knowledge the most succinct criticism was a drawing that appeared some years ago in *The New Yorker* (Fig. 139). Its target is the very setting in which the term self-expression has had the greatest vogue. A little dancer fondly believes she is communicating her idea of a flower, but observe what arises instead in the minds of the various onlookers. A series of experiments made by Reinhard Krauss in Germany some decades ago confirms the sceptical view portrayed in the cartoon.[15] Subjects were asked to convey through drawn abstract configurations some emotion or idea for others to guess at. Not surprisingly it was found that such guessing was quite random. When people were given a list of various possible meanings, their guesses became better, and they improved progressively with a reduction in the number of alternatives with which they were confronted. It is easy to guess whether a given line is intended to convey grief or joy, or stone or water.

Many readers will know the painting by Van Gogh of his humble bedroom painted in Arles in 1888 (Fig. 140). It happens to be one of the very few works of art where we know the expressive significance the work held for the artist. In Van Gogh's wonderful correspondence there are three letters dealing with this work that firmly establish the meaning it held for him. Writing to Gauguin in October 1888 he says:

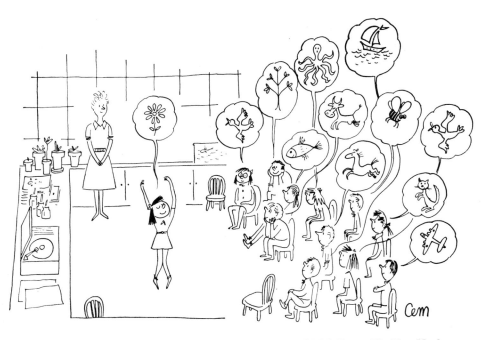

139. Sceptical view of non-verbal communication by CEM. From *The New Yorker*

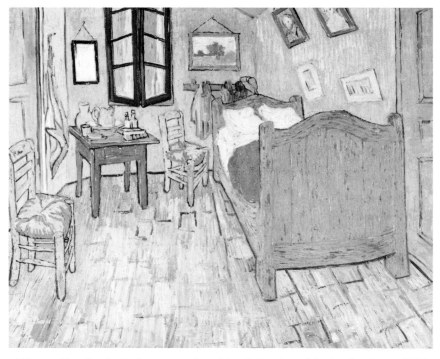

140. Vincent Van Gogh: *Bedroom at Arles*. 1889. Collection of the Art Institute of Chicago

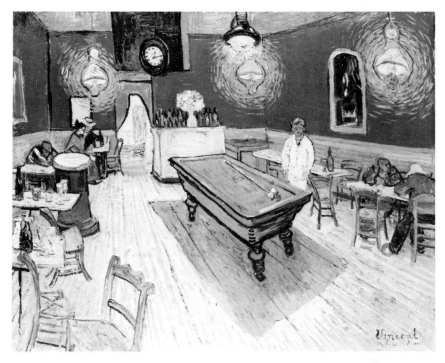

141. Vincent Van Gogh: *The Night Cafe*. 1888. New Haven,
Yale University Art Gallery. Bequest of Stephen Carlton Clark, 1903

Still for the decoration [of my house] I have done . . . my bedroom with its furniture of whitewood which you know. Well, it amused me enormously to do that interior with nothing in it, with a simplicity à la Seurat: with flat paint but coarsely put on, the neat pigment, the walls a pale violet. . . .

I wanted to express an absolute calm with these very different tones, you see, where there is no white except in the mirror with its black frame. . . .

A letter to his brother Theo confirms his intention and explains it further:

My eyes are still strained, but at last I have a new idea in my head. . . . This time it is quite simply my bedroom, colour alone must carry it off, by imparting through simplification a grander style to things, it should be suggestive of rest and sleep in general. In other words, the sight of the picture should rest the head, or rather the imagination. . . . The walls are pale violet, the floor tiles red . . . the doors are green, that is all. There is nothing in the room with the shutters closed. The squareness of the furniture should also express the undisturbed rest. . . . The shadows and modelling are suppressed, it is coloured with flat tints like the Japanese prints. This will contrast, for instance, with the *diligence* of Tarascon and the Night Café.

Here we have an important clue. Van Gogh had written of *The Night Café* (Fig. 141) that he wanted to show that it was a place where one could go mad. To him, in other words, his little room was a haven after the strain of work, and it was this contrast that made him stress its tranquillity. The manner of simplification he adopted from Seurat and from the Japanese print stood for him in clear opposition to the expressive graphological brushwork that had become so characteristic of his style. This is what he stresses in still another letter to his brother. 'No stippling, no hatching, nothing, flat areas, but in harmony.' It is this modification of the code that Van Gogh experiences as being expressive of calm and restfulness. Does the painting of the bedroom communicate this feeling? None of the naïve subjects I have asked hit on this meaning; although they knew the caption (Van Gogh's bedroom), they lacked the context and the code. Not that this failure of getting the message speaks against the artist or his work. It only speaks against the equation of art with communication.

'The Sky is the Limit' : The Vault of Heaven and Pictorial Vision

'THE VISUAL field is the product of the chronic habit of civilized men of seeing the world as a picture.' This statement by J.J. Gibson, dating from 1952,[1] which he has subsequently described as a 'half-way stage' to his developed views,[2] must serve as an explanation for the presence of an art historian among professional psychologists. In *Art and Illusion* I picked up this remark which assigned such crucial importance to the role of pictorial art in our visual habits, and paid tribute to 'this bold reversal of the traditional way of putting things'.[3] I had reason to welcome this departure from orthodoxy, for originally I had accepted the current opinion that what Gibson called 'the visual field', the two-dimensional mosaic of sensations registered by the retina, should be described as what we 'really' see, while the three-dimensional 'visual world' was to be explained as the product of our knowledge, mainly derived from the experience of touch. This account of perception, which played such a vital part in the theory of Impressionism, I found increasingly hard to square with the observed facts of image making. Indeed I was prompted to add that 'the psychologist might with profit test his theories against the material offered by the historian. He might find ... that the "chronic habit of civilized men" is not sufficient for most of them to adopt the necessary attitude to paint without training.'

In his book of 1966, *The Senses Considered as Perceptual Systems*, Gibson came to even more radical conclusions, arguing that 'the optical (not retinal) gradients and the other invariants that carry the information for perception are often not open to analytic introspection, and that perception is therefore, in principle, not reducible to sensations.'[4] It is this impossibility consciously to analyse our act of perception, I would suggest, which accounts for the

This study appeared in Perception: Essays in Honor of James J. Gibson (*Ithaca and London, 1974*)

artist's need to approach the problem of naturalistic painting by trial and error. Though he cannot foretell exactly what device may have the desired effect, he can judge whether he can *recognize* the effect in his picture.

But if that is so, the problem remains how painters and psychologists (including, after all, Gibson himself) could ever have thought that we can reduce our perception to pure sensation. The answer which I gave to this question in *Art and Illusion* was hardly a model of clarity. 'Our belief that we can ever make the world dissolve into such a flat patchwork of colours rests in itself on an illusion, connected, maybe, with the same urge for simplicity that makes us see the indeterminate sky as the vault of heaven.'[5]

I hope J. J. Gibson will accept an elaboration of this cryptic remark as a modest contribution to these essays in his honour and as a continuation of the friendly debate in which we have been engaged in the journal *Leonardo*.[6]

Gibson does not much like the student of perception to call heaven as his witness. 'The night sky,' he writes, 'is not the case with which to begin the analysis of stimulus information . . . Points of light can structure the darkness . . . but it is not the kind of structure that evokes a perception of space.'[7]

It is undeniable that what Gibson has described as the 'old, old idea, that perception cannot be separated from misperception'[8] derived much strength from that example. For the night sky may well have been the case with which mankind began the analysis of stimulus information. It was in the discussion about astronomy in ancient Greece that the famous phrase 'saving the phenomena' was first coined.[9] No hypothesis about the real movement of the planets in space that did not account for their apparent movement on the night sky was acceptable. In this case, at least, Gibson would surely agree that 'our faith in the direct act of seeing the world is misguided', though in the course of our debate in *Leonardo* he brands this opinion as a muddle of thinking, not a fact of psychology.[10]

The student of art certainly has reasons to take note of Gibson's attack on the traditional distinction between appearance and reality, for at least since the time of the Greeks art has always been said to be concerned precisely with the imitation of appearances.[11] This dualism has indeed caused a good deal of muddle in the theory of art, not least in the teaching of painting. At a time when painters were taught anatomy and perspective in order to enable them to create a semblance of the natural world, the demand that the painter should stick to appearances to the extent of trying to forget what he merely 'knew' proved to be in flagrant conflict with actual practice. Nor were the arguments against these methods and in favour of the 'innocent eye' ever consistent or effective. The phenomenal world eluded the painter's grasp and he turned to other pursuits.

Art and Illusion is largely concerned with the reason for the collapse of a theory of art which concentrated on the need to copy the phenomenal world. Most of these reasons have of course long been known to students of perception, but it still remains difficult to avoid confusions when applying them to the painter's problems. This is happily not the place to return yet once more to that perennial question of the validity of various systems of perspective. I have argued elsewhere[12] that what Brunelleschi invented was a method of working out what will be occluded by what in our field of vision from any given station point. The objectivity of this demonstration is not in doubt; what caused and still causes the trouble is the concept of 'apparent size' that has been imported into these discussions.[13]

I recently watched the moon rising over Hampstead Heath when I noticed a child holding a toy balloon. My effort to find the point at which the balloon would exactly occlude the moon was unfortunately frustrated by the unwelcome attention my eccentric behaviour appeared to arouse. Yet I still can recommend this exercise to less inhibited students of vision who are interested in the various factors influencing apparent size, such as the constancies and Emmert's Law, which has been connected with the notorious moon illusion.[14] But my walks on the Heath have also convinced me that, though apparent size is an elusive entity, apparent orientation is still more elusive. While observing the vapour trails of jet planes which so frequently disturb the calm of a cloudless sky I have come to appreciate the reasons why some students of art, including the great Panofsky, asserted with such conviction that we 'really' see straight lines as curved.[15] To appreciate, but not to accept. I believe, with Gibson, that normally the visual array contains all the information we need to perceive the invariant forms of edges and solids. If we did not recognize a straight line as straight and a plane as plane we would soon come to grief. But somewhere near the limit of my visual world this assurance obviously breaks down. Even though I have reason to think that the course of the jets is straight, I tend to see the trail rising over the horizon and arch around me, flattening overhead, but turning down steeply before it vanishes. I tend to see a similar curvature when the flight path is closer to eye level and appears to swing round parallel to the horizon. I say I 'tend to', because it is only the distant flight that appears more or less traced on the dome of the sky. As soon as the aircraft is seen to recede and the trail is visibly structured in its rhythmical puffs of vapour, the real orientation of the line asserts itself.

It is the same with real, as distinct from these artificial, clouds. Some appear to be distributed like flat patches along the vault of heaven or to race around the horizon in a storm, but lighting conditions and mutual occlusion

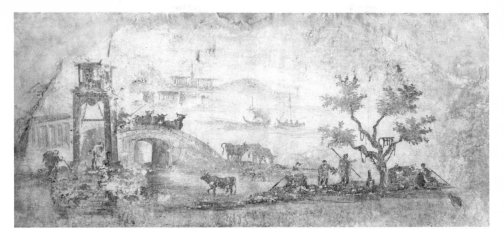

142. *Landscape*. Wall-painting. 1st century A.D. Rome, Villa Albani

of shapes may suggest alternative orientations. This occurs most dramatically when aircraft weave in and out of these concentrations and give us additional information about their approximate distance so that a bank of clouds which had appeared to be far up suddenly becomes part of our world.

I believe a similar elasticity can be experienced with all features of the scenery which obey the conflicting pulls of the foreground and the background. Students of landscape painting know indeed that the transition between these two zones, with their very different representational problems, have caused a good deal of trouble to various conventions of landscape painting. Both the Graeco-Roman and the Chinese masters of the genre refused to acknowledge the middle ground and preferred to veil it in haze or mist (Figs. 142 and 143). Thus they achieve a sharp distinction between houses or rocks in the proximity, which are made to look solid, and

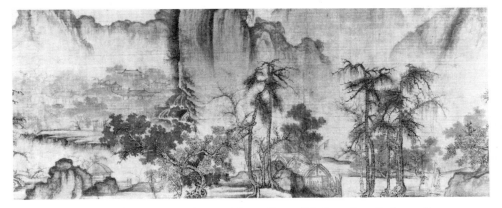

143. *Clearing Autumn Skies over Mountains and Valleys*. Detail of a scroll.
Attributed to Kuo Hsi. Sung, 12th century. Washington, Freer Gallery of Art

the mountains or trees in the distance, which are projected as flat shapes against the sky. In other words, such features are (or can be) seen at an unspecified distance but in an imaginary orientation aligned with the distant panorama which we scan.

The phenomenon is both akin to and different from the experience of the night sky, for now it is the objects in front of the imaginary back-cloth which arrange themselves in a sphere or spheres parallel to the enveloping limit.

With regard to this limit then, Gibson's formulation 'that the way the surfaces of the world are laid out is seen directly' does not apply,[16] since in his own analysis the perception of invariants depends on information conveyed through texture, parallax and illumination. All these fail us with distance, and the decrease in information is gradual and uncertain. At dusk or in mist the silhouetted world around us will come closer; when the air is clear and the light sharp, the forms even of distant features will reveal their layout. Sometimes, perhaps, we may also be able to switch from one attitude to the other, particularly in the middle ranges, where we can ignore information even without half-closing our eyes as painters sometimes do when they want to concentrate on 'appearance'.

Is it really likely that we owe this mode of perception entirely to the painters? Long before anybody ever painted a cloud, the Biblical chronicler described dramatically how the prophet Elijah's prayer for rain was answered. 'Behold, there ariseth a little cloud out of the sea, like a man's hand' (1 Kings 18: 44). Clearly the perception of such a sign or portent can never be veridical. The witnesses had no information about the cloud's real size or shape, their perception was what Gibson might call 'pictorial'.

The reason why Gibson considers this to be merely derivative lies, I believe, in his strong evolutionist bias. The eye was given us so that we should find the way to our food and our mate without bumping into things or falling prey to predators. But though this function of the system is certainly paramount, there are some tasks for which veridical perception is irrelevant. I am referring to the need for orientation, for which Gibson only considers the general layout of ambient light.[17] What is also needed for that task is the perception of landmarks or perhaps skymarks, as in the navigational use which birds appear to make of the night sky.[18] These perceptions of the enveloping limit, in other words, may follow their own laws and requirements without being purely cultural developments.

Be that as it may, I would suggest that man must have reflected on this tension in his visual world as he scanned the horizon and searched the heavens. Once these reflections began, the difference between appearance and reality must have become an object of his thought.

If I am right in stressing this duality of purposes, Gibson was amply justified in rejecting the traditional account of the visual field as a uniform patchwork of colours spread out, we do not know where. But he may be mistaken in denying that we can experience visual fields. These fields form the limit of our visual world.

The relevance of this dematerialized distant view to art is the subject of a much-discussed book by the nineteenth-century German sculptor Adolf von Hildebrand, who incidentally counted Helmholtz among his sitters. *Das Problem der Form in der bildenden Kunst* (The Problem of Form in the Visual Arts, 1893) has many subtle observations, but I am not out to revive an interpretation which certainly has its full share of those muddles of which Gibson has spoken. One of those muddles may lie precisely in the confusion between the two modes of perception, the treatment of appearance on a par with objects. Panofsky's belief in the visual curvature of straight lines may be a case in point. If I am right, the curvature does not represent what we really perceive, but what we really do not perceive. It marks the transition from the world of solid objects to the field we scan for orientation.[19] These two distinct modes of perception may thus account for the existence of two warring schools in the theory of perspective, though it can be shown that their claims and counterclaims have very little practical relevance.

Gibson has warned us that the night sky is not the case with which to begin the analysis of stimulus information, but what about ending it in this way, or rather regarding it as a limiting case in every sense of the term? What interests the student of art in this phenomenon is precisely that it can be simulated by artifice and not only for humans but also for migratory birds. I have referred before in this context to the device of the planetarium which aims at giving the impression of the starry sky by the projection of light beams from a source in the centre of the room.[20] If it were necessary to demonstrate the importance of visual angles, this arrangement would indeed furnish the proof, since anyone placed close to the centre should see the same constellation in the dark regardless of the height of the vault. The same arrangement would also confirm Brunelleschi's procedure of a flat projecting plane, for if the room can be made sufficiently dark to make the projecting plane disappear from our awareness, the apparent configuration of dots should remain invariant regardless of the shape and orientation of the overhead screen. But what interests me in this situation, which may well be amenable to experimental tests, is the prediction that any suitable arrangement would also result in the illusion of a phantom vault of heaven which might in theory become indistinguishable from the open sky.

In discussing the problem of images Gibson has, in fact, denied this very possibility. 'A mediated perception', he wrote in 1971, 'cannot become a direct perception by stages.'[21] And yet Gibson himself has admirably described the mediation of such a perception precisely in the context that interests me.

> The appearance of sky is produced, as every theater-goer knows, by a finely textured curved surface at the back of a stage which can be flooded with illumination. It is called a cyclorama. The actual surface may be only a few feet behind the garden wall of a stage setting, but to the audience 50 feet away the illusion of depthless space will be compelling.[22]

Even for him the sky is the limit of our visual world, and a suitable limit can mediate the perception of the sky.

Perhaps I may at this point draw attention to a difference in emphasis between Gibson's definition of an image and my own attempts to discuss these matters. For Gibson, 'a picture is a surface so treated that a delimited optic array to a point of observation is made available that contains the same kind of information that is found in the ambient optic arrays of an ordinary environment.' What matters in this definition is that it does away with 'visual sensations or appearances'. 'An artist can capture the information about something without replicating its sensations.'[23]

What I suggested in *Art and Illusion* may seem rather similar, but differs in one important respect:

> To say of a drawing that it is a correct view of Tivoli does not mean, of course, that Tivoli is bounded by wiry lines. It means that those who understand the notation will derive *no false information* from the drawing—whether it gives the contour in a few lines or picks out 'every blade of grass' ... The complete portrayal might be the one which gives as much correct information about the spot as we would obtain if we looked at it from the very spot where the artist stood.[24]

I agree with Gibson that this complete portrayal, even if it were possible, would never yield an illusion of looking at Tivoli through a window, precisely for the reason which I italicized in the preceding sentence. Any such portrayal would inevitably carry with it an amount of 'false information', or rather, the true information that we are faced with a picture.

We can reduce some of this false information, the simplest method being a narrowing of our field of vision as when we screen off the surround with our hands, the most difficult being the elimination of visible texture in a treated transparency shown in a darkened room. However we may choose to interpret the resulting experience, it seems to me hard to deny that it can be described as enhancing the illusion by stages, even though the illusion will still fall short of the one produced by Gibson's cyclorama.

This, of course, duplicates the absence of information of the real experience by a similar absence from the stage setting. Yet it would be misleading to identify this absence with a complete negation of information. Such negation begins outside the fringe of our visual field while the empty sky expands within the field. We are thus led to fill in, to project, or whatever other word we may prefer to use for this activity. Gibson rejects with particular emphasis 'the tiresome contradiction of supposing that perception comes only partly from outside the perceiver and partly from inside'[25] but it would be a pity if the debate here got entangled in verbal definitions.

For Gibson himself has discussed such limiting cases in which something—whatever we call it—certainly comes 'partly from inside'. I refer to the section of his book on 'The Consequences of Inadequate Information', which ranges from the consequences of sensory deprivation to conditions

> when the system hunts more widely in space and longer in time. It tests for what remains invariant over time, trying out different perspectives. If the invariants still do not appear, a whole repertory of poorly understood processes variously called assumptions, inferences, or guesses come into play ... the general formula of the *search for meaning* seems to fit them all fairly well.[26]

The hypothesis which has appealed to me, as a student of art, is connected with this search. I have regarded these phantoms as gropings or testings which normally await confirmation or refutation through the incoming flow of information but which obtrude themselves on our awareness in the absence of any further results of the search. I have suggested that such gropings exhibit the strategy of testing for simplicity.[27] I readily accept Gibson's *caveat* that these processes are poorly understood and I realize that the concept of simplicity itself is far from simple.[28] But I believe that the vault of heaven illustrates this process to perfection. In *Art and Illusion* I have referred in this connection to an observation in V. Cornish's interesting book on *Scenery and the Sense of Sight* to the effect that in the absence of contrary information 'we instinctively regard an object as extended in the plane at right angles to the line joining the object to the eye'.[29] The author connects this phenomenon with the shape of the retina, but I preferred to interpret it as an example of a non-refuted test for simplicity.

Why, then, do we not see a flat expanse but a convex field? Because—my answer would have to be—we can never separate the static view from the flow of information that precedes and follows it. If the apparent vault is really composed of a succession of narrow fields of vision at right angles to the momentary line of sight, we must not only expect such a curvature while we scan the heavens, we are bound also to perceive it while we try to keep our eyes fixed on one point in the sky. Introspection suggests to me that in such an unnatural situation the very processes described by Gibson for conditions of inadequate information come into their own because the area of focused vision is then surrounded by a halo of uncertainties onto which anticipatory phantoms are projected in accordance with the simplicity principle. Could this experience, perhaps, be used as a basis for further generalizations?

I am sure all students of vision have learned from Gibson a new and healthy respect for the richness of information which is ordinarily present in the visual array, but perhaps an appreciation of these resources and of these redundancies on which we can rely when finding our way through the world does not compel us to postulate a discontinuity between ordinary perception and those methods of search under conditions of reduced information. True, it is only in moments of uncertainty that we become aware of the constant productivity of the system, but if I understand Gibson correctly the hunt for invariants is always, at least to some extent, a process over time that responds to the match or mismatch between anticipation and information. If this is indeed of relevance, as Gibson suggests in his discussion of the relation between perceiving and expecting,[30] many of the visual sensations of which we are aware may not be directly caused by the stimuli of which sensationalists speak, but rather originate in the system itself. In normal circumstances these anticipatory phantoms and the incoming information fuse so readily and so efficiently that we are neither aware of the visual stimuli nor of our visual expectancies. Only when this fusion is inhibited by external or internal causes do we actually see what I have described as 'pre-images',[31] as distinct from after-images (which are generally attributable to purely physiological processes). I have come to wonder, however, whether this distinction is likely to hold. If the 'waterfall illusion' and other sensations attending on movement can be described as anticipations based on the simple assumption that a process will continue, is the same not also true of the stationary after-image? May it not be connected with the same assumption of continuity that guarantees our stable world? Maybe, then, these images are not 'luxuries', as Gibson calls sensations, but important aids in what he so eloquently describes as 'the serious business of perceiving the world'.[32]

My excuse for such brainstorming must be found in the real subject under discussion, which is the relation between our experience of the visual world and our reaction to pictures. For Gibson, there can be no continuity between the two, but for me it is precisely where the rainbow ends that art begins.

'Heard melodies are sweet, but those unheard are sweeter.' When Keats wrote this line about the music makers on the *Grecian Urn* he was only giving a new twist to the old response that we actually hear the sounds the artist asks us to imagine. For Keats the 'ditties of no tone' are 'more endear'd' than if the pipes were to play to the 'sensual ear'. It sounds far-fetched, but the human imagination is a powerful thing when expertly manipulated. Conjurors know many devices for creating convincing phantoms through the setting up of uncontradicted expectations[33] and so, on a different level, do the purveyors of erotic art with their varieties of suggestive veiling.[34]

When Plato called pictures 'dreams for those who are awake',[35] he was perhaps more profound than many students of art, even though he disapproved of such dreams. For no account of the artist's image can be complete that ignores what Baudelaire called the 'Queen of the Faculties', the faculty of the imagination. Though he may dislike the use of this loaded term, Gibson, it seems to me, appeals to this faculty when he asserts that 'even when one sees a pictured object one ordinarily does not see its front surface only but the whole of it'.[36] Perhaps I may go beyond his paradox by suggesting that the less information is given, the more what I would still like to call 'the beholder's share' comes into play, provided of course the search for meaning is suitably guided. The visual information the painter can simulate may never actually duplicate the information we pick up from solid objects close by. But is it not possible that he can mobilize the system to produce the same phantom sensations which come into play in those processes of search or probing for simplicity precisely in situations of inadequate information? If that is true, our perception of pictures would indeed differ from the perception of the visual world, but the right stimulation from the canvas may still engender a reaction similar to that which we experience in front of nature. A fine landscape or seascape by one of the Dutch masters certainly does not give me the illusion that the museum wall opens into parts of Holland. But I would claim that in getting absorbed in such a painting my search for meaning between and behind its brush-strokes weaves on its surface a rich fabric of uncontradicted sensations. Following the artist's suggestion I begin to forget the textured surface. I see the horizon curving and the sky arching over the earth, not a mediated perception so much as a mediated phantom. I doubt whether the illusion would be stronger if the panel were rounded rather than flat or that it is much influenced by the position from which I view the painting. Little is needed, but little of the right kind, for my visual system to pick up the scent and to enjoy the pleasures of the chase, even when it is hunting that notorious Snark—the non-existent vault of heaven.

Mirror and Map:
Theories of Pictorial Representation

1. VISUAL INFORMATION

IN MY native city of Vienna the Museum of Natural History and the Museum of Art History confront each other across the square with the monument to Maria Theresa (Figs. 144 and 145). Often on a Sunday morning my father would take us children to that nearby place and I vividly remember hoping that he would turn left and go to the Museum of Science with its thrilling skeletons of prehistoric creatures rather than to the picture gallery. It was only later that my bias changed and that I frequently took the turn to the right, to the Museum of Art History where I got stuck, as it were.

However, I did not tell this story merely to indulge in reminiscences. I also wanted to show the normal use of pictorial representation for the illustration and supplementation of a verbal description. We represent or describe *something to someone*. If I had no 'visual aids' at my disposal I could have described the museums to you in somewhat greater detail, for instance as large two-storey buildings topped by a cupola, and this might have given you some general framework you could have filled in, drawing in your imagination on buildings of the kind you may have seen in other Central European cities. But however long I would have gone on with my description I could never have given you enough details to construct the buildings fully from my verbal account, for language operates with universals and thus no description could ever be complete. There is no end, in principle, to the further questions you could ask about any one feature such as the cupola. Now pictorial representations are also incomplete. The two I have shown would not suffice for you to imagine or build an identical complex of museums unless they were supplemented in their turn by a verbal account. One such possibility is neatly illustrated in my example. If it were true that

Review Lecture given at the Royal Society in May 1974.

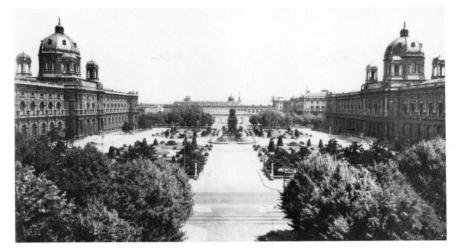

144. The Maria-Theresien-Platz in Vienna with the Museum of Natural History on
the left and the Museum of Art History on the right. From R. Wagner-Rieger,
Die Wiener Ringstrasse (Vienna, 1969). Courtesy of the publishers

the two museums are identical (which they are not in their statuary) one of
them might serve as the representation of the other, and if one were destroyed it could be reconstructed from the companion on this verbal
information alone. But this, clearly, is a limiting case. We do not normally
describe any two members of a class as representations of each other, and any
other kind of representation has by its very nature its limits, which its user
must either accept or try to transcend by other means. The nature of these
limits, on the other hand, will differ with the medium and method employed.
It is these methods I have proposed to characterize in my title as that of the
mirror and the map. The wide-angle photograph (Fig. 144) which tells us
something of the elevation and decoration of the buildings may be loosely
compared to a frozen mirror image, the map (Fig. 145) indicates their
ground-plan and their spatial relation across the square.

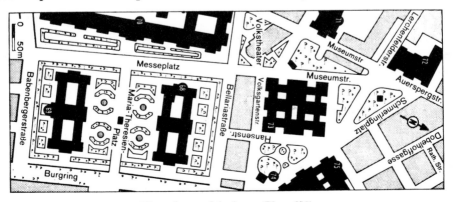

145. Plan of part of the inner City of Vienna

We rightly take this use of pictures so much for granted that it is only in recent years that pictorial representation has become something of an issue in psychology,[1] in philosophy,[2] in technology[3] and in the study of art.[4] Maps would appear to present less elusive problems.[5] We know about the kind of information they offer; we know that they have a key to explain their use of certain symbols for such 'universals' as churches, post offices, railway lines or rivers. We also know they have a scale that allows us to translate the distance of symbols on the map into distances in the city or country; we know that the grid permits us to locate any of the listed items within a given square. We quickly learn the use and the limits of these handy tools. But what exactly does the wide-angle photograph tell us? Where are its limits? Should we regard the gradations of grey as the equivalent of the codes used in maps? And what about the perspective view? Is it a convention of representation, mechanized and standardized by the camera according to pre-established rules? It is to these questions mainly that I propose to devote this review.

Like the verbal account and indeed like the map we can use the photograph only because we do not come upon it quite unprepared. We also supplement much of what it does not convey, at least in general terms. Even in a black and white photograph we do not imagine the trees to be red, the walls blue and the lawn black, and given this general framework of previous knowledge the photograph imparts more, but less precise, information than the map. We could tell, for instance, how many windows the front elevation has, but we could not find out the precise measurements of the windows, for even if we are lucky and find that the photographer included a human being to give the approximate scale that scale would still allow a margin of variation. It is precisely because of this vagueness that an eminent philosopher has recently criticized the use of the term information in the context of pictorial representation.[6] He is quite right in reminding us that the technical use of the term in information theory should not be confused with non-technical parlance, but after all the theory started its career as a theory of communication along a channel and it is well to remember that pictures are now sent by wire or satellite. It would be easy in this way to specify the position and shape of a building on a pre-existent map by using precisely the traditional method of the grid indicating, for instance, which square is empty and which filled, nor would it present a problem to tell how many 'bits' of information would be needed for this operation.[7] Obviously a detailed plan would need more than a schematic one, and a photograph in its turn would demand an even denser grid or screen. The power of resolution of the lens and the grain of the film being limited, we would want, perhaps, to supplement the overall picture with a close-up of a window or column. Since we see enough of the general lay-out on the coarser rendering we might say that it would be redundant in the technical sense of the term to provide more than one detailed illustration of these repeated elements.

As a frequent user of both photographs and maps the historian of art, like other people using pictorial material, has many a tale to tell of the limits of information provided by smudged photographs. He knows that all methods of reproduction will inevitably carry a certain amount of visual 'noise', which would be crippling were it not for certain assumptions on which we can draw—for instance that a gap in an outline need not represent a void in the building.

It has also been asked how we can ever know whether a picture or a map represents a particular building. To this the answer is simple. We cannot. In our case there are two buildings of the same plan and elevation, the two museums, and it may be impossible to distinguish them in a picture which happens to lack a tell-tale detail. Nor is that the full extent of the limits which are inseparable from pictorial representation as distinct from language. Pictures cannot assert.[8] While a verbal account need leave us in no doubt that it claims to describe an existing state of affairs, the uncaptioned pictorial representation may just as easily refer to an existing building as to a memory, a plan or a fantasy. There is a watercolour by the Austrian painter Rudolf von Alt showing the museums from above (Fig. 146).[9] It is what architects call an 'artist's impression'. At the time when it was made the buildings had not yet gone up, but the need was felt to visualize how the plans would translate into reality. Books on the history of our buildings provide yet another variant—a wooden model was made of the whole complex of buildings which incorporated real features but was intended to demonstrate

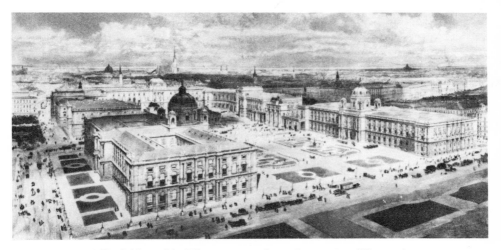

146. Rudolf von Alt: The museums from above. 1872. Watercolour

certain possibilities of extension and modification. Only those who have independent evidence can tell what kind of information we are intended to receive from this type of model.

2. VISUAL REPRESENTATION AND VISUAL EXPERIENCE

This brief consideration of the informational aspects of maps, models and pictures has brought out the need to distinguish between different kinds of information we can receive from representations. There is a common-sense distinction between information about some feature of the physical world (such as a building) and its appearance from a given station point and under given conditions. Maps give us selective information about the physical world, pictures, like mirrors, convey to us the appearance of an aspect of that world as it varies with the conditions of light and may therefore be said to give information about the optical world. It is tempting to regard this 'optical world' as something given, something indeed that can be mapped with the same selective objectivity as can the real world, and those who spoke of the painter 'copying' or 'imitating' appearances obviously succumbed to this temptation. The optical world, the light reflected from the features of the

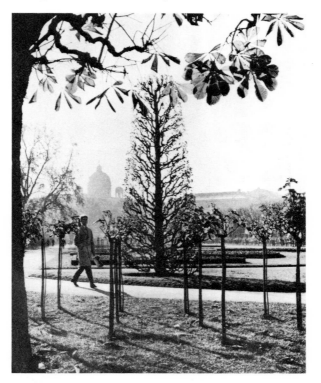

147. The Museum of Natural History from the Volksgarten.
From Barbara Pflaum and Jorg Mauthe, *Wie ist Wien?* (E. Hunna Verlag, Vienna, 1961)

physical world, is really part of that physical world, though subject to more rapid changes than are its solid components. A record of these optical data can indeed convey the changing appearance of such a feature as the museum with evocative force. Take two artistic impressions of our building from a book of photographs of Vienna: one (Fig. 147) shows the museum in the distance as seen through the morning haze on an autumn day. We can infer that visibility was low, restricting the information to the general outlines of the building. In the other artistic impression (Fig. 148) it is the photographer who has restricted the information about the museum by focusing his camera on the boys in the foreground, leaving the building somewhat blurred.

What these photographs help to clarify is the further need to distinguish between the optical world and its 'appearance'. For even a photographer does not register all light energies but actively selects the ones he wishes to record. Needless to say, the human eye does the same.

It is true that this qualification would have presented little difficulty to the traditional account of what constitutes 'appearances', for this account relied on a rather simplistic view of visual perception. According to this time-honoured view the light rays that enter the eye stimulate the optic nerve and

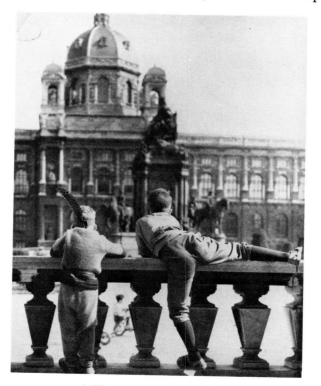

148. The Museum of Art History.
From Barbara Pflaum and Jorg Mauthe, *Wie ist Wien?*

cause those visual sensations which in their aggregate correspond to the image on the retina. The optical world, or that part of it that is sampled by the eye, can therefore be inferred from the visual sensations we experience. There is a fixed correlation between the physical world, the optical world and the appearance of this world in our experience. The same stimuli that cause the sensations will also register on the photographer's plate and if we look at his treated image it will of necessity arouse in us the same sensations we would have experienced when standing beside his camera. The camera, like the skilled artist, simply transcribes the optical data which mediate the visual experience, in other words he maps the optical world by mapping the visual sensations which correspond to it.

As long as this view prevailed, visual representation appeared to pose no very interesting philosophical or psychological problems. But of course it no longer does prevail. It has become a commonplace in most discussions of perception to start with a warning against the analogy between the eye and the camera—except, perhaps, if we regard both the camera and the nervous system as a 'black box'. We cannot watch what happens to the input.[10]

To quote question and answer from a recent authoritative account:

How does our visual system accomplish the extraordinary operation of converting these highly variable two-dimensional light distributions at either retina into one stable, three-dimensional perception of the surrounding visual world? There can only be one complete answer, which is that we do not yet know.[11]

One thing can be taken as established. There is no fixed correlation between the optical world and the world of our visual experience. Granted that the controlled manipulation of optical data can result in an evocative photograph, that photograph in its turn belongs, of course, both to the physical and the optical world and will therefore be fed into the black box which mediates our visual experience, which is only partially determined by the sensory input. Some of the reasons for this limitation can be found in any modern textbook of psychology, from whichever point of view it is written. There is the influence of past experience and of expectations, the variables of interest, 'mental set' and alertness, not to speak of variations in the observer's physiological equipment and in the adjustment of the perceptual system to changing conditions.

What makes these findings a little hurtful to our pride is the discovery that we ourselves have no privileged access to the black box. We cannot give a complete account of our visual experience either when looking out into the world or when looking at its pictorial representation. If it were not for this impossibility of telling at any moment which visual experience is due to the optical world and which to memories or guesses, oculists who wish to test our eyesight would not have to use random letters rather than coherent texts. The 'appearance' of the display changes dramatically as soon as we can infer what is in front of us. Psychologists go further and confront their subjects with so-called nonsense figures in the tachistoscope to test the limits of information we can process in a given time and the strategies we apply in what Bartlett called the 'effort after meaning'.

Nobody doubts that this effort will influence our experience when looking at the photographs under discussion. We can never be quite sure what data are actually present and what experiences we 'project' onto the photograph. Where exactly can we discern individual blades of grass and where lies the limit beyond which we merely expect and imagine their presence? Can we really see the flagstaff on top of the museum's cupola, or do we merely know it must be there? Admittedly, we can always resort to a magnifying glass or to other means of isolating and checking our impressions. To insist on the subjective element in our visual experience does not mean to deny its objective veridical component. I believe much light is thrown on this question by Karl Popper's lifelong insistence[12] that a parallelism exists between the reactions of the organism to external stimuli and that of the scientist evaluating his observational evidence. The elimination of false guesses, the refutation through tests and probings of mistaken hypotheses, play a decisive part in any area of doubt that demands attention. Where such doubts do not arise we may go along with a vague provisional hypothesis without much awareness that it is in need of examination. Thus, as we move through the world, we experience a continuous range of visual hypotheses extending from the most general to the minutest particular. We react to movement on the periphery of the field of vision even before we can tell what has moved and normally such a reaction is coupled with movement of the eyes.[13] While we thus focus and concentrate on one object in sight the others become indefinite, but they may be present to our echo memory and held in readiness for refuting or confirming a momentary hypothesis—a process that is best studied by recording the eye movements of a rapid reader. I have pointed to the blurring of the museum in our illustration, but this is at best a vague analogue, not a representation of the way the background would appear to us if we watched the boys in the foreground. The question of what the museum looks like while we do not look at it is a teaser that has much engaged the attention of conscientious artists, but I do not think it allows of a precise answer. Trying to focus on one picture on pages 176–7 while watching the impression of the other from the corner of our eye we soon discover the limits of introspection. Not only is it hard to overcome the nearly automatic coupling of eye movement and interest, it is harder still to separate now what we remember, anticipate or really see than it was while inspecting the building in the haze.

To put the matter briefly, seeing, like representing, is a transitive verb and demands an object. I want to see something out there, I cannot quite make it out, at last I believe I see it clearly. In this continuous process we must be as ready to disregard disturbing or irrelevant sensations as we must be to attend to any possible source of information. Dazzle, after-images, double contours, the result of astigmatism or other anomalies tend to be pushed beyond the threshold of our awareness if they regularly and manifestly contradict a visual hypothesis that has stood the battery of reality tests we have at our disposal, at least while we are awake and sane.[14]

But here is the real paradox. While such sensations can be regarded as mere 'noise' in what J. J. Gibson[15] has called the 'serious business of living', this noise can still be aroused and exploited with comparative ease by those who wish to play with visual effects. After all, vision depends indeed on nervous mechanisms, and just as a knock against the eye makes us see sparks and a strong glare an after-image, so the experienced manipulator, whether conjuror, artist or scientist, has been able to find out how to predict and trigger certain non-veridical visual experiences through the arousal of visual sensations. Such modern devices as the stereoscope, the cine-camera or the television screen arouse in the beholder visual experiences which he cannot stop and which he never could have predicted if he had been shown the arrangement on which they are based. I would suggest that it is these surprise effects which we tend to describe as visual illusions. Given the unexpected difference between our visual experience and what we know to be really in front of us—a twin image, a sequence of stills, a scanning beam—we reflect on the discrepancy between information and response and remark that the artifice deceives the eye. Admittedly it is difficult to specify at any given moment where such surprise is due to physiological mechanisms and where to mistaken cognitive strategies.[16] We may also be surprised at having overlooked a misprint, or an inconsistency in a picture, as in Escher's notorious teasers.[17] Often the visual effects exploited by image makers draw on both mechanisms. An example is in front of the reader—the screen used by the makers of half-tone illustrations to which I have already referred is partly invisible, partly ignored. We look for the representation and disregard the dots as 'noise'.

Where art is concerned the surprise of 'trompe l'oeil' can be part of the pleasure; the pleasure does not lie in discovering that what we took to be a real dead duck is merely a painted one—this surely would be the cause of disappointment rather than of enjoyment—it lies in our continued feeling of incredulity that the visual effect of plumes, of gleam or softness has been achieved on a flat hard panel by a skilled hand using a brush dipped in paint. We may want to touch the panel to be quite sure there is no other trickery involved, for the visual effect is so striking as to set up a real conflict between our reaction and our better knowledge: the artist has made us see something different from what is there. He has aroused in us a visual experience of a kind that we know from our encounters with reality.

The difficulty of being more precise in describing this kind of experience stems precisely from the problem of the 'black box'. It is the recognition of this limit to introspection that makes the problem of pictorial representation both more interesting and more complex than earlier theories suggested. These theories were still based on the distinction between visual sensations and visual perception. They postulated that the artist should look into the black box and record what he saw there, and they also suggested that such a record would be processed by the beholder in the same way as it might have been by the artist if he had not trained himself to arrest this transformation. Indeed it may be claimed that much experimentation in the art of the last two centuries has been concerned with this area between the registering and the arousal of visual sensations, though the exact relation between these two activities was not necessarily clear to artists and critics. We find both effects combined in the developed theory of Impressionism, with the painter endeavouring to be absolutely faithful to his vision and to map, as it were, the visual field that extends in front of his 'innocent eye', without entering on this map anything he merely knows about the external world.[18] In doing so, however, he expects, and rightly expects, that the resulting painting would not be seen as a canvas covered with dabs and strokes, but that the understanding beholder would want to step back from the picture to eliminate these interfering messages from the picture surface and experience the sensations of light and flicker that the artist wished to arouse in him as an equivalent of his own reaction to his motif.

Two examples from the painting of our own time illustrate the way these aims have now diverged. A painting by Professor Lawrence Gowing (Fig. 149), a passionate student of Cézanne's visual researches, shows the artist carrying the Impressionist programme to its extreme. He has painted the still life as it appeared to him when he focused his eyes on a spot behind the table, thus producing the doubling of images of proximal objects and an apparent curvature of the table edge. We may say he has tried to produce a faithful map of his visual field at a given transitory moment and to enter on this map even

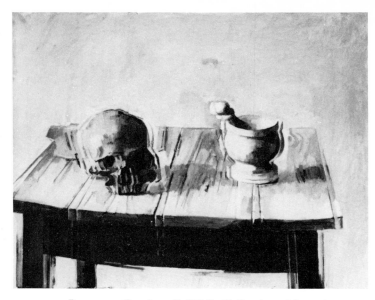

149. Lawrence Gowing: *Still Life*. Collection of the artist

the sensations we are usually set to ignore because they interfere with the perception of the external world. Such experiments[19] are of undoubted psychological and artistic interest, even though it could be argued that no artifice can ever reproduce the experience of binocular vision on a flat canvas. But there is another problem here of more general significance—it is the problem of how we should view his canvas. If we try to repeat the artist's visual experience by focusing in our turn not on the painted objects on the table but behind it, we will then see a double image of his double images. This is a paradox that arises in every case where the artist tries to register his subjective experience regardless of the one his record will arouse in the beholder. J. J. Gibson has referred to the consequences of this aim as the Greco Fallacy, alluding to the naïve belief that El Greco elongated his figures because his astigmatism distorted them in this way. If that were the whole story, his astigmatism would also have led him to seeing his painted figures distorted. Only a correctly proportioned painting would have been seen like a correctly proportioned man.[20] The painter is also his first beholder, and all he can aim at is a matching of sensations, not a mapping.

It so happens that another movement in contemporary art permits us to isolate this problem of visual sensations from the point of view of the beholder. I am referring to the experimental school known as 'op art'. These paintings are not concerned with the way the artist sees the world but with the sensations aroused by certain visual tricks resulting in flickering after-images, moiré effects and unexpected colour sensations (see Fig. 39).[21] The effects are real enough, but could they ever be registered or mapped in the way Lawrence Gowing attempted to map the effects of unfocused binocular vision?

Both Lawrence Gowing's *Still Life* and 'op art' can be interpreted as experiments to probe the limits between subjective, non-veridical visual experiences and their objective causes. They are to be welcomed precisely because these limits are often misrepresented and misunderstood. The undeniable fact that our subjective visual experience is not solely determined by the physical or optical world has frequently been used as an argument in favour of relativism and subjectivism in the theory of representation. It must be the aim of any improved theory to give subjectivism its due without making concessions to relativism. It is here, I believe, that the example of maps may prove of use.

3. OBJECTIVE STANDARDS AND SUBJECTIVE RESPONSES IN CARTOGRAPHY

Maps are normally designed to impart information about the invariant features of an area, in other words they leave 'appearances' on one side. There are no maps of Vienna in moonlight or of the museums out of focus. Nor would it be welcome if maps aroused unexpected visual sensations such as flicker. Handling a map, we are intent on the veridical perception of what is there on the piece of paper, and if we cannot see it well we take it to the light or use a magnifying glass. We speak of reading a map, and its foremost requirement is indeed that it should be easily legible in a succession of fixations. There should be no interference of the symbols with each other and each should be as distinct as possible. Where such differentiation fails the use is put in jeopardy. Only recently a printed warning was added to Ordnance Maps of Wales because some users had confused the lines marking county boundaries with lines indicating footpaths. Provided however that the distinctions are clear it would not seem to matter what key is chosen. The map of the London Underground marks the Piccadilly Line in blue and the Central Line in red; the key could have been switched round without impairing the efficiency of the display. It is true that for habitual users of the map the colours become associated with their designation. I tend to visualize these Underground lines in terms of their fortuitous colours, but this phenomenon belongs to the pathology of symbolization rather than to its logic—a pathology, however, which has never ceased to worry theologians and mystics who want to visualize the spiritual world without having their symbolic maps confused with mirror images.[22]

The question to which I am alluding goes back to Plato's *Cratylus*, which considers language in the light of the problem so dear to the Greeks—the problem of what exists by 'nature' and what by 'convention'. It is a problem which is still very much with us, but I think that in the theory of signs and of maps it has also led to a certain amount of confusion, particularly in the modern classification of 'iconic' and 'non-iconic' signs. For granted that the symbols on maps need not be iconic in the sense of being faithful representations, they are not necessarily arbitrary. We would be puzzled to find a map of London in which the parks were marked blue and the ponds green, because the other arrangement is so much easier to learn and keep in mind. It would be interesting to investigate cartographic codes from this point of view of mnemonics. A map in the Times Atlas representing temperatures in various latitudes shows the warmer regions in darker red and the cold ones blue. No doubt we could also learn the opposite code, but why not make use of these 'natural' metaphors.[23]

To the student of representational devices the history of maps offers many observations of a more general application. He can watch how simple pictographic renderings of areas with little pictures of towns and mountains become formalized through the use of a precise key, indicating what distinctions are aimed at, such as the difference between fortified and 'open' cities (Fig. 150).[24] The schematic pictures as such are not purely arbitrary, but their use becomes conventionalized in the interest of conceptual categorization.

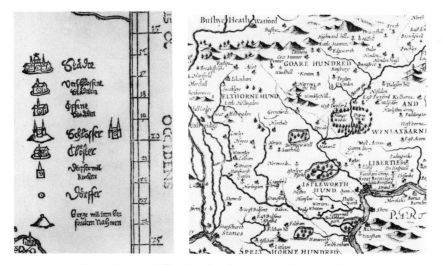

150. Key of a map of Oberlausitz of 1593 by B. Schulze (Sculetus).
From F. D. Dainville, S.J., *Le langage des géographes* (Picarol, Paris, 1964).
151. J. Norden's map of Middlesex (detail), augmented by I. Speed, 1610.
After a facsimile

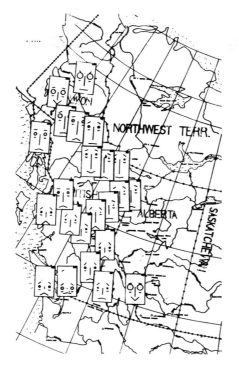

152. Map of the annual growth rhythm of *Pinus contorta* in Canada. After M. Hagner in *Studia Forestalia Suecica* (81, 1970, p. 12). Nose, lignified cells (%) (|, low;|, high); eyebrows, dry matter (%),(∨, low;∨, high); eye diameter, shoot length (%) (·,low, ⊙, high); mouth, bark colour (∧, green, ∨, brown); eye wrinkle, seedlings with terminal bud (%)(∨, low; ∨, high).

Because of the advantage that lies with easily memorized conventions, psychology enters map making by the back door, as it were. The conventionalized symbol of hills or mountains has always been a steep outline (Fig. 151), and even in modern renderings of mountain ranges we find the device of conventionally exaggerating height in relation to width by a stated amount—reflecting the tendency of our mind to overrate the vertical extension and therefore the steepness of slopes. Recent experiments in the construction of easily legible symbols have gone very far in thus trying to meet the propensities of our perceptual system. A Swedish forestry journal[25] published a survey of the annual growth rhythm of *Pinus contorta* in Canada which is coded in terms of facial expressive features 'because of the human ability to recognize several features at once if presented as part of a face' (Fig. 152). As a non-forester I find the device more amusing than enlightening precisely because the pathology of symbol-reading tends to take over again. The reaction to faces is so compelling that I find it hard to re-translate my response into the desired information.

The immediacy of this response often comes into question in debates about

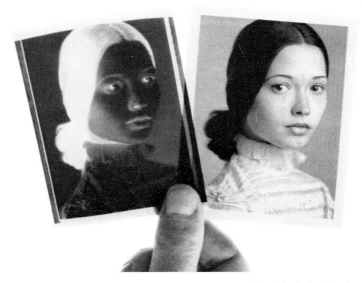

153. Negative and positive of a Polaroid pack film by Melvin Sokolsky from an
advertisement for Polaroid in *Scientific American*, January 1974

the relative share of 'nature' and 'convention' in representational devices and
in the reading of images. It is my impression that several wires tend to get
crossed in these discussions, as when it is alleged that those who have never
seen a photograph cannot decode and read it. Evidence even about this fact is
conflicting,[26] but whatever the truth of certain anecdotes, it would also have
to be asked whether any difficulty is experienced in recognizing, for instance,
toy animals made of wood or outline drawings of familiar objects,
particularly of features of immediate cultural and psychological significance.
Investigators appear to have been shy, for instance, of using erotic imagery,
though the reactions to this kind of material by the most untutored does not
appear to suggest great difficulty in learning its significance.

   It is quite true that we do not normally see our fellow creatures in black and
white, and so the notation of greys looks superficially very much like a
mapping device. But need it therefore be arbitrary? Should we not rather ask
how quickly we can pick up this kind of code and adjust to its notation?

   In any case if it were just a conventional notation the inventors of
photography would not have evolved the process of turning a negative into a
positive. It is most unlikely that it is merely our habituation which makes it
easier for us to read the latter. Granted that in looking at the negative of a
portrait we will not find it hard to interpret it either, but it turns out that for
the layman, at least, such confidence can be misplaced precisely where his
immediate reactions are engaged, as in the perception of eyes.[27] Not being a
trained photographer, I found that looking at Fig. 153, I misinterpreted the

direction of the girl's gaze on the negative where the highlights, of course, appear black while the black pupils appear white and elicit the false response.

It may sound chilling to regard the photograph of a human face as a map of its features, but we get nearer to this idea in a series of pictures recently published in the *Scientific American* which shows the systematic transposition of these gradients to establish the information generally used in physiognomic recognition.[28]

There are many media and devices in the history of art which might be illuminated by such experiments. As mentioned before, mosaic is only the simplest example of the selective information that can be encoded in a particular technique (see Fig. 120). Marquetry is another which exploits a particular range of shades for striking spatial effects.[29]

But most of all it is in the comparison of styles with mapping conventions that the historian of art may find a useful corrective to evolutionist theories. Thus the style of ancient Egypt with its rather rigid conventions has often been compared with the 'conceptual' art of children because of its remoteness from visual experience.[30] In my book on *Art and Illusion* I have proposed that it should rather be interpreted as a mapping system so admirably adapted to its purpose that it remained in force for almost 3000 years. The study of maps confirms that certain of its devices will turn up any time a particular kind of information is required. The Egyptian convention, for instance, of drawing a pond in the shape of its ground plan but men in elevation (Fig. 154) is

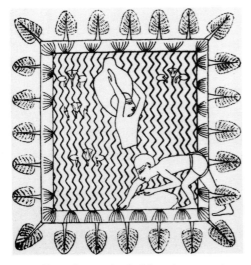

154. Egyptian method of drawing a pond.
After a painting of the New Kingdom from
H. Schäfer, *Principles of Egyptian Art*
(Oxford, 1974)

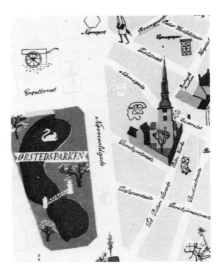

155. Tourist map of Copenhagen (detail) by
Gustav Hjortland. After R. Broby-
Johansens, *Gennem det Gamle
Kobenhaven* (Gyldendal, Copenhagen, n.d.)

universally used not only in primitive maps but also in tourist guides, because it is so easily intelligible (Fig. 155).

The example strongly indicates that the great variety of styles we encounter in the images of past and present civilizations cannot be assessed and interpreted without a clear understanding of the dominant purpose they are intended to serve. It is the neglect of this dimension which has suggested to some critics that the range of representational styles must somehow reflect a variety of ways in which the world is seen. There is only one step from this assumption to the assertion of a complete cultural relativism which denies that there are standards of accuracy in visual representation because it is all a matter of convention.

Once more it is useful at this point to refer to the example of the map. For it is hard to be completely relativistic about maps. There can be mistakes in maps which can be systematically rectified. We also know how this accuracy has been improved over the centuries—as in the case of the map of Middlesex (Fig. 151)—through the development of the technique of surveying. This technique, moreover, has nothing to do with the way the world is seen, for the surveyor who wants to map the invariant features of a region can and will never rely on that elusive guide, his visual impression of the landscape. His surveying instruments are set up in given locations at distances which can be measured, and are pointed at given natural or artificial landmarks for the purpose of triangulation. Surveying is not an easily acquired skill, but what matters here is only that the individual readings obtained when aligning a sighting instrument must be noted and held, till further data from other station points are obtained and a correct relational model of the terrain can be constructed. It does not matter by what means these locations are plotted. Modern technology has long supplemented the surveyors' visual methods by photography, radar, echo-soundings, not to mention various methods of mapping the invisible through infrared photography, X-rays or the electron-scanning microscope, which translate the information obtained into visual form for those who know the rules of transformation.[31]

There can be no doubt that the piecemeal methods of construction used in all these mapping procedures can result in an image that coincides with a visual record. Aerial pictures of cities, not to speak of the exhilarating photographs of our globe from space, turn out to look very much like the maps which were compiled in a long process of measurement and refinement over the centuries. True, we know that maps are usually projected on flat surfaces for convenience sake and that there is no way of developing a spherical surface onto a plane without a choice of evils (see Fig. 237), but this inconvenience does not contradict the observation that, knowing the

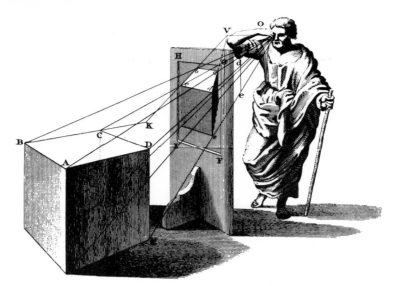

156. The visual cone. From B. Taylor,
New Principles of Linear Perspective (London, 1715)

curvature of the globe and the distance of the station point, the exact outlines of any continent from that point could have been predicted long before spacecraft and satellites enabled us to put the theory to the test.

4. Perspective: Geometrical Proof and Psychological Puzzle

The theory to which I refer is of course that of perspective, to which M. H. Pirenne's *Optics, Painting and Photography*[32] provides an authoritative guide. It is based on the fact that light is normally propagated along straight lines and that we can therefore work out for any object in space what light rays from its surface will reach a given point. This is the optical theory of the visual cone or visual pyramid which became relevant to pictorial representation in the Italian Renaissance when such a representation was first defined as a cross-section through a visual cone (Fig. 156).

This theory was developed as a response to the demands of narrative art. No longer satisfied with the hieratic assemblage of symbols through which the crucifixion of St. Peter was depicted in the fourteenth century, the public of the early fifteenth century hailed the rendering of such a scene as if the artist had actually been watching it (Figs. 157 and 158).[33]

There is no doubt that it was the ancient Greeks who first assigned to the artist this role of an imaginary eye-witness, and it is equally clear that Euclidean geometry would have provided them with the tools for working out the implication of this demand—to what extent this was actually done is,

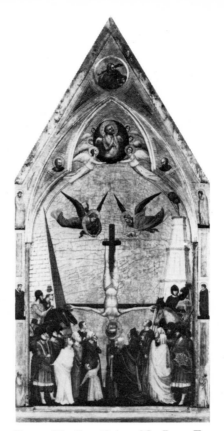

157. Giotto: *The Crucifixion of St. Peter*. From the
Stefaneschi Polyptych. Rome, Pinacoteca Vaticana

however, still a matter of debate.[34] On the other hand, the discovery or
rediscovery of the theory of perspective in the Renaissance and its spread
from fifteenth-century Florence to the rest of Europe happened in the full
light of history.[35] Though some of the geometrical implications could only be
proved in the seventeenth century, the basic assumptions are simple enough.
Given the situation envisaged in the demonstration illustrated in Fig. 156,
the conclusions follow from Euclidean geometry. The cube will in fact
present the predicted aspects on that intersection of the visual cone which the
theory demands. If proof were needed, it would be found in the modern
application of this theory to computers. Given the plan and elevation of a
building a computer can be programmed to work out what aspects the array
will present from any chosen station point.[36]

And yet it is in the assessment of perspective representation that the
approach through the theory of information has highlighted a problem which
has been strangely neglected not only by Renaissance theorists but even by
more recent commentators. Briefly, the theory was treated as if it were a

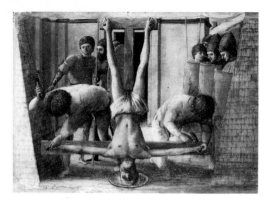

158. Masaccio: *The Crucifixion of St. Peter*. 1426.
Berlin, Staatliche Museen

mapping procedure. It was claimed that it enabled the artist to represent what has been called 'measurable space'. Yet if you have a geometrical theory you must take the geometrical consequences, and it is clear from the theory of central projection that you cannot reverse the process: while we can work out what the projection of a given three-dimensional object will be like on a given plane, the projection itself does not give us adequate information about the object concerned, since not one but an infinite number of related configurations would result in the same image (Fig. 159), just as not one but an infinite number of related objects would cast the same shadow if placed in the beam emanating from a one-point source.[37]

From a logical point of view a perspective representation, therefore, has this in common with a map that it indicates a class of objects, though a class of which only very few members would ever be known in our environment. It is even possible to formulate the problem of illusion caused by perspective representations in this way. We take one specimen of the class—the flat design on the plane in front of us—for another, the solid object over there. Indeed Renaissance artists and their successors used this indeterminacy of the view from a single station point for the construction of a visual trick of this kind—the so-called anamorphosis, a picture that looks distorted when seen head-on, but which appears to right itself when seen through a peep-hole from the side (Fig. 160).[38] The sideway view results in an illusion, not so much of a reality as of a differently oriented painting which tends to be seen as a hovering phantom.

But what is the cause of this illusion? Why do we not see the oblique panel, and why, even if we lack a cue, do we fail to notice the indeterminacy and rather assign the head a given distance and form? The question has been raised into a psychological puzzle by Adelbert Ames, the painter turned

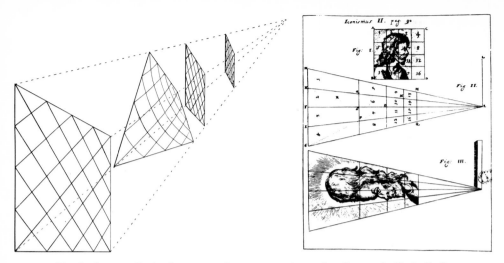

159. Equivalent configuration as seen from one station point. Drawn by B. A. R. Carter.
160. The principle of anamorphic. From Gaspar Schott, *Magia Universalis* (Würzburg, 1657).
After Baltrusaitis, *Anamorphoses* (Paris, 1955)

psychologist, who applied the principle of anamorphosis in a set of well-known demonstrations which make use of the visual cone and the peephole.[39] What is inside his box is really a criss-cross of wires and unlikely shapes, but they are so arranged that they project the same image from a station point as would a model chair, and so it is such a model chair we seem to see and not a criss-cross, however much we may be intellectually aware of the true arrangement.

These constructions confirm the theory of the visual cone and yet they have a perplexing corollary. For what is it again that makes us select out of the infinite number of possible readings just the image of the chair rather than anything else? It is tempting to invoke past experience; after all we know chairs but are unfamiliar with the random shapes that are really there. No doubt there is something in this explanation but it hardly suffices. Needless to say, the problem of how we get from sensations to perception, from the multivalent pattern of light on the retina to an image of the world out there is one of the oldest problems of psychology. It is a problem which the theory of the visual cone alone cannot solve. For in its developed form this theory states that the light rays of varying wavelength and intensity act as stimuli resulting in visual sensations. If we succeed by artifice in so treating a surface that it produces the same stimuli under a given light they must of necessity result in the identical sensations and therefore create an illusion. Granted the first step, the last is still inexplicable.

The simplest artifice for the production of such duplicate stimuli would seem to be a mirror. The mirror deflects and reflects the light emanating from objects and since we normally assume the light to have come to us along a straight path we believe we see the object behind the mirror. It is indeed tempting to compare a representation with a mirror because both can present a framed surface on which an image appears. But does it really appear on the surface of the mirror? Certainly not if we look with both eyes. Our binocular vision really fuses two different mirror images just as it fuses two different aspects of the three-dimensional world in our proximity. Leonardo da Vinci, who urged the painter to use a mirror as his standard of accuracy,[40] also knew that in this important respect no painting could emulate this trick[41]—how he would have relished the stereoscope and holograph! All the painter can do is what the normal camera does. He can match the light reflected from a surface seen from one point rather than two. But why a mirror? Except for the reversal of the image there is no difference between the view from the window seen in the mirror and the view itself, witness two views towards the Senate House from an upper floor of the Warburg Institute (Figs. 161 and 162). To match this view in paint we have simply to close one eye and scan the window with the other, tracing the outlines and then the colours on the window pane.

It is worth every time to repeat this experiment, because the result tends to be strangely surprising (Fig. 162). It turns out that the outline of Senate House on the window pane is no larger than the span of my colleague's hand and each of its windows no higher than the thickness of his fingers. This shock of surprise we tend to experience when measuring size relations in a plane such as a window pane must be attributed to the so-called 'constancies'. Since we know that we see a large building out there rather than a small patch close by, our visual experience is modified. The distant building 'looks' much larger than its projection on the nearby pane. The facts are not in doubt, but the way in which we should describe this discrepancy, or rather this surprise, is more open to questioning. The main cause of difficulty here is the term of 'apparent size' which teachers of perspective have used long before the constancies began to figure in the debate. Since by apparent size they meant projected size, we arrive at the paradox that thanks to the constancies distant objects appear to us larger than their apparent size. The formulation almost insinuates that it is our visual experience which rests on an illusion while our tracing tells us what we really see. But we need only shift our position by the window ever so slightly to question the soundness of this assertion, for as we move forward or backward by a yard or two, the view itself will remain more or less stable, but the tracing will radically change. As the hand indicates on the next picture (Fig. 163), the photographer has roughly halved the distance between camera and window pane and the outline has become much too wide. Coming nearer still (Fig. 164), it seems incredible that it should just

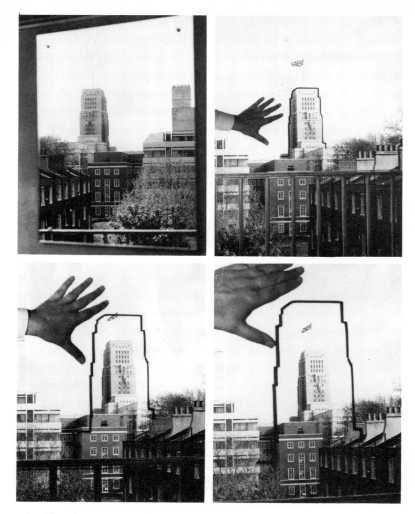

161. View from an upper floor of the Warburg Institute as seen in a mirror.
162–4. The Senate House of the University of London as traced on a window,
photographed with the camera moving closer in stages

have fitted so well. But it is precisely at this point that this surprise rather
hides than reveals to us what I have called the unsolved psychological puzzle
of perspective representation. How can we ever know that we see a distant
building and not a patch on the pane? The brief answer is that we may
sometimes not know, but merely guess. We *assign* it a distance and a size.
Take the flag waving from the top of Senate House—it does not need a lot of
imagination to turn it in your mind into a flaw on the pane, and if you have
imagination to spare you can even turn the outline into a huge scaffolding and
the hand into that of a giant. As soon as we succeed in this game of our
imagination we may in fact begin to wonder whether the 'constancies' are

rightly named. Should we not rather speak of the 'inconstancies' of the phenomenal world if the apparent size of objects in our field of vision can be so unstable as to be changed by a whim?

The way our perceptual experience can be altered by the adoption of alternative interpretations or hypotheses about what it is we see out there has often been described. Among those phenomena which attest to the plasticity of our visual reactions none is more germane to the subject in hand than Emmert's Law.[42] If we stare for a time into a bright light till an after-image forms on our retina we can observe that the apparent size of this luminous patch will differ dramatically according to the distance we assign to it. Look at a book in your hands and the image will only cover a few lines of print, lift your eyes to the distant wall opposite and it will appear to grow to the size of a large picture. It is possible even to train oneself to do without such external props and to change the size of the image while keeping one's eyes closed, merely by imagining it to lie at various distances. Apparent size seems indeed to depend on the arbitrary assignment of a distance.[43]

Maybe it is not too difficult to account for this vagary of perception if we remember the multivalence of the visual cone. In terms of the theory of surveying we may say that the stationary eye gives us only a preliminary reading, since we need at least two to plot a point on the map. The situation would be analogous to an incomplete instruction about the location on a map of a particular building, indicating, for instance, only the letters of the grid but not the numbers. Such inadequate information would indeed tell us, as does the visual cone, in what zone to look for the item, but not on what square. Given other sources of information, even such an incomplete message could narrow down our search and lead to a hypothesis about the location of the item to which we might hold on in the absence of convincing alternatives. We thus achieve a constancy *pro tem* though not one that is anchored in valid evidence. This, maybe, is what we are compelled to do in the constraining situation of monocular stationary vision where we are under the compulsion to adopt any one reading, however unsupported by collateral clues. I have argued in *Art and Illusion*[44] that here Popper's analogy between scientific procedures and such hypothesis formation is particularly enlightening, for it can be claimed that one of the criteria for the selection of such a tentative visual interpretation is the comparative ease with which it could be disconfirmed. This, indeed, may be the value of that principle of simplicity that pervades our perceptual processes and that has been so thoroughly explored by the Gestalt school of psychology. A 'simple' hypothesis is one that can most easily come into conflict with complex facts. Thus I believe it to be a result of this strategy that in the absence of contrary indications we regard the orientation of shapes in our field of vision as normal to the line of sight.[45] This applies to after-images no less than to views through peepholes or even windows where there are no contrary clues. The frame or scaffolding into which we can playfully turn the outline of Senate House would take on this orientation unless we made an extra effort. But of course none of these readings we might tentatively adopt as alternatives of the view through the window would stand up to reality tests in a real situation. We need only shift our position ever so slightly for the effects of movement parallax to come into play. The forms on the window would detach themselves and refute any interpretation that made them part of the distant view.

5. PERSPECTIVE REPRESENTATION AND PERCEPTUAL INVARIANTS

The relative helplessness of the single stationary eye has in fact led J. J. Gibson of Cornell University to propose a fresh start to the theory of visual perception.[46] He is no doubt right in stressing that we were not endowed with eyes by evolution so that we may look through peepholes or window panes at multivalent shapes. We have two eyes and these permit us to begin the process of triangulation at the first glance as far as proximal objects are concerned. Moreover, we are normally moving through the world and mapping our environment through a continuous series of readings of changing aspects. From this point of view the geometry of the visual cone is much less relevant to perception than are the changing aspects of forms in motion, which give us all the information about the invariant features of the world out there we may need. Coming to a lecture room (Fig. 165) you may first receive a vague mental picture of a space and then use your eyes to modify and refine this map by entering some of the features that concern you. You may look for a seat and have no visual or logical problem in plotting its location on your cognitive map, for as you move your eyes and yourself the vista changes in a way to which only the film camera could do justice. In Gibson's view this changing vista provides us with quite unambiguous information about the lay-out of the hall, indeed he has gone so far as to maintain that we are programmed to pick up these invariants, the map, from the stream of information which hardly obtrudes on our awareness. From this point of view, therefore, the so-called constancies present no problem. I see all the chairs in the row as being of the same size because they are the same size whatever momentary pattern of light they may reflect onto my two retinas.

Gibson's insistence on the perception of the invariants of our environment is of interest to the student of representation because it helps to explain why

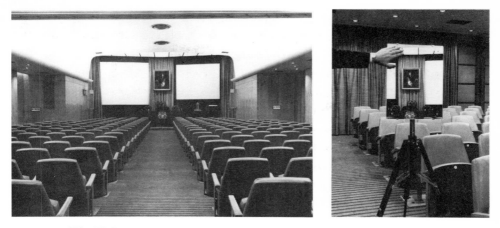

165. The Wellcome Lecture Hall of the Royal Society.   166. The portrait of the
Society's founder and the dais of the Lecture Hall photographed in a mirror

most pictorial styles of the past contain such a strong element of mapping or what are called conceptual features. Perspective had to be reasoned out and has to be learned, it cannot be discovered by the eye alone, unaided by measurements in the plane. Hence it looks once more as if the apparent size of which teachers of perspective speak was no more than a myth. If we follow Gibson the world appears to us as it is, not as it appears traced on a window pane.

But precisely because of his radicalism Gibson also poses fresh problems for the student of representation. For he has brought out the tremendous difference between our experience of the visible world and the appearance of a picture.[47] The photograph, as I said, resembles a frozen mirror image—indeed I brought a mirror into the lecture hall of the Royal Society to do justice to the title of this lecture (Fig. 166). The laws of optics and geometry would enable you to work out exactly where the camera was placed to record the information about the portrait of the Society's founder, Charles II, and its position. If it could be traced on the surface and matched with pigments it would be an accurate representation in reverse of the end of the hall. But we have seen how vulnerable such a view would be to that kind of movement which Gibson stressed as indispensable to perception. Shift your position and you alter the image. Even within the assumptions of perspective theory, therefore, the painting could only claim to replicate the appearance of the hall from the exact point where the camera stood. Yet we disregard this fact when looking at photographs or perspective renderings.[48] Indeed we could not show such representations on the screens of our lecture halls if they were as volatile as mirror images, for every member of the audience must see them differently. Why is it that such pictures are so resistant to anamorphosis that they tend to right themselves? Perhaps we come nearer to an answer if we think of maps. A map would also become foreshortened when seen from the side, and so would the printed page of a book, but we are not disturbed by these changing aspects because we see them as they are—or, to use a less radical terminology, because of the constancies. Up to a point we read perspective pictures as if they were maps, but we have also learned that as maps they would be highly unsatisfactory. There is no key, only assumptions to guide us. The picture of the hall (Fig. 165) could also be taken to represent a very unusual and inconvenient space, one in which the floor is slanting upwards towards the dais, while the real chairs diminish in size so that only children could use the front row. Glancing back at Fig. 159 we would even have to admit that the walls and boundaries of the hall might be cunningly curved while yet looking straight from one viewing point. Once we have prised loose our reading, we must admit that any number of model halls could be constructed all of which would result in the same keyhole picture and therefore in the same multivalent map.

But this is manifestly not how we experience the picture. We might say that on the contrary it compels a reading by means of a visual effect that is almost as strong as are the physiological reactions to the stereoscope, the cinema camera or the television screen. Remembering the terminology I then proposed, I would claim that the picture creates an illusion. Not an illusion of reality, to be sure, but an illusion that can be assessed by the surprise we feel when we compare what is there with our visual experience. One of these surprise effects is often exploited by guides to galleries—it concerns the apparent shift in orientation of the objects represented. It is a fair guess that anybody in the hall will see the gangway between the seats as oriented towards him, an effect which points to the limits of the constancies and the difference between the picture and the map. The element of anamorphosis takes us unaware, we do not notice to what extent the arrangement in the plane has shifted and we assign this shift to the represented array.[49]

More than that. It can be shown that even when we look at a photograph there is a tendency to assign different distances to the images of different objects and thereby to change their 'apparent size' (see Fig. 6).[50] The head of my colleague at the end of the hall fills the same area in the plane as do the number plates under the seats in the first row (Fig. 167). It is easy to demonstrate this fact by repeating one of these number plates by the side of the head on the panel of the door. But the result of this transplantation is only that now the plate, too, looks much larger than in its original setting. If that is so, it follows that even a simple photograph produces an illusion, that is an unexpected visual experience: an experience we find surprising because it is

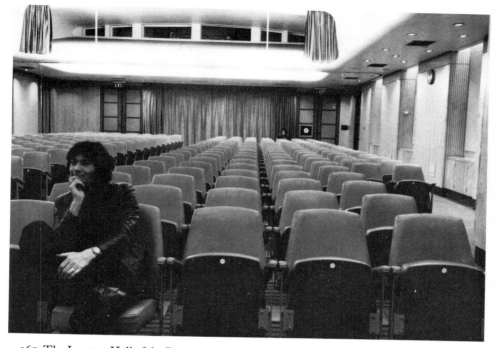

167. The Lecture Hall of the Royal Society, with a front seat number plate repeated on the door at the back of the Hall

manifestly non-veridical, as when we are shown identical shapes in a perspective setting and are led to misjudge their relative size (Fig. 168 and see Fig. 6). I have a protracted friendly debate with Richard Wollheim[51] about the nature and strength of these illusions since I obviously find it less easy than he does to counteract the pull of virtual depth in pictures. I am all the more happy to find that efforts have been made by Richard Gregory[52] and Kenneth Adams[53] to measure these deviations from projected size. I am most interested in their procedures, though I confess that I am not quite sure yet what it is they measure. Is it a perceptual compulsion or a habitual reading? We would need more studies of the variables which come into play here. To what extent does familiarity of objects represented or of representational media influence the experience? What effect would it have if we reversed the picture, turned it sideways or upside down? How do colour photographs compare with black and white ones, what are the artifices available to painters which can either strengthen or counteract this effect which they no longer welcome?

Where pictorial devices can fairly well replicate a visual experience as in the cinema, the effect may well be strongest. Even stills may contain more indications of the perceptual invariants than we usually give them credit for. One of them, as Gibson[54] and his disciples have rightly stressed, derives from

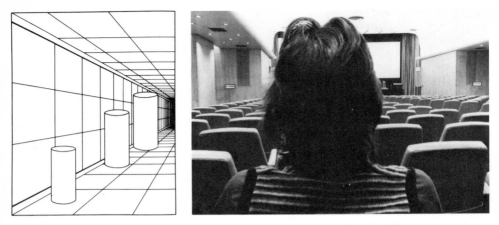

168. Three identical shapes in a perspective setting. After J. J. Gibson,
The Perception of the Visual World (Boston, 1950).
169. Close-up of a head in the Lecture hall of the Royal Society

texture gradients, that is from the visible microstructure of surfaces such as a carpet or wall covering. It is here that the 'simplicity hypothesis' will serve us in good stead, for the assumption of uniformity in grain and texture is so safe a bet in normal circumstances that we can take it as a cue for depth.

Now the painter can certainly not replicate this texture gradient in his medium, but he can suggest it in another order of magnitude, and this suggestion, too, will tend to have a comparable effect. How is it with line drawings? We are back at the problem of representational conventions, where views are most in flux.[55] It used to be said that there are no lines in nature and that outlines are therefore a human creation, a mapping device. But here, as in the case of photographs in black and white, we must be careful lest we fly in the face of the evidence. In a stimulating book, *A Psychology of Picture Perception*,[56] Professor John M. Kennedy has argued vigorously against the view that the understanding of outlines has to be learned like any other code. The experimental and observational material he has collected to show that not only young children and untutored tribes but even animals accept outline drawings without training is certainly impressive. He speaks of the surrogate function of outlines as indicators of visual discontinuities. Julian Hochberg has argued,[57] independently I believe, that one of these discontinuities is of special significance. Outlines can serve as predictors of the effect of movement parallax, for objects within our reach will always detach themselves from their background but cohere internally if we move our head ever so slightly. Maybe there are other compensatory devices which import an element of mapping even into perspective renderings from one station point. One of them may well be the convention of holding the camera level. It does not correspond with our habits when we look around in the world, but in real life it is our sense of balance which gives us the indispensable coordinate of the plumb-line. When we are deprived of this aid the parallelism of uprights provides a substitute which gives us comfort, though we can do without it, as we can do without outlines (see Fig. 210).

Who knows whether response to perspective convergence is not of similar importance in our reaction to representations? This, at any rate, is what Richard Gregory[58] would make us expect in his explanation of the Müller-Lyer and other illusions. If he is right the arousal of illusions in photographs of this kind may be as deep-rooted as is the illusion of movement on the television screen. The trick had to be reasoned out and tried, but it stuck because it worked. It has seemed to me for some time in any case that the discussion of perspective has got too much entangled with the psychological problems of apparent size and subjective sensations. Richard Wollheim and I may slightly differ about the size we assign to the head of the person in the last row. We are sure to agree what happens to us when we ourselves sit behind that head (Fig. 169). Since it is not transparent it occludes the hall and how much of it it occludes from any given point can be worked out with ease from a knowledge of central projection.

6. Objectivity and Indeterminacy

It may be worth dwelling for a moment on what I have called this objective aspect of the theory of perspective, the possibility of working out not how things will appear to me from a given station point, but what things cannot appear to me at all because they will be occluded at that point.[59] I asked an artist to construct a little box which resembles the Ames demonstration, though its purpose is a little different (Figs. 170 and 171). Seen from the viewing point, the three schematic trees appear as one, though objectively

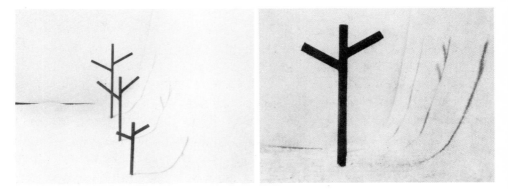

170. Demonstration box: three schematic trees and their shadows (constructed by H. King).
171. The same as Fig. 170, photographed through a peephole

they differ not only in size, but as far as the middle one is concerned, also in shape and orientation. The first point I want to stress is that this objective fact of occlusion is quite unaffected by the subjective appearance. It is quite irrelevant to this demonstration whether the viewer is astigmatic or even whether he looks through the peephole through a distorting lens. More surprising perhaps, it is also irrelevant whether he looks at the trees straight on, or whether he tries to roll his eyes to gaze in a different direction. Certainly if he does, the image will get blurred but there will be no movement parallax and no other tree will come into view.[60] Naturally the situation will change if he turns his head rather than his single eye, for then he sees the arrangement from a different angle and the two other trees will emerge. He may also see them indirectly as it were, if they cast strong shadows which indicate their presence, and given a strong texture gradient he will be able to estimate their distance. In other words, his knowledge may again influence his visual experience. Our box could possibly be used to investigate this tendency from yet another angle. If we allowed our subjects to inspect and to handle the box before applying their eye to the peephole they would be likely to be influenced in their experience by the information they have. Thus removing the foremost tree in their presence might lead to an alteration in the apparent size of the silhouette despite the fact that the retinal image has remained constant. If this prediction could be confirmed it would suggest a generalization of Emmert's Law discussed above. As in the case of Emmert's Law and germane phenomena we would also expect that the apparent orientation of the tree seen through the peephole would remain normal to the line of vision despite the fact that the real orientation of the branches is irregular, unless our memory, or contrary indications due to illumination, make us revise our spontaneous hypothesis.

It is true that in this and in some other respects our model box can present no more than a partial analogue to a real situation which allows free scope to binocular vision and accommodation, but the analogue may still be instructive because these and similar helps let us down with an increase of distance or a decline in illumination as at dusk.

I have chosen trees for this little demonstration precisely because unlike halls, chairs and even people they come in all sizes and orientations and offer little scope for the use of past experience. They therefore constitute good material for testing Gibson's claims for the information we receive through the eye. Take photographs first. How much can we in fact tell about that tree in the courtyard of the Warburg Institute (Fig. 172)? Could anyone have predicted even approximately what the view of the same tree would turn out to be when photographed from above (see Fig. 173)?

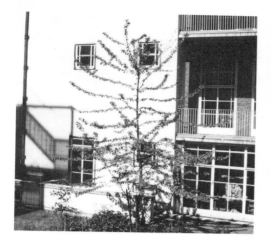

172. Tree in the courtyard of
the Warburg Institute

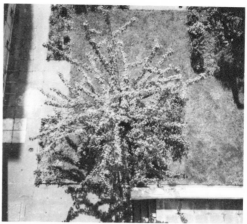

173. The same tree as in Fig. 172,
photographed from above

It seems to me that such simple questions are surprisingly rarely asked. True, members of primitive tribes are occasionally grilled by anthropologists about their reading of spatial relations in pictures,[61] but the same interviewers show less curiosity about the precise limits of their own interpretation of photographs. What one would like to see is a systematic comparison between the informative values of a photograph, a stereoscopic picture, a moving picture and that of the real view when seen from a given station point either through a peephole or in free-ranging vision. All we would have to do is to ask subjects more searching questions than, I take it, J. J. Gibson[62] asked, in front of a photo mural of an area they knew from experience. We might even ask them to attempt wire models of trees or, best of all, to sketch maps of the whole area they see in front of them, preferably under various conditions of illumination and visibility.

Such tests are likely to confirm the degree to which we account for our perceptions of the physical world in terms of 'universals'. We identify 'a' mountain, 'a' tree, 'a' house, as if we were reading a map, and we attribute to these objects qualities and spatial relationships of a general nature allowing much latitude to subsequent adjustments. We only feel we have made a mistake if what we took for a house turns out to be a stone or what we described as a blue flower turns out to be white. This cognitive map, moreover, is always likely to react back on our visual experience. We rarely have occasion to compare notes about all the details of such an experience, but if we did it is likely that we would be surprised at the range of interpretations the same sight can evoke.

Once this is established we can be more specific about the demands we can make on what we call a faithful rendering of the scene. Far from forcing us to adopt any one of these various interpretations, such a representation should afford the same range of interpretations as does the real scene. This range would of necessity also include the correct one, though we might never know without external aids where along the continuum of readings it is to be found.

I hope this rather laborious way of describing a very commonplace thing such as a picture postcard may pay some dividends in clarifying the issues on which so many arguments in the theory of representation have turned. It is undeniable for instance that a distant mountain looks subjectively both larger and steeper than its tracing on the window pane would suggest. No wonder it has been claimed that only a record of this subjective experience can communicate to us what the artist really saw.[63] But here as always we must beware of the 'Greco Fallacy'. When one of Whistler's students claimed she only painted what she saw he gravely replied: 'But the shock will come when you see what you paint.' There is more psychological wisdom in this witticism than in many books on art.

Even leaving art on one side and speaking of picture postcards, it must be expected that a view of Zermatt which exaggerates the height and slope of the Matterhorn would lead us to overrate its soaring quality even more, so that if we now copied this view and our copy were copied again we would soon produce a fantasy landscape. The tracing or photograph on the other hand, may possibly cause us a fleeting disappointment, but if it were placed in the right setting, say as the backdrop of an illusionistic stage, it should ideally result in the same visual experience as does the real view.

It is the advantage of the informational approach that it allows us to sort out these issues without falling into relativism. Let us return here to the view of the Vienna Museum as seen in the morning haze (Fig. 147). Gibson is certainly right in reminding us of the value of light and texture in gaining a great deal of information about the foreground array. Moreover, there is our awareness of what he calls 'ecological optics', the behaviour of things in our world. The figure of the man striding on the path would prevent us from misinterpreting the brighter strip as a wall standing normal to the line of sight as we might otherwise do. But the same principle of simplicity asserts itself more strongly in the case of the trees, for there is nothing much in these silhouettes which clearly indicates the orientation of branches and twigs and so we read them more or less as stage props without really taking them to be flat. What seems to me noteworthy here is not so much the limit of information at our disposal, which is natural enough, as our reaction to these limits. Jerome Bruner[64] has spoken in this connection of 'gating'. We do not normally ask questions in perception to which we cannot expect any answers.

Just as we have learned not to reach for the moon, so we do not fret about information which is excluded from the situation we recognize. This resignation of course is called for when our eyes reach a distance where change of focus, binocular disparity, texture gradients and even movement parallax yield progressively little return. All we have at our disposal here is the information contained in the light and this information is not particularized. It does not yield to the reality tests which Gibson has shown to play such a part in our dealings with the stage of our actions. The backdrop to this stage remains an unsubstantial world of 'appearances' to which Gibson's radical realism cannot be applied. It is here, indeed, that the phenomenal world, the distant blue hills and snow-capped peaks, the clouds and the gleam of the ocean are perceived in the way in which we perceive not a map but a painting.

It would be interesting to find out to what an extent the habit of taking up a purely contemplative, aesthetic attitude towards such prospects is culturally determined by our exposure to landscape paintings and photographs. Maybe members of a nomadic tribe who have to scrutinize the distant horizon for landmarks experience such sights in a very different way. We may recapture something of this difference when we watch our own response to a distant prospect of familiar scenery, or even of a view we have just examined through binoculars.[65] It is then that we will come to realize that our healthy refusal normally to scrutinize the distant view for precise information about the size and orientation of its components tends to give it the misleading appearance of a static and unalterable phenomenon. We have the illusion that this view at any rate is 'given' to us, and that it allows us to watch our visual sensations 'neat' as it were. A little effort at introspection will disabuse us of this thought, which hides from us the very flexibility of appearances which it has been my purpose to bring out in this discussion. Both in reality and in pictures we can, if we so wish, see these distant phenomena in various ways. They can acquire all the plasticity and variability that belong to our unconfirmable visual hypotheses. We can play at Emmert's Law with the indeterminate clouds in the sky and with the fading mountain ranges. After a little training in visual gymnastics we can make them take on a subtly different appearance according to the shapes and relations we tentatively attribute to them.

I realize that my contention that our visual world is much less definite and stable than it is often supposed to be, and that it should rather be described as slightly elastic at the edges, is likely to arouse not only scepticism but even resistance. It is not hard to see the roots of such discomfort. For it must be granted that our aim will always be to see a stable world since we know the physical world to be stable. Where this stability fails us, as in an earthquake, we may easily panic, for we appear to lose the cognitive anchorage we need in our effort after meaning.

I believe, however, that the nature of this anchorage changes as we leave the proximal world with which we interact and scan the distance. I have suggested in the preceding essay[66] that we may have to return here to a distinction much discussed at the turn of the century. At that time artists such as the sculptor Adolf von Hildebrand became critical of Impressionism and stressed the importance of 'tactile values' in our perception of the immediate environment. Gibson has shown us why this appeal to other sense modalities is somewhat redundant in accounting for proximal vision. But where lies the limit between this world which we see as it is and the world which we can only conjecture? I have suggested that there can be no such limit, but that the visual hypothesis with which we respond to distant impressions will tend towards certain characteristics, such as the prevalence of the simplicity principle. Where all other information lets us down we adopt the provisional assumption of objects silhouetted normal to our line of vision, with the consequence that this limit of our environment will assume the form of a dome enclosing the stage of our actions. It is this limit which proves particularly flexible. It may enclose us at dusk, and recede on a clear day or after the use of a telescope.

7. WHY APPEARANCES CANNOT BE MAPPED

I should like to propose that this variability of distant vision has an important bearing on a problem that has bedevilled the discussion of representation for a long time. I mean the quarrel about the curvature of the phenomenal world.[67] Neither the sky that vaults over us nor the horizon that surrounds our vista is straight. How can we claim, therefore, that the theory of the visual cone with its isomorphic projection of planes onto parallel planes correctly represents the phenomenal world of our experience? I have indicated before that I find it difficult to give a clear operational meaning to the concept of phenomenal size or shape, as distinct from real size and shape which can be measured or mapped. And I should like to propose that the source of that unending quarrel rests on a confusion between the mirror and the map.

Before the psychology of perception was ever thought of, the ancient Greeks realized the problem to which I am alluding. It was they who coined the phrase of 'saving the appearances' in relation to the appearance of the stars. I have postulated that saving the appearances is what we are always concerned with when faced with the indeterminacy of the single view point. What we see can and indeed must be consonant with an infinite variety of

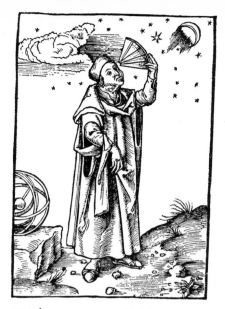

174. An astronomer with his quadrant.
From Sebastian Münzer, *Organum Uranicum* (Basle, 1536)

possibilities out there, between which we cannot decide on the visual evidence alone. From this point of view the starry heavens may be described as a gigantic Ames experiment which nature has set up for man. Falling back on the simplicity principle we assign the luminous dots a tentative place and order in the sky normal to the line of sight. This expedient allows us even to turn the apparent constellations into pictures of things, but we also know perfectly well that their real configuration in space must remain unknown to us as long as we rely on the naked eye alone.

The early astronomers who wished to map the heavens certainly lacked the resource of parallax. They used the method of alignment with their quadrants (Fig. 174), but they had to be satisfied with the relative position of the stars on an imaginary sphere. In other words they measured the visual angle a constellation subtends because that is all they could measure with the means at their disposal. It seems immensely plausible to go on from there and to say the phenomenal size depends on the visual angle, yet this is precisely the moment when we must watch our step.[68] Like all measurements from one station point the visual angle provides us with information of an infinite class of things in space and here as always this geometrical fact is masked from us by our tendency to fill the void in our knowledge by a general hypothesis. The vault of heaven, to repeat, is such an assigned distance, not phenomenally very precise or rigid, but coherent enough to create a puzzle.

A diagram of the situation should make it clear how I propose to settle this conflict (Fig. 175). One set of lines points to a number of stars which can be

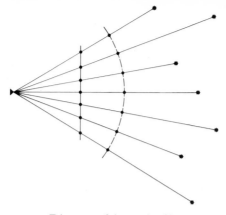

175. Diagram of the vault of heaven

aligned by moving the quadrant by 15 degrees. Having no further information about their real distance we hold them, as it were, along those first readings at an approximately similar distance, that is on the imaginary vault of heaven on which the assigned distances from star to star will be the same. If we want to match this appearance we need the spherical surface of a stellar globe, for on a flat map of the heavens the configuration would of course be distorted, much as geographical maps of the surface of the earth become distorted. But this elementary consequence of projective geometry by no means invalidates the theory of perspective which postulates that a row of equidistant objects aligned parallel to the picture plane will project as equidistant shapes on our window pane (Fig. 162). To repeat, projection cannot tell us what is out there, only what might be out there.

Instead of marking the apparent configuration of these stars on a drawing surface, we might exchange our pencil against a needle. If, as I have argued, perspective can be interpreted as the geometrical theory of visibility and occlusion of light reaching a given station point (ignoring the complications of refraction through the atmosphere), we should be able to clarify by means of a simple arrangement some of the issues which separate the views of the 'straightliners' from those of the 'curvilinearists'. The claim of the former would seem to imply that a series of equidistant lights (stellar or terrestial) would be visible through equidistant openings in a flat screen held parallel to their array. Here the limiting factors would only be the lateral foreshortening of the holes with increasing distance from the centre and the thickness of the perforated board. If we bent the screen into a hollow sphere, however, the same lights would immediatly disappear from sight, though the other limitations would not interfere with any other lights coming into view.

Of course the experiment would demand a fixed monocular viewing point, which seems a particularly artificial restraint when scanning the heavens. But

I think that trying some such experiment would also show why the comparison between the phenomenal vault of heaven and the solid globe is in any case misleading. Since the sky is the result of a vague hypothesis it is much less determinate than we tend to think—in any case the notorious moon illusion reminds us that it is not imagined as a perfect hemisphere.[69]

I should like to propose that what goes for the sky applies also to the distant panorama from a mountain top. No doubt the horizon is round because the earth is round. No doubt also that we can point in any direction and identify a particular peak. It is easy to imagine a tracing of that view on the inside of a spherical glass dome. Guide books sometimes print such panoramas as the one from the Gornergrat in Switzerland (Fig. 176). Going up we can confirm the accuracy of the horizon line, but find the foreground features distorted.

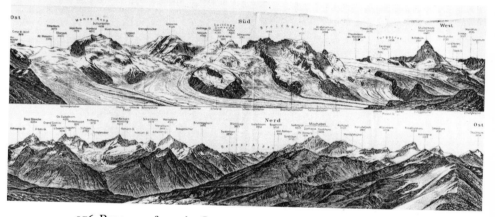

176. Panorama from the Gornergrat. After Baedeker's *Switzerland*

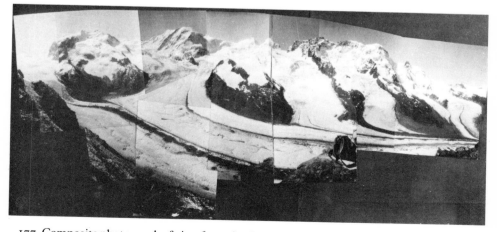

177. Composite photograph of view from the Gornergrat. Photographed by Ilse Gombrich

How, then, can we justify taking our cameras up to the Gornergrat and making a succession of snapshots, claiming them to represent the view correctly? If we take a succession of such views and paste them together (Fig. 177), they will again fail to fit. We must arrange them in a fan-like fashion and we have to choose which horizontal line we want to cohere. Could we ask for a better proof of the conventionality of the single perspective view or the snapshot? In my opinion this argument rests on the same confusion as does the argument about the vault of heaven. What a picture can show us objectively is what lies behind what when we look out into the landscape. The further we move into the distance the less do we guess or want to guess about the real lay-out. The chain of the Alps as seen from a plane on the flight to Zurich looks indeed like an apparition, merging with the sky, but this apparition does not tell us anything of directions and occlusions, it is a highly multivalent configuration which I can see both as straight or curved because I cannot tell how the mountains are really arranged. I can tell even less if I keep my gaze fixed in one direction, for peripheral vision is even more indeterminate. We are back at the problem of what mountains look like while we do not look at them.

Books on perspective rarely dwell on the very narrow limits of foveal vision, because their topic is geometry, not psychology. Instead they frequently discuss certain somewhat unexpected consequences of the geometry of central projection onto a plane which increase with the width of the angle on either side of the line of sight.[70] A row of identical columns, for instance, will represent the outer ones as thicker than the ones close to the centre, just as spheres will only project as circles when placed in the line of vision but will project as ovals of increasing flatness the further they are removed from the centre.

I have tried to analyse the geometrical reasons for this effect in *Art and Illusion*[71] and have emphasized that it cannot be used as an argument against the isomorphism of parallel planes. Unlike spheres, circular wire hoops parallel to the picture plane would not project as ovals but as circles. The disconcerting effect of solid columns or spheres is merely due to their extensions beyond the plane and our inability to distinguish their various aspects. Once more I would contend that the surprise that is felt about these consequences of the theory of perspective rests on a confusion of the mirror with the map. In maps we want identicals to show as identical regardless of the angle from which we happen to look at them. It is different with the projected image. All the theory claims, and rightly claims, is that it records the multivalent information the single eye would receive when placed at the apex of the 'visual pyramid'. What else can we ask for?

The malaise caused by the effect of wide-angle views indicates, however, that we do want something else. We want perspective representations to share certain characteristics with maps. In other words, we do not want them to function only in peep-boxes for monocular viewing from a fixed point, but to convey their information much as maps do to the moving and scrutinizing eye. Now even pictures taken at a normal angle extend beyond the area of foveal vision unless we look at them from an unreasonable distance. Hence they, too, do not replicate the visual information received at a single glance, but are read sequentially as an account of what was visible to the scanning eye from a given point. We have seen (page 198) that this attitude to pictorial representations makes them nearly as resistant to anamorphosis as the printed page.

If the lateral distortions which are inseparable from central projection cause us discomfort in reading such pictures, this is due to the fact stressed by Gibson that we are unaware of our retinal sensations while we scan the environment for its invariant features. No wonder mapping styles are easier to learn and that alternatives to central perspective remain of interest to artists and engineers.[72]

Geometrically a wide-angle photograph is neither more nor less correct than one taken with a normal focal length. The difference is one of psychology. The photograph of the two museums facing each other across the square with which I opened this enquiry (Fig. 144) is certainly informative, but to those who know the situation it may look odd, for there is no point from which we could take in both without turning our heads. True, if the architecture of the city allowed it (which it does not), we could take up a station point far enough to see both buildings at one glance, but from that point the façades towards the square would be much more steeply foreshortened. And yet I can see no advantage in adopting an alternative system of representation. To introduce curvature in order to indicate the effect of turning my head seems to me to destroy the informational value of the wide-angle photograph without adequate compensation. The photograph, corresponding to central projection, gives me the information that certain lines are straight and that parallel planes are isomorphic. Of course if I turn my head, the line that has just projected at a certain length will be stretched or shortened on the projection plane, but mercifully the elasticity of our visual experience does not extend to this incessant transformation of the optical world. Far from seeing straight lines bend and contract while we turn our head we use these evolutions for the perception of their invariant shape.

Even so, one champion of a curvilinear system of perspective, R. Hansen, has accused me of dogmatism.[73] He assures his readers that he can make them

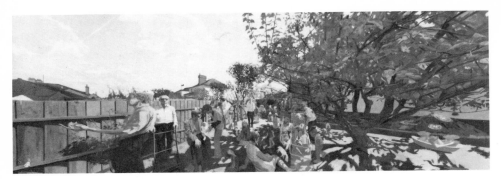

178. John Wonnacott: *The Family*. 1973–4. Courtesy of the artist and the Royal Academy

see the walls and doors of their rooms curve as they move their heads from left to right and back again. I would not want to be dogmatic here, for I have no doubt that he can so see them. What I doubt is only his contention that this possibility reveals to us what we 'really' see. Mr. Hansen, of course, is in excellent company in the belief that our visual experience is uniquely correlated to the optical world which it is his business to map. It so happens, however, that a great biologist, Erich von Holst,[74] used very similar diagrams but came to the opposite conclusion. In an important paper on the 'Active functions of human visual perception' he asks precisely why we do *not* see our walls curving and our rooms tapering. His answer, which is partly indicated by his title, includes a reminder of the fact that the eye does not register impressions during saccadic movements and that we therefore do not normally experience that continuous displacement which Mr. Hansen has taught himself and his disciples to observe. Mr. Hansen's world, in other words, is even more elastic than mine and infinitely more so than Gibson's, but he regards this rubbery world as more real than the stable world about which we seek information both in reality and from pictures.

I agree, however, that it would be dogmatic to deny the psychological and artistic interest of this chase after appearances. Lawrence Gowing's attempt (Fig. 148) to catch and to map his sensations in unfocused vision is a case in point. Contrary to a widespread prejudice, painters of our day continue to be fascinated by the elusive questions of what we really see. We need only pay a visit to the Summer Exhibitions at the Royal Academy to see many such experiments. A painting by Mr. John Wonnacott (Fig. 178) deals precisely with the problem of wide-angle vision and its consequences. It shows the painter's family in the garden; near the centre of the field of vision the figures and objects are undistorted, but the closer we come to the margin, the more the painter has used the technique of anamorphosis, pulling the shapes apart and curving the fence to compensate for the fact that his picture is flat and his

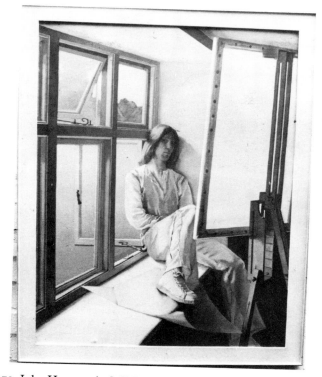

179. John Hopwood: *Self-Portrait.* 1974. Courtesy of the artist

horizon round. It would be interesting to put his large canvas into a peep-show and to experiment with the result of foreshortening it through a swivelling eyepiece held close to the picture. Obviously Mr. Wonnacott regards it as his task to map the optical world rather than his experienced world as uncompromisingly as he can. The self-portrait by Mr. John Hopwood (Fig. 179) does the same, though in a less startling way. He takes the mirror theory at its word and shows us the kind of apparent distortion which certainly follows from projective geometry once we choose a very close station point. The question whether or not Mr. Wonnacott or Mr. Hopwood really saw their motifs like that is less easily answered. Gibson would certainly deny it, for within our immediate world of action the invariants win every time over our momentary retinal image. I find it hard when using my hands to remain aware at the same time of the way their apparent size grows and shrinks in my field of vision. But before dismissing such experiments as misguided, consider the way such effects can gain meaning and urgency as soon as our emotional reactions become involved, as in these two memorable images of menace (Fig. 180) and of welcome bounty (Fig. 181).

Maybe that is the point from which this review of representation should

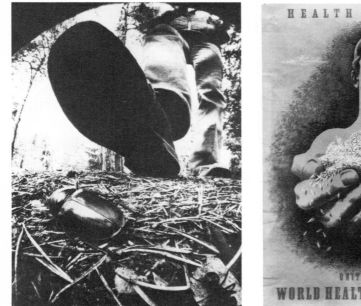

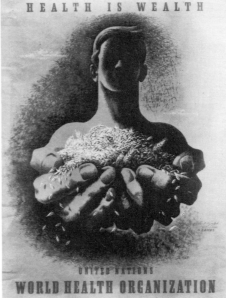

180. *Beetle and Boot.*
From E. and A. Dyring,
Synligt och osynligt (Stockholm, 1973)

181. Abram Games: *Health is Wealth.*
Poster for WHO. 1954–5.
Courtesy of the artist

have started, but then it might never have come to an end. For our reaction to the visible world is not primarily cognitive. We can be triggered by an infinite combination of stimuli. Ethologists have shown the way such reactions can be explored by the systematic variation of dummies which act on the internal release mechanisms of animals. We are daily subjected to a battery of such experiments trying to arouse our appetites, our anxieties or our curiosity by ever fresh inventions of visual images combining realistic photography with the weirdest distortions and the most unexpected symbolism. How is it human beings can be expected to respond to such a range of devices? Is it not precisely because we always use our eyes to explore, to search, to seek and to avoid at the slightest hint? These reactions, as I have said, are largely outside the range of our introspection, but they can be manipulated and even made conscious through artifice. It is sometimes said that images teach us to see. This is a pardonable over-simplification, but images may indeed teach us to recognize and specify a visual and emotional effect which has always been present in our experience. The search for these effects is much older than the science of psychology. It is known as the history of art.

Experiment and Experience in the Arts

IT SEEMS to me a pleasant fancy to imagine that no event in this world ever disappears without trace, and that even the words spoken in a particular room continue to reverberate, ever more slightly, long after their audible echoes have faded. If that were true, a supersensitive instrument might still be able to pick up the resonance of words spoken in this very hall a little less than 142 years ago in what I imagine to have been a vigorous Suffolk accent, very different from mine. 'Painting is a science'—you would hear the voice say—'and should be pursued as an inquiry into the laws of Nature. Why, then, may not landscape painting be considered as a branch of natural philosophy, of which pictures are but the experiments?' The artist who was thus appealing to the *genius loci* of this place was John Constable (Fig. 182) and the occasion the last of four lectures he gave at the Royal Institution in May and June 1836, for which the invitation is still preserved in its library.[1]

I regard it as peculiarly fitting, therefore, that it is this Institution which has been selected by the Richard Bradford Trust for a series of Seven Lectures on the Influence of the Arts and of Scientific Thought on Human Progress, of which this is the last. One of their aims should be, as I read in the memorandum given to the lecturers, 'to test the theory that there is a close analogy between the processes involved in the development of a scientific hypothesis and of an artistic creation', the analogy, in fact, to which Constable appealed in the words I have just quoted. It is for this reason that I should like as far as this is possible within this compass, to take the notion of the experiment as my guide in looking at the relation between the sciences and the arts. The role which experiment plays in science has been outlined by both speakers on scientific topics in this series. To quote Professor Samuel's

The concluding lecture in a series of seven on the Influence of the Arts and of Scientific Thought on Human Progress sponsored by the Richard Bradford Trust and given at the Royal Institution in its historic hall in 1980.

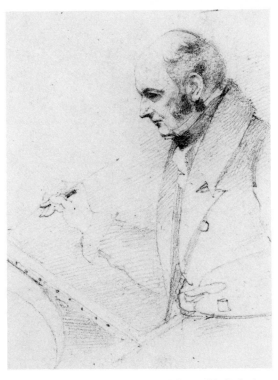

182. Daniel Maclise: *Portrait of Constable Painting.*
c. 1831. London, National Portrait Gallery

lecture on brain research:[2] 'Scientists must remember that though they should be audacious in seeking hypotheses, they must be meticulous in experimentation.' The reason for this injunction became clear in Sir Peter Medawar's exposition of the philosophy of Karl Popper where he stated succinctly that 'Acts undertaken to test a hypothesis are referred to as experiments'.[3] Such tests, which should be public and repeatable, determine the scientist whether to hold on to his 'audacious' hypothesis, or modify, if not abandon it. In either case we may speak of the success of the experiment, for the refutation of a wrong hypothesis is vital for the progress of science, leaving the path open for further searching and probing. In the language of engineering this approximation to a goal through the elimination of errors is known as 'negative feedback'. Can we observe a similar mechanism in the evolution of the arts?

It is suggested in the memorandum that a work of art is actually 'subject to verification or falsification very much like a scientific theory', the test being 'whether the work is accepted or rejected by the large majority of those to whom it is submitted'. I shall come to further amplifications and qualifications of this principle later. For the moment it must be granted that it is certainly possible to see the evolution of art also in the light of 'negative feedback'. But put in this form, the answer may be insufficiently specific to be tested in its turn. For we have learned from Darwin that all evolution can be seen in terms of the survival of the fittest and a good case can always be made out for applying this approach also to the history of civilization.

Whether you think of technology, of religion or of social institutions, you have at any moment of time a possible spread of variants, of which most are still-born while others are taken up and survive. Technology seems the most obvious example. It is tempting and easy with hindsight to say that bronze tools were bound to prove better than those of stone, and iron ones better still, though there probably were moments when it was not clear yet which technology had more advantages on its side. It is harder to say why one religion or sect overtook another or why certain institutions were so eagerly adopted by one culture and rejected by others. Yet I would agree that artistic developments can also be viewed from that angle and that we can say with hindsight that Egyptian art was just the right art for Egyptian religion and society, and the same must apply to Sumerian, Minoan or Mexican art, the examples chosen by Jacquetta Hawkes in her lecture in this series.[4] Whatever we see as the ultimate cause of the formation of these contrasting styles— and I am not sure that we can rest satisfied with the answers which have been proposed—we may still agree that the images adopted by a particular culture must have evolved from something like selective pressure. Certain qualities were found more appealing or intuitively more in accord with the desired aims than others and these were codified as conventions.

What was said in that lecture about Sumerian art also applies to other ancient civilizations. 'All works were created for cultic purposes to celebrate the divinities, or the Kings who were their stewards on earth.' Maybe 'to placate' would be clearer than 'to celebrate', for ultimately it was neither their beauty nor their impressiveness which mattered, but their efficacy in securing the favours of the higher powers, a good harvest, victory in war, the discomfiture of the enemy, and perhaps mercy for the departed souls. It is in the nature of such a ritualistic conception that the very idea of wanting to test the power of these artistic enterprises would be blasphemous. In rites, chants or the construction of amulets and spells you follow precedent in the confidence that they will work their magic. Hence an attitude like the Egyptian was, in the words of the lecture, 'almost bound to lead to highly traditional arts, with a fixed symbolic meaning in every attitude, action and object'. Indeed, the arts which are 'completely enmeshed in their religious mythologies' could never be tested from the inside as it were. If you seek for experiments you would have to go to the followers of other religions, to the prophets, saints or missionaries who wanted to convince the populace that their idols were merely sticks and stones by smashing them with impunity. Jacquetta Hawkes has told us of the astounding episode in Egypt in which Akhenaten caused the names of all gods save the sundisk Aten to be erased and instructed the sculptor to depart from the ritualistic style of precedent. The difficulty of interpreting a stylistic revolution over such a distance of time makes one wonder whether the realism he demanded in the portrayal of his person and of his family was a symptom of humility or of pride—if, indeed, these terms can apply to such an exceptional situation. To what extent this style would have consolidated into a set of conventions if Aten's religion had endured we can never know. At any rate, not all students of the period regard it as an analogy to our Romantic movement in art.[5] If, as she assumes, the art was profoundly shocking to conservatives in Egypt it was, no doubt, because they feared dire consequences from the non-observance of sanctified rules.

The replacement of this attitude by critical awareness is one of the crucial elements in what Jacquetta Hawkes justly describes as that greatest revolution in human thinking achieved by the Greeks which, in her words, 'not only initiated science but also vastly increased the conscious, thoughtful aspect of art'. Professor Kitto in his lecture on the Greeks rightly warns us to watch our terms here, for it is always risky to assume that the Greeks operated with the same concepts of religion, science and art as we do.[6] They had no word for art in our sense, because *techne* meant skill in any aspect of culture, in fortification no less than in image making. But maybe it is precisely because all arts were seen as skills that the decisive element entered the situation which explains much of that increased consciousness I have mentioned—I mean criticism. To criticize is to make distinctions and the critic is the professional fault-finder. Remembering what we have heard about the importance of negative feedback, this detection of mistakes is no minor function. In any case the need for the critic who could articulate his judgement arose in many aspects of Greek life, for the Greeks—as Jakob Burckhardt stressed in his *Griechische Kulturgeschichte*—had a passion for public competitions.

It is no mere pun to remind you here how closely the term contest is related to the term test; there were tests and contests everywhere not only at the Olympic games but at any village feast. Now the idea of skill is only applicable to art if you look at art from an instrumental point of view as trying to achieve a particular end, and this was certainly the Greek approach.

I mentioned that in ancient cultures the implicit end of art was efficacy, the licensed magic of religious rites. Speaking schematically one might say that this element of magic was still very much in evidence in the Greek view of the arts. There is indeed an easy transition from the idea of a religious incantation to that of the spell cast by art. A thinker such as Plato judged art, dancing, poetry, music and to some extent image making by its effects. If I may be allowed another oversimplification I would describe this development as a transition from religion to medicine. Art for Plato is like a drug, its effects can be rousing or tranquillizing, invigorating or debilitating and it is precisely for this reason that in his view it had to be strictly controlled by the state. It is well known that he looked back with nostalgia and approbation to the ancient Egyptians who had, he thought, exercised such a control for thousands of years and had prevented innovation as dangerous and subversive. You must not tamper with such powerful agents. Homer should be banished from the ideal Republic, politely, it is true, but banished all the same. Plato is the predecessor of those enemies of the stage mentioned by Professor Wickham in his lecture[7] and of those of us who fear the corrupting influence of violence on TV, a possibility conceded by Lord Clark in his opening talk.[8]

But clearly there is a vital difference between censorship and criticism. Greek culture opted for the second rather than the first. The distinctions of the critic cannot be based on blanket approval or disapproval but on a verdict of good, better and best. We must not forget in this context that Greek drama, the central theme not only of Professor Kitto's lecture but also of the Bradford statement, evolved in and through competitions. These solemn re-enactments of communal myths performed at the festival of Dionysus differed from other communal rites precisely because they did not encourage but rejected artistic conservatism. We have a schematic picture of the resulting development in Aristotle's *Poetics* where he tells us that Thespis had only one actor, Aeschylus two, Sophocles three, and so on. But these developing means were harnessed in his view to a desired effect, which he defines in half religious, half medical terms as *katharsis*, or purgation of the passions. Of course this is not only a matter of technical means, but of the most compelling interpretation of the myth. We have four versions of the Electra story[9] and each can be seen as an attempt to improve on the earlier. It is not far-fetched to speak here of experimentation, though not yet of experiment. By experimentation I mean the attempt to look for alternatives which are more effective, more suitable for the achievement of the desired end.

Whatever may be true of the playwright, there is no doubt that this spirit of experimentation pervaded the art of image making during the Greek revolution. It looks as if the painters and sculptors were set to solve a predetermined problem, the problem which is traditionally described as

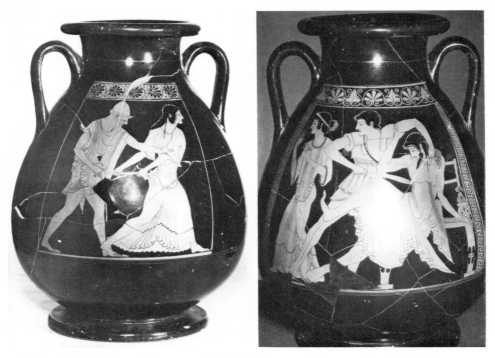

183. The Berlin Painter: *Klytemnestra held back*. From a red-figure pelike. End of 6th century B.C. Vienna, Kunsthistorisches Museum.   184. *Orestes killing Aegisthus*. Detail from the same pelike

mimesis, the correct representation of Nature, but which I prefer to connect with the wish to turn the beholder into an imaginary eye-witness of the mythical events.[10] It was for this reason that Greek masters since the late sixth century attempted with ever more intensity to struggle free from the conventions of art which had governed the Egyptians. A red-figured vase in Vienna (Figs. 183 and 184) of around 500 B.C. illustrates a scene from the story of Orestes which no extant Greek play shows on the stage, the killing of Aegisthus by Orestes, all marked by names. It is Klytemnestra who rushes to the aid of her dying lover with an axe, but is restrained by Talthybius, while Chrysothemis rather than Electra assists the terrible scene. What may strike us first is perhaps the archaic rigidity of the style, the way the bodies are still twisted somewhat like Egyptian figures to show the trunk from in front and the head invariably in profile, but this impression is belied by the rendering of the hands and feet. The left hand of Aegisthus grips the edge of the throne while his right attempts desperately to loosen the arm of Orestes.

We are fortunate in being able to document the spirit of competition which inspired the experimentation of these vase painters. There is a vase in Munich by the painter Euthymides which bears the famous inscription: *Hos oudepote Euphronios*, 'Euphronios [a rival vase painter] has nowhere done this'. It is clear from the picture to which this proud boast is attached that 'this' must mean the mastery of complex movements seen in foreshortening.[11] But even without this written evidence we have the proof in the further development of Greek art that professional fault-finding led to progressive solutions. Two generations later another episode from the Oresteia—the purification at Delphi (Fig. 185)—is represented with the freedom that was the result of further experimentation. Some heads are in profile, some *en face*, and the impression of relaxed ease of movement that characterizes the whole scene is due to the mastery of the skill of foreshortening. A painting in Pompeii, reflecting a Greek original of the fourth century (Fig. 186), shows another scene: Orestes and Pylades on Tauris in front of the King, about to be sacrificed on the altar before they are recognized by their long-lost sister Iphigenia, the priestess. One does not have to enlarge on the fall of light and the convincing rendering of space, but this only provides the setting for the expressiveness of the two beautiful figures. Even those who prefer the vigour of the earlier style must acknowledge that what might be called 'directed experimentation' had led Greek artists towards the solution of the problem of how to evoke a convincing and moving vision of this episode.

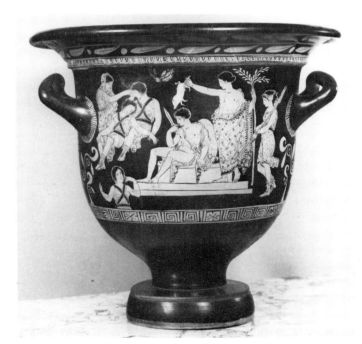

185. The Eumenides Painter: *The Purification of Orestes.*
Red-figure bell krater from Lucania. 4th century B.C. Paris, Musée du Louvre

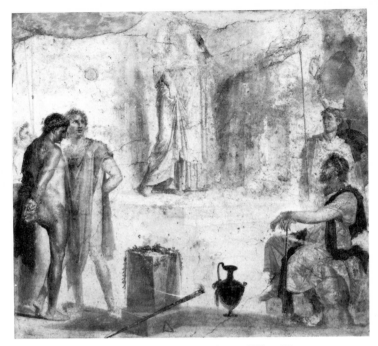

186. *Orestes and Pylades in front of King Thoas.*
Mural from Pompeii. 1st century A.D. Naples, Museo Nazionale

Now it so happens that the effectiveness of these means of art was also reported to have been tested by experiments—in fact by animal experiments. The story concerns the mastery of representing lifelike horses, of which the Alexander mosaic in Naples may convey some idea(see Fig. 212). Not that we need believe the anecdote told by Pliny in his *Natural History* (XXXV, 95) but it is symptomatic all the same. Here we learn that the greatest painter of that period, the famous Apelles, competed with rivals to see who could do a better painting of a horse, and when he suspected his rivals of some kind of foul play in securing the prize, he asked for horses to be taken to the exhibition. Lo and behold, the horses whinnied only in front of his own painting while those of rivals left them cold. 'Afterwards', remarks our source, drily and unconvincingly, 'this experimental test of art (*experimentum artis*) was always used.' In other words, the tests of public repeatability were applied—or so they say.

But I don't want to give the impression that art criticism in the ancient world was left exclusively to horses. There is a story in Lucian about the famous precursor of Apelles, the painter Zeuxis, which brings in a very different element. Zeuxis had painted a picture of a family of Centaurs. The painting made an immediate hit because of the charm and the originality of the subject matter. But the very compliments he received on that score annoyed the artist. 'Pack it up and take it home', he says in the dialogue *Zeuxis, or Antiochus*, 'the people are delighted with the earthy part of my work, novelty of subject goes for more with them than truth of rendering. Artistic merit is of no account.'

Note that the contrast between the judgement of the crowd and the approval of the discerning, between the horse and the connoisseur, worried the ancients as it still worries us. It is a problem that does not really bother the scientist, for it is obvious that to evaluate a scientific experiment you have to understand its aim. In art this kind of distinction is now labelled élitism, an ugly vogue word which still points to a real problem as long as you look at art as an instrument designed to create a psychological effect.

In this respect the model art for the ancient world was not painting nor even poetry but oratory, the art of gaining friends and influencing people, which was of such vital importance in the ancient democracies. Accordingly the art of rhetoric in all its aspects was the subject of the most sophisticated analysis in ancient literature. Cicero, the leading Roman practitioner of this art, has left us his reflections on these matters in many of his writings. In one of them, the dialogue *Brutus*, he traces the rise of oratorical skills in the Roman Republic and carefully compares the means used by the spellbinders of yore. And yet, he admits, you don't really have to know all these technicalities to make up your mind about the quality of a speaker in a court of law. In fact you don't even have to listen to the speaker. A casual glance will tell the listener whether the orator who is on his feet knows his job. If one of the judges is seen to yawn or to talk to his neighbour there is no orator present who can, in Cicero's words, 'play on the minds of the court, as the hand of the musician plays on the strings' (*Brutus*, 200). What the horse was to the picture of Apelles, the jury is to the orator. It is the effect alone which counts as a test, and audience ratings are really all that matter in the end. But Cicero warns us also not to generalize too far. There is a court of appeal against the verdict of the crowd. He tells of a poet who read to an assembled audience an epic of his own composition only to find that all listeners had left, except for Plato. 'I shall go on reading all the same,' he said, 'for me the one Plato counts one hundred thousand' (*Brutus*, 191). Cicero believed in what the media call minority programmes. More than that, he implied in an even more moving anecdote that even Plato is not the ultimate court of appeal. When the playing of a flautist was coldly received by an audience his teacher pleaded: 'sing for me and for the muses' (*Mihi cane, et Musis*) (*Brutus*, 187). The muses remain in heaven even when the gods have departed. Those of us who believe in the muses as the final arbiters set less store by horses, by judges, and even by Plato. But I am the first to admit that such a faith creates its own problem precisely because we have no direct line to the muses and cannot test their reaction. No wonder that the objective canons of science promised for a time to offer a valid substitute, at least in the visual arts.

In attempting to explain this appeal to science, for which Constable served me as my first witness, I must point to the remarkable similarities between the scenario I have described and the one that followed. There was a tendency in the Christian art of the West, and even more so of the East, to revert to a ritualistic concept of image making, but the purpose assigned to the visual image in the West potentially favoured a return to dramatic evocation. Briefly, pictures could be used to impress on the minds of the faithful the teachings of the Church. Professor Wickham's lecture dealt in this context with the role of the miracle plays and here, as in ancient Greece, the stage and the arts followed a parallel course. In the later Middle Ages, sculpture and painting began to rival the popular preachers in their efforts to evoke the stories of the scriptures or the miracles of the saints as vividly and movingly as possible.[12] We are used to connecting this new spirit of exploration and experimentation with the idea of the Renaissance, the return to classical standards, but it would be a mistake to omit from this epic of conquest the contribution made by the Gothic North.

What was distinctive of the Italian Renaissance was the way the aid of science was invoked to create a semblance of reality. Even the most moving picture could be found to jar if attention fastened on inconsistencies in spatial relations, indeed the more so the closer they otherwise came to a convincing setting. To correct these inconsistencies an understanding was needed of the laws of optics which govern the process of vision, in other words of perspective, and it is here that we learn of the first experimental demonstration connected with painting. The demonstration was due to the great Florentine architect Filippo Brunelleschi, who solved the problem on the basic of Euclidean geometry. His experiment took the form of a peepshow—alas no longer extant—in which you could see through the eyehole a view of the Florentine Baptistry as seen through the open doors of the Cathedral. He showed that it was possible to work out theoretically what aspect of any object could be seen from any particular point in space.[13]

But a knowledge of the laws of projective geometry cannot help the painter in creating that desired semblance of reality unless he also has a knowledge of the structure of the objects he wishes to include in his picture—most of all, of course, the structure of the human body. Anatomy, therefore, became the other branch of science eagerly studied by the artists of the Italian Renaissance. It was in fifteenth-century Florence, then, that that tradition was born to which John Constable appealed in his description of painting as a

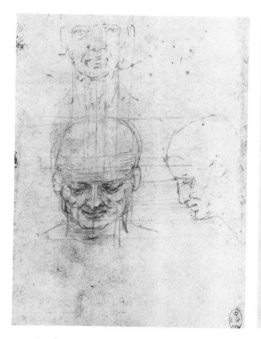

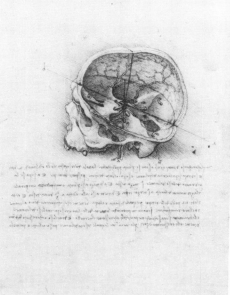

187. Leonardo da Vinci: *Foreshortened heads. c.* 1510. Drawing. No. 12605r. Windsor Castle. Reproduced by gracious permission of Her Majesty the Queen

188. Leonardo da Vinci: *Section of a skull. c.* 1489. Drawing. No. 19058r. Windsor Castle. Reproduced by gracious permission of Her Majesty the Queen

science which should be pursued as an inquiry into the laws of nature, and it was that greatest of Florentines, Leonardo da Vinci, in whose writings this conviction is given the most vigorous expression. There is no doubt that Leonardo's investigations into so many aspects of nature took their starting-point from the demand for objective criteria in the rendering of structure and appearance (Figs. 187 and 188). Too often, he knew, we deceive ourselves if we rely on our impressions rather than on measurement. Thus he notes for the instruction of budding painters who should not trust traditional routine:

That painting is the most praiseworthy that conforms most skilfully to the object it represents, and I say this to confound the painters who want to improve the work of Nature, for instance those who represent a one-year-old boy with the proportions of a man of thirty, giving the body eight head lengths instead of five [Fig. 189]. They have so often committed this error and seen it committed so often, that they have become used to it, and the habit has lodged itself so deeply in their corrupt judgement, that they make themselves believe that Nature, or whoever imitates Nature, is gravely in the wrong in not doing what they do.[14]

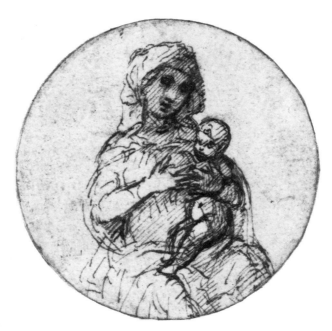

189. Francesco Marmitta: *Madonna and Child. c.* 1505.
Drawing. London, The British Museum

One senses that Leonardo, who liked to represent his Christ child with a very
large babyhead (Figs. 190 and 191), encountered the criticism of traditional
painters. We shall find that the need for measurement and observation
becomes henceforward linked with a warning against the lazy habits and
prejudices of artistic bumbledom.

For Leonardo, of course, the need to test, to observe, to experiment, not to
take anything for granted, had become second nature. It is not always
possible in his writings to tell when he uses the word '*sperienza*' whether he is
talking of 'experience' or of 'experiment', but there are enough passages
which show unambiguously that he had a clear notion of the modern meaning
of the term experiment. Thus there are two pages of the Codex Forster, in the
Victoria and Albert Museum (Vol. II fols. 135*r* and 67*v*), where he studies
the laws of suspension and leverage, one arrangement being marked
'*sperimentato*' (tested), the other '*nonn isperimentato*' (not tested).

Here we have a real experiment in the scientific sense, but in studying
Leonardo's writings we soon realize that he extended the principle of
experimentation far beyond that of objective testing. Confronted with any
problem, he liked to resort to a systematic permutation of the elements as if
he wanted first to make sure that he had not overlooked a single possibility.[15]
We find him applying this method of experimentation rather than
experiment in his geometrical and architectural studies no less than in his

compositional sketches (Fig. 191). These are not simply preparatory stages for the finished work, they are 'studies' in the modern sense, attempts to seek the best solutions for an effective gesture or a balanced grouping (see Fig. 74). What is at stake, in other words, is not the achievement of fidelity to nature; rather it is the realization of the artist's own vision which is pursued through trial and error. We are so used to this procedure that we may fail to see the psychological puzzle it presents. Why should an artist put something on paper only to reject it?

The explanation was furnished by Giorgio Vasari in the middle of the sixteenth century. Vasari was a Tuscan, like Leonardo, and had gone to Venice for a time, where he must have engaged in many debates about art. At any rate he alleged, not without gross exaggeration, that Venetian painters did not believe in the value of making studies on paper. None other than Giorgione is reported to have believed that to paint immediately in colour was the best method. In his Life of Titian, Vasari writes that Giorgione

failed to realize that it is necessary to anyone who wants to arrive at a good composition and to adjust his inventions, first to draw them in different ways on paper so as to see how it all goes together. The reason is that the mind can neither perceive nor perfectly imagine such inventions within itself unless it opens up and shows its conceptions to the corporeal eyes which aid it to arrive at a good judgement.

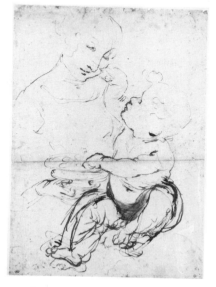

190. Leonardo da Vinci: *Madonna and Child. c.* 1480. Drawing. Paris, Musée du Louvre

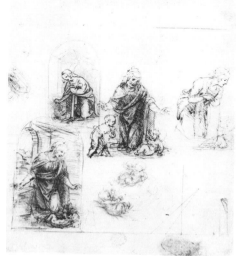

191. Leonardo da Vinci: *Composition of studies. c.* 1483. New York, The Metropolitan Museum of Art, Rogers Fund, 1917

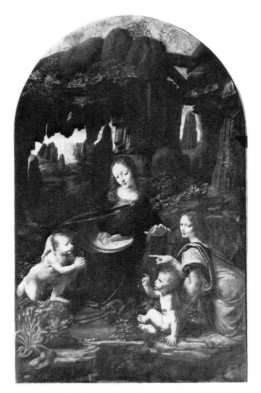

192. Leonardo da Vinci: *The Madonna of the Rocks*.
c. 1483. Paris, Musée du Louvre

Here we have the idea of experimentation, of negative feedback applied to the artist himself. He is his own experimental guinea-pig submitting the inventions of his mind to the critical judgement of his eyes. The more an artist ventures into the unknown by abandoning the well-tried methods of tradition the more vital is this procedure likely to be. Indeed it may be claimed that this discipline of self-criticism has become the most precious heritage of Western art.

It is all the more important, in my view, to clarify in what respect it differs from the principle of scientific experimentation. It differs, I would claim, because the goal which the artist seeks with such self-critical persistence is not a true proposition (as in science), but a psychological effect. Such effects can be discussed, but they cannot be demonstrated.

We need not stray further than the art of Leonardo to give substance to these general considerations. For however intent the master may have been in making his pictures conform to visual reality, there are limits to this aspiration. Let us grant (to avoid misunderstandings) that it is possible to produce a faithful replica of a flat or solid object. But paintings are not replicas. Who would dare to say whether *The Madonna of the Rocks* (Fig. 192)

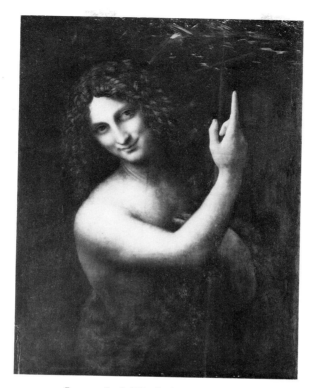

193. Leonardo da Vinci: *St. John the Baptist.*
c. 1514. Paris, Musée du Louvre

matches objectively what we would see when entering such a cave? It would depend on our adaptation to the darkness and many other factors, but in normal conditions there never could be an objective correspondence, for there is a limit to the matching of light by pigments.

The effect which the painter here seeks, therefore, is an impression of equivalence. He has to grope his way to come as close as possible, but he has only his own 'corporeal eyes' to tell him how far he has realized his vision. Other eyes may or may not be satisfied. Once more Vasari, who is so frequently maligned, shows a remarkable understanding of the situation when he comments on the dark appearance of Leonardo's paintings.

He went ever more deeply into the shadows and searched for blacks yet darker than other blacks in order to achieve brightness and luminosity, till his paintings look like renderings of night scenes rather than daylight: yet he did it all to achieve more relief and to attain perfection in art [Fig. 193].

Here we have a good example of an aesthetic problem, the solution of which is hard to measure and quantify. All we can say is that, like Vasari, other Renaissance painters were not convinced that the method really worked, while in the seventeenth century further experimentation led from Caravaggio to Rembrandt.

It fits my book that Constable came to speak of this very problem of matching light with paint when in his second lecture he discussed the works of the seventeenth-century master Claude Lorrain (see Fig. 18), who, as he said, 'carried landscape to perfection, that is *human perfection*'.

> No doubt the greatest masters considered their best efforts but as experiments, and perhaps as experiments that had failed when compared with their hopes, their wishes, and with what they saw in Nature. When we speak of the perfection of art, we must recollect what the materials are with which a painter contends with Nature. For the light of the sun he has but patent yellow and white lead, for the darkest shade, umber or soot.[16]

In these experiments, as Constable rightly stressed, 'Claude, though one of the most isolated of all painters, was still legitimately connected with the chain of art.' He could not have existed without his predecessors. 'He was, therefore, not a *self-taught artist*, nor did there ever exist a great artist who was so. A *self-taught artist* is one taught by a very ignorant person.'

What Constable singled out in Claude was his integrity, 'there is no evasion', as he puts it, and only in his declining years were 'his former habits of incessant observation of Nature ... departing from him'. For with all his emphasis on tradition, Constable's main critical target was what he called 'mannerism', 'the imitation of preceding styles with little reference to Nature'. He singled out the Italianate Dutch masters such as Both and Berchem (Fig. 194) for strictures: in their works 'all the commonplace rules of art are observed; their manipulation is dextrous and their finish plausible', but their truth is second-hand and their reputation merely kept up by dealers. After his lecture, we hear from Leslie, a member of the public said to Constable: 'I suppose I had better sell my Berchems', to which he replied, 'No, sir, that will only continue the mischief, *burn them*.'

It is not hard to see what the conception of science was which influenced Constable in his lectures at the Royal Institution. Even if he had been less fond of quoting Bacon we could tell that his view of human progress was Baconian. The only enemy of true knowledge is prejudice, laziness. As Popper has suggested in an important lecture,[17] in Bacon's view it is our sinful nature which prevents us from seeing the truth God has placed in front of our eyes. Like the scientist the landscape painter must not take received opinion on trust. He must apply himself as an investigator of natural

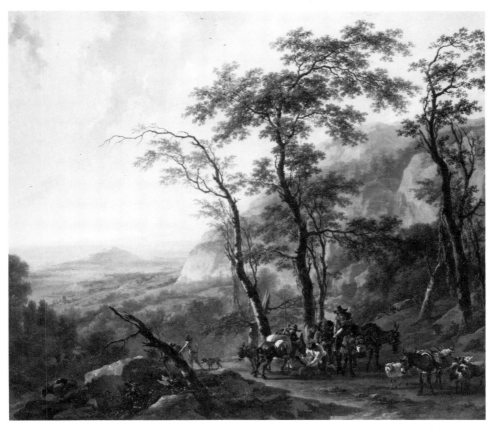

194. Nicolaes Berchem: *Mountainous Landscape*. 1658. London, The National Gallery

phenomena and ceaselessly observe and record them. It is likely that when Constable suggested that pictures are experiments he was thinking of such observational records in the service of 'induction' rather than of the testing of theories, though the two were less sharply distinguished then than they have become since. His art confirms this interpretation. He noted with marvellous precision the fleeting effects of light and of weather in the landscapes he painted (Fig. 195). We know that he passed on this conception of the painter's mission to his friend and biographer C. R. Leslie, in whose *Handbook for young Painters* we find it even more explicitly stated. Leslie mentions there celestial phenomena

> not yet made tributary to Art; the lunar rainbow, for instance, and the aurora borealis ... There is also a beautiful appearance in calm weather, when large masses of bright clouds are reflected on broad columns of light on the sea, just as the sun throws his pillar of fire below him. I may be mistaken, but I cannot recollect this in a picture, constant as its

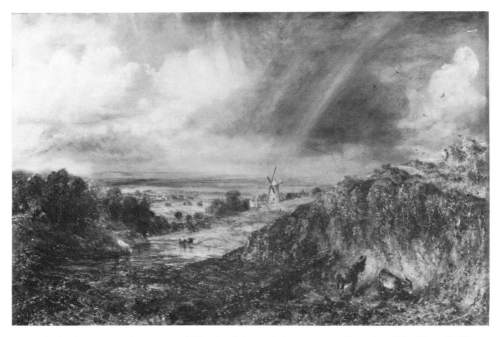

195. John Constable: *Hampstead Heath with a Rainbow. c.* 1828. London, The Tate Gallery

appearance is in Nature . . . The truth is, we go on painting the things that others and ourselves have painted before, . . . Now and then an original painter adds something new and beautiful, but the most original might be more so, were it not for that natural indolence that makes even such too easily content to rest in what has been done.

Natural indolence, sloth; the most eloquent witness of this faith in art as an ally of science in the search for truth is not Leslie nor even Constable but John Ruskin. One would love to know whether it is at all possible that Ruskin, then a young man of seventeen about to go to Oxford, was among the two hundred people who came to Constable's lectures at the Royal Institution. He had taken drawing lessons from Harding and had actually written or was about to write an essay in defence of Turner.

It was this theme which Ruskin developed seven years later in *Modern Painters*, the most ambitious work of scientific art criticism ever attempted. The main sections of the book consist of a survey of natural phenomena, 'Of Truth of Skies', 'Of Truth of Clouds', of mountains, of water, and vegetation described and analysed in marvellous detail, always with the purpose of demonstrating that even the most famous landscape painters of the past had fallen short of perceiving the truth and that they had all been surpassed by Turner (Fig. 196). In the first chapter of his section 'Of Truth of Water' he

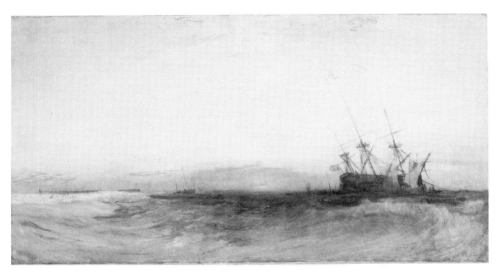

196. J. M. W. Turner: *A Ship Aground. c.* 1831. London, The Tate Gallery

lets himself go in his contempt for such famous marine painters as
Backhuysen (Fig. 197) and Van de Velde (Fig. 198)—who 'are thought to
have painted the sea, and the uninterpreted streams and maligned sea hiss
shame upon us from all their rocky beds and hollow shores'. How can he
convince his readers that the water painting of the elder masters is so

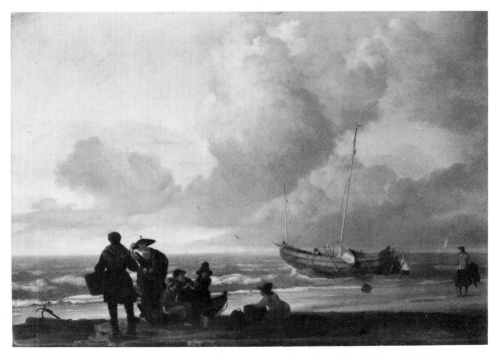

197. Ludolf Backhuysen: *Beach Scene. c.* 1665. London, The National Gallery

execrable? 'When I find they can even endure the sight of a Backhuysen on
their room walls, (I speak seriously) it makes me hopeless at once ...'
'Another discouraging point is', he goes on, 'that I cannot catch a wave, nor
Daguerreotype it, and so there is no coming to pure demonstration.' He was
writing in 1843, and there was no way yet of satisfying his search for an
objective record of appearances by any mechanical means. It was painting or
nothing.

But eleven years later it was possible to catch a wave on the photographic
plate by means of a new process (Fig. 199), and, if so desired, to compare it
with Turner. The new way in which science had taken a hand in the process
of image making must have posed a serious problem to the outlook we have
considered. I have always found it significant and moving that Constable's
son became interested in photography.

When Ruskin came to discuss the relation of science and art in 1871, he was
clearly on the defensive. It appears that Thomas Huxley had drily remarked
to him that recording nature was a purely mechanical matter, and Ruskin felt
compelled to explain why it was not. It was not the phenomena themselves
the artist analysed, as the scientist did, but their appearance, their effects on
him. In doing so, scientific knowledge might in fact hinder rather than help
him, for it created intellectual prejudices which prevented him from
recording what he really saw rather than what he expected to see.

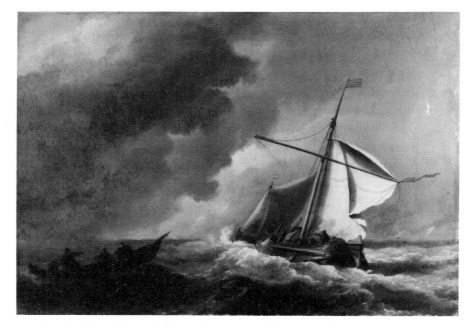

198. Willem Van de Velde the Younger: *A Dutch vessel in a squall. c.* 1660.
London, The National Gallery

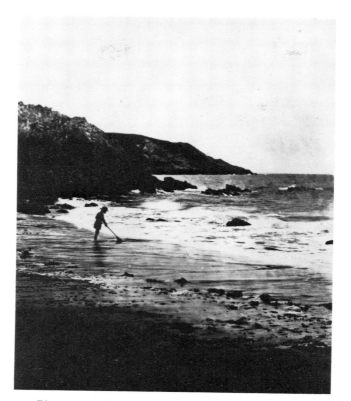

199. Photograph of a wave taken at Brandy Cove, 24 May 1854,
by John Dillwyn Llewelyn. Swansea, Royal Institution of South Wales

Like Constable he appeals to the notion of experiment but his meaning is
less apparent. 'Experiments in art'—he writes—'are difficult and often take
years to try.'[18] Perhaps he was thinking also of his friends the Pre-
Raphaelites, equally bent on combating the corruptions of routine. Indeed,
one of them, William Holman Hunt, in discussing the place in the movement
of the utmost elaboration in painting puts it on record that 'I have retained
later than either of my companions did, the restrained handling of an
experimentalist'.[19]

But the experiments in art which attracted most attention were not made in
Ruskin's England, but in France with that revolution which was marked by
the clash over Manet's *Déjeuner sur l'herbe* shown and derided in the Salon
des Refusés of 1863, and which achieved its fruition in the triumph of
Impressionism.

The epic of this struggle forms the centre of Zola's novel *L'Oeuvre*,
published in 1885 but containing recollections of earlier episodes the author
must have witnessed. The novel has a bad name among lovers of art, for Zola
incorporated traces of his friend Cézanne in the figure of his tragic hero, who

commits suicide in the end.[20] But whatever we may think of Zola's act of disloyalty, the novel remains priceless as a document because it illustrates the enormous impact which the rise and prestige of science had achieved at that time on writers and artists alike. *L'Oeuvre* is in fact part of that enormous series of novels Zola wrote to demonstrate the workings of heredity in one family, the Rougon-Macquarts; the series was to exemplify his programme of experimental novel, the *roman expérimental* he had outlined in 1880. He had borrowed this challenging designation from one of the most famous land-marks in the history of medicine, the *Introduction à l'étude de la médecine expérimentale*, by that great physiologist Claude Bernard who had discovered the vaso-motoric nerves, the functions of the pancreas and of the liver. But could a novel rival these achievements? It could, in Zola's view, if it accepted the findings of science about the forces determining human life and behaviour. Placing two characters together in a given situation could be compared to putting two chemicals into a proving glass. The result was predetermined by known causes. It is interesting to recall that a chemical metaphor was used in Constable's time by Goethe in his novel *Elective Affinities*. An even harsher materialistic determinism governs the plot of Büchner's unfinished play *Woyzeck*, which centres on a dietary experiment performed by the doctor on the helpless downtrodden hero till he commits murder. If Zola's hero Claude Lantier suffers a similar fate it was because the author had also placed him in a hopeless plight. It was the plight of the painters around 1865 as the author saw it from the perspective of 1885. 'Science is today the only possible source,' says Claude, 'but what should we take from it, how can we march with it?'[21] Yet in his buoyant mood he has no doubt of his mission and its value. Declaiming against the academic routine of copying the masterpieces in the Louvre, he vows he would rather cut off his thumb than return there and spoil his eyes in this way, which for ever blinds one to the sight of the world we live in. Was not a bunch of carrots, yes, a bunch of carrots studied directly and painted naively with the personal note in which you saw it, worth all the interminable confections of the schools? The time would come when a single original carrot would be pregnant with revolution.

Why revolution? Because, we understand by now, it would reveal a truth we usually hide from ourselves and from others. It would tear away the veil of sloth and prejudice and would be incorruptible like science. Of course, even on the most charitable interpretation of this wild talk it is not the painted carrot which would do that. We have had and can have any number of scientific images of carrots by now: photographs, holograms or scannings by the electron-microscope; they have not really brought us much nearer to utopia, but then this is not what Zola's hero means. What he considers pregnant with revolution is the simple act of daring to use one's eyes. The act of painting an unconventional motif in an unconventional way, as Manet did in his still lifes (Fig. 200), becomes a metaphor, a symbol of a social and political attitude, of non-conformism and defiance of conventions—but it is the authority of science which gives the artist courage to perform this act.

In the eighties, when Zola wrote this novel, the search for this authority had gone further. I am alluding to the birth of what is known as Post-Impressionism in the art of Georges Seurat. What was believed to be his programme can be gathered from the letter which his friend and admirer the great Camille Pissarro wrote to his dealer Durand Ruel in 1886: 'To look for the modern synthesis by the means based on science, which are grounded in the theory of colours discovered by Chevreul, and later on the experiments of Maxwell and the measurements of O.N. Rood.'[22]

Of those mentioned, Chevreul was the acknowledged authority on the perception of colour, the discoverer of what is known as simultaneous contrast and of similar effects of colour interaction. The famous Maxwell,

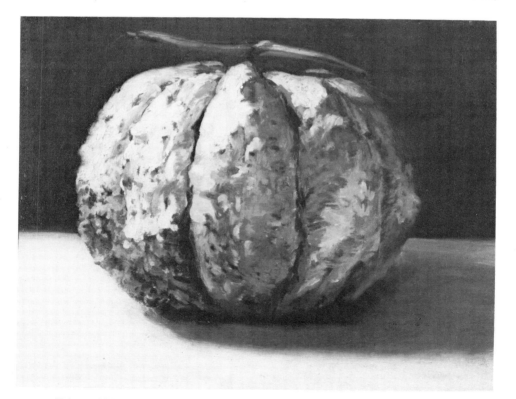

200. Edouard Manet: *The Melon*. 1868. Melbourne, The National Gallery of Victoria, Felton Bequest, 1926

who became the first Professor of Experimental Physics in Cambridge, is here quoted for his studies of colour vision including colour blindness, and the American O.N. Rood was the author of a book on *The Scientific Theory of Color*, which had recently been translated into French. The artists were thoroughly up-to-date and they hoped to use these new theories for the solution of the problem of which I have spoken in relation to Leonardo and Claude—the problem of matching the effects of light by means of pigments. If you mix pigments they begin to look muddy, and so it seemed more promising to build up a mosaic of dots in primary colours on the canvas and leave it to the eye to combine their effects without loss of luminosity. Seurat was a great artist and the very effort of analysis which compelled him to deny local colour and even outlines made him search for compensatory moves of simplification which proved of great interest. Even so, the hoped-for effect did not quite materialize. In fact Professor Weale has recently told us that from the point of view of optics the experiment was doomed because it was based on an oversimplification.[23] An investigation of the interdependence of colour and size published in 1894, three years after Seurat's premature death, could have explained to him why the luminosity he hoped for disappeared at a distance from the canvas when the apparent size of the dots dwindled. Pissarro himself was soon disillusioned and thought he had wasted his time. Not that there was no profit to be gained from the scientific study of colour interaction. One of Seurat's friends was working towards a method of colour photography which, of course, draws on these principles, but then we must not forget that the coloured snapshots we show from our holidays borrow their luminosity from the strong lamp in the lantern, as does colour television.

There has been much argument about the effect of the photography explosion on the development of painting in this century. I personally have little doubt that it was crucial. For in a sense painting had lost what biologists call its ecological niche. Having been threatened before by the decline of religious art, it now had to look for an alternative function where science could not compete. The *volte face* was facilitated by a change in the climate of opinion towards the end of the nineteenth century. Around 1890 the French critic Aurier wrote that many scientists and scholars were discouraged. 'They realize'—he writes—'that this experimental science of which they were so proud is a thousand times less certain than the most bizarre theogony or the maddest metaphysical reverie.'[24] Having been told in this series of lectures that it is not certainty which science claims, but a method to detect errors, we may be unimpressed, but we have to note the paradox that in their search for alternatives artists, musicians and writers claimed to use this method although they knew nothing of its purpose. The word experiment became a vogue word to be used indiscriminately for any departure from tradition, any unconventional enterprise on the stage, in dancing, in poetry or in the application of new media.[25] So thoroughly has the term entered common parlance that I was amused to read in the notice of a recent novel in *The Times* (15 October 1977) that it suffered from a 'reach-me-down experimentalism'. The fact is that artists and critics could not but remain impressed by the triumphal progress of science in the twentieth as in the nineteenth century, and that all the more as they continued to embrace the philosophy of progress. There are few twentieth-century movements whose champions have not appealed to the example of contemporary science. Kandinsky wanted to link his abstract painting with the splitting of the atom which, to him, symbolized the disappearance of solid matter.[26] Cubism has been coupled again and again with Einstein's theory of relativity in statements which it would be uncharitable to quote. Surrealism has made play with the Freudian unconscious, though Freud remained unimpressed; the game goes on with structuralism, linguistics or what have you, but needless to say these are efforts to profit from the prestige of certain scientific fashions rather than experiments testing their validity.

There are exceptions such as the exploitation of flicker effects in what is called 'op' art by artists such as Bridget Riley (see Fig. 39) and Vasarely, who apply and explore certain physiological and perceptual effects of vision. I admire the ingenuity and enjoy the fun of these demonstrations, and I realize that the artists cannot be blamed if we find them somewhat marginal in importance. Claude Lorrain, to remind you of Constable's fine formulation, 'was legitimately connected with the chain of art', these painters cannot be, for there no longer is such a chain. It broke into disconnected links when the consensus broke down about the aims and functions of image making in our culture.

It is the lack of common purpose which also makes one hesitate to speak of experimentation in the sense which we observed in ancient Greece and again in the period reaching from the Renaissance to the late nineteenth century. For what I described as directed experimentation presupposes the existence of a problem for which good or better solutions can be offered.

There remains, then, the third possibility to which I briefly referred at the outset of this lecture, that rhythm of undirected trial and error that plays such a part both in organic and cultural evolution as natural selection leads to the elimination of misfits and the survival of the fittest.

Now this, if I understand it aright, is the tenor of the proposition advocated by the Bradford Trust. It puts forward for discussion 'the idea that an important criterion of fitness in cultures is in fact survival', and it proposes further that this survival may be legitimately compared to verification in science. 'Verification is here used in the sense of acceptance by a human audience though such acceptance may sometimes be delayed', a point to which I shall have to return.

I am not sure, as I have indicated before, that this interpretation fits art more than it fits other aspects of culture such as religious or social institutions; they must all be accepted in order to survive and what the historian tries to explain within the limits of his resources is precisely how and why a particular culture incorporates certain modes of life or styles of art. But despite this qualification I find this proposal particularly relevant to the situation of art today, and that, paradoxically, because if there is such a mechanism in art it has almost ceased to function in our time. We are familiar with such impediments to the 'survival of the fittest' in other fields than art. In politics the obsolete can cling to power by force. In economics the free play of the market can be distorted by protectionist tariffs or even by unscrupulous advertising. The forces which militate against the unfolding of art in modern society are more subtle and more insidious. They spring from a new kind of 'protectionism' unknown to previous ages. I refer to the belief in the verdict of the future, which is also incorporated in the document before us. The passage I have in mind reads:

> The verification (of works of art) is of course not merely limited to our own view, or to that of contemporary opinion, but must be agreed or rejected by a large majority of those to whom it is submitted. Thus even if a work of art is 'ahead of its time' and generally rejected by contemporary opinion, future generations may recognize its truth and it may thus attain verification. On the other hand, it may simply come to be regarded as an irrelevant period piece.

Now there is an interpretation of this statement which I fully endorse, as I have done earlier on when commenting on Cicero's anecdote about the poet who preferred the approval of Plato to that of a hundred thousand others. If you are sufficiently 'élitist' to assume that the percentage of discerning critics in any population is likely to be small, any good work has more chance of being recognized by such critics in the course of centuries than at any given moment. I suppose this is the process our document describes as 'averaging', but much also depends on accident, on who gets to know what work, just as the recognition of Mendel's experiment was long delayed because he published it in an out-of-the-way place.

But if I may remain with this illustration for a moment, we have also experienced in our time another and more sinister reason for the failure of Mendelianism. I refer to the situation under Stalin when it was unsafe to doubt the results of Lysenko's experiments purporting to disprove Mendel's laws. Whether culpable or not, the experimenter was surrounded by a chorus of yes-men who impeded self-criticism and criticism.

In science such a stifling of the mechanism of negative feedback is still an exception. It is my contention that this is not so in art. For here the once innocuous belief in the verdict of the future has been turned into a weapon against any criticism, or 'fault-finding'. Criticism is never pleasant and it is often uninformed. One can thus sympathize with the artist who stakes his faith in posterity, and yet the more he does so, the less he finds himself understood. One of Zola's heroes clings to this consolation as he defiantly confronts the hostile crowd at an exhibition with the battle cry: 'we have the verve and boldness, we are the future'. In this view rejection by the present is almost the guarantee of future fame, because, so the legend goes, all great artists, indeed all true geniuses, are derided by their contemporaries. That this is bad history goes almost without saying. What matters more is that it is also bad philosophy. For the belief that good art not only may but must be 'ahead of its time' is not rational as is the faith in 'averaging'. It is rather part and parcel of that philosophy which Popper has criticized as 'historicism', the belief that there is a law of progress in history which it is not only futile but actually wicked to resist.[27] It is wicked, because whatever sufferings may be caused by revolutions, wars and massacres, they are merely the inevitable accompaniments, the birthpangs of a better and brighter age. It is a philosophy which would hardly have been accepted by so many if it had not carried the consolations of religion into the arena of politics, promising victory to its adherents and damnation to its opponents. Transferred to the sideshow of art, this ideology of inevitable progress is of course responsible for the notion of the avant garde, those advance parties of art which will plant the banner of the new age on the territory which will be settled by the next generation of artists.[28] I find it noxious, because it really abolishes the very belief in values which the other interpretation upholds. There is no bad art and good art, only antiquated and advanced art. One day the scales will drop from the eyes of the purblind majority and they will accept what they now deride, but when this happens it is time for the avant garde to get busy and court martyrdom for the sake of the next age.

Now it stands to reason that this version of 'futurism' can lead to a crippling elimination of all negative feedback, and with its disappearance the notion of an artistic experiment also loses its meaning. However the artist chooses to paint his bunch of carrots, none of his contemporaries can judge it.

What is worse, it becomes doubtful that he can judge it himself. Our standards, our conscience, moral or artistic, are derived from our environment. We are free to criticize and modify them but without criteria of what is good and what is better we cannot submit our ideas to the judgement of our 'corporeal eyes'. It is this unintended breakdown of standards that has made it so hazardous to compare the life of art today with the life of science.

For contrary to the rigorous standards by which any scientific paper is judged when it is submitted for publication, the lack of criteria has led to a loss of nerve among art critics and, what is more serious, it has also intimidated the public. Intimidated precisely because their self-respect is threatened. If they fail to acknowledge the art of the future they show themselves to be mentally backward. I am not the first to recall in this situation Andersen's famous parable of the Emperor's new clothes which are sold to His Majesty by cunning merchants, who claim that the new material has the added advantage of being visible only to those who are fit for their office. In the end it takes the innocent child to call out 'but he has nothing on'. We cannot be helped by such innocence, for how could a mere child discern the art of the future?

The story is germane to my subject because it is of course the story of a psychological experiment. All hoaxes can be so interpreted, and what hoaxes in the field of art tend to show is the degree to which acceptance or rejection is influenced by our suggestibility. Vasari tells us of such an experiment which Michelangelo made while at work on his famous David. When the communal leader of Florence, the gonfaloniere Piero Soderini, came to inspect it, he praised the statue but thought that the nose was too big. Whereupon Michelangelo climbed up on his scaffolding, took a few grains of marble lying around and pretended to chisel off a piece of the nose, letting the dust fall on Soderini, who promptly said, 'now I like it better, you have given it life.' Can anyone be sure he would not have fallen for the trick? And can we be surprised that Apelles preferred the incorruptible horse to the corruptible judgement of human beings? The trouble is only that what is corruption to some, is conversion to others.

When Georges Braque, in 1906 or 1907, first saw the revolutionary composition by his friend Picasso which is called rather squeamishly *Les Demoiselles d'Avignon*—for it represents a group of prostitutes in a brothel— he is reported to have said, 'it is as if you asked us to drink petrol'. But art is an acquired taste and I confess that actually I have come to like drinking this petrol—the so-called experiment of cubism, which started with this picture, and led to the discovery of interesting and amusing visual puns and ambiguities, which I enjoy as long as I am not told that they correspond to Einstein.

Art is not science and the art exhibition differs in more than one respect from the laboratory, where the results of experiments are soberly assessed and repeated by the investigator's peers who will find the faults, eliminate error and work in the direction of progress. I do not want to be misunderstood. I do not want to suggest that in contrast to science the world of art today is entirely governed by brainwashing and bandwagons, but I do think that our art is not safe from corruption from these forces and that we must be aware of these distorting influences if we are to take the comparison of works of art with scientific experiments further. What we call art, as I have stressed, has served a variety of functions in a variety of cultures. If today we see artists trying out and trying on an unprecedented variety of modes, media and effects, we should enjoy the opportunity of accepting or rejecting these mutations without a feeling of guilt or pride. I believe that the young have largely come round to this point of view. Indeed this reaction against portentousness is the nugget of value I discern in my more optimistic moments in the noisy carnival of anti-art; if only portentousness did not so often catch up with it, as it has caught up with 'Dada'! Not that I would ever wish to discourage solemn emotions in front of transcending masterpieces. I fully agree with the Bradford document that there exist such works which, as the saying is, have 'stood the test of time'[29] and I share the feelings of gratitude and admiration for these supreme achievements no less than for the intellectual conquests of science. But while science is a coherent body to which every practitioner can make a major or minor contribution, art is not. It has its valleys and plains as well as its soaring peaks. If we equate the artist with the scientist by regarding both as equal servants of human progress we may tempt our art students to see their role as that of prophets and oracles with disastrous results for their mental equilibrium and their capacity for self-criticism.

It was not that which Constable meant when he addressed an audience which included Faraday. If you listen sharply you can perhaps still hear his final plea for humility. 'It appears to me that pictures have been overvalued, held up by a blind admiration as ideal things ... and this false estimate has been sanctioned by extravagant epithets that have been applied to painters as "the divine", "the inspired" and so forth ... yet the most sublime productions of the pencil are ... the result, not of inspiration, but of long and patient study, under the direction of much good sense.'

Standards of Truth:
The Arrested Image and the Moving Eye

HUMOURISTS HAVE a way of summing up a problem in an amusing drawing which can save many words. The desperate artist in Smilby's picture from *Punch* (Fig. 201) is shown wrestling with the need to produce what I have called in my title an 'arrested image' of his view through the window during a thunder-storm. As he is trying to make a truthful record of the flashes of lightning which race across the sky, we can see his hand swishing from one position to another, for Smilby is also presented with the task of representing movement in a 'still'.

In contrast to what I may call the man-made image, the machine-made image can now be used with confidence to give us a truthful record of the path of lightning across the sky. The photographic camera can cut down the time it takes for the phenomenon to leave its trace on the emulsion. Some of the camera's resources are well illustrated in the two photographs of the same flash of lightning (Fig. 202). The one on the left was taken by a stationary camera, the one on the right by a moving one which shows several phases of the event—not unlike the humorous drawing. It reveals that branch 'a' consisted of one single discharge and branch 'b' of a sequence of partial discharges which were recorded on the plate while the camera was turned to the right. The whole duration of the discharges was 0.556 seconds.

Data of this kind are characteristic of the way the scientific image is used. We can only extract the required true information from it if we have all the specifications of the instrument and of the exposure. The information thus obtained is quite independent of what anyone might have seen when watching that flash of lightning. It is not a visual truth, it is an objective record, but one which has to be interpreted in the light of additional information.

This paper was first read at Swarthmore College, Pennsylvania, in October 1976 at a symposium to mark the retirement of Professor Hans Wallach.

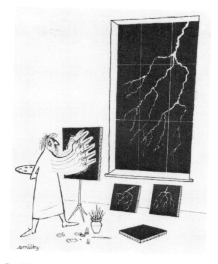

201. Smilby, drawing from *Punch*, 1 February 1956

Philosophers have sometimes questioned the use of the term 'information' in relation to visual images.[1] Naturally, this like any other term has to be used with circumspection; I am convinced, however, that even the student of the hand-made picture can profit from an acquaintance with the methods which science has used and is using in the extraction of information from visual records. In my book *Art and Illusion* I have paid tribute in this context to my late friend Gottfried Spiegler, who started his career in the early days of X-ray technology and who taught me to look at the interpretation of images as a philosophical problem. I learned from him that both technological and psychological variables must be considered and that the standards of truth

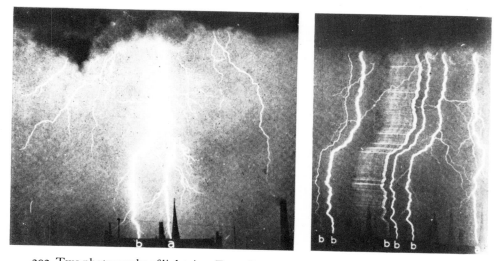

202. Two photographs of lightning. From *Der grosse Brockhaus* (Leipzig, 1929, Vol. 3)

are anything but obvious in the evaluation of X-ray photographs.[2] What strikes the layman or even the inexperienced physician as an optimal picture because of its clarity and its easily legible contrasts may actually suppress rather than convey all the desired information (Figs. 203 and 204). Thus the 'sharp' image on the left fails to show that the outlines of the bones in question are anything but sharp, and it is this pathological condition the X-ray should reveal.

Scientific images do not, of course, aim at recording what is visible, their purpose is to make visible. This applies to the ordinary enlargement as well as to the miracle of the electron-scanning microscope, which has enabled scientists to answer so many questions—always presupposing that they know the specifications of the instrument, its magnification, power of resolution, and so on.

In no other field have we been made more poignantly aware of the wizardry of science in obtaining information far beyond the reach of the human eye than in the exploration of the universe. Pictures of the surface of Mars have been transmitted over the distance of some 212 million miles. It is worth recalling that the pictures shown in our newspapers were of course mediated through a most complex chain of processes. The picture taken by the landing craft on the surface of the planet (Fig. 205) was transmitted in the form of

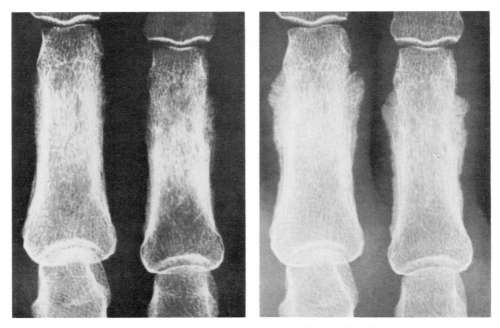

203, 204. X-ray with high contrast (*left*) and X-ray with soft contrast.
From Gottfried Spiegler, *Physikalische Grundlagen der Röntgendiagnostik*
(Stuttgart, 1957)

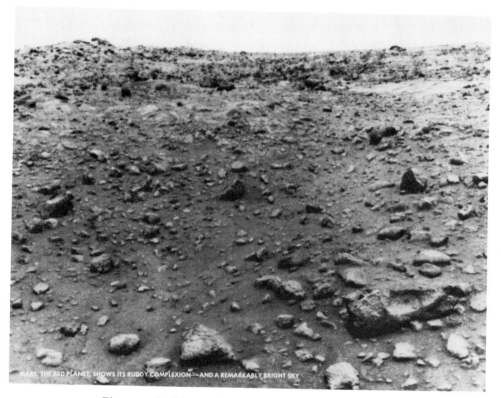

205. Photograph of the surface of Mars. From *Time*, 2 August 1976

weak electrical impulses to the 'orbiter', where these impulses were so reinforced that they could reach our earth at any point turned at that moment towards Mars—for instance, Australia. From there they were bounced back to a satellite and thence picked up at the jet propulsion laboratory at Pasadena, the whole journey taking some twenty minutes. At that point the information-carrying impulses had to be reconverted by computer into an arrested image, and this reconversion needed care. At the time, the story went through the newspapers that the sky on Mars looked blue, but it was subsequently found to be of a pinkish hue. It appears that it was not even very difficult to rectify this departure from visual truth in the final picture. The camera on Mars carried with it a colour calibration chart, of which the values were known at Pasadena. Studying the appearance of that chart, they could work out the other colour values, for which they had no independent evidence.[3]

To me, as a layman, this device of 'calibration' illuminates the whole process of obtaining information from an arrested image, both by its power and its limitation. We can calibrate for colour but not for depth, for here we

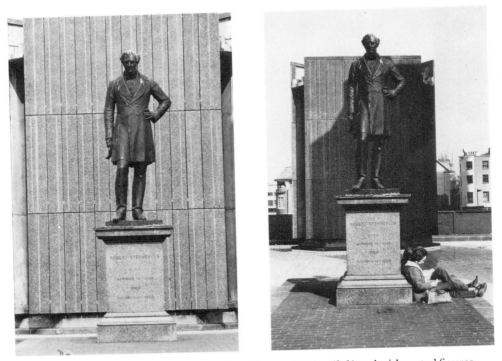

206, 207. Statue of Robert Stephenson at Euston Station (*left*) and with seated figures

come up against what in *Art and Illusion* I have called the ambiguity of the
third dimension. It is in the nature of things that the image, the permanent
trace of the light which entered the lens, can give us no information on the
distance the light had travelled before it released the chemical process on the
emulsion. Hence the picture must always be ambiguous or, to be
linguistically more correct, multivalent, like any other projection of a solid on
a plane. We really cannot tell the size of the boulders or ridges which are
visible on the picture from Mars unless we know their distance, and vice
versa, though for proximate objects there may be additional information
through such clues as texture or 'grain'—assuming again that we guess
correctly at their composition. An arrested image might thus be compared to
a single equation with two variables such as $n = x \times y$. We can calculate the
size of an object if we know the distance and the distance if we know its size, to
calculate both we would have to have additional information.

For any professional engaged in extracting information from arrested
images, this limitation is perfectly obvious, but psychologically, or, if one
may use the word, experientially, it is less so. The reason is simple; we
usually have a fair idea of the order of magnitude of the objects in our
environment and hence of their size and distance in pictures, at least those
which represent people or houses, animals, flowers or fruit. We thus

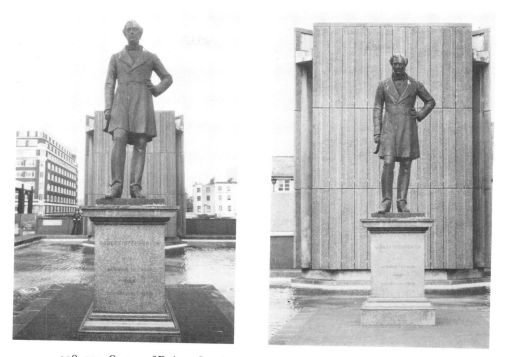

208, 209. Statue of Robert Stephenson, wide angle (*left*) and normal view

normally approach any arrested image with the confidence of being able to solve its implicit equation at least approximately—and we are not frequently jolted out of our complacency.

A series of photographs (Figs. 206–9) of the statue of Robert Stephenson, the famous English engineer, which stands in front of Euston Station in London, was made for me in 1976 by Mr. Parker-Ross of the Warburg Institute to illustrate this point. In contrast to real men, men of bronze come in almost any size and so do buildings of uncertain character, like the one that is seen behind the monument. In the first photograph that structure can be interpreted as a tall building some distance away. The second reveals that it is merely an air vent which is accordingly much closer to the monument. The size of the monument can be approximately inferred from the figures sitting beside it. The statue is about twice life-size. In the third photograph, taken with a wide-angle camera, an obliging assistant has placed himself next to the air vent, which is about six times his height. According to my .rough estimate on the spot (aided by the flagstones of the pavement), the distance between the statue and the background structure is some twenty-eight feet. The last of the photographs would seem to me to suggest these relationships without much strain, though this must always remain a subjective feeling. It may be derived from the habit of viewing a monument from a standard distance, close enough to see the features but not so close as to have to crane one's neck, and possibly also from a viewing point which allows us to read the inscription on the plinth.

The relevance of our viewing habits to the perception of pictures is easily demonstrated by considering the effect or effects produced by a tilted camera. One reads in older books on photography that the resulting distortions are intolerable, but we have become quite used to them and accept without demur a monument shown from below with the houses in the background foreshortened (Fig. 210). Naturally a correct reading of the situation rests on the assumption that the picture was not taken during an earthquake, while the façades swayed and telescoped, for only if we start from the conviction that the monument and houses are normal can we infer the tilt. It is still a trifle less easy to accept the downward view of a tall building like Rockefeller Center in New York (Fig. 211); it is hard to believe that the building is not both bulging and expanding upward.

It is not surprising that we are reluctant to accept the visual truth of such pictures and that we deny that we ever see a building in this way. We are right in our protest, and yet we must proceed with caution. We have good reasons for our basic conviction that the objects in our environment are solid and real and that we see them as such rather than as flat, rubbery, enigmatic shapes.

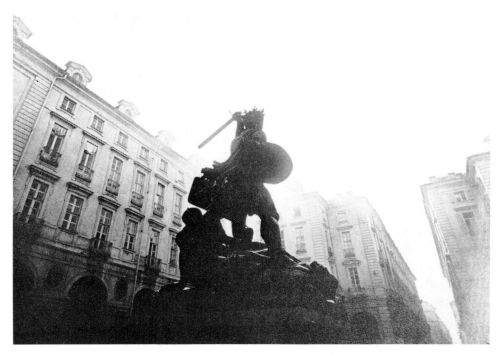

210. Piazza di Torino photographed with tilted camera

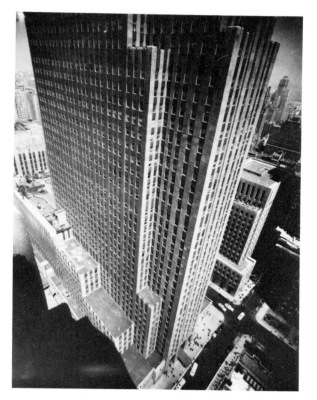

211. Rockefeller Center from the top of
Time-Life Building. Photograph by Andreas Feininger

The traditional justification of this conviction took recourse to our experience of touch and to such knowledge as we have acquired in the course of our lives, knowledge that comes to our aid in making sense of our sense impressions. The ghost of this theory still haunts discussions of the art of painting not only in the nineteenth century but even today, even though today this ghost has been exorcized, largely by that great student of vision, J. J. Gibson.[4]

It is interesting to note that Gibson arrived at his alternative view through his involvement in a technical rather than an artistic problem. He derived it from his wartime work when he investigated the visual information available to a pilot landing at high speed. It was this example which brought home to him how misleading it was to start any account of visual perception with an analysis of the image formed on the retina of a stationary eye. In Gibson's developed view the comparison between the eye and the *camera obscura*, though perfectly justified from the point of view of optics, is at best irrelevant and at worst misleading for the study of visual perception. It is not such a static image which gives the pilot the required estimate of the distance and position of the runway but the flow of information he receives, the sequence of transformations all around which show him across these rapid changes the invariants of the lay of the land, invariants he must pick up if he is to survive.

And what is true of the pilot is true of any organism, whatever may be the construction of the visual organs with which it is endowed—the multiple eyes of insects can perform this service no less than can the eyes of mammals. It is an awareness of their own movements which enables their central nervous systems to solve the problem of separating the invariant shape of rigid objects from the transformations of their momentary aspects. For that equation with two variables stating merely the inverse relationship of size and distance, which I instanced as a problem for the interpretation of the arrested image, offers no similar difficulties to the organism in movement. It has at its disposal not merely one equation with two variables but a whole sequence of transformations which enable it to separate out the invariants of shape and colour from the changing aspects and colours which characterize the momentary view. These changing aspects, indeed, serve no purpose in the business of orientation, and thus they rarely obtrude on our awareness. To start the investigation of visual perception from a study of such arrested monocular vistas seems to Gibson little short of perverse.

Whether or not it will ultimately be found that Gibson somewhat overstated his case against what he calls 'snapshot vision',[5] the historian of art will always have to be grateful to him for having contributed to the solution of the puzzle that has plagued the history of painting for so long. For this history has been written by critics (ancient, Renaissance, and later) who accepted the snapshot vision as the norm and who could not but notice how rarely it was adopted in the past. The images of great civilizations such as those of Egypt and China were never constructed on these principles, and so their essentially different approach was seen as a deviation from a natural norm. Special theories and notions were constructed to explain the prevalence of 'conceptual' styles in all parts of the globe which had failed to adopt the Western standard of truth. When this degree of ethnocentricity began to worry historians, they escaped into a facile relativism, declaring that all standards are equally conventional and that the Western method—that of the camera—is no less arbitrary than any other.[6]

Such relativism can draw no comfort from Gibson's researches nor, of course, from a consideration of the use of images in science. For there is at least one perfectly rational standard of truth which can be applied to the arrested monocular image, and this standard was discovered and applied for the first time by the ancient Greeks. I have argued elsewhere that what prompted the Greeks to explore this standard was a new function of the visual image which demanded what I propose to call the 'eye-witness principle'. It is the principle which has usually been described in the light of ancient aesthetics as one of mimesis, the imitation of nature. But in my view, this formulation diverts attention from the most important corollary of the eye-witness principle, which is so often neglected; I refer to the negative rule that the artist must not include in his image anything the eye-witness could not have seen from a particular point at a particular moment. While complete mimesis will always be a will-o'-the-wisp—for where should it ever stop?—the negative rule will immediately lead to a study of aspects, of foreshortening, and of perspective.

Note that this standard is not affected by the ambiguity or multivalence of the third dimension in any image. The photograph of our monument may leave room for interpretation, but it is surely a correct record in not showing us the back of Stephenson's head, which is not visible from the station point, and indeed any other features of the bronze man which cannot be seen in that aspect. Trivial as this may sound, the art student learning to draw from a cast would have to attend very carefully to avoid including in his drawing the slightest feature he could not see without moving.

There was no reason for the Greeks to worry too much about the inability of the method to convey information of previously unknown motifs or objects. The purpose for which they developed the eye-witness principle was, as I have tried to argue, essentially dramatic.[7] Art concerned itself with human beings in action. It served to render mythological or actual events. The imaginary eye-witness of the battle of Issus, the victory of Alexander the Great over Darius, thus makes us vicarious participants of the mêlée (Fig.

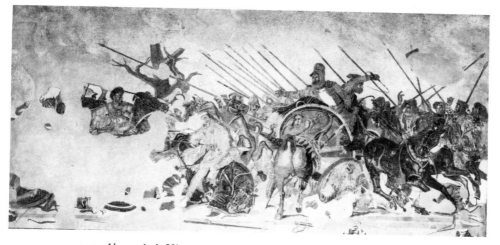

212. *Alexander's Victory over Darius, c.* 100 B.C. Pompeiian mosaic.
Naples, Museo Nazionale

212); the resources of Hellenistic painting of the third century B.C. allowed the artist to use foreshortening, overlap, light, shade and reflection; we see the warriors falling and the horses rearing and take part in the moment when the tide of world history turned and the Persian king on his chariot tried in vain to escape the conqueror. Mark that in conveying this experience of the eye-witness the image serves a dual purpose—it shows us what happened out there, but also, by implication, what happened or would have happened to us, both physically and emotionally. We understand, without much reflection, where we are supposed to stand in relation to the event depicted and what moment we are made to share vicariously with the eye-witness. There is no difference in principle between the image and the one shot in a million of which the photographic war reporter may dream.

It happens to suit my purpose that the Alexander Battle is a mosaic, an image composed of a granular medium. The medium does not permit smooth transitions and makes it impossible to show objects smaller than the smallest tessera at the disposal of the craftsman. Go too near and you will no longer see what you are meant to see but rather individual patches. Not that there is something unique in this granular medium. Photographs reproduced in newspapers are also granular; they have a 'screen' which will again restrict the information which can be coded and incorporated in the pictures, whether scientific, artistic, mechanical, or hand-made.

In this respect the standard of truth under discussion is also related to the medium. The image cannot give us more information than the medium can

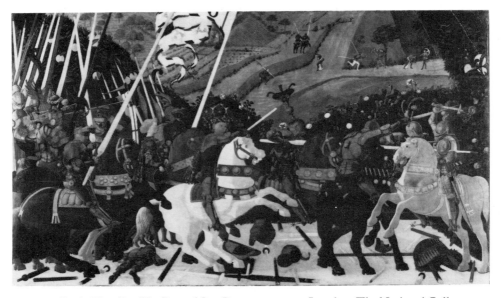

213. Paolo Uccello: *The Rout of San Romano. c.* 1450. London, The National Gallery

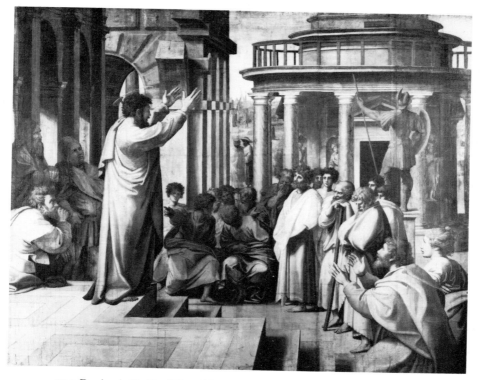

214. Raphael: *St. Paul Preaching at Athens. c.* 1515. Cartoon. London,
The Victoria and Albert Museum

carry. But this limitation does not lead to a denial of any standard. On the contrary, while the principle may suggest that the information from the visible world can rarely be completely matched in any medium, we also learn why it can still exclude false information. It was due to the eye-witness principle that standards of truthfulness or accuracy could be accepted by the artist irrespective of the medium.

We observe the continued striving for these standards at the end of the Middle Ages when artists struggled to recover and to improve on the achievement of ancient art. It is notorious how intensely the Florentine painter Uccello studied the newly discovered laws of perspective for this purpose, and in comparing one of his famous battle pieces (Fig. 213) with the ancient mosaic, we notice his somewhat self-conscious demonstration of his knowledge but also his failure to avoid certain inconsistencies in arriving at a completely convincing eye-witness account.[8]

Leaping a generation or two we can study the finished achievement in a work by Raphael, who was to set the standards of academically correct drawing for four centuries. There is no doubt in my mind that a work like his *Saint Paul Preaching at Athens* (Fig. 214) can best be understood as an application of the eye-witness principle. Note once more how the artist turns us into participants of the momentous scene when the apostle of Christ addressed the élite of pagan philosophers. We must envisage ourselves sitting on the invisible steps outside the picture, but the image shows us nothing that would not be visible from one point at a given distance, a distance which could be worked out mathematically but which we feel instinctively. It is this consistency which art historians like to describe as 'the rationalization of space'. Every object in view is seen as it would be seen from the same point. This standard of correctness is a standard of draughtsmanship. It has again nothing to do with the medium employed and applies whether you look at Raphael's cartoon in colour, at a black and white reproduction, or at the tapestry which was woven in Flanders after this design.

I have mentioned that this standard of consistency is based on the art of perspective, an art which has caused so much agony to students of drawing and such dissension among art historians. Debates about the question of how far perspective can claim to embody a particular standard of truth have tended to be somewhat abstruse and arid; like other participants in this debate, I happen to be convinced that I have at last hit on the magic formula which should close it forever, though I know that this hope is somewhat unrealistic. I should like to propose that what I have called the negative principle of the eye-witness record could lead to an agreement about the nature of perspective and its problematic features. According to my formula, perspective enables us to eliminate from our representation anything which could not be seen from one particular vantage-point—which may still leave the question open as to what can be seen.[9]

The story of how Brunelleschi developed the method of central perspective in Florence around 1420 has been rehearsed by students of the subject any number of times.[10] He is said to have demonstrated the principle by depicting the Baptistry as seen through the door of the Florentine cathedral, having extended a net or veil over the entrance. A photograph of another centralized building, Santa Maria della Salute in Venice, as seen through a wrought-iron gate (Fig. 215), makes it easy to visualize the method. All the draughtsman has to do is to turn the grill into a corresponding grid on his drawing pad and enter into each of the openings what he can see of the church through any particular gap, while closing one eye and keeping the other at one point. If he moves, and incorporates in his drawing something he could not have seen before, the picture will become distorted.

What is needed for the understanding of this method is merely the fact, already known to the ancients, that light travels along straight lines through a

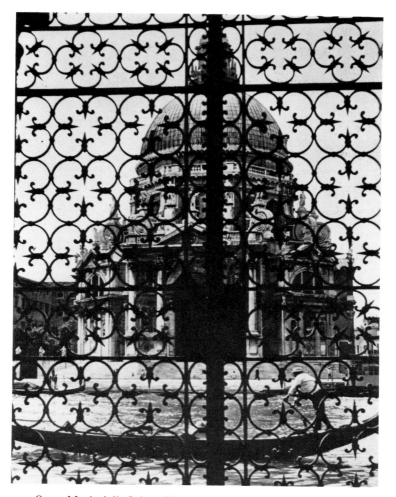

215. Santa Maria della Salute, Venice, seen through a wrought-iron gate.
Photograph by Vianello. *Art et Style* (Paris, No. 35, 1955)

uniform medium and is stopped by opaque objects. This permits us to work
out by means of projective geometry what can be seen from where, except in
those freakish circumstances when light does not travel in straight lines and
produces a mirage through refraction.

In the absence of such exceptional effects the method is quite foolproof.
Brunelleschi was an architect, and architects have never, to my knowledge,
questioned its rationale. An application of this method which proves this
point is exemplified by the picture we see in Fig. 216. It is a photomontage of
King's College, Cambridge, on which has been superimposed a drawing of a
projected addition to the New Museums site to test whether and how much
this intrusion would spoil one of the most beautiful views of the city. I do not
think anybody can doubt that such a drawing can conform to the standards of

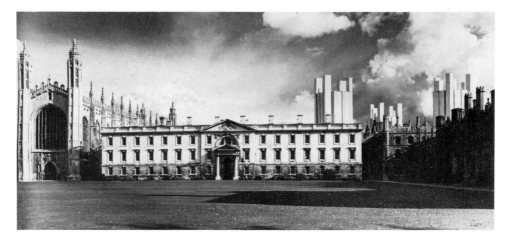

216. Photomontage of King's College, Cambridge, showing the proposed new science
complex, since abandoned

truth. In fact, in building another museum, that at Cornell University, the
method was used with the aid of a computer to work out the aspects of the
projected building from given vantage-points on the campus.[11] The fact that
we normally look with two eyes rather than one, that our eyes move, or that
our retinas are curved—all these alleged flaws in the principles of central
perspective do not affect the validity of the demonstration.

Why, then, has perspective so often been called a convention which does
violence to the way we see the world? Clearly because the eye-witness
principle demands that we stand still and only look in one direction—and
that we must indeed close one eye if the object of interest is sufficiently near
for binocular parallax to make a difference. What happens when we move, as
we normally do? The composite photograph of a view through a window
suggests an answer (Fig. 217). Looking down, looking up, and looking
sideways, different views will become visible, and these could only be fully
rendered on the inside of a sphere rather than on a flat surface. The argument
has convinced many students of perspective, notably since Erwin Panofsky
made himself the champion of this interpretation,[12] but it happens not to be
quite accurate. It is perfectly true that our field of clear vision is very limited
and that we automatically turn the head to make up for this restriction. As
soon as we do so, of course, different vistas come into view. The panoramic
camera shows the result of this movement in a photograph of the
Remembrance Day service at the Cenotaph in Whitehall, London (Fig. 218).
Whitehall is a straight thoroughfare, but looking down the road first in one
direction and then in the opposite, we have two vistas of converging roads, as
if the monument stood at the apex of a curve; but then the photograph

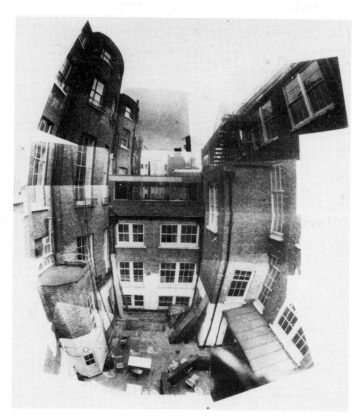

217. Composite photograph of a courtyard seen through a window,
by Paul Green-Armitage. *Architectural Association Journal*, February 1965

infringes on the eye-witness principle by showing us things we could not see from one point. When we move the head our eye or eyes are carried around a semicircle pivoted on the neck. We turn, and the information changes.

What happens if we merely move the eye but not the head? Students of optics have known for some time that in this case the information available for sampling remains the same.[13] To demonstrate this point which has an important bearing on the debate about perspective, though admittedly on

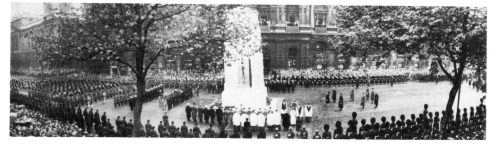

218. Panoramic photograph of Remembrance Day Ceremony in Whitehall, London.
From *The Times*, 14 November 1966

little else, I had an artist construct the box containing a row of three schematic trees of various shapes and sizes so aligned that they occlude each other from one point, the peephole of the box (see Figs. 170 and 171).[14] The photograph shows the silhouette of the nearest tree but none of the other trees, which are only revealed by means of the shadows they cast on the wall of the box. In theory it makes no difference to that silhouette if we remove first the foremost and then the second tree because their projections are designed to be identical, as the laws of perspective imply.

Now if you keep your eye at the peephole but roll it up, down, and sideways, you will find that the image loses definition. It will become indistinct because it will fall outside the foveal area, but none of the schematic trees which were occluded when we looked straight into the box will emerge during that exercise. Hence if you want to follow the programme of the eye-witness principle of not including in your picture anything that is not visible from a given point, you can and indeed you must stick to the method of central perspective which the camera has taken over from the painter.

So far, I would claim my box (if I may so call it) vindicates the traditional method of the perspectival painter who looks straight on at the landscape he wants to paint and measures the relative size of the objects in the landscape against the upright pencil held in his outstretched arm (Fig. 219). The method tells him quite simply what objects out there are or would be occluded by a given object held at arm's length. He may be surprised that a given tree occupies less than half the length of his pencil in what is called the projection plane. This surprise, which we all can feel if we repeat his exercise, helps to explain the reluctance to carry the eye-witness principle to its ultimate conclusion, but though the relative increase or diminution of objects due to distance may much exceed our expectation, there is no flaw in the method.

The method, to repeat, enables the artist to conform to the negative standard of truth I have outlined. The positive postulate, the question of how much visual information he should include in his painting, presents a very different problem and leads to very different standards of truth.

Consider two records made by Turner during his visits to Holland, one his famous and characteristic seascape *The Dort Packet-Boat from Rotterdam Becalmed* of 1818 (Fig. 220), showing what is no doubt a faithful view of the harbour of Dordrecht as the painter saw it, another a rapid sketch he made on a different visit to the same harbour (Fig. 221). We may assume that both these contrasting records conform to the negative eye-witness principle and both can be taken, for argument's sake, to be correct. The painter obviously did not show any part of the shore which was obscured by the sail or any part

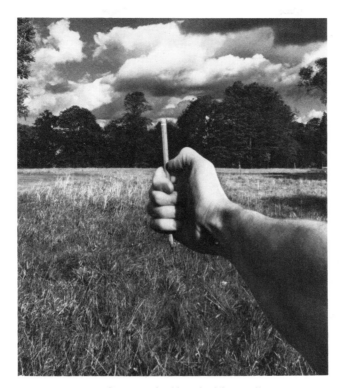

219. Outstretched hand with pencil

of the boat which was occluded from him. But this formulation only applies if it is meant to refer to the objects and aspects which were *potentially visible* from his station point. As soon as we ask how much of that scene he actually saw at the moment of painting or drawing we are confronted with a radically different set of questions.

An anecdote told by John Ruskin well illustrates this point. Always eager to exalt Turner's work for its absolute fidelity to visual truth, Ruskin mentions that a naval officer had criticized one of the master's drawings of the harbour of Plymouth—with some ships at a distance of a mile or two seen against the light—because 'the ships of the line had no portholes'. But Turner replied: 'If you will walk up to Mount Edgecombe and look at the ships against the sunset, you will find that you can't see the portholes.'[15] He may well have been right, and still there is an important difference between my inability to see a person's eyes because he is too far away and because he turns his back to me. The first fact depends on the structure and quality of our visual equipment, the second on the physical behaviour of light.

Not that this makes the first of these statements less important to the painter in the classical tradition. The loss of definition through distance preoccupied Leonardo at least as much as did the laws of geometrical

perspective.[16] He tellingly described the phenomenon as *'prospettiva de'*
perdimenti', the perspective of disappearance, though he more usually spoke
of 'aerial perspective'. It could be argued that this second term is doubly
misleading, first, because it attributes the loss of detail solely to the 'air', that
is, the degree of its permeability to light, and neglects the limits of the acuity
of the eye; second, because in equating the indistinctness of distant objects
with perspective (the diminution of distant objects), we lose an important
difference between the two phenomena. Linear perspective, as I have been at
pains to show, rests on rigidly objective standards, the perspective of
disappearance does not.

Eyesight, illumination, atmospheric conditions, the nature of the objects
themselves—their colour, their texture, their contrast with their surroundings—these and other variables play a role here, even if we do not take a
pair of spectacles or binoculars to upset the principle either by magnification
or, if we turn the binoculars round, by reduction in scale but increase in
relative luminosity. As we have seen, the scientist remains aware of these
variables and introduces into records the specifications of the instruments
which produced the image he wishes to evaluate. The painter cannot take
recourse to similar methods, and thus the observation of 'the perspective of
disappearance' has led him inexorably onto the path of introspection, of the
exploration of his subjective visual experience.

Not that this experience could not be communicated and, if I may so call it,
authenticated. It is an undeniable fact that by the introduction of Leonardo's
programme paintings gained in visual credibility. The method enhanced the
vicarious experience of sharing a privileged view with an eye-witness. The
progressive loss of information about objects at increasing distance produces
a gain in the evocation of the experience of an imaginary eye-witness. Claude
Lorrain's magnificent vision of *The Sermon on the Mount* in the Frick
Collection (Fig. 222) conveys a very different experience from that mediated
by Raphael's cartoon of *Saint Paul Preaching at Athens*, but in both cases
visual truth enhances our feeling of participation.

Small wonder that the principle of eliminating all that the eye-witness
could not see led to further heart-searching on the part of the artist. In the
seventeenth century it was observed that it was absurd to paint the spokes of a
rapidly revolving wheel because we cannot see them, and so Velázquez
painted the spinning wheel in the *Hilanderas* as a mere shimmering area.[17] So
much for the moving object, but what, once more, about the moving eye?
The difference I have mentioned in connection with my experiment between
foveal and peripheral vision played a part in the history of optics in the special
role assigned to what was called the central ray, but as far as I know it was not

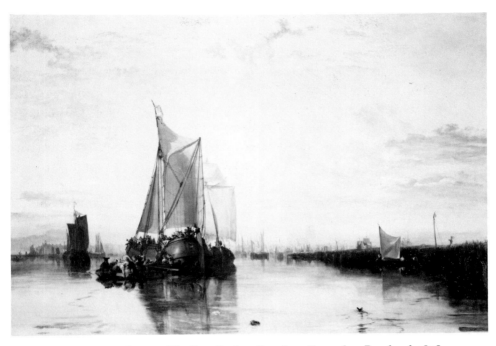

220. J. M. W. Turner: *The Dort Packet-Boat from Rotterdam Becalmed*. 1818.
New Haven, Conn., Yale Centre for British Art, Paul Mellon Collection

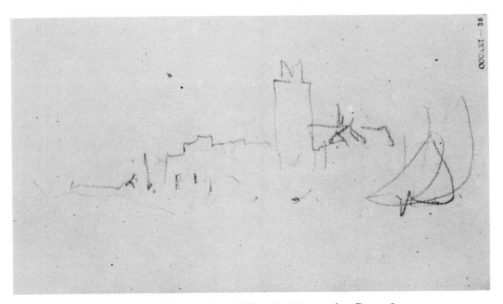

221. J. M. W. Turner: *Rapid Sketch of Approach to Dort*. 1841.
London, The British Museum, Turner Bequest

before the early eighteenth century that the painter was asked to pay heed in his work to the difference between the focused area and the rest of the scene in front of him.

In *The Sense of Order* I have sketched part of that story,[18] quoting and criticizing Roger de Piles, who erroneously equated the lateral loss of definition with the perspective of disappearance and who in his turn influenced Hogarth. Though de Piles' and Hogarth's descriptions of the visual experience still left something to be desired, the relevance of the phenomenon to the problems of the painter is well illustrated by a passage from Hermann von Helmholtz where this greatest student of optics discusses what he calls 'indirect vision':

> The eye is an optical instrument of a very large field of vision, but only a small very narrowly confined part of that field of vision produces clear images. The whole field corresponds to a drawing in which the most important part of the whole is carefully rendered but the surrounding is merely sketched, and sketched the more roughly the further it is removed from the main object. Thanks to the mobility of the eye, however, it is possible to examine carefully every point of the visual field in succession. Since in any case we are only able to devote our attention at any time to one object only, the one point clearly seen suffices to occupy it fully whenever we wish to turn to details; on the other hand

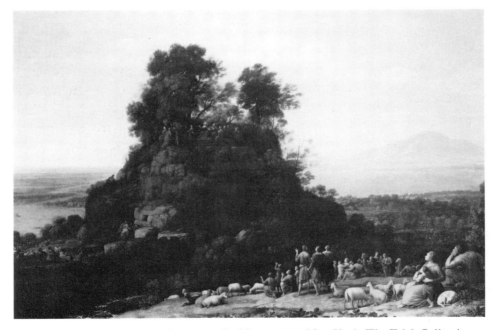

222. Claude Lorrain: *The Sermon on the Mount*. 1656. New York, The Frick Collection

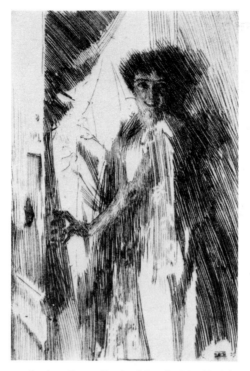

223. Anders Zorn: *Rosita Mauri*. 1889. Etching

the large field of vision is suitable, despite its indistinctness, for us to grasp the whole environment with one rapid glance and immediately to notice any novel appearance on the margin of the field of vision.[19]

At the time when Helmholtz wrote, these facts of vision were frequently appealed to by critics of painting. Particularly during the battle for and against Impressionism, the question of finish, of definition, came much to the fore, and such sketchy methods as those of the popular Swedish etcher Anders Zorn were explicitly defended on the grounds of truth to visual experience (Fig. 223). Looking at the face of the lady, the eye-witness could not possibly also see her hands or the details of her dress with any accuracy. Of course there can be no doubt about the truth of the negative argument. The artist could indeed not see or at least examine these features without moving his eye, but does the sketch also record truthfully how these unfocused elements looked to him at one particular moment in time? We are back to the question of what things may look like while we do not look at them. We have learned from Helmholtz that it need not bother us in real life because we always tend rapidly to focus on any feature to which we wish to devote attention. This fact alone suffices to make nonsense of that notorious ideal of the so-called innocent eye which I was at pains to criticize in *Art and*

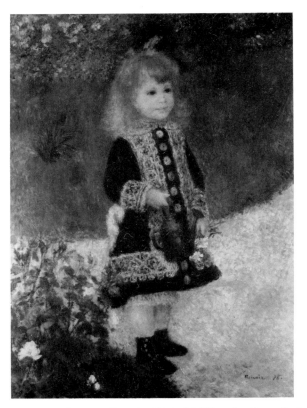

224. Pierre Auguste Renoir: *Girl with Watering Can.* 1876.
Washington, The National Gallery of Art, Chester Dale Collection

Illusion. Even the eye of the Impressionist must be selective. It must focus on the significant rather than the insignificant in the field of vision. More than that. The Impressionist technique of trying to capture the fleeting vision of a moment must rely doubly on what, in that book, I called 'the beholder's share'. He can be sketchy only where we can supplement. We know or guess that Zorn's lady had arms and hands and can take this as read. But where the artist cannot rely on the beholder's experience, he will be compelled to inspect and convey the motif in much greater detail, presumably by moving his eyes.

It may not be very artistic to scrutinize paintings by great masters for the amount of information embodied in their pictures, but indirectly we learn a good deal even from this perverse exercise. I have paid attention for some time to the way Impressionists rendered decorative motifs, patterns on dresses, on wallpapers, and on china, and I found to my surprise that they went much further into detail than I had expected (Fig. 224). You can afford to leave out a hand or an eye, but you cannot ask the beholder to guess the pattern on a dress of which he has no knowledge.

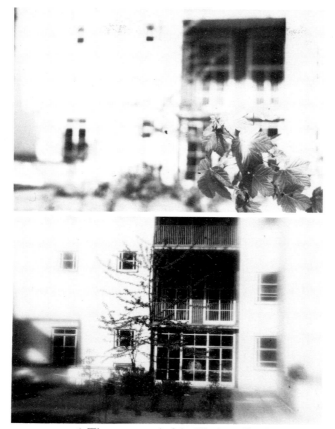

225, 226. The courtyard of the Warburg Institute,
with close focus on leaf (*above*) and with lateral
blurring, by a photographer of the Warburg Institute

Needless to say, the camera can never achieve the tact and selectivity which the painter can display in this effort to evoke a subjectively truthful visual experience, but the photographer has no difficulty in recording the effect of differential focusing along the line of sight. I have asked the photographer of the Warburg Institute to focus his lens on the leaves in the foreground of the courtyard of its building, leaving the background blurred (Fig. 225). It is not a picture he would have taken normally because by using a different opening and exposure time he could easily have increased the depth of his picture far beyond what the eye can record at any one moment. But what about the lateral decrease of definition discussed by Helmholtz? Here the normal camera is less adapted to follow the eye. Our photographer resorted to the expedient of covering part of his lens with vaseline to get partial blurring of the field, but the results only demonstrate the futility of this device (Fig. 226). Things are not simply blurred outside the foveal area, they are indistinct in a much more elusive way.

What compounds this elusiveness is the intriguing fact that peripheral vision is extremely sketchy in the perception of shapes and colours but very responsive to movement. We are aware of any displacement in the medley of forms outside the foveal area and ever ready to focus on such an unexpected intrusion. Once we have done so, we can track the moving object without letting it go out of focus, while the rest of the field of vision recedes from our awareness. There is no means of conveying this experience in a stationary display. The perception of movement is different in character from the inspection of a static scene. True, photography, as we have seen, can record the track of a moving flash, and the trail of forms left on the emulsion during a long exposure has suggested to painters a number of devices for rendering motion—one of them being the device adopted by Smilby for suggesting the rapidity of the painter's movement, that is, by showing many hands linked by a blur.[20] But though we have come to take this convention for granted, it is rather untrue to the experience we would have had in watching the painter at work. If we had tried to track his hand, we could not have attended to his head, let alone to the lightning flashes seen through the window.

While I was reflecting on these perplexities several years ago, my attention was caught by an advertisement which was at that time frequently displayed in London buses (Fig. 227). As is so often the case with such products of the advertiser's skill, I subsequently had considerable difficulty in tracking it down and procuring a copy when I wished to use it as a demonstration piece. I fastened on it because to my mind it came reasonably close to what I had been looking for, an arrested image which recorded both the effects of blurring through movement with that of selective focus. In the original, the effect is enhanced by the vivid colours which certainly provided attraction for those passengers who were not meditating on the standards of truth in visual representation. The theme is the daily ceremony of the changing of the guards in London, a reminder of past pomp and glory which remains a favourite tourist attraction. Innumerable visitors must have tried to snap this approach of the cavalry with their resplendent uniforms, helmets, and flags, but if they did not get more on their films than we see on the poster they probably discarded it as a bad shot. The German designer van Brissen did not. Whether or not he had pondered the implications of the eye-witness principle, he may have found that the picture conformed to its negative demand that no more should be shown than can be seen from one spot during one moment of time—however we may wish to define such a moment. We focus on the white horse in the van, though its rider is less clearly visible. The flag on the left and the brown horse on the right are also less easy to discern, and it is hard to tell whether the eight helmets we can make out are all there

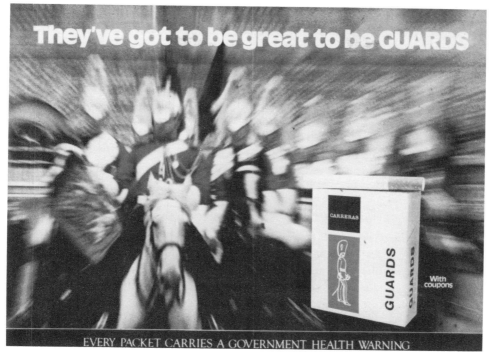

227. Van Brissen: Poster for Guards cigarettes

were. The eye-witness could not linger and count during the cavalry's rapid advance, for I presume he had to get out of the way in a hurry.

Here, then, we have an arrested image which tries to convey both the effect of the moving motif and of the limitations of the non-moving eye, and however eccentric the result may be, it provides food for thought on what I have called the subjective standard of truth—truth to our visual experience. In a sense it may also be described as a *reductio ad absurdum* of this very standard, which has played such a part in discussions of the hand-made image. In the first instance it confirms Gibson's view that we have no privileged access to our own visual sensations which are supposed to underlie our perceptions. We cannot really tell to what extent the experience the eye-witness had is correctly mediated by the picture, and he could not tell us either. As soon as he tried to do so he would have to make it more definite than it was—a problem all of us have had who have ever tried to tell a dream. It is here that we come up once more against the second and fatal flaw of the eye-witness principle;[21] taken to its limits it flounders on what Gibson called 'the Greco Fallacy', the belief that Greco's figures are so elongated because his astigmatism made him see them so distorted, forgetting that in that case he would also have seen his paintings elongated and would have had to correct them till they matched his vision of the model.[22]

It was no other than John Ruskin who anticipated Gibson and applied his warning to the representation of peripheral indistinctness:

> We indeed can see, at any one moment, little more than one point, the objects beside it being confused and indistinct; but we need pay no attention to this in art, because we can see just as little of the picture as we can of the landscape without turning the eye; and hence any slurring or confusing of one part of it, laterally, more than another, is not founded on any truth of nature, but is an expedient of the artist—and often an excellent and desirable one—to make the eye rest where he wishes it.[23]

In the case of our poster it is especially easy to know where the designer wishes the eye to come to rest—it is not the leading horse of the cavalcade which is most in focus but the packet of cigarettes. In obediently focusing on this area, indeed in reading the captions, it is the whole photograph which moves outside the foveal area and becomes indistinct. We can prevent this no more than we can prevent focusing on the indistinct passages and thus contradicting the experience they are meant to convey.

Clearly, then, there are more limits to the functioning of the eye-witness standard than could be foreseen when the visual image was first used to turn the beholder into the vicarious participant of an event. The shift from the object out there to the experiencing subject has resulted in perplexities which make it understandable why the very subject of visual representation has become problematic to psychologists and philosophers alike. The objective and the subjective standards of truth became hopelessly muddled in many of their discussions.

It is perhaps easier to see from the point we have reached how this confusion also affected the debate on perspective. I have stressed here and elsewhere that perspective cannot and need not claim to represent the world 'as we see it'. The perceptual constancies which make us underrate the degree of objective diminutions with distance, it turns out, constitute only one of the factors refuting this claim. The selectivity of vision can now be seen to be another. There are many ways of 'seeing the world', but obviously the claim would have to relate to the 'snapshot vision' of the stationary single eye. To ask, as it has so often been asked, whether this eye sees the world in the form of a hollow sphere or of a projection plane makes little sense, for it sees neither. The one point in focus can hardly be said to be either curved or flat, and the remainder of the field of vision is too indistinct to permit a decision. True, we can shift the point of focus at will, but in doing so we lose the previous perception, and all that remains is its memory. Can we, and do we, compare the exact extension of these changing percepts in scanning a row of columns extended at right angles from the central line of vision—to mention the most recalcitrant of the posers of perspectival theory?[24] I very much doubt it. The theory refers to the convenient choice of projection planes, not to the experience of vision.

As I have tried to show at the outset, the scientist is never troubled by questions of this kind. What matters to him is that he knows the behaviour of light and the specifications of his instrument. Even in the absence of such a complete record he would not disdain using a photograph like our poster. If no other document were available, he might surely try to find out from it as much as it might yield about the changing of the guards. After all, military intelligence officers have frequently had to work with even more fragmentary evidence, extrapolating from what they could guess of its probable history; and in this work they certainly would not have to worry about anybody's visual experience.

But if this subjective experience is in fact as private and elusive as I have made it out to be, how could it ever have been elevated into a standard of truth? I have attempted to give an answer to this question in *Art and Illusion* and in several other of my writings, but I welcome the opportunity to test it here against another kind of image. The standards, I argued, are based not on a comparison of the motif with the image but on the potential capacity of the image to evoke the motif. In this reading of the history of image making, the artist has no more privileged access to his visual experience than has anyone else.[25] But he has trained himself to watch his own response to the image as it grows under his hand. If his aim is a matching of the visual world, he will follow up any device that suggests it to him. If his work is successful, we may infer that it also suggests such an experience to other beholders. A feedback loop is set up which leads to an ever closer approximation to the desired effect.

This, then, is the reason why I have selected this poster for analysis. However debatable it may be whether it matches a visual experience, we must presume that those who selected it found that it had become acceptable to their public. I find it useful in this concluding section to concentrate on this photographic device because photography yields more easily to the separation of the standards of truth than does the hand-made image.[26]

One thing is sure. At the time when photography was a new medium a shot like van Brissen's would not have been acceptable, even if it had been considered readable. In tracing the development which made it acceptable, the historian would have to consider at least three different factors—the technical equipment, the general notion of social decorum, and, most important of all, the education of the public in the reading of images which are capable of evoking an experience even through the absence of information.[27]

In contrasting evocation and information as two different functions of the image, I am again referring to a distinction which was made by Sir Joshua Reynolds in his famous discussion of Gainsborough's portraits. As long as a portrait 'in this undetermined manner' contains enough to remind the spectator of the sitter, 'the imagination supplies the rest, and perhaps more satisfactorily . . . than the artist, with all his care, could possibly have done'. True, Reynolds continues, the effect presupposes a knowledge of the sitter; in the absence of such knowledge the imagination may 'assume almost what character or form it pleases'.[28] Evocation, in other words, relies even more on prior information than perspectival records.

No doubt this is true. But the formula does not yet tell us what type of information we need to bring the incomplete image to life.[29] Perhaps it is less information than understanding that is involved. An intelligent woman who had her first baby relatively late in life observed that baby shapshots began to assume more vividness for her after she had experienced how babies move and react. It is this capacity to generalize, to move from the known to the less known, which must never be left out of account when discussing 'the beholder's share'. A photograph from that famous anthology *The Family of Man* may illustrate this point (Fig. 228). To me, at any rate, it immediately evokes the situation of the hunting bushman—the aiming hand, the tense watchfulness, the presumed fate of the quarry—but I have never hunted antelopes with bushmen. It is not to the memory of information previously stored that the image appeals but to the very faculty Reynolds invokes, the imagination. It is a term not frequently used in psychological debates today because it is insufficiently precise to be subject to measurements and tests, but I believe the student of the evocative potential of images cannot do without it. Whatever term he uses, he must account for the capacity of the human mind to respond not only to individual memories but to kinds or classes of events. Whatever we study, we are always likely to land ourselves right in the middle of the oldest and most persistent philosophical debate, the debate about the so-called problem of universals.

Without a prior disposition to respond to such generic classes as faces or bodies, we could not cope with novelty. Experience is always novel, it can never repeat itself exactly. I hold with those who believe that there are certain classes of experience to which we are programmed to respond from birth, while others are readily assimilated to this initial stock.[30] I doubt whether we know enough about these mysteries to plot the course of this learning process

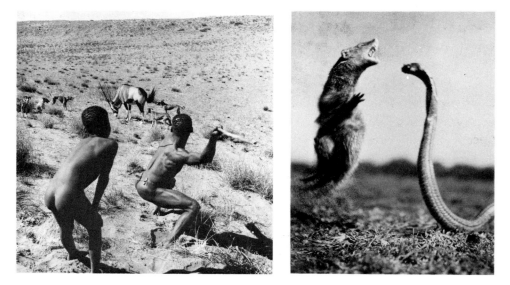

228. *Hunting in Botswana (formerly Bechuanaland)*. Photograph by N. R. Farbman.
229. *Fight Between Cobra and Mongoose*. From Ylla, *Animals in India* (Lausanne, 1958)

and to tell in every case which of our reactions is learned and which is not. I believe that some degree of what used to be called empathy, the automatic reaction to another person's physical state, is built into our perceptions and that we see the tenseness of the throwing arm rather than infer it.[31] Indeed I would venture to go further still and postulate that we have some empathy even with animals, that the dramatic life-and-death fight between a cobra and a mongoose is intelligible to us, that it appeals to our imagination, because we instinctively understand the urgency of this confrontation (Fig. 229). It is a configuration of which the meaning is easily learned because the pathways are laid.

But surely man is a strange creature. His ability to assimilate, to learn to respond to symbols and to novel situations, suggests a degree of plasticity of the moving mind which defies analysis and confounds prediction. A generation or two ago instantaneous snapshots were pronounced illegible because the public had not yet made the connection between the images and the process by which they came about. It is here rather than in the features recorded by the image that understanding presupposes a process of cultural habituation or training. Almost any recent collection of photographs of landscapes and people can serve to remind us of this public habituation on which the photographer can rely. Four photographs from *Viaggio in Toscana*, the attractive book by Gianni Berengo Gardin, illustrate the range of this ready response. The first is traditional in style (Fig. 230). It shows the

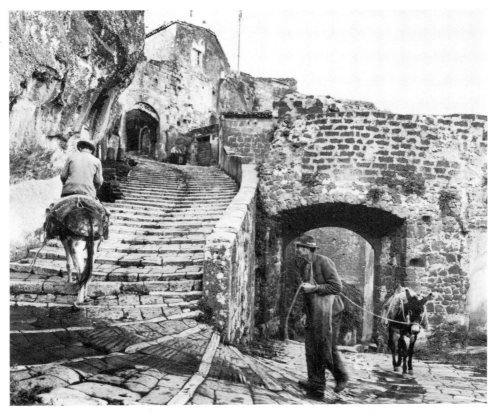

230. *Donkey riders*. From Gianni Berengo Gardin, *Viaggio in Toscana* (Lausanne, 1967, p. 51)

unmistakable old-world scene of the road and allows us vicariously to experience its course as we automatically follow in our minds the movement of the men and the donkeys up the hill. We are left in no doubt where they came from and where they are going. But those of us who know the Italian scene may respond with equal vividness to the snapshot taken from an unfamiliar angle, probably out of a window, showing a woman in a narrow road carrying loaves of bread on her head (Fig. 231). A few decades ago such a picture would hardly have been selected for publication, even less, perhaps, the snapshot which records the reaction of the woman in the church to the photographer, the woman who turns round to stare at the intruder (Fig. 232). If this picture relies on our understanding of how it came about, the fourth example from the collection presents the extreme of this expectation. It shows a famous palace façade in Montepulciano (Palazzo Buccelli) partly composed of Etruscan reliefs and tombstones (Fig. 233). A documentary volume would have shown it neat and (incidentally) captioned it. Here the photographer included the blurred images of two passers-by, a device which would have shocked earlier publishers and users but which serves eminently

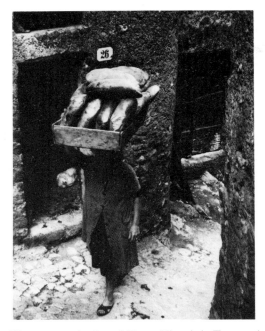

231. *Woman carrying bread.* From *Viaggio in Toscana* (p. 59)

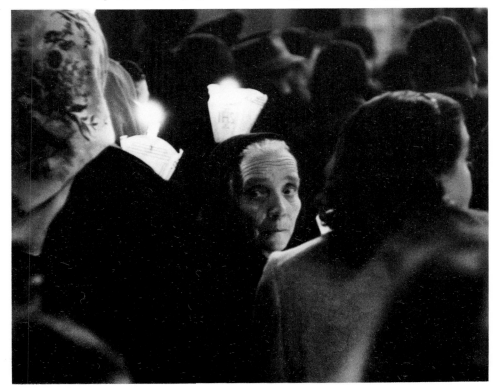

232. *Woman turning round.* From *Viaggio in Toscana* (p. 58 top)

well to evoke the reality of an old building which still belongs to a living town. Next time when we take a photograph on our travels we may also refuse to wait till the view is clear and hope for a similar result.

But whether or not we are used to taking snapshots ourselves, we have seen so many that we can classify them and understand them. We have adjusted to the peculiarities of the arrested image and accept it as 'true' for its evocative rather than its informative qualities. Thus the photograph of a giraffe, which I take from a book by Federico Hecht published in 1971, no longer looks like a spoilt picture he should have discarded (Fig. 234). Our tolerance is due to an understanding of the situation in which the picture was presumably taken; he probably saw these creatures in a fading light and risked a longer exposure time which resulted in a blur. But does not this ghost-like image permit us to imagine the appearance in the wild of these fabulous animals with a kind of vividness denied to the textbook illustration which gives us so much more information? In other words, has not the technical accident led to a psychological discovery?

We must not yield to the temptation to which the philosophy of art has given in far too often, of declaring that this picture is more truthful than the

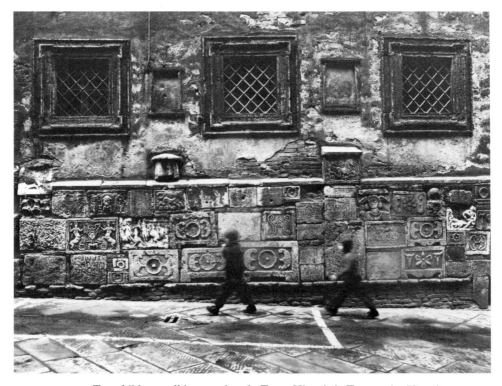

233. *Two children walking past façade.* From *Viaggio in Toscana* (p. 88 top)

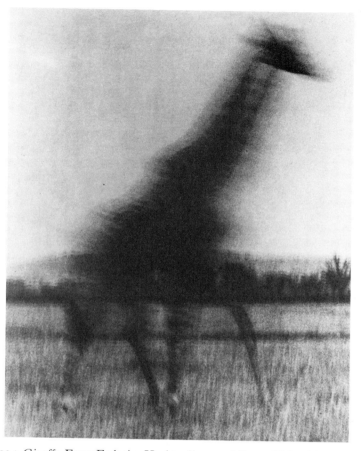

234. *Giraffe*. From Federico Hecht, *Above and Beyond* (Munich, 1971)

detailed photograph. This kind of aesthetic one-up-manship gets us nowhere. But it may be truthful in a different way, more evocative of something which is not information but rather a peculiar kind of experience which we can understand whether or not we have ever been to Africa. We are back at what I have called the eye-witness principle, but from the other side, as it were. Not from that of the object, but from that of the subject. It was the shift from the one to the other which ultimately led to pictures like the poster of the guards which I analysed and criticized for its inherent contradictions. The contradictions are there, but they still illuminate the fascinating problem of the various standards of truth which we have learned to accept in our commerce with visual images.

Image and Code : Scope and Limits of Conventionalism in Pictorial Representation

THE TITLE I gave to this essay is intended to allude to that perennial question in philosophy which much exercised the Greek mind—the question of what in our world is part of nature *(physis)* and what is convention *(thesis, nomos, ethos)*. It is raised in connection with the topic of this conference in one of Plato's strangest dialogues, the *Cratylus*, which is concerned with the philosophy of language. There seems to be no more obvious instance of an arbitrary convention than the names we give to people and to things. Socrates might also have been called Aristophanes, and the other way round, just as the word for 'horse' might have been not *'hippos,'* but *'kyon,'* the word for dog. It is common-sense conviction which is challenged in Plato's *Cratylus*: at least one of the speakers wants to prove that the words of language are not arbitrary but reveal something of the nature of the things to which they refer. It is an idea which has haunted students of language ever since and has led to extraordinary flights of fancy, but it need not concern me here. What matters is that the participants in Plato's dialogue take it for granted that—whatever may hold for words—pictures, visual images, are natural signs. They are recognizable because they are more or less 'like' the things or the creatures they depict.

This common-sense distinction between images, which are naturally recognizable because they are imitations, and words, which are based on conventions, has pervaded the discussion of symbols or semiotics ever since Plato.[1] To be sure there are imitations also in language, the onomatopoeic words such as 'cuckoo' in English, but while what Peirce called iconic signs are fairly exceptional in speech, iconicity is the basis of the visual image. We can read the image because we recognize it as an imitation of reality within the medium.

Lecture given at the International Conference on the Semiotics of Art held in May 1978 in Ann Arbor, Michigan.

I am afraid I must plead guilty to having undermined this plausible view. In my book on *Art and Illusion*[2] I made the point repeatedly that there is something like a language of pictorial representation. Art historians know that in past styles images were frequently made with the aid of conventions which had to be learned. The most famous example is that of the Egyptian style, which the German Egyptologist Heinrich Schäfer[3] has fully analysed as a visual code to explain how Egyptian artists would solve certain problems like that of recession in space within their rules. The closed and hieratic style of Egypt made this analysis particularly compelling, but I have no doubt that comparable conventions existed elsewhere, say in the painting of the Far East, and can be tabulated and recognized by the expert.

Any art historian will remember examples from other fields; thus, I elsewhere[4] discussed the convention of rendering rocks which extended from late antiquity, as in the mosaics at Ravenna, to the Quattrocento and beyond. Even Leonardo made use of them in the grandiose visions of landscapes he drew from his imagination. I never asserted that Leonardo's drawings do not represent nature more accurately than earlier conventions, let alone that no picture of a landscape—for instance a picture postcard—can be a more faithful rendering of a view than the background of the *Mona Lisa*.

This, however, is the claim made, or nearly made, by Nelson Goodman in *Languages of Art*. I cannot here do full justice to this difficult and subtle work, but briefly the thesis Professor Goodman defends is one of complete relativism. Realism, he says, is relative. We may find an ancient Egyptian representation unrealistic because we have not learned to read it. The same may happen to our traditional standards of realism. To quote his own words:

> Realistic representation ... depends not upon imitation or illusion or information but upon inculcation. Almost any picture may represent almost anything; that is, given picture and object there is usually a system of representation, a plan of correlation, under which the picture represents the object.[5]

There is nothing implausible in this formulation, for after all we know that when Impressionist pictures were new they were found hard to read. And I have no doubt that Professor Goodman's bold assertion that there is no such thing as resemblance to nature owes some of its success to what I have called the apologetics of twentieth-century art. Whether Picasso represented the head of a woman as in 1904 (Fig. 235) or in 1927 (Fig. 236), only a philistine could say that women looked more like the first than the second.

Now it is again true to say that we are no longer shocked by the second picture and that this is a matter of convention. We have accepted the styles of

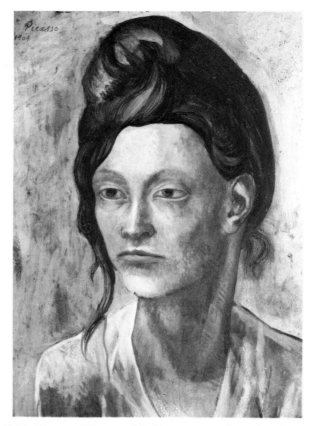

235. Pablo Picasso: *Woman with chignon*. 1904. Gouache. Collection of
The Art Institute of Chicago, Bequest of Kate L. Brewster

twentieth-century art and are prepared to look at such a picture with this
attitude.

The simplest way of formulating what might be called extreme
conventionalism would be the assertion that there is no generic difference
between pictures and maps. Both, as Nelson Goodman concedes, can give us
information, but only if we are familiar with the code. Maps, of course,
frequently set out the code in what is called a 'key' to the symbolism
employed.[6] Faced with a map of the religions of the world, we could not read
it unless we consulted the key which tells us that Islam is green and Roman
Catholicism red. Often, however, the choice of the code is not wholly
arbitrary but employs mnemonic devices which make it easier to remember,
as when in a map of the products of the world oilfields are marked with
triangles suggesting derricks. It is interesting to observe how frequently
synaesthetic metaphors are also drawn upon to anchor the symbolism in
psychological dispositions—as when in maps of the climate the cooler regions
are marked blue and the warmer ones red.

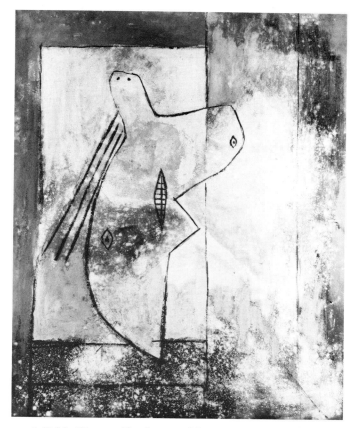

236. Pablo Picasso: *Head*. 1927. Oil and plaster. Collection of
The Art Institute of Chicago, Gift of Mr. and Mrs. Samuel Marx

To read any such map, however, we must first realize what it is: a projection of the curved surface of the earth. This convention is born of convenience, since it is awkward to operate with globes. If we want flat maps that we can spread out on a table or bind together in an atlas we have no choice but to opt for a form of projection which can never preserve all geometrical relationships marked on the globe. A map dating from 1507 and designed to be pasted on a globe (Fig. 237) neatly illustrates the dilemma and so does any comparison of the continents as represented by various systems.

This is one of the aspects Professor Goodman had in mind when he speaks of inculcation. I have ventured to contribute a lengthy paper to the Essays in his Honour[7] to explain why I cannot agree with him. Perspective is the necessary tool, if you want to adopt what I now like to call the 'eye-witness principle', in other words, if you want to map precisely what any one could see from a given point, or, for that matter, what the camera could record. We can photograph a geographic globe and will know beforehand which countries will show on the plate, and we can repeat the experiment from a

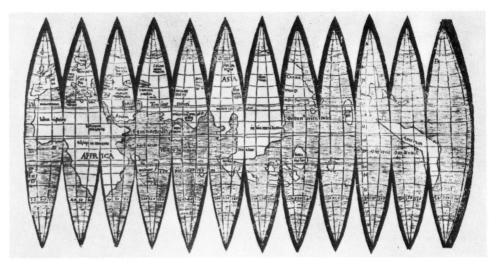

237. Waldseemüller: *Map of the World.* 1507

satellite and calculate precisely the area of the real globe it can survey at any one moment. We can also instruct a computer to give us the corresponding data about any such problem, and the information we need for programming it will embody the rules of perspectival projection.

But granted the objective, non-conventional element in a photograph, how closely does it ever come to the visual experience which it purports to reproduce? Surely a black and white photograph, at any rate, is not a replica of what is seen but a transformation which has to be re-translated to yield up the required information. This is another point I made in *Art and Illusion*, but which I found necessary in a later paper to qualify a little.

It is true that there is rarely a one-to-one correspondence between the amounts of light reflected from various areas of the motif and those reflected from the relevant parts of the photograph. Relationships must be compressed to be accommodated by the film or print. But I believe that the fact that they are thus transformed does not entitle us to call them an arbitrary code. They are not arbitrary, because a gradation from dark to light observed in the motif will still appear as such a gradation, even if reduced in span. It was to secure this analogy, after all, that from the very beginnings of the technical process photographers converted their 'negatives' into 'positives'.[8] It is perfectly true that the trained eye can also read a negative, but I am convinced that more learning is required for this transformation than for the reading of a 'normal' photograph. The lack of correspondence between image and reality is less obtrusive in the latter case than in the former. In fact the widespread view has recently been challenged that the conventional elements in photographs bar naïve subjects such as unsophisticated tribesmen from reading them.[9] At any rate it appears that learning to read an ordinary photograph is very unlike learning to master an arbitrary code. A better comparison would be with learning the use of an instrument. It is quite possible that many tribesmen who are handed a photograph will not know at first what to do with it, or how they are expected to look at it, but I assume their reaction would be similar if they were handed a pair of binoculars. You have to learn to use it. A microscope presents even greater difficulties to the beginner, but these difficulties have to do with the need for adjustment and for the right 'mental set' rather than with the learning of a 'convention'.

As soon as we approach our problem from this angle, the angle of the ease of acquisition, the traditional opposition between 'nature' and 'convention' turns out to be misleading. What we observe is rather a continuum between skills which come naturally to us and skills which may be next to impossible for anyone to acquire. Surely a cipher machine can operate with constantly varying codes which no human brain could master and apply. If we grade the so-called conventions of the visual image according to the relative ease or difficulty with which they can be learned, the problem shifts on to a very different plane. What must be learned, as we have seen, is a table of equivalences, some of which strike us as so obvious that they are hardly felt to be conventions,[10] while others are chosen 'ad hoc' and must be memorized piecemeal for the occasion.

It is instructive to apply this approach to the most basic element of the two-dimensional image, the outline. It has often been said that the outline is a convention because the objects of our environment are not bounded by lines. No doubt this is true, and as any photograph shows, outlines can easily be dispensed with as long as there are sufficient gradients in the distribution of light to indicate the limits of individual things in space. And yet it turns out that the traditional view of the contour as a convention is based on an oversimplification. Things in our environment are indeed separated from their background, at least they so detach themselves as soon as we move. The contour is the equivalent of this experience; it indicates what would happen if the image were not a still but were to change, as the world around us usually does. It is only in the distance that this change becomes imperceptible and that contours are therefore lost. To draw them around far away objects looks accordingly unrealistic.

So important are these boundaries indicating what psychologists call 'common fate' in features of the immediate environment that it has been shown that animals too respond to objects in outline as they do to their three-dimensional prototypes. The equivalence is so obvious that no special learning appears to be required.

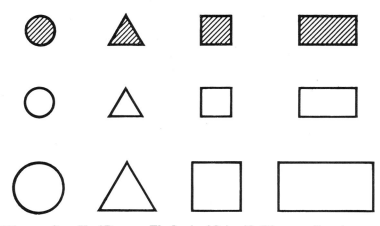

238. Diagram from Karl Popper, *The Logic of Scientific Discovery* (London, 1959)

I venture to think that from the point of view of the equivalence or response some of the problems which have agitated philosophers, particularly since the appearance of Nelson Goodman's book, can be exorcized: in a symposium I attended at Swarthmore College, Professor Marx W. Wartofsky made a drawing of a dog on the blackboard and wrote underneath the word 'dog'. He might also have written 'chien' or 'Hund'. He did it to assert that the words were neither more nor less like the real animal than the drawing. I am not sure that Nelson Goodman would go quite as far as this in asserting the purely arbitrary or conventional character of images, but he certainly insists that the term 'resemblance' or 'likeness' is useless for any definition of pictorial standards.★ For the philosopher the term 'likeness' is indeed without value[11] unless he is told in what respect two things are supposed to be compared. In his book *The Logic of Scientific Discovery*[12] Karl Popper has illustrated this important point by a simple diagram (Fig. 238).

★ When I sent this paper to Professor Goodman he kindly commented as follows in a personal letter: 'I read *Image and Code* with interest. I think it brings our views much nearer together on these matters. As you know, I do not hold some of the views often attributed to me. I do not say that representation is entirely a matter of convention, but rather hold that no firm line can be drawn between what is conventional and what is not. This is emphasized in my *Ways of Worldmaking*;[13] and you write that "the traditional opposition between nature and convention turns out to be misleading". Bravo! Also I do not deny that realism of representation has something to do with resemblance, but only urge that each affects the other, and that neither goes by unique or absolute standards. Finally, I surely don't deny that some tasks are easier than others. Hopping on one hand is harder than walking. Finding a square root is harder than adding. But I think as you do that it is "not very helpful to divide meanings into those which exist 'by nature' and others which are learned". That seems to diminish the importance of the residual disagreement: I cannot believe that the standard rules of perspective embody the one native and easiest way of achieving and reading a realistic depiction. But does innateness really matter much?'

You can see at a glance that the shapes are like in one respect when you read the diagram from the top to the bottom as circles, triangles, etc., in a different respect if you look at their surface, and different again if you compare their size. In the same way a picture of a dog might be like in shape but not in size, it might be like in colour but not in shape and so on through any number of variations which leave us no wiser as to which resembles the dog more.

You will not be surprised to hear me say that this would be all very well if images were made by students of logic for students of logic. But they are not, and when you study them in the way they function in communication you will soon notice a radical difference between the picture and the word. As mentioned earlier there is a famous mosaic from Pompeii, *Cave Canem*, Beware of the Dog (see Fig. 120). To understand the notice you must know Latin, to understand the picture you must know about dogs.[14] Let us concede to Professor Goodman's school that the designer of the warning has a great deal of choice in the shapes and colours he uses for his picture. He can use a fully coloured rendering or a mere silhouette, he can turn the relationships round or leave them intact and there is no reason why any of these methods might not be used in a textbook of zoology or in a children's book to represent a dog of a particular kind or breed and to indicate its distinctive features, the short legs of a dachshund or the slim body of a whippet. These images function like maps or like the silhouettes of planes used in handbooks of aircraft recognition.

But the picture of the dog is not meant to teach but to warn. It will do its job best if it looks menacing. I am convinced that we do not have to acquire knowledge about teeth and claws in the same way in which we learn a language. And the representations of teeth and claws in their turn will be more easily recognized than the features of various aircraft. There are few cultures and few styles which do not exploit this ease of recognition in the creation of threatening masks or protective spells.[15] I am led to the conclusion that in analysing the role of conventions in image making we must consider two distinct though interlocking gamuts of skill. The first is the one with which I have been concerned so far, which may be called the representational method or idiom; the second concerns meaning. We cannot regard the visual environment as neutral. Our survival often depends on our recognition of meaningful features, and so does the survival of animals. Hence we are programmed to scan the world in search of objects which we must seek or avoid. We are programmed to be more easily triggered by some configurations than by others. It appears indeed that the greater the biological relevance of a feature, the greater is also the ease of recognition, however remote the objective resemblance may be. We must assume such basic responses, as I said, not only in man but even in animals. To ask whether animals can respond to images seems like a return to the old anecdotes from antiquity about sparrows coming to peck at the grapes painted by Zeuxis, but if we don't take such reactions as a testimonial of artistic excellence (as we have seen that Pliny did) we may still persist with that question. Images have always been used to attract or frighten animals. What else is a decoy duck or the angler's bait than an image securing the reaction of another creature?

The main point I wish to make here is indeed that the fish which snaps at the artificial fly does not ask the logician in what respect it is like a fly and in what unlike. It classifies the stimuli that reach its brain through its eyes according to simple criteria, mainly whether they stimulate its appetite or its flight reaction. But though the fish cannot ask the logician, the logician or scientist can ask the fish or any other animal what those configurations have in common which trigger a reaction. In other words he can also replace the difficult word 'resemblance' by the idea of 'equivalence' and study the biological meaning which various shapes may have in common for a particular species.

I am referring to the exciting work done by students of animal behaviour such as Konrad Lorenz and Nikko Tinbergen on what they call inborn release mechanisms. By producing very simple models, dummies, the scientist can define the minimal features which are necessary to make a young bird open its beak or a stickleback fish attack. These reactions are not learned, they are instinctive. They suggest that the organism is programmed to categorize the world around it according to some principles of equivalent meaning which allow it to survive. To perceive is to categorize, or classify, and as soon as we look at the problem of *physis* and *thesis* from that biological point of view, some of the puzzles can be seen in their just proportion.

The pressure of evolution can also result in the emergence of illusionistic resemblance to other things, such as the moth which looks like a leaf (Fig. 11). Such deceptions owe their existence to the survival of mutations which will not be noticed by predators. In other words they camouflage or blot out the meaning which the animal would have to the hungry bird.

I always like to remind extreme relativists or conventionalists of this whole area of observations[16] to show that the images of nature, at any rate, are not conventional signs, like the words of human language, but show a real visual resemblance, not only to our eyes or our culture but also to birds or beasts. I am well aware of the fact that there is a difference here between men and animals, and that difference is precisely the role which culture, conventions, laws, traditions can make in our reactions; we have not only a nature, *physis*, but also what in English parlance is so aptly called 'second nature', our personality which is formed by our cultural environment. He would be a bold person who would claim that he can tell at any time which of his own reactions, or of those of his fellow humans, are due to conditioning, to what Nelson Goodman calls 'inculcation' and which we would experience in any case wherever we had been born and however we had been brought up.

Recognizing an image is certainly a complex process and draws on many human faculties, both inborn and acquired. But without a natural starting-point we could never have acquired that skill. It seems to me that if we want to investigate that skill outside the laboratory we should by preference turn not to products of 'high art' but to the images on display on the hoardings and in the press, that is to posters and advertisements. I have used such images in *Art and Illusion* and for various reasons. For one, these designs are certainly intended to be read and recognized, something one cannot say with the same assurance of all works of art encountered in museums and galleries; secondly it seems to me more appropriate to select for such a study of the workings of perception not the great masterpieces of art. I remember too well how irritating I found it when I was a schoolboy that we appeared to read Homer mainly as a storehouse of grammatical exceptions. But the art of the poster designer is not debased if we use it to analyse response to meaning and understanding of conventions, uninhibited by classical prejudice or aesthetic taboos. Its very purpose is to surprise and shock by the use of novel methods and to combine this shock with a clarity of meaning without which the design would lose its appeal and the artist his livelihood.

Take the poster advertising the zoo for London Transport designed by one of our most inventive artists, Abram Games (Fig. 239). It seems well suited to exemplify what Ulric Neisser[17] has termed the 'perceptual cycle' because its complexity slows down the process and thus permits us to watch it by introspection. I believe I can distinguish three main stages in that experience. The first is the moment of alertness or attention. Unhappily it cannot easily be recaptured in the present context, for when shown on the screen or in a book the attention is presupposed. It is different when the image is shown outdoors together with many others, for here the arousal of attention is the most vital effect for the advertiser. He must achieve this magnetic pull by the traditional means of loud colours, simple shapes, emphatic contrasts, but also by the promise of meaning. The feeling 'attention, this has meaning', seems to me absolutely basic for the working of the image, and this feeling, unless I am much mistaken, is here achieved by the perception of eyes in a face. It is to this configuration that we are first alerted and which compels our glance. The second phase, if I may be

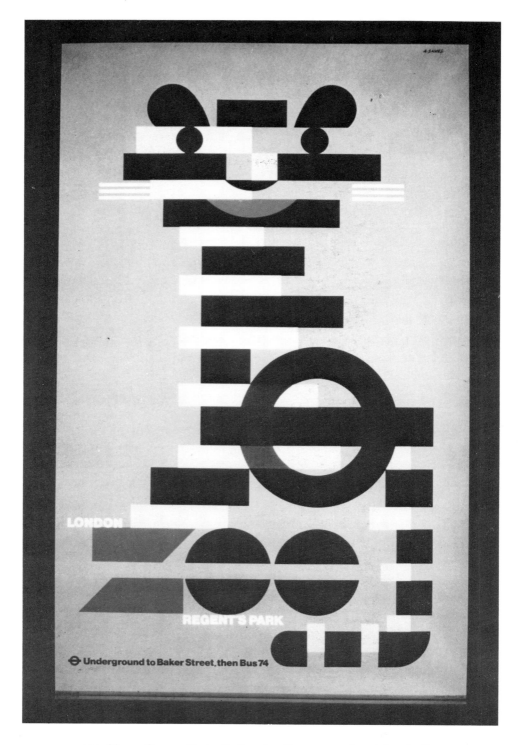

239. Abram Games: Poster for London Transport, advertising the Zoo

schematic, is one of puzzlement. We are made to stay with the image and wonder what it is all about. It is this phase of the enigma, the uncertainty, which discloses the absence of the usual conventions. There are no outlines here, no space, nothing we expect of a representation, and yet the meaning is found. What is this striped body under the face? Surely it is a tiger. And so we enter the third phase of working out, the integration of meaning. It does not take long to find that the creature has a tail and white whiskers, but it needs the knowledge of other conventions to take in the forms of the rest. One is the symbol of London's Underground, of which I showed several other applications in *Art and Illusion*.[18] Here it is embodied in the tiger's outline. If you persist in your reading you will also discover that the letters underneath are not just ornamental shapes, but unconventional letters spelling the word Zoo. The poster urges you to use London Transport to go to the Zoo in Regent's Park, and in the coloured original the green and blue are reminders of the green grass and the blue ponds in that lovely park.

I confess that I admired that poster for quite some time without doing all this working out, which I really only completed when I decided to use it as an example. But the example shows, I think, that it is the meaning which leads us to the convention and not the convention which leads us to the meaning. Without the meaning of the image we could not have understood the convention used in the lettering.

What is more, I would contend that here as so often recognition also results in a transformation of the configuration. Once we read the shapes as letters they visually cohere in a new way. This experience of shapes falling into place and integrating into an image is most easily experienced in puzzle pictures. Trying to find out what they represent we consciously apply what Bartlett called 'the effort after meaning'. It is this effort we can also watch at work when we solve the riddles of the advertisers to our fleeting satisfaction. Again it does not seem to me very helpful here to divide meanings into those which exist 'by nature' and those which are learned. Rather we should speak of a hierarchy of responses, some of which are easily triggered, whereas we must be conditioned to discover others. In any case it is unlikely that we shall make much progress in understanding how images work unless we start from the assumption that our senses were given us to apprehend meanings rather than shapes. Apparently our mind is so avid for meaning that it will go on searching and integrating, as if it were hungering for it all the time, ready to devour anything that can satisfy this need once it is roused. We speak in this context of the readiness to 'project', that readiness of which Leonardo da Vinci wrote in the famous passage describing the use of crumbling walls to stimulate the imagination. The poster designer does not go so far. It is part of

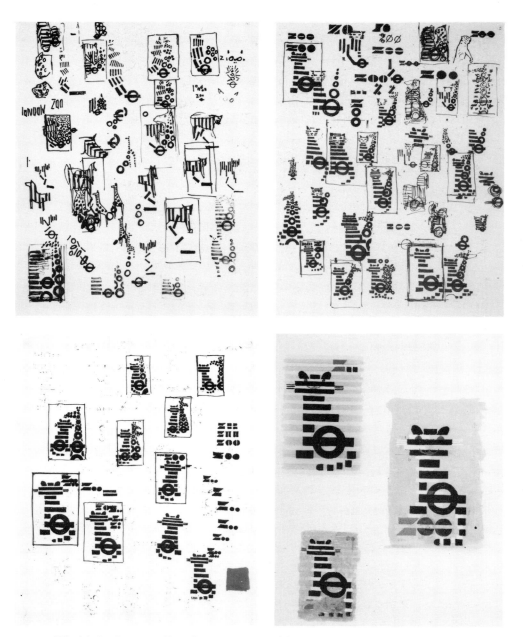

240. The birth of a poster. Development stages of the poster by Abram Games illustrated on p. 288 (Fig. 239). Courtesy of the artist

his purpose to guide the projection, first to suggest and then to establish a meaning. In fact, Mr. Games has been kind enough to respond to my analysis. In a recent letter to me he wrote:

Your philosophical analysis intrigued me because a designer's approach

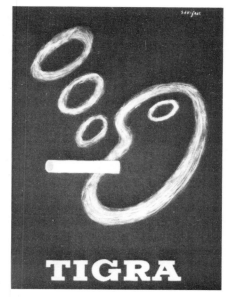

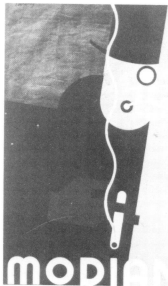

241. Raymond Savignac: Poster for Tigra. From *International Poster Award* (1952, p. 139)

242. R. Berény: Poster for cigarette paper. From *World Graphic Design* (1968, p. 20)

takes most of the described considerations 'en courant' as it were and without deliberate consciousness except at the back of the mind. All the same as an 'analytical worker' I recalled and recognised my developments as I read your words.

He has sent me a record of the earlier stages of his design (Fig. 240), showing that originally several striped and spotted animals, such as zebras, giraffes and leopards, were to be included, the giraffe holding out longest.

A few more examples may be helpful here. The poster by a leading French designer, Savignac (Fig. 241), is less complex than that of Games and is presumably more rapidly understood. The strange profile head which we see at once is easily explained; it is formed of smoke rings, no, it is forming smoke rings itself, for it is holding a cigarette. Surely here is a cultural experience, but we could not make the association unless we saw the face first as meaning. It may be helpful to contrast this excellent poster with one I find less good precisely because it takes too long to puzzle out and because it fails to arouse curiosity (Fig. 242). The man with a top hat and a monocle smokes a cigarette, but though one can work it out rationally I miss something in the first phase of alerting to meaning. Maybe the designer was too anxious to insist on the elegance of the smoker with his monocle. Possibly the addition, however sketchy, of the second eye would have added to the alerting power of the design.

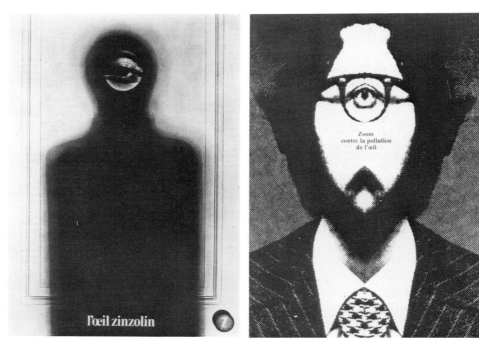

243. R. Cieslewicz: L'oeil zinzolin.
From *Modern Publicity* (1972–3, p. 127)

244. R. Cieslewicz: Advertisement for *Zoom Magazine*. From *Modern Publicity* (1972–3, p. 52)

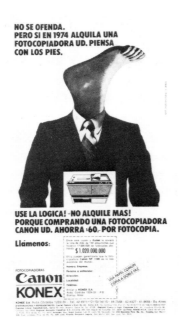

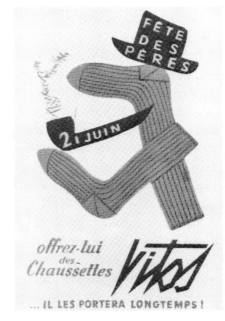

245. Oscar N. Marcovecchio:
Advertisement for copying machine.
From *Modern Publicity* (1975–6, p. 71)

246. Barlier: Advertisement for socks.
From *Modern Publicity* (1954–5, p. 59)

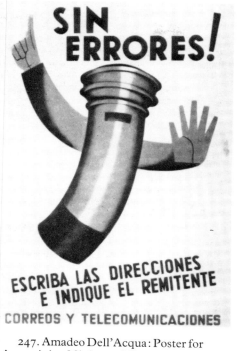

247. Amadeo Dell'Acqua: Poster for
Argentinian Ministry of Communications.
From *Modern Publicity* (1954–5, p. 51)

248. F. and R. Grindler: Poster for a
play. From *Modern Publicity* (1972–3, p. 46)

Not that the single eye cannot release a similar process of search and interpretation—at least it does with me in the strange poster for *l'œil zinzolin* (Fig. 243), which combines an eye at a keyhole with a vague outline I can see as a bottle or as a body, but where the body is clear the single eye becomes disturbing and menacing, as in another poster (Fig. 244). Indeed it is interesting what power the body shape has over us to project the image of a head onto the place where we expect to find it. You might exchange it for a foot (Fig. 245), and still get some kind of puzzling effect of plausibility even if you do not transform the shape of the foot by further manipulation, as in a harmless poster (Fig. 246) where the hat indicates what we are to expect and project.

Or take emphatic hands: how easily they transmute the pillar box into a person as on a Spanish poster imploring us to write a correct address (Fig. 247). Even a non-existent part of the body can make a ghost-like appearance on the surrealist image of half a man sitting in an easychair (Fig. 248).

Absent bodies are even more wittily suggested in another design by Games, advertising a newspaper (Fig. 249). It is really an image of an image, for the hands of the central figure, who holds the newspaper, appear to be indicated by roughly torn-out pieces of paper. And yet to the English public

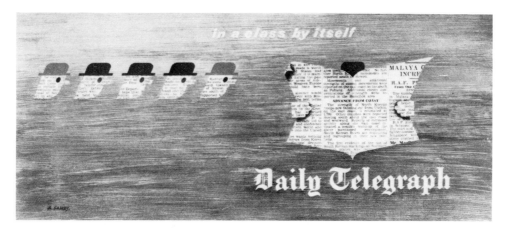

249. Abram Games: Advertisement for the *Daily Telegraph*.
From *International Poster Annual* (1951)

of our time the situation is immediately conjured up; the bowler hat suggests
the city gent, and the profiles of other members of the species gazing at the
same paper with envy leaves no doubt that they are all commuters in a train.

One would not have to go far outside our culture for the picture to become
illegible. The share of 'convention' is obvious, but they are not conventions
in the making of the image (which is in fact quite unconventional) but of dress
(bowler hat) and habits (reading the paper on the way to the city). In other
words the advertiser, like most artists, draws on the signs and symbols
current in the culture. More than that, where he finds that such symbols are
lacking or unsuitable for his purpose he will create them and train the public
to accept the convention.

Tourist propaganda abounds in such examples. The special attractions of a
country and the promise of enjoyment are often conveyed in a few
stereotyped images. It is legitimate, for instance, to associate Vienna with the
waltzes of Johann Strauss, but since travel folders cannot play music, a visual
symbol had to be found. The monument to the composer erected in one of
Vienna's parks in 1923 (Fig. 250) is admittedly no masterpiece. It aroused
much criticism in the days of my youth for its rather vulgar naturalism,
showing us a man of bronze playing the violin surrounded by marble nymphs
of the 'blue Danube'. However, the criticism is now forgotten, and the
abbreviated image of the monument serves as a shorthand symbol for that
aspect of Vienna. We find it combined with the universal bait used by all
advertisers, the picture of a smiling girl (Fig. 251). In another folder the
feminine element is represented by two air-hostesses, with the monument
behind them almost dissolved and transfigured by the radiant sun (Fig. 252).
Finally, the symbol is subjected to further distortions; it is printed in a red

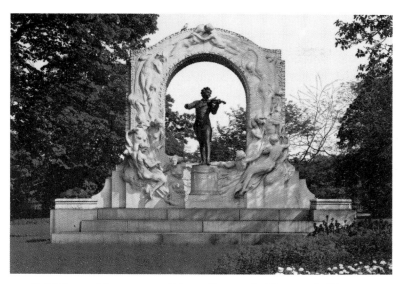

250. E. Hellmer: Monument to Johann Strauss the Younger in Vienna. 1923

silhouette and barely legible (Fig. 253), but the chain from the music to the monument and from the monument to the formula is expected to hold even in this puzzling transformation.

We would not expect any of the pictures discussed above to be shown in an

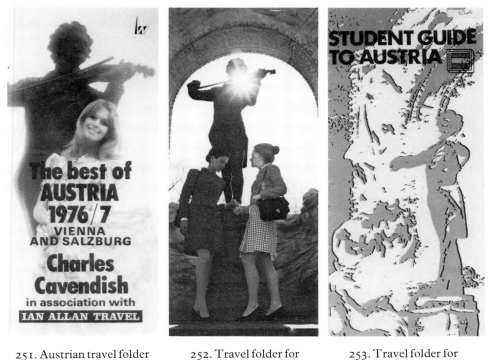

251. Austrian travel folder   252. Travel folder for   253. Travel folder for
                                        Austrian Airlines   students

art exhibition or illustrated in a book on twentieth-century movements. This fact is connected with another aspect of the role of conventions in image making, the emergence of 'genres'. In our society art no less than literature or music is divisible into such genres, which have their own implicit rules and therefore arouse different expectations.[19] The mental set with which we read a novel differs from that with which we read a police report—though when a police report forms part of a novel it will be read accordingly. In the same way our mental focus when looking at an abstract painting differs from our attitude in front of a decorative design, though the two might be interchangeable. Many battles have been fought about these aesthetic issues—e.g., whether statues should be coloured, or painted sketches be shown in exhibitions. It has been suggested, for instance, that these latter conventions had to be changed before Impressionist paintings could be accepted—and no doubt also read—by the general public.[20]

One is led to the conclusion that it is easier to transfer the skill of the search for meaning from one example of a genre to another than to learn the necessary adjustment required by a new genre. The most striking example of this generic adjustment I know is the ease with which schoolchildren read comics. I would hate to be solemn about the comic, but clearly as a genre it deserves more attention than I can devote to it in my present context because of its use of so many conventions.[21]

No doubt the success of comics in our society must be due to certain advantages they offer to the learner. There is first of all the mutual support one frame gives to the next; a sequence of narrative images must be easier to take in than a single picture aiming at the representation of a complex event, as is the case in academic painting. There is the further aid provided by the writing in the 'balloons'—never so long as to require complex unravelling, and usually printed in capitals. There are the conventional 'streaks' indicating movement, the stars in front of the eyes after a blow, question marks showing puzzlement; but most of all there are the obvious stereotypes of heroes and villains, figures of fun and frightening bogeys. The idiom of the comic shares some of these with the movies and the TV show; indeed the genres appear to support and elucidate each other, thus forming a closed world of their own into which it is not too easy for the non-initiated to penetrate. I would guess that many academics would take longer in comprehension tests than their grandchildren.

If the comic appears to support the case of the conventionalist because it cannot be understood without a good deal of cultural learning, the other form of cheap imagery which proliferates in our society warns us not to generalize this finding. I am referring to the erotic nudes displayed with such monotonous regularity on the covers and pages of magazines on sale in our cities. It seems very unlikely that response to this genre much depends on 'inculcation'. To be sure, there are conventions at work in the choice of the models and of the poses, but the aim must be to produce the maximum permitted effect.

Fortunately it is not necessary for my argument to dwell further on this particular topic. For we are surrounded by many other kinds of images which can serve. Is it really true that we have no right to say that the pictures of peaches on a can resemble the contents, sometimes more and sometimes less? Does it make sense to deny that a coloured picture postcard of the Piazza di San Marco in Venice can be recognized by those who have been there (or who stroll on the piazza) without initiation? Or, to use more technical terms, is there really no transfer from seeing the fruit, or the piazza, to recognizing the picture? I have claimed elsewhere[22] that there must be such a transfer and I think that Ulric Neisser's notion of the 'perceptual cycle', which I have used in this paper, permits me to specify its nature. Recognition arouses expectations. A drawing in outlines of the piazza will be subsequently tested for the hypothesis that we have here an image of this and no other view. If the drawing is faulty the cycle slows down, if the expected features include colour and atmospheric effects such as we experience in nature it will not only run smoothly, it will come more closely in a specifiable way to the experience of standing on the spot. The degree of cohesion, of mutual support of the features seen in the image, leads to the kind of transformation which always follows the detection of meaning and its subsequent confirmation.

Meaning, as we have seen, does not depend on 'likeness'; the Egyptian who looked at a picture of a hunting party in the lotus swamps might easily have had his memories and imagination stirred, much as it may happen to us when we read a verbal description of such a party; but Western art would not have developed the special tricks of naturalism if it had not been found that the incorporation in the image of all the features which serve us in real life for the discovery and testing of meaning enabled the artist to do with fewer and fewer conventions. This, I know, is the traditional view. I believe it to be correct.

Notes

VISUAL DISCOVERY THROUGH ART

1. See my broadcast series, 'The Primitive and its Value in Art', published in *The Listener*, 15 and 22 February and 1 and 8 March 1979.
2. See my 'The Leaven of Criticism' in *The Heritage of Apelles* (Oxford, 1976).
3. New York and London, 1960.
4. P. Selz, *The Work of Jean Dubuffet* (New York, 1962), p. 102.
5. See my 'The Museum: Past, Present and Future' in *Ideals and Idols* (Oxford, 1979).
6. See my *Means and Ends: Reflections on the History of Fresco Painting* (London, 1976).
7. This is discussed at some length in my 'From the Revival of Letters to the Reform of the Arts' in *The Heritage of Apelles*, op. cit.
8. See my 'Experiment and Experience' in this volume, pp. 215–43.
9. See my 'Image and Code' in this volume, pp. 278–97.
10. N. Tinbergen, *Social Behaviour in Animals* (London, 1953), pp. 94–5.
11. See also my 'Illusion and Art' in R. L. Gregory and E. H. Gombrich, *Illusion in Nature and Art* (London, 1973).
12. See my 'The Mask and the Face' in this volume, pp. 105–36.
13. See my 'Mirror and Map' in this volume, pp. 172–214.
14. See my 'The Renaissance Theory of Art and the Rise of Landscape' in *Norm and Form* (London, 1966).

MOMENT AND MOVEMENT IN ART

1. See E. Panofsky's review of Hanns Kauffman's *Albrecht Dürers rhythmische Kunst* in *Jahrbuch für Kunstwissenschaft* (1926); M. J. Friedlaender, *Von Kunst und Kennerschaft* (Oxford and Zurich, 1946), pp. 60–6; H. A. Groenewegen-Frankfort, *Arrest and Movement* (London, 1951); H. van de Waal, *Traditie en bezieling* (Rotterdam, 1946) and 'De Staalmeesters en hun legende', *Oud Holland*, 71, 1956; Etienne Souriau, 'Time in the Plastic Arts' in *Journal of Aesthetics and Art Criticism*, 7, 1949, pp. 294–307; R. Arnheim, *Art and Visual Perception* (1956), ch. 8; E. H. Gombrich, *Art and Illusion* (New York and London, 1960), see under 'movement' in index.
2. Anthony, Earl of Shaftesbury, *Characteristicks of Men, Manners, Opinions, Times* (1714). For the commission and its result see F. Haskell, *Patrons and Painters* (1963), p. 138.
3. James Harris, *Three Treatises* (1744).
4. *Laocoon*, xvi.
5. See my 'Lessing' (Lecture on a Master Mind) in *Proceedings of the British Academy*, 43 (1957).
6. *Laocoon*, iii.
7. See, for example, Friedrich Schlegel's defence of the subject of martyrdoms in painting, *Gemaeldebeschreibungen aus Paris und den Niederlanden, II. Nachtrag* (1804).

8. J. Constable, *Various Subjects of Land-scape* (1832). See also R. Beckett, 'Photogenic Drawings', in *Journal of the Warburg and Courtauld Institutes*, 27, 1944, pp. 342–3.
9. *Modern Painters* (1842–60), section v, ch. 1.
10. Beaumont Newhall, 'Photography and the Development of Kinetic Visualization', in *Journal of the Warburg and Courtauld Institutes*, 7, 1944, pp. 40–5. See also S. Reinach, *La représentation du Galop dans l'art ancien et moderne* (1925).
11. Aaron Scharf, *Art and Photography* (London, 1968).
12. My attention was drawn to this connection by Dr. William Bartley III.
13. Donald G. Fink and David M. Lutyens, *The Physics of Television* (1961).
14. Book XI, 10–31.
15. Book XI, 27; the translation follows the one by William Watts (1631) used in Loeb Classical Library (1912).
16. Book XI, 28.
17. Book XI, 28.
18. *Bulletin of the British Psychological Society*, 30 September 1956.
19. *The Third Annual Report of the Center for Cognitive Studies at Harvard* (1963), p. 142, contains a preliminary account of a study of this phenomenon under the graphic name of the 'echo box'.
20. D. O. Hebb, *The Organization of Behavior* (1949), pp. 61, 62.
21. *Psychological Review*, 63, 1956, pp. 81–97.
22. 'The Problem of Serial Order in Behavior' in *Cerebral Mechanisms in Behavior*, ed. L. A. Jeffres (New York, 1951).
23. Henry Quastler, 'Studies of Human Channel Capacity', in *Control Systems; Laboratory Report*, No. R.-71, p. 33 (circulated in stencilled form).
24. F. C. Bartlett, *Remembering* (Cambridge, 1932), pp. 29ff.; M. D. Vernon, *A Further Study of Visual Perception* (Cambridge, 1952), Appendix B.

25. J. J. Gibson, *The Perception of the Visual World* (Boston, 1950), p. 155.
26. For the following see Ian M. L. Hunter, *Memory, Facts and Fallacies* (1957), pp. 148–9.
27. See my *Art and Illusion*, op. cit. (note 1) and my 'Illusion and Visual Deadlock' in *Meditations on a Hobby Horse* (London, 1963).
28. W. Wundt, *Völkerpsychologie*, I, 1, 1911, p. 247.
29. See also my 'Ritualized Gesture and Expression in Art' and 'Action and Expression in Western Art' in this volume, pp. 63–77 and 78–104.
30. See my 'The Mask and the Face' in this volume, pp. 105–36.
31. S. Kracauer, *The Nature of Film* (1961), Fig. 25.
32. A. Warburg, 'Dürer und die italienische Antike' (1905), in *Gesammelte Schriften*, 2, 1932, and see my *Aby Warburg, An Intellectual Biography* (London, 1970).
33. See my 'Action and Expression', op. cit. (note 29).
34. See my *The Sense of Order* (Oxford, 1979), ch. 5 'Towards an Analysis of Effects'.
35. 'Auf das Sehen kommt es an', issued for Ilford by Ott & Co., Zofingen.
36. C. Gottlieb, 'Movement in Painting', in *Journal of Aesthetics and Art Criticism*, 17, 1958.
37. See Cyril Barrett, *Op Art* (London, 1970), and Maurice de Sausmarez, *Bridget Riley* (London, 1970).
38. Donald M. MacKay, 'Moving Visual Images produced by Regular Stationary Patterns', in *Nature*, 1957, pp. 180, 849–50, and 1958, pp. 181, 362–3; A. Crawford, 'Measurement of the Duration of a Moment in Visual Perception', and B. Babington Smith, 'On the Duration of the Moment of Perception' in *Bulletin of the British Psychological Society*, XVII, 54 and 55, 1964; and see also my *The Sense of Order* (London, 1979), p. 134 and note.

RITUALIZED GESTURE AND EXPRESSION IN ART

1. *On Aggression* (London, 1966).
2. See my 'Expression and Communication' in *Meditations on a Hobby Horse* (London, 1963).
3. M. H. Krout, 'Autistic Gestures, An Experimental Study in Symbolic Movement', in *Psychological Monographs*, 46, 1935, p. 4; C. Wolff, *A Psychology of Gesture* (London, 1945).
4. E. Kris, 'Laughter as an Expressive Process', in *Psychoanalytic Explorations in Art* (New York, 1952).

5. See my 'Achievement in Medieval Art' in *Meditations on a Hobby Horse*, op. cit. (note 2).

6. E. Künssberg, *Schwurgebärde und Schwurfingerdeutung* (Freiburg, 1941).

7. K. Amira, 'Die Handgebärden in den Bilderhandschriften des Sachsenspiegels', in *Abh. bayr. Akad. Wiss.*, 23, 1909, pp. 163–263, and *Die Dresdener Bilderhandschriften des Sachsenspiegels* (Leipzig, 1926).

8. F. Cabrol, 'Bénir', in *Dictionnaire d'Archéologie Chrétienne* (Paris, 1910).

9. C. Sittl, *Die Gebärden der Griechen und Römer* (Leipzig, 1890); B. Paradisi, 'Rito e retorica in un gesto della mano', in *Studi in onore di A. C. Jemolo* (Milan, 1962).

10. See J. J. Tikkanen, 'Zwei Gebärden mit dem Zeigefinger', in *Acta Soc. Sci. Fenn.*, 43, 1913, on pensive and pointing gestures in art.

11. An indispensable foundation was laid by K. Bühler, *Ausdruckstheorie, Das System an der Geschichte aufgezeigt* (Jena, 1933), who traced the history of these studies from ancient rhetorics to Darwin, and established a link with the theory of language. Whether Birdwhistell's attempt to develop a new terminology and notation for the analysis of bodily movements in a new science of 'Kinesics' will bear fruit it is still too early to say (R. L. Birdwhistell, 'Background to Kinesics', in *Rev. Gen. Semantics*, 13, 1955, pp. 10–18).

12. J. Lange, 'Handen paa brysted' in *Tilskueren*, 4, 1887, pp. 455, 570; C. v. Mander, *Schilder Boeck* (Amsterdam, 1618).

13. The complexity of this relationship has certainly been underrated by Riemschneider-Hoerner, *Der Wandel der Gebärde in der Kunst* (Frankfurt, 1939), who wants to trace the stylistic cycles of gestures through art and literature.

14. See my 'Moment and Movement in Art' in this volume, pp. 40–62.

15. A. P. McMahon (ed.), *Leonardo da Vinci, Treatise on Painting* (Princeton, 1956).

16. J. W. Goethe, 'Joseph Bossi über Leonardo da Vincis Abendmahl'. First published in *Über Kunst und Alterthum*, I, 3, pp. 113–88.

17. *Art and Illusion* (New York and London, 1960).

18. R. Brilliant, *Gesture and Rank in Roman Art. Mem. Conn. Acad. Arts Sci.*, 14, 1963.

19. T. Ohm, *Die Gebetsgebärden der Völker und das Christentum* (Leiden, 1948).

20. I am indebted for this information to Dr. A. Heimann.

21. G. B. Ladner, 'The Gesture of Prayer in Papal Iconography of the Thirteenth and Early Fourteenth Centuries', in *Didascaliae. Studies in Honor of Anselm M. Albareda*, ed. Sesto Prete, 1961.

22. O. Ollendorf, *Andacht in der Malerei* (Leipzig, 1912).

23. A. Flach, *Die Psychologie der Ausdrucksbewegung* (Vienna, 1928).

24. E. de Martino, *Morte e pianto rituale nel mondo antico* (Turin, 1958).

25. E. H. Brauer, *Studien zur Darstellung des Schmerzes in der antiken bildenden Kunst Griechenlands und Italiens* (Breslau, 1934).

26. L. Morgenstern, 'Die Ausdrucksbewegung des Schmerzes in der Christlichen Kunst bis zum Ausgang der Renaissance', in *Studien zur deutschen Kunstgeschichte*, Book 220, Strassburg, 1921, and Moshe Barash, *Gestures of Despair in Medieval and Early Renaissance Art* (New York, 1976), which I reviewed in *The Burlington Magazine*, November 1978.

27. Warburg's remarks on this subject, scattered through his *Gesammelte Schriften* (Leipzig, 1932), can best be traced through the index under *Antike, Nachleben*; *Wirkungen*. See also my *Aby Warburg, An Intellectual Biography* (London, 1970).

28. K. Clark, *The Nude* (London, 1956).

29. A bibliography of the subject of gestures can be found in *Gestures, their Origins and Distribution* (London, 1979) by Desmond Morris, Peter Collett, Peter Marsh and Marie O'Shaughnessy.

ACTION AND EXPRESSION IN WESTERN ART

1. See *Art and Illusion* (New York and London, 1960), 'The Leaven of Criticism in Renaissance Art' in *The Heritage of Apelles* (Oxford, 1976), and 'Visual Discovery through Art' in this volume, pp. 11–39.

2. See my 'Moment and Movement in Art' in this volume, pp. 40–62.

3. K. Bühler, *Ausdruckstheorie* (Jena, 1933).

4. *Ideen zu einer Mimik* (Berlin, 1785–6). Letter XIV, my translation.

5. Ibid. Letter XXVI.

6. Ibid. Letter XX.

7. Ibid. p. 131.

8. In 'Moment and Movement', op. cit., pp. 40–2.

9. Heinrich Schäfer, *Principles of Egyptian Art*, translated by John Baines (Oxford, 1974), to which I wrote a Foreword.

10. For a bibliography of symbolic gestures see Desmond Morris, Peter Collett, Peter Marsh, and Marie O'Shaughnessy, *Gestures, their Origins and Distribution* (London, 1979).

11. See my 'Ritualized Gesture and Expression in Art' in this volume, pp. 63–77.

12. H. A. Groenewegen-Frankfort, *Arrest and Movement* (London, 1951).

13. John Carter, 'The Beginning of Narrative Art in the Greek Geometric Period', in *Annual of the British School of Archaeology at Athens*, Vol. 67, 1972, pp. 25–58, has taken the hypothesis I put forward in *Art and Illusion* as a starting-point for his analysis.

14. See 'Moment and Movement', op. cit. (note 2).

15. W. Deonna, *L'Expression des sentiments dans l'art grec* (Paris, 1914); G. Neumann, *Gesten und Gebärden in der griechischen Kunst* (Berlin, 1965).

16. E. Buschor, *Griechische Vasenmalerei* (Munich, 1921); P. E. Arias, *A History of Greek Vase Painting* (New York and London, 1961); and John Boardman, *Athenian Red Figure Vases* (London, 1975).

17. *Memorabilia*, III, x, 1–5, ed. E. C. Marchant (1923).

18. Jennifer Montagu, 'Charles Le Brun's *Conférence sur l'expression*', unpublished PhD thesis, University of London, 1960.

19. H. A. Murray (Boston, 1943).

20. J. Montagu, op. cit.

21. This example is taken from a series of experiments made at Karl Bühler's seminar in Vienna in the early 1930s in which I took part as a subject. I was introduced to these studies by Ernst Kris, who also organized a series of experiments on the reading of facial expression in art. I have applied these insights in 'Botticelli's Mythologies' (*Symbolic Images*, London, 1972), where the divergent interpretations of the expression of Venus in the *Prima-*vera are quoted, and in 'The Evidence of Images: The Priority of Context over Expression' (in *Interpretation*, ed. C. S. Singleton, Baltimore, 1969), which centres on the various interpretations of a figure in one of Hieronymus Bosch's compositions.

22. R. Brilliant, *Gesture and Rank in Roman Art*, Mem. Conn. Acad. Arts Sci., XIV, 1963.

23. See my review of J. Bodonyi's 'Entstehung und Bedeutung des Goldgrundes', in *Kritische Berichte zur kunstgeschichtlichen Literatur*, V, 1935, pp. 66–75.

24. See my *The Story of Art* (London, 1950) and my *Means and Ends: Reflections on the History of Fresco Painting* (London, 1976) and also 'The Visual Image' in this volume, pp. 137–61.

25. See 'Moment and Movement', op. cit.

26. Michael Baxandall in *Painting and Experience in Fifteenth-Century Italy* (Oxford, 1972) discusses a sermon dealing with the sequence of emotions expressed in the episode of the Annunciation.

27. L. B. Alberti, *De Pictura* (c. 1435), ed. Cecil Grayson (London, 1972), section 44.

28. *Treatise on Architecture* (c. 1460), ed. J. R. Spencer (New Haven and London, 1965).

29. *Treatise on Painting* (c. 1500), ed. A. P. McMahon (Princeton, 1956), p. 58.

30. Cod. Urb. fol. 33.

31. Ibid. (Cod. Urb. fol. 33).

32. J. W. Goethe, 'Joseph Bossi über Leonardo da Vincis Abendmahl', in *Über Kunst und Alterthum*, I, 1817, p. 3.

33. See my 'Ritualized Gesture and Expression in Art' in this volume, pp. 69–70.

34. E. Mâle, *L'Art religieux après le Concile de Trente* (Paris, 1932).

35. André Félibien, *Entretiens sur les ouvrages des peintures* (Paris, 1968), II, pp. 407–27.

36. S. Ringbom, *Icon to Narrative* (Åbo, 1965).

37. 'Motives', in *Acts of the Twentieth International Congress of the History of Art at New York*, Vol. 4, 1961 (Princeton, 1963).

38. But see C. Nordenfalk, 'Tizians Darstellung des Schauens', in *Nationalmusei Arsbok*, 1947–8.

39. See my *Ideas of Progress and their Impact on Art* (New York, 1971). Privately circulated.

40. R. Lister, *Victorian Narrative Painting* (New York, 1966).

41. See my 'Expression and Communication' in *Meditations on a Hobby Horse* (London, 1963) and also 'Ritualized Gesture and Expression in Art', op. cit. (note 11).

42. See my 'Four Theories of Artistic Expression', in *Architectural Association Quarterly*, 12, No. 4, 1980.

THE MASK AND THE FACE

1. *Art and Illusion* (New York and London, 1960). The standard books on portraiture are: Wilhelm Waetzoldt, *Die Kunst des Porträts* (Leipzig, 1908), and Herbert Furst, *Portrait Painting, Its Nature and Function* (London, 1927). A brief bibliography of the subject can be found in Monroe Wheeler, *Twentieth Century Portraits* (New York, 1942); to this might be added Julius von Schlosser, 'Gespräch von der Bildniskunst' (1906), *Präludien* (Berlin, 1927); my 'Portrait Painting and Portrait Photography' in Paul Wengraf (ed.), *Apropos Portrait Painting* (London, 1945); Clare Vincent, 'In Search of Likeness', *Bulletin of the Metropolitan Museum of Art* (April, 1966); and John Pope-Hennessy, *The Portrait in the Renaissance* (New York and London, 1966).

2. Charles de Tolnay, *Michelangelo*, III (Princeton, 1948), p. 68.

3. Vincenzo Golzio, *Raffaello nei documenti* (Vatican City, 1936). Letter by Bembo, 10 April 1516.

4. Alfred Scharf, *Filippino Lippi* (Vienna, 1935), p. 92.

5. Erwin Panofsky, *Idea*, Studien der Bibliothek Warburg (Hamburg, 1923; English translation, Columbia, 1968). For a recent statement of this point of view, see Ben Shahn, 'Concerning "likeness" in Portraiture', in Carl Nordenfalk, 'Ben Shahn's Portrait of Dag Hammarskjöld', *Meddelanden från Nationalmuseum*, No. 87 (Stockholm, n.d.).

6. See Leon D. Harmon, 'The Recognition of Faces', in *Scientific American*, November 1973.

7. This observation served Benedetto Croce as a convenient argument to deny the justification of any concept of 'likeness' (*Problemi di Estetica* (Bari, 1923), pp. 258–9). The English portrait painter Orpen took a similar line when his portrait of the Archbishop of Canterbury was criticized: 'I see seven Archbishops; which shall I paint?' (The anecdote was related by W. A. Payne in a letter to *The Times* on 5 March 1970.)

8. Jennifer Montagu, 'Charles Le Brun's *Conférence sur l'expression*', unpublished PhD thesis, University of London, 1960. The full Cartesian implications of Le Brun's exposition were only brought out in this analysis.

9. Francesco Petrarca, *Le famigliari XXIII*, 19, pp. 78–94. For the full text see also my paper on 'The Style *all'antica*' in *Norm and Form* (London, 1966).

10. Liselotte Strelow, *Das manipulierte Menschenbildnis* (Düsseldorf, 1961).

11. Yvette Guilbert, *La chanson de ma vie* (Paris, 1927).

12. J. J. Gibson, *The Senses Considered as Perceptual Systems* (Boston, 1966); and see also his final formulation in *The Ecological Approach to Visual Perception* (Boston, 1979).

13. See my 'Moment and Movement in Art' in this volume, pp. 40–62.

14. Yousuf Karsh, *Portraits of Greatness* (Edinburgh, 1959).

15. Roger de Piles, *Cours de peinture par principes* (Paris, 1708), p. 265. I quote from the English translation (London, 1743), pp. 161–2.

16. See the dialogue on portraiture by J. von Schlosser, quoted above, note 1.

17. Janet Robertson, *Practical Problems of the Portrait Painter* (London, 1962).

18. R. Töpffer, *Essay de physiognomie* (Geneva, 1845). English translation by E. Wiese, under the title *Enter the Comics* (Lincoln, Neb., 1965).

19. Egon Brunswik, *Perception and the Representative Design of Psychological Experiments*, 2nd edn. (Berkeley, 1956), p. 115.

19a See my 'Illusion and Art' in R. L. Gregory and E. H. Gombrich, *Illusion in Nature and Art* (London, 1973), p. 203, and *The Sense of Order* (London, 1979), p. 169.

20. Françoise Gilot and Carlton Lake, *Life with Picasso* (New York, 1964).

21. In a note to my paper on 'The Variability of Vision' (C. S. Singleton, ed., *Interpretation, Theory and Practice* (Baltimore, 1969), pp. 62–3), I ventured to compare some interpretative processes in perception with linguistic

phenomena investigated by N. Chomsky. I was all the more interested to see that Professor Chomsky was reported in *The New Yorker* of 8 May 1971, p. 65, to have compared man's disposition to understand facial expression with his linguistic equipment.

22. Ferdinand Laban, *Der Gemütsausdruck des Antinous* (Berlin, 1891). I have attempted to document the wide range of interpretation of works of art in 'Botticelli's Mythologies', *Journal of the Warburg and Courtauld Institutes*, VIII (1945), pp. 11–12, reprinted in *Symbolic Images* (London, 1972), pp. 204–6; and in 'The Evidence of Images', in C. S. Singleton, ed., *Interpretation*, op. cit. (note 21).

23. G. B. della Porta, *De humana Physiognomia* (1586).

24. Igor Stravinsky and Robert Craft, *Themes and Episodes* (New York, 1966), p. 152.

25. See Paul Leyhausen, 'Biologie von Ausdruck und Eindruck', in Konrad Lorenz and Paul Leyhausen, *Antriebe tierischen und menschlichen Verhaltens* (Munich, 1968), especially pp. 382 and 394.

26. For these discussions see Ernst Kris, 'Die Charakterköpfe des Franz Xaver Messerschmidt', *Jahrbuch der kunsthistorischen Sammlungen in Wien*, 1932.

27. See *Art and Illusion*, op. cit. (note 1), ch. 10, section III.

28. For a summary and illustration see N. Tinbergen, *The Study of Instinct* (Oxford, 1951), pp. 208–9.

29. Gabriele von Bülow, *Ein Lebensbild* (Berlin, 1895), p. 222. For the same tendency, see also my paper 'Leonardo's Grotesque Heads' (1954) in *The Heritage of Apelles* (Oxford, 1976).

30. What I wish to suggest, but cannot prove, is that Velázquez was able to solve the very problem which Orpen (see note 7) considered unsurmountable.

THE VISUAL IMAGE

1. See my *The Sense of Order* (Oxford, 1979), ch. 9.

2. See the section 'Light and Highlights' in my *The Heritage of Apelles* (Oxford, 1976).

3. *The Art of Memory* (London, 1966).

4. Walter and Marion Dietholm, *Signet, Signal, Symbol* (Zurich, 1970), see in particular pp. 23–31.

5. Cambridge, Mass., and London, 1953.

6. See my *Art and Illusion* (New York and London, 1960), ch. 2.

7. Gottfried Spiegler, *Physikalische Grundlagen der Röntgendiagnostik* (Stuttgart, 1957).

8. See 'The Form of Movement in Water and Air' in my *The Heritage of Apelles* op. cit.

9. For an appreciation of the contribution of the Neuraths see Lancelot Hogben, *From Cave Painting to Comic Strip* (New York, 1949).

10. See my *Symbolic Images* (London, 1972).

11. See 'The Cartoonist's Armoury' in my *Meditations on a Hobby Horse* (London, 1963).

12. Sigmund Freud, *Der Witz und seine Beziehung zum Unbewussten* (Vienna, 1905) (*Jokes and their Relation to the Unconscious*, Vol. 8 of The Standard Edition (London, 1953–74), translated by James Strachey), and Ernst Kris, *Psychoanalytic Explorations in Art* (New York, 1952), especially ch. 6.

13. See my *Symbolic Images*, op. cit.

14. See 'Expression and Communication' in my *Meditations on a Hobby Horse*, op. cit.

15. Reinhard Krauss, 'Über den graphischen Ausdruck', in *Beihefte zur Zeitschrift für angewandte Psychologie*, 48 (Leipzig, 1930).

'THE SKY IS THE LIMIT'

1. J. J. Gibson, 'The Visual Field and the Visual World', in *Psychological Review*, LIX, 1952, pp. 148–51, 237.

2. J. J. Gibson, *The Senses Considered as Perceptual Systems* (Boston, 1966).

3. *Art and Illusion* (New York and London, 1960), ch. 9, section XIII.

4. *The Senses Considered as Perceptual Systems*, op. cit., p. 237. For Gibson's ultimate formulation (not yet available at the time of writing) see *The Ecological Approach to Visual Perception* (Boston, 1979).

5. *Art and Illusion*, op. cit. ch. 9, section XIII.
6. J. J. Gibson, 'The Information Available in Pictures' in *Leonardo*, IV, 1971, pp. 27–35; my response, ibid. pp. 195–7; Gibson's rejoinder, ibid. pp. 197–9, and my reply, ibid. p. 308. After the publication of this article Gibson wrote 'The Ecological Approach to the Visual Perception of Pictures', in *Leonardo*, XI, 1978, p. 227, on which I commented in *Leonardo*, XII, 1979, pp. 174–5.
7. Gibson, *The Senses Considered*, op. cit., p. 220.
8. Gibson, Letter, *Leonardo*, op. cit., p. 198.
9. J. Mittelstrass, *Die Rettung der Phaenomene* (Berlin, 1962).
10. Gibson, Letter, op. cit., p. 198.
11. I first learned about these connections between astronomy and aesthetics through a paper on Friedrich Schiller's philosophy of art by Marie-Luise Waldeck: 'Shadows, Reflexions, Mirror-Images and Virtual "Objects" in "*Die Künstler*" and their relation to Schiller's concept of "Schein"' in *Modern Language Review*, LVIII, 1963, pp. 33–7.
12. See my 'The "What" and the "How": Perspective Representation and the Phenomenal World' in R. S. Rudner and I. Scheffler (eds.), *Logic and Art: Essays in Honor of Nelson Goodman* (New York, 1972).
13. For a lucid survey see the admirable article by B. A. R. Carter, 'Perspective', in H. Osborne (ed.), *The Oxford Companion to Art* (Oxford, 1970).
14. L. Kaufman and I. Rock, 'The Moon Illusion', in *Scientific American*, VII, 1962, p. 204.
15. Erwin Panofsky, *Early Netherlandish Painting* (Cambridge, Mass., 1953).
16. Gibson, Letter, op. cit. (note 6), p. 198.
17. Gibson, *The Senses Considered*, op. cit. (note 2), pp. 156ff.
18. G. V. T. Matthews, *Bird Navigation* (Cambridge, 1968).
19. See 'The "What" and the "How"', op. cit. (note 12).
20. See my *Art and Illusion*, op. cit. (note 3), ch. 8, section IV.
21. Gibson, 'The Information Available', op. cit. (note 6), p. 31.
22. *The Senses Considered*, op. cit. (note 2), p. 293.
23. Gibson, 'The Information Available', op. cit. (note 6), p. 31.
24. *Art and Illusion*, op. cit. (note 3), ch. 2, section VI.
25. Gibson, *Leonardo*, IV, op. cit. (note 6), p. 198.
26. Gibson, *The Senses Considered*, op. cit. (note 2), pp. 303, 304.
27. *Art and Illusion*, op. cit. (note 3), ch. 8, section X, especially.
28. J. E. Hochberg, *Perception* (Englewood Cliffs, N.J., 1964).
29. *Art and Illusion*, op. cit. (note 3), ch. 8, section X.
30. Gibson, *The Senses Considered*, op. cit. (note 2), pp. 279ff.
31. *Art and Illusion*, op. cit. (note 3), ch. 7, section VI.
32. Gibson, 'The Information Available', op. cit. (note 6), p. 31. Ulric Neisser in *Cognition and Reality* (San Francisco, 1976) speaks of images as 'anticipations'.
33. *Art and Illusion*, op. cit. (note 3), ch. 7, section I.
34. See my *Meditations on a Hobby Horse* (London, 1963), pp. 10, 40ff.
35. *Art and Illusion*, op. cit. (note 3), Introduction, section II.
36. Gibson, 'The Information Available', op. cit. (note 6), p. 31.

MIRROR AND MAP

1. J. J. Gibson, *The Senses Considered as Perceptual Systems* (Boston, 1966), and 'On Information Available in Pictures', *Leonardo*, IV, 1971, pp. 27–35; R. L. Gregory, *Eye and Brain; The Psychology of Seeing* (London, 1966), and 'The Confounded Eye', in R. L. Gregory and E. H. Gombrich, *Illusion in Nature and Art* (London, 1973), pp. 49–95; J. Hochberg, 'The Representation of Things and People', in E. H. Gombrich, J. Hochberg and M. Black, *Art, Perception and Reality* (Baltimore, 1972); R. Jung, 'Neuropsychologie und Neurophysiologie des Kontur- und Formsehens in Zeichnung und Malerei', in H. H. Wieck, *Psychopathologie musischer Gestaltungen* (Stuttgart, 1974); J. M. Kennedy, *A Psychology of Picture Perception* (San Francisco, 1974).
2. M. Black, 'How Do Pictures Represent?', in *Art, Perception and Reality*, op. cit. (note 1); N. Goodman,

Languages of Art (New York, 1968); R. Wollheim, *On Art and the Mind* (London, 1973).

3. E. and A. Dyring, *Synligt och osynligt: Vetenskapens nya bilder* (Catalogue of an Exhibition of the Moderna Museet, Stockholm, 1973); R. M. Evans, *Eye, Film and Camera in Color Photography* (New York, 1959); H. C. Reggini, 'Perspective', in *Summa*, LXXIV–LXXV, 1974, pp. 68–75.

4. E. H. Gombrich, *Art and Illusion* (New York and London, 1960), and 'Illusion and Art', in *Illusion in Nature and Art*, op. cit. (note 1); M. H. Pirenne, *Optics, Painting and Photography* (Cambridge, 1970).

5. C. Board, 'Maps as Models', in R. J. Chorley and P. Huggett, *Models in Geography* (London, 1967), pp. 671–725.

6. M. Black, op. cit. (note 2).

7. F. Attneave, *Applications of Information Theory to Psychology* (New York, 1959).

8. See my 'The Visual Image' in this volume, pp. 137–61.

9. R. Wagner-Rieger, *Die Wiener Ringstrasse* (Vienna, 1969).

10. C. Blakemore, 'The Baffled Brain', in *Illusion in Nature and Art*, op. cit. (note 1).

11. H. Bouma, 'Perception as a Physical Phenomenon', in *Light and Sight* (Amsterdam and London, 1974).

12. K. R. Popper, *Objective Knowledge* (Oxford, 1972).

13. R. L. Gregory, *Eye and Brain*, op. cit. (note 1).

14. E. H. Gombrich, 'Illusion and Art', op. cit. (note 4).

15. J. J. Gibson, 'On Information Available in Pictures', op. cit. (note 1).

16. R. L. Gregory, *Eye and Brain*, op. cit. (note 1).

17. R. L. Gregory, *The Intelligent Eye* (London, 1970), pp. 52–3, and see also my *The Sense of Order* (Oxford, 1979), p. 124.

18. E. H. Gombrich, *Art and Illusion*, op. cit. (note 4).

19. E. Meinel, 'Peripheral Vision and Painting', in *British Journal of Aesthetics*, XIII, 1973, pp. 3, 287–97.

20. M. H. Pirenne, op. cit. (note 4), p. 43.

21. See my 'Moment and Movement' in this volume, pp. 40–62, and C. Blakemore, op. cit. (note 10).

22. See my *Symbolic Images* (London, 1972), p. 151.

23. C. Board, op. cit. (note 5), p. 698.

24. F. de Dainville, S.J., *Le langage des géographes* (Paris, 1964).

25. M. Hagner, 'A Genecological Investigation of the Annual Rhythm of *Pinus contorta* Dougl. and a Comparison with *Pinus sylvestris* L.', in *Studia Forestalia Suecica*, LXXXI, 1970.

26. J. M. Kennedy, op. cit. (note 1).

27. See my 'Illusion and Art', op. cit. (note 4), p. 202.

28. L. D. Harmon, 'The Recognition of Faces', in *Scientific American*, November 1972, pp. 71–82.

29. See my *The Heritage of Apelles* (Oxford, 1976), p. 28.

30. H. Schäfer, *Principles of Egyptian Art* (Oxford, 1974).

31. E. and A. Dyring, op. cit. (note 3).

32. Pirenne, op. cit. (note 4).

33. See my *Art and Illusion*, op. cit. (note 4), and my 'The Leaven of Criticism in Renaissance Art' in *The Heritage of Apelles*, op. cit. (note 29).

34. J. White, *The Birth and Rebirth of Pictorial Space* (London, 1957).

35. B. A. R. Carter, 'Perspective', in H. Osborne (ed.), *The Oxford Companion to Art* (Oxford, 1970), pp. 840–61.

36. D. P. Greenber, 'Computer Graphics in Architecture', in *Scientific American*, May 1974, pp. 98–106.

37. See my *Art and Illusion*, op. cit. (note 4), and R. L. Gregory, *The Intelligent Eye*, op. cit. (note 17).

38. J. Baltrusaitis, *Anamorphoses* (Paris, 1955).

39. F. P. Kilpatrick, 'The Problem of Perception', in F. P. Kilpatrick, *Explorations in Transactional Psychology* (New York, 1961), pp. 36–57; R. L. Gregory, *The Intelligent Eye*, op. cit. (note 17). For an illustration and discussion see ch. 8, section III in *Art and Illusion*, op. cit.

40. J. P. Richter, *The Literary Works of Leonardo da Vinci* (Oxford, 1939).

41. See *Art and Illusion*, op. cit. (note 4), ch. 2, section IV.

42. R. L. Gregory, *Eye and Brain* (op. cit., note 1), p. 124. Goethe described this effect in his *Farbenlehre* (1810), *Didaktischer Teil*, II, 22.

43. R. M. Evans, *Eye, Film and Camera*, op. cit. (note 3), p. 29.

44. Op. cit. (note 4), Introduction, section VI.

45. See my 'The Sky is the Limit' in this volume, pp. 162–171.

46. *The Senses Considered as Perceptual Systems*, op. cit. (note 1) and *The Ecological Approach to Visual Perception* (Boston, 1979).

47. Gibson, 'On Information Available', op. cit. (note 1).
48. Goodman, op. cit. (note 2); Pirenne, op. cit. (note 4), ch. 8.
49. See my 'The "What" and the "How": Perspective Representation and the Phenomenal World' in R. Rudner and I. Scheffler, *Logic and Art: Essays in Honor of N. Goodman* (New York, 1972); and E. Bruce Goldstein, 'Rotation of Objects in Pictures Viewed at an Angle: Evidence for Different Properties of Two Types of Pictorial Space', in *Journal of Experimental Psychology: Human Perception and Performance*, Vol. 5, No. 1, February 1979, pp. 78–87 (with bibliography).
50. J. J. Gibson, *The Perception of the Visual World* (Boston, 1950); E. H. Gombrich, 'The Evidence of Images. I. The Variability of Vision', in C. S. Singleton, *Interpretation: Theory and Practice* (Baltimore, 1969), pp. 35–68.
51. Wollheim, op. cit. (note 2).
52. Gregory, *The Intelligent Eye*, op. cit. (note 17), p. 92.
53. K. R. Adams, 'Perspective and the Viewpoint', in *Leonardo*, V, 1972, pp. 209–27.
54. Gibson, *The Perception of the Visual World*, op. cit. (note 50).
55. Jung, op. cit. (note 1).
56. Kennedy, op. cit. (note 1).
57. Hochberg, op. cit. (note 1).
58. Gregory, *The Intelligent Eye*, op. cit. (note 17) and 'The Confounded Eye', op. cit. (note 1).
59. See my 'The "What" and the "How"', op. cit. (note 49).
60. G. ten Doesschate, *Perspective, Fundamentals, Controversials, History* (Nieuwkoop, 1964).
61. J. B. Deregowski, 'Illusion and Culture', in R. L. Gregory and E. H. Gombrich, *Illusion in Nature and Art*, op. cit. (note 1).
62. 'On Information Available in Pictures', op. cit. (note 1).
63. Goodman, op. cit. (note 2).
64. J. S. Bruner, 'On Perceptual Readiness', in *Psychological Review*, LXIV, 1957, pp. 123–52.
65. See my 'The Evidence of Images', op. cit. (note 50).
66. 'The Sky is the Limit', op. cit. (note 45).
67. E. Panofsky, 'Die Perspektive als symbolische Form', in *Vorträge der Bibliothek Warburg* (Hamburg, 1924/5); White, op. cit. (note 34); and see my 'The "What" and the "How"', op. cit. (note 49).
68. V. Ronchi, *New Optics* (Florence, 1971).
69. Gregory, *The Intelligent Eye*, op. cit. (note 17), p. 104.
70. Pirenne, op. cit. (note 4), ch. 9.
71. Ch. 7, section III.
72. F. Dubery and J. Willats, *Drawing Systems* (London, 1972); H. C. Reggini, op. cit. (note 3).
73. 'Hyperbolid Linear Perspective', in *Journal of Aesthetics and Art Criticism*, XXXII, 1973, No. 2, pp. 145–61.
74. E. von Holst, 'Active Functions of Human Visual Perception', in *The Behavioural Physiology of Animals and Man*, Selected Papers, I, 1973, pp. 192–219.

EXPERIMENT AND EXPERIENCE IN THE ARTS

1. Constable's notes for his lectures were published in C. R. Leslie, *Memoirs of the Life of John Constable* (London, 1843). I quote from the edition by Jonathan Mayne (London, 1951), p. 323.
2. 'Some Facts and Theories Regarding the Brain', in *Speaking of Science*, Vol. 50 of the *Proceedings of the Royal Institution*, 1977, pp. 217–35.
3. 'The Philosophy of Karl Popper', in *Speaking of Science*, op. cit., Vol. 50, pp. 202–15.
4. 'By their arts you shall know them?: A Study in Bronze Age Civilizations', in *Speaking of Science*, op. cit., Vol. 50, pp. 79–102.
5. H. A. Groenewegen-Frankfort, *Arrest and Movement* (London, 1951), offers a very negative assessment of the Amarna style.
6. 'That Famous Greek "Wholeness"', in *Proceedings of the Royal Institution*, 49, 1976, pp. 323–37.
7. 'Nature in a Mirror', in *Speaking of Science*, Vol. 51 of the *Proceedings of the Royal Institution*, 1979, pp. 21–34.
8. 'Television', in *Proceedings of the Royal Institution*, 49, 1976, pp. 17–31.
9. Brian Vickers, *Towards Greek Tragedy* (London, 1973), ch. 10, 'Four Electra plays'.
10. See my *Art and Illusion* (New York and London, 1960), ch. 4.

11. For an illustration see my *Ideals and Idols* (Oxford, 1979), Fig. 7.

12. See my *Means and Ends: Reflections on the History of Fresco Painting* (London, 1976).

13. For this and the following see my chapters on 'The Renaissance Conception of Artistic Progress' in *Norm and Form* (London, 1966), and 'From the Revival of Letters to the Reform of the Arts' and 'The Leaven of Criticism in Renaissance Art' in *The Heritage of Apelles* (Oxford, 1976), and also 'Standards of Truth' in this volume, pp. 244–77.

14. Leonardo da Vinci, *Treatise on Painting*, ed. A. P. McMahon (Princeton, 1956), Vol. 1, p. 161 (amended).

15. *The Heritage of Apelles*, op. cit.

16. *Memoirs of the Life of Constable*, op. cit., p. 307.

17. Karl Popper, 'On the Sources of Knowledge and Ignorance', in *Conjectures and Refutations* (London, 1963).

18. *The Works of John Ruskin*, ed. E. T. Cook and A. Wedderburn (London, 1903–12), XXII, p. 209.

19. W. Holman Hunt, *Pre-Raphaelitism and the Pre-Raphaelite Brotherhood* (London, 1905), ch. 7.

20. Anita Brookner, *The Genius of the Future* (London, 1971).

21. My quotations are taken from section II of the novel.

22. Sven Lövgren, *The Genesis of Modernism* (Stockholm, 1959), pp. 71ff.

23. R. A. Weale, 'The Tragedy of Pointillism', in *Palette* (Basle, 1972), pp. 17–23.

24. Quoted after H. R. Rookmaaker, *Synthesist Art Theories* (Amsterdam, 1959). p. 1.

25. Renato Poggioli, *Teoria dell'Arte d'Avanguardia* (Bologna, 1962), ch. 7.

26. Sixten Ringbom, *The Sounding Cosmos* (Abo, 1970), pp. 33ff, traces the history of this notion.

27. Karl Popper, *The Poverty of Historicism* (London, 1957); see also my lecture on 'Hegel und die Kunstgeschichte' in *Neue Rundschau*, 88/2, Spring 1977 (English translation in *Architectural Design*, 51, 6/7, 1981, pp. 3–9).

28. See Poggioli, *Teoria dell'Arte d'Avanguardia*, op. cit.

29. See my Romanes Lecture of 1974, 'Art History and the Social Sciences', in *Ideals and Idols* (Oxford, 1979).

STANDARDS OF TRUTH

1. See Max Black's 'How do Pictures Represent', in E. H. Gombrich, J. Hochberg and M. Black, *Art, Perception, and Reality* (Baltimore, 1972), especially pp. 105ff; N. Goodman in *Language of Art* (Indianapolis, 1968) merely warns against making information a standard of realism.

2. G. Spiegler, *Physikalische Grundlagen der Röntgendiagnostik* (Stuttgart, 1957); see also my tribute to Spiegler, 'Zur Psychologie des Bilderlesens' in *Röntgenblätter*, 20 February 1967.

3. I am indebted for this explanation to Professor Gold of Cornell University.

4. The most complete statement of J. J. Gibson's view is to be found in his last book, *The Ecological Approach to Visual Perception* (Boston, 1979).

5. Ibid, p. 1. Some of my reservations to the wholesale application of Gibson's approach are discussed in 'The Sky is the Limit' in this volume, pp. 162–71.

6. I have taken issue with this view in 'Image and Code', see this volume, pp. 278–297.

7. See my *Art and Illusion* (New York and London, 1960), ch. 4; and my *Means and Ends: Reflections on the History of Fresco Painting* (London, 1976).

8. See my *The Story of Art* (London, 1950).

9. See my 'The "What" and the "How": Perspective Representation and the Phenomenal World' in R. Rudner and I. Scheffler (eds.), *Logic and Art: Essays in Honor of Nelson Goodman* (New York, 1972), and my 'Mirror and Map' in this volume, pp. 172–214.

10. See the astringent article by Martin Kemp, 'Science, Non-Science and Nonsense: The Interpretation of Brunelleschi's Perspective', in *Art History*, 1, No. 2, June 1978, where many of these discussions are summarized. A recent interesting addition is John A. Lynes, 'Brunelleschi's Perspectives Reconsidered', in *Perception*, 9, No. 1, 1980.

11. See D. P. Greenber, 'Computer Graphics in Architecture', in *Scientific American*, May 1974.

12. See Erwin Panoksky's 'Die Perspektive als Symbolische Form', in *Vorträge der Bibliothek Warburg* (1924–5), and his *Early Netherlandish Painting* (Cambridge, Mass., 1953).

13. See Gezienus ten Doesschate, *Perspective, Fundamentals, Controversials, History* (Nieuwkoop, 1964), and M. H.

Pirenne, *Optics, Painting and Photography* (Cambridge, 1970).

14. See my 'Mirror and Map' in this volume, pp. 172–214.
15. *The Works of John Ruskin*, ed. Cook and Wedderburn (1872), Vol. XXII, ch. 7, 'The Eagle's Nest', p. 210.
16. See Jean Paul Richter, *The Literary Works of Leonardo da Vinci*, 2 vols. (Oxford, 1939), I, p. 209.
17. See my *Art and Illusion*, op. cit., ch. 7, section VI.
18. *The Sense of Order* (London, 1979), ch. 4, sections III and IV.
19. Hermann von Helmholtz, *Handbuch der physiologischen Optik*, 2nd edn. (Hamburg and Leipzig, 1896), par. 10, p. 86; my translation.
20. See note 17 above and my 'Moment and Movement in Art' in this volume, pp. 40–62.
21. See 'Mirror and Map', op. cit.
22. P. B. Medawar, in his *Advice to a Young Scientist* (New York, 1979), suggests the exposure of this fallacy as an elementary intelligence test.
23. John Ruskin, *Modern Painters*, 5 vols. (London, 1843), I, pt. 2, section 2, ch. 4, n. 1.

24. I now prefer this formulation to my somewhat laboured discussion in *Art and Illusion*, op. cit., ch. 8, section IV.
25. My most explicit formulation is in the opening paragraph of ch. 11 of *Art and Illusion*.
26. I had a welcome occasion to discuss photography as an art in the introduction to the catalogue of an exhibition of Henri Cartier-Bresson (Edinburgh, 1978), arranged by the Scottish Arts Council and the Victoria and Albert Museum.
27. See Giuliana Scimè's article 'Il Movimento' in the Italian periodical *Il Diaframma*, No. 252, October–November 1980, for some striking examples of photographs evoking the sensation of movement.
28. Reynolds' Discourse 14, 1788, quoted in *Art and Illusion*, ch. 6, section III.
29. See my 'The Mask and the Face' in this volume, pp. 105–36.
30. See 'The Mask and the Face', op. cit.
31. See Ulric Neisser, *Cognition and Reality* (San Francisco, 1976), in particular ch. 7, 'Images as Perceptual Anticipations'.

IMAGE AND CODE

1. Umberto Eco, *A Theory of Semiotics* (Bloomington, 1976).
2. *Art and Illusion* (New York and London, 1960).
3. *Principles of Egyptian Art* (Oxford, 1974). Translated and edited by John Baines (with a foreword by E. H. Gombrich).
4. *The Heritage of Apelles* (Oxford, 1976).
5. *Languages of Art, An approach to a Theory of Symbols* (New York, 1968), p. 38.
6. See my 'Mirror and Map' in this volume, pp. 172–214.
7. See my 'The "What" and the "How": Perspective Representation and the Phenomenal World', in R. Rudner and I. Scheffler (eds.), *Logic and Art: Essays in Honor of Nelson Goodman* (New York, 1972).
8. See 'Mirror and Map', op. cit.
9. John M. Kennedy, *A Psychology of Picture Perception, Images and Information* (San Francisco, 1974).
10. F. Dubery and J. Willats, *Drawing Systems* (London, 1972).

11. Eco, op. cit. (note 1).
12. London, 1959.
13. *Ways of Worldmaking* (Hackett, Indianapolis; Harvester, Sussex, 1978).
14. See my 'The Visual Image' in this volume, pp. 137–62.
15. See my *The Sense of Order* (Oxford, 1979), ch. 10.
16. See my 'Visual Discovery through Art' in this volume, pp. 11–39.
17. *Cognition and Reality, Principles and Implications of Cognitive Psychology* (San Francisco, 1976).
18. Ch. 7, section VIII.
19. E. D. Hirsch, Jr., *Validity in Interpretation* (New Haven, 1967).
20. Albert Boime, *The Academy and French Painting in the Nineteenth Century* (London, 1971).
21. David Kunzle, *History of the Comic Strip*, Vol. I (Berkeley, 1968), Vol. II (forthcoming). See also Denis Gifford, *Victorian Comics* (London, 1976).
22. See my 'The Sky is the Limit' in this volume, pp. 162–71.

Bibliographical Note

DETAILS OF the previous publications of the papers in this volume are as follows:

VISUAL DISCOVERY THROUGH ART. Lecture given at the University of Texas, Austin, in March 1965, in the series Program on Criticism. First published in *Arts Magazine*, 1965, and republished in James Hogg (ed.), *Psychology and the Visual Arts* (Harmondsworth, 1969).

MOMENT AND MOVEMENT IN ART. Lecture given at the Warburg Institute in a series on Time and Eternity in June 1964 and published in *Journal of the Warburg and Courtauld Institutes*, 27, 1964, pp. 293–306.

RITUALIZED GESTURE AND EXPRESSION IN ART. A contribution to a Discussion on Ritualization of Behaviour in Animals and Man organized by Sir Julian Huxley in June 1966. Published in *Philosophical Transactions of the Royal Society of London*, 251, 1966, pp. 393–401.

ACTION AND EXPRESSION IN WESTERN ART. A paper presented to a study group set up by the Royal Society under the chairmanship of W. H. Thorpe in 1970. Published in R. A. Hinde (ed.), *Non-Verbal Communication* (Cambridge University Press, 1972), pp. 373–93.

THE MASK AND THE FACE: THE PERCEPTION OF PHYSIOGNOMIC LIKENESS IN LIFE AND IN ART. First of three Alvin and Fanny Blaustein Thalheimer Lectures of 1970, published by Johns Hopkins University in *Art, Perception and Reality* by E. H. G., Julian Hochberg and Max Black, editor Morris Mandelbaum (Baltimore and London, 1972), pp. 1–46.

THE VISUAL IMAGE. *Scientific American*, Special Issue on Communication, 227, 1972, pp. 82–96. © 1972 by Scientific American, Inc. All rights reserved.

'THE SKY IS THE LIMIT' : THE VAULT OF HEAVEN AND PICTORIAL VISION. Robert B. MacLeod and Herbert L. Pick, Jr. (eds.), *Perception. Essays in Honor of James J. Gibson* (Ithaca and London, 1974) pp. 84–94. © 1974 by Cornell University.

MIRROR AND MAP: THEORIES OF PICTORIAL REPRESENTATION. Review Lecture given in May 1974. Published in *Philosophical Transactions of the Royal Society of London*, 270, 1975, pp. 119–49.

EXPERIMENT AND EXPERIENCE IN THE ARTS. The final lecture in a series of seven on The Influence of the Arts and of Scientific Thought on Human Progress, endowed by the Richard Bradford Trust. Published in *Proceedings of the Royal Institution*, 52, 1980, pp. 113–43.

STANDARDS OF TRUTH: THE ARRESTED IMAGE AND THE MOVING EYE. An early version of this paper was presented at Swarthmore College in October 1976 at a symposium to mark the retirement of Professor Hans Wallach. Published in *The Language of Images* (Chicago, 1980) and reprinted in *Critical Inquiry*, 7, No. 2, 1980, pp. 237–73. © 1980 by The University of Chicago.

IMAGE AND CODE: SCOPE AND LIMITS OF CONVENTIONALISM IN PICTORIAL REPRESENTATION. Lecture given at the International Conference on the Semiotics of Art held in May 1978 in Ann Arbor, Michigan. Published in W. Steiner (ed.), *Image and Code* (Michigan Studies in the Humanities, Ann Arbor, 1981). © 1981 The University of Michigan.

The author wishes to thank these publishers for their permission to reprint.

Sources of Photographs

Index

abstract art, 61
action painting, 77
Adam, Kenneth, 199
advertising, 23, 103, 140, 154, 287–96
'after-image', 61, 170, 180, 195, 196
Alberti, Leone Battista, 85, 92
Alexander mosaic, the, 222, 253–4, Fig. 212
Alt, Rudolf von, 175, Fig. 146
ambiguity, 38–9, 86, 97–100, 117–18, 248, 253;
    see also indeterminacy
Ames, Adelbert, 35, 191; Ames demonstration,
    201, 207
anamorphosis, 191, 197, 211, 212, Fig. 160
Andrei, Johannes, Fig. 127
anecdotal painting, 101, 103
animals: behaviour, 16, 24–5, 72–3, 138–9, 222,
    273, 283–6; in physiognomics, 128–9
'anti-art', 77, 243
anticipation, 45, 49, 52, 60; and information, 170
Antinous, 126, Fig. 110
Apelles, 222, 242
apparent size, 164, 193, 201; see also Emmert's
    Law
Aristotle, 12, 35, 71, 219
astronomy, 163, 207, Fig. 174
Aurier, G. A., 238
avant garde, 241
Averroes, 71

Backhuysen, Ludolf, 233, 234, Fig. 197
Bacon, Francis, 230
Baltrusaitis, J., Fig. 160
Barlier, Fig. 246
Baroque art, 76
Bartlett, F. C., 51, 179, 289
Bayeux Tapestry, 66
beholder's share, the, 78, 87–8, 90, 95, 99, 100,
    116, 145, 159, 171, 180, 181, 220, 266, 272
Berchem, Nicolaes, 230, Fig. 194
Berengo Gardin, Gianni, 273, Figs. 230–3
Berenson, Bernard, 128
Berény, R., Fig. 242
'Berlin Painter', The, Figs. 183–4
Bernard, Claude, 236

Bernini, G. L., 43
binocular parallax, 258
Both, Jan, 230
Botticelli, 94, Fig. 76; workshop of, 92, Fig. 72
Braque, Georges, 242
Braun, Kaspar, Fig. 109
Brilliant, R., 71
Brunelleschi, 164, 167, 224, 256, 257
Bruner, Jerome, 204
Brunswik, Egon, 120, 121, 125, Fig. 102
Büchner, Georg, 236
Bühler, Karl, 80, 138
Burckhardt, Jakob, 218
Byzantine mosaics, 23

camera: photographic, 116, 178, 244
Canaletto, 43
Caravaggio, 230
caricature, 29, 126, 131, 132, 158; and por-
    traiture, 105, 112, 127, 130, Figs. 89, 92, 109,
    112
Carter, B. A. R., Fig. 159
cartoonist, art of, 153
catacomb painting, 89, Fig. 68
Cenotaph, Whitehall, 258, Fig. 218
Cézanne, Paul, 235
Chartres Cathedral, 157, Fig. 137
Chevreul, E., 237
Chinese art: calligraphy, 77, 152; painting, 165,
    252, Fig. 143
chorus effect, the, 89–90
Christian art, early, 88, 93, 98, 224, Figs. 74, 79
Churchill, Sir Winston, 18, 117, 118, Fig. 98
Cicero: quoted, 223
Cieslewicz, R., Figs. 243, 244
Cinerama, 37
Clark, Kenneth, 101, 219
Claude Lorrain, 37, 230, 239, 262, Figs. 18, 222
Cleiton, 85
code, coding, 16, 18, 28–9, 37, 145–7, 150–1, 156,
    161, 186, 278–97; cartographic, 184
Colonel Blimp, 111, Fig. 89
colour: calibration, 247; Chevreul on, 237;
    expressive function of, 140; in maps, 149,

183–4; photographs, 147, 238; Post-Impressionism and, 237–8; Van Gogh and, 161
coloured shadows, 27, 30, 34, 35, 146
comics, 79, 103, 104, 151, 296
commercial art, see advertising
communication, 83, 137–40, 141, 143, 146–8, 161; art as, 158–9, Fig. 139
computers, 106, 130, 190, 282
'conceptual' methods and styles, 17, 21, 38, 52, 70, 82, 100, 141, 148, 187, 197, 252; see also pictographs
Constable, John, 43, 224, 231, 232; quoted, 215, 230, 243, Figs. 182, 195
constancies, perceptual: of colour, 125; physiognomic, 125; of size, 18–20, 28, 38, 164, 193–4, 196, 198, 270
convention: in expression, 81; in maps, 187; in representation, 19, 20, 77, 79, 104, 142, 147, 151, 184–7, 217, 237, 278–97; and symbolism, 152; see also code
Cornish, V., 169
Counter Reformation, 95
Cubism, 35, 61, 239, 242
curvature: of the earth, 164, 170, 206; in perspective, 167, 211, 258

Dada, 243
Daguerreotype, 43–4, 234
Dainville, F. D., S.J., Fig. 150
Dante, 68, 91
Darwin, Charles, 217; Darwinism, 24
Daumier, Honoré, Fig. 14
decorum, 95–7; Leonardo on, 92
Degas, Edgas, 59
Dell'Acqua, Amadeo, Fig. 247
della Porta, G. B., 127, Fig. 111
demonstration: of perspective, 19–20, 201–2, 256, 259–60; of waves, 234; see also Ames
depth reversal, 146, Fig. 125
diagrams, 16, 23, 149, 150
Discobolos, 60, Figs. 35, 36
discovery, visual, 11–39
Disney, Walt, 140
Donatello, 58, 59, 76, 92, Figs. 31, 32, 59
Draper, Ruth, 110, Figs. 87, 88
Dubuffet, Jean, 13, Figs. 1, 2
Duchamp, Marcel, 60
dustbin, 30
Dyring, E. and A., Fig. 180

'echo memory', see memory
'ecological optics', 204
effort after meaning, the, 51, 60, 61, 179, 206, 289
Egyptian art, 74, 77, 82, 151, 187, 217–18, 252, 279, 297, Figs. 56, 61, 154
eidetic faculty, 50–1
Emmert's Law, 164, 195, 202, 205
empathy, 83, 128–33, 273
Engel, J. J., 80, 81, 87, 90
equivalence, 105, 124, 131, 283, 286
erotic imagery, 104, 140, 171, 186, 297

Escher, M. C., 180
Eumenides Painter, The, Fig. 185
Euphronils, 220
Euthymides, 220
Evans, Ralph, 19, 20, Fig. 6
evocation, 21–3, 87, 271, 277; see also suggestion
evolution, 24, 25, 217, 286
ex voto, 14, Fig. 3
experiments: in art, 27, 215–43; in science, 215–16; see also Ames; Brunswik; demonstration; Emmert's Law; Evans; Krauss; trial and error
Expressionism, 25, 63, 66, Fig. 40
eye: and camera, 44, 178, 251; contacts, 101; Helmholtz on, 264; 'innocent eye', 163, 181, 265; moving, 50, 179, 180, 212, 244–77; perception of eyes, 25, 186, 287–93; stationary, 195, 251, 270; in vision, 25, 59, 169, 177, 205, 212, 214, 264
eye-witness, principle of, 84, 189, 220, 253–6, 258, 260, 268–9, 277, 281

familiarity, 36, 153; and the effect of isolation, 37–8; see also recognition
family tree, 149, Fig. 127
Farbman, N. R., Fig. 228
Feininger, Andreas, Fig. 211
Filippino Lippi, 71, 105, Fig. 50
film, 37, 44, 69, 116
Freud, Sigmund, 152, 239
function: of the image, 79, 137–61; of music, 104; see also evocation, information
Futurists, the, 60

Gainsborough, Thomas, 118, 272
Games, Abram, 287, 290, 291, 293; quoted, 290, Figs. 181, 239, 240, 249
Genoa Cathedral, 156, Fig. 136
Gestalt psychology, 47, 195; see also simplicity principle
gesture, 52, 63–77, 78–103
Ghent Altarpiece, 66, Fig. 42 (detail)
Ghirlandaio, Domenico, 55, 94, Figs. 27, 75
Gibson, J. J., 116, 162–71, 180, 182, 196–7, 199, 202–6, 211–13, 251–2, 269–70; quoted, 162, 168, 169
Gilot, Françoise: quoted, 123–4; Figs. 107–8
Giorgione, 227
Giotto, 21, 55, Figs. 9, 26, 69, 157
Goethe, J. W. von, 30, 34, 69, 94, 236
Gombrich, Ilse, Fig. 177
Goodman, Nelson, 279, 280, 281, 284, 285, 287; quoted, 279, 284
Gowing, Lawrence, 32, 33, 181, 183, 212, Figs. 16, 149
graphology, 65, 77, 130, 161
Great Seal of the U.S., 153, Fig. 131
Greco fallacy, 182, 204, 269
Greek art, 20, 27, 75, 79, 82–8, 96, 163, 219–23, Figs. 62–5, 183–5
Greek drama, 219
Green-Armitage, Paul, Fig. 217

Gregory the Great, Pope: quoted, 155
Gregory, Richard, 199, 201
Grindler, F. and R., Fig. 248
Grünewald, Mathias, Fig. 45
Guilbert, Yvette, 111–12, Figs. 90, 91

Haeckel, Ernst, 144
Hagner, M., Fig. 152
Hansen, R., 211, 212
Harding, J. D., 232
Harris, James, 42, 45, 50
Hawkes, Jacquetta, 217, 218
Hearnshaw, L. S., 47
heaven, vault of, 162–71, 207–8
Hebb, D. O., 48
Hecht, Federico, 276, Fig. 234
Hellmer, E., Fig. 250
Helmholtz, Hermann von, 167, 267; quoted, 264–5
Hering, E., 34
Hildebrand, Adolf von, 167, 206
Hochberg, Julian, 200
Hogarth, William, 103, 129, 264
Holman Hunt, William, 235
Holst, Erich von, 212
Homer, 84, 219
Hopwood, John, 213, Fig. 179
Horace, 140
Hortulus Master, The, Fig. 78
Humboldt, Wilhelm von, 133
Huxley, Thomas, 234

illusion, 180–1, 199; see also Müller-Lyer; Poggendorf
imagination, 272
Impressionism, 39, 100, 181, 206, 265, 296; Impressionists, 11, 27, 35, 266, 279
indeterminacy, 166, 169, 191, 201–6
information: false, 168, 261; images for, 137, 144, 172–6, 183, 244–7, 251, 255, 271; theory of, 141, 174; visual, 50, 163, 170, 246, 251, 259, 262
insects, 24, 252, Figs. 11, 12
interest: influence on perception, 30, 34, 39
interpretation: of facial expression, 117–18, 126–7, 135; of images, 84–8, 126, 140, 141, 146, 203, 245–7, 253, 287; see also ambiguity; indeterminacy
invariants: Gibson's theory of, 196
Isenheim Altar, 67, Fig. 44
isolation, effect of, 34, 35, 86
Ivins, William M., Jr., 143

James-Lange theory, 74
Japanese prints, 161
Jung, Carl Gustav, 152

Kandinsky, Wassily, 239
Kapplow, 86
Karsh, Yousuf, 117, Fig. 98
Keats, John, 171
Kennedy, John M., 200

King, H., Figs. 170, 171
King, Haynes, 102, Fig. 81
King's College, Cambridge, 257, Fig. 216
Kit-Kat Club, 114
Kitto, H. D. F., 218, 219
Kluver, H., 51
'Kobbe', Fig. 92a
Kokoschka, Oskar, 133–4, Figs. 113, 114
Kollwitz, Käthe, 63, 73, Fig. 40
Kneller, Sir Godfrey, Figs. 93, 94
Krauss, Reinhard, 159

landscape painting, 35, 165, 171, 215, 230–1, 260–3
Laocoon, 42–3, 89, 104
Lashley, K. S., 48, 49
La Tour, Maurice Quentin de, 118, Fig. 99
La Viridiana, 69
Lawrence, Sir Thomas, 133
Le Brun, Charles, 85, 96, 107, Fig. 84
Lee, Vernon, 128
Lenbach, Franz, 115, Fig. 96
Lenin, Fig. 44
Leonardo da Vinci, 11, 68–9, 85, 91–4, 104, 148, 193, 225–9, 261–3, 279, 289; quoted, 68, 92, 225; Figs. 47, 74, 187, 188, 190–3
Leslie, C. R., 230; quoted, 231–2
Lessing, G. E., 42–3, 45–6, 50, 52, 89
Lichtenberg, G. C., 30, 34, 129
Liebermann, Max, 18, 136
likeness, 25, 105–36, 284, 297; see also mimesis; portraiture
Lipps, Th., 128
Lister, Raymond, 102
Liszt, Franz, Figs. 95, 96
Llewelyn, John Dillwyn, Fig. 199
Locke, John, 129
Loewy, Emanuel, 16
Lomazzo, 85
Lorenz, Konrad, 63, 74, 132, 139, 286, Fig. 119
Los Olvidados, 53, Fig. 24
Louis Philippe, 130, 132, Fig. 112
Low, David, Fig. 89
Lucian, 222
Lysenko, 241

Maclise, Daniel, Fig. 182
macula, the blind spot, 50
Manet, Edouard, 235, 237, Fig. 200
maps, 148–9, 172–214, 280, 281, Figs. 145, 150–2, 155, 237
Marcovecchio, Oscar N., Fig. 245
Marmitta, Francesco, Fig. 189
Masaccio, Fig. 158
Masaryk, Thomas, 133, Figs. 114, 115
Mauthe, Jorg, Figs. 147, 148
Maxwell, J. C., 237–8
Medawar, Sir Peter, 216
Mellan, Claude, 147, Fig. 126
memory, 13, 18, 46–9, 130, 142, 179; memory colour, 38; memory images, 16; see also recall; recognition

Mendel, G. J., 240–1
mental set, 36, 115, 145, 178, 283, 296
Michelangelo, 105, 157, 242, Fig. 138
Miller, G. A., 48
mimesis, 11, 101, 219, 253
mirror, 172–214, Figs. 161, 166
mosaic, 141, 187, 254
mourning, ritual of, 74–6, 82
movement, 37, 40–62, 78, 81, 116; impression of, 51, 55–60, 62, 239; moving eye, 179, 244–77; moving objects, 44, 234, 244, 263, 268–77; perception of, 268; *see also* film; gesture
movement parallax, 200, 202, 205, 207
Müller-Lyer illusion, 121–2, 201, Fig. 104
Münzer, Sebastian, Fig. 174
Museum of Art History, Vienna, 172, 175, Figs. 144, 147
Museum of Natural History, Vienna, 172, 175, Figs. 144, 148
music, 16, 49, 53, 96, 104, 171
Muybridge, E., 44

'Nadar' (F. Tournachon), 115, Fig. 95
Naram Sin, stele of, 70, Fig. 48
narrative art, 78–104; Greek, 20, 84, 220–1, 253–4; medieval, 21, 66; pictographic, 52, 91; Rembrandt, 98; Renaissance, 52–5, 70, 189, 255–6
NASA, 150
naturalism, 17, 18, 21, 23, 34, 35, 70
negative feedback, 216–18, 228, 241; *see also* trial and error
Neisser, Ulric, 287, 297
Neo-Platonism, 106
Neurath, Marie and Otto, 150
non-verbal communication, Fig. 139; *see also* communication, gesture

Ohm, T., 71
Olympic Games, 58, 142, 218, Figs. 33, 121
'Op' art, 62, 182–3, 239
Orchardson, Sir William, 102, Fig. 82
Orpheus, 86–8, Figs. 25, 65, 66
Osiris, 152–3, Fig. 129
Ottonian miniature, 66, Fig. 43
outline, 201, 283

Panofsky, Erwin, 164, 167, 258
Paolo de Matteis, Fig. 20
Parker-Ross, S. G., 249, Figs. 206–9
Parrhasios, 85
Peirce, C. S., 278
perception: of colour, 125; Gibson's theory of, 162–71, 196, 251; masking effect in, 113; modes of, 166–71; of movement, 40–62, 268; of pictures, 19, 197–8, 250; of physiognomic likeness, 105–36; universals in, 106, 109, 203, 272; veridical, 166, 183
perceptual cycle, 287, 297
Permoser, Balthasar, 71, Fig. 49
perspective: theory of, 19, 23, 167, 189–201, 208–13, 224, 256–60, 270, 281; aerial, 263

Petrarch, 109, 120, 129
Pflaum, Barbara, Figs. 147, 148
Philipon, Charles, 130, 131, Fig. 112
photography: apparent distortion, 19, 37, 213–14; blurred, 178, 267–8, 271–6; commercial, 103; effects of constancies, 20, 198; focusing, 177, 267; information through, 144, 146, 174, 177–9, 188, 197, 203, 248–51, 254; leaflet for amateurs, 55; legibility, 53, 100, 186, 198, 273, 282; mirrors and, 197; panoramic, 209, 258; painting and, 27, 43–4, 103, 234, 238; portrait, 106–7, 114–18, 133; tilted, 201, 250; wide angle, 173–4, 249; X-ray, 146, 245–6, Figs. 203, 204; *see also* camera
physiognomy, 28, 105, 133; history of, 127, 129; physiognomic reactions, 132, 185; *see also* portraiture
Picasso, 60, 123, 124, 242, 279, Figs. 37, 38, 108, 235, 236; on painting Mme Gilot, 103–6
pictograph, 21, 23, 52, 88–9, 91, 93, 98, 142, 151–2, 157, 184, Figs. 10, 21, 33, 121, 129, 155
picturesque, 37, 39
Piero della Francesca, 76
Piles, Roger de, 264; quoted, 118
Pioneer spacecraft, 150, 151, Fig. 128
Pirenne, M. H., 189
Pissarro, Camille, 12, 237, 238
Plato, 171, 219, 223; *Cratylus*, 183, 278
Pliny, 222
Poggendorf illusion, 59, Fig. 34
Pollock, Jackson, 77
Pompeii: painting from, 221, Fig. 186; mosaic from, 140, 141, 285, Figs. 120, 212; *see also* Alexander mosaic
Pop art, 104
Popper, Karl, 179, 195, 216, 230, 241, 284, Fig. 238
portraiture, 14, 28–30, 105–36, 158; Leonardo on, 92
Post-Impressionism, 237
posters, 214, 287, 289, 291, 293, Figs. 40, 133, 181, 227, 239, 241–9; *see also* advertising
Potter, Paulus, 14, Fig. 4
Poussin, Nicolas, 96, Fig. 77
praying, gesture of, 71, 72, 82
Pre-Raphaelites, 235
Prestwich, Sir John, 153
primitive art, 11, 26, Fig. 21
punctum temporis, 42, 45–7, 53, 61

Quastler, Henry, 50

'rabbit or duck', 35–6, Fig. 17
Raphael, 105, 255, 256, 262, Figs. 46, 214; school of, Fig. 70
Rauschenberg, Robert, 31, 33, Fig. 15
recall, 12, 16; difficulties of, 14, 130; *see also* memory
recognition, 12–14, 20, 27–9, 32–4, 38, 106, 108–10, 162, 285, 289, 297
reduction screen, 34, 38, 125

Reisner, Bob, 86
Reiter, Fig. 102
relativism, 25, 101, 183, 252, 286
Rembrandt, 73, 78, 98, 99, 230, Figs. 55, 80, 117;
    self-portraits, 107, 134, Fig. 116
Renaissance: art and artists, 11, 20, 55–9, 77, 92,
    100–1, 105, 189–91, 224; music, 104; *see also*
    Botticelli; Brunelleschi; Filippino Lippi;
    Leonardo; Michelangelo; Raphael; Uccello
Renoir, Pierre Auguste, Fig. 224
Reynolds, Sir Joshua, 118, 272
Richter, Sviatoslav, 116, Fig. 97
Riley, Bridget, 62, 239, Fig. 39
ritualization, 63–77, 82
Robertson, Janet, 119, 122; on portrait painting,
    119–20
Rockefeller Center, 250, Fig. 211
Roman art, 71
Rood, O. N., 237, 238
Ruskin, John, 44, 232; quoted, 234, 261, 270
Russell, Bertrand, 108, 130, Figs. 85, 86

saccadic movement: of eye, 212
Sachsenspiegel, 66, Fig. 41
St. Augustine, 46–8
St. Francis of Assisi, 72
Samuel, Dr. David, 215
Savignac, Raymond, 291, Figs. 133, 241
Schacht, Hjalmar, 113, Figs. 92a, 92b
Schäfer, Heinrich, 279
schema, 16, 17, 70
Schnabel, Arthur, 49
science and painting, 27, 215, 236–9, 243;
    Constable on, 224–5; Leonardo on, 225;
    Ruskin on, 232–5; use of photography in, 44,
    188, 244–7; *see also* X-ray
screen: of half-tone blocks, 147, 174, 254
Sebastiano del Piombo, 52, Fig. 23
Seurat, Georges, 161, 237, 238
Shaftesbury, Lord, 40–2, 44, 45, 46, 50, 52, 53,
    81, 90
Shinwell, Emanuel, 106–7, Fig. 83
signal, 138–9
simplicity principle, 169–70, 195, 200, 206–7
Smilby, 244, 268, Fig. 201
Socrates, 85
Soderini, Piero, 242
Sokolsky, Melvin, Fig. 153
Spiegler, Gottfried, 147, 245, Figs. 203, 204
Spooner, Dr., 48
Steichen, Edward J., 118
Strauss, Johann, 294, Fig. 250
Stravinsky, Igor, 127
suggestion, 88, 171, 200; *see also* evocation
Sumerian art, 217
Surrealism, 239
Sydney Opera House, 146, Fig. 124
symbol, 16, 58, 82, 86, 91, 152–3, 183, 189, 294;
    pathology of, 183–5; and symptom, 64–5, 138;
    see also pictograph
symmetry, 55
symptom, 64, 76–7, 138

Tachism, 77
Talma, F. J., 112
Taylor, B., Fig. 156
television, 45–6, 147, 180, 198, 219, 296
temporal integration, 47
Thematic Apperception Test, 86
time, 89; St. Augustine on, 47; *see also* movement
Tinbergen, Nikko, 286, Fig. 119
Tintoretto, 55, Fig. 29
Titian, 55, Fig. 28
Tomb of Ti, Fig. 61
Töpffer, Rodolphe, 120, 125, Fig. 101
Toulouse-Lautrec, Henri de, 112, Fig. 91
tourist: guides, 188, Fig. 155; propaganda, 294
trial and error, 15, 23, 24, 78, 124, 162, 227, 239;
    see also experiment
tribal art, 26, 115, Fig. 13; American Indian, 52,
    Fig. 21
trompe l'oeil, 180
Turner, J. M. W., 43, 44, 232, 234, 260–1, Figs.
    196, 220, 221

Uccello, Paolo, 255, Fig. 213
universals: in language, 172; in perception, 106,
    203

Vallotton, Félix, 119, Fig. 100
van Brissen, 268, 271, Fig. 227
Van Eyck brothers, Fig. 42
Van Gogh, Vincent, 77, 159, 161, Figs. 140, 141
van Leyden, Aertgen, Fig. 67
Van de Velde, W., 43, 233, Fig. 198
Vasarely, Victor, 239
Vasari, Giorgio, 11, 20, 242; quoted, 227, 229
Velázquez, Diego, 122, 135, 262, Figs. 105, 106,
    118
Vergil, 43, 153
Vernon, M. D., Figs. 103, 104
Vianello, Fig. 215
'Vicky' (Victor Weisz), 153, Fig. 132
visual cone, 189, 190, 192, 196, 206, Fig. 156
von Löfen, Bennewitz, Fig. 90

Wagner-Rieger, R., Fig. 144
Waldseemüller, Fig. 237
Warburg, Aby, 76
Wartofsky, Marx M., 284
Weale, R. A., 238
Whistler, J. A. M., 12; quoted, 204
Wickham, G. W. G., 219, 224
Wilson, Richard, 37, 39, Fig. 19
Winckelmann, J. J., 43
Wölfflin, Heinrich, 128
Wollheim, Richard, 199, 201
Wonnacott, John, 212, 213, Fig. 178
Worringer, Wilhelm, 128

X-ray, 146–7, 188, 245–6, Figs. 203, 204
Xenophon, 85

Yates, Frances, 142

Yin and Yang, 152, Fig. 130
Ylla, Fig. 229

Zeno's paradox, 45, 46

Zeuxis, 222–3, 286
Zola, Emile: *L'Oeuvre*, 34, 37, 38, 235–7, 241
Zorn, Anders, 265–6, Fig. 223
Zurbaran, Francisco de, Fig. 54

DATE DUE